WITHDRAWN

THE NOVEL IN FRANCE

STENDHAL

(Reproduced by permission of the Grenoble Museum)

THE NOVEL IN FRANCE

MME DE LA FAYETTE
LACLOS CONSTANT STENDHAL
BALZAC FLAUBERT PROUST

BY

MARTIN TURNELL

'Un roman est comme un archet, la caisse du violon
qui rend les sons, c'est l'âme du lecteur'
STENDHAL

Essay Index Reprint Series

LIBRARY
BRYAN COLLEGE
DAYTON, TN. 37321

BOOKS FOR LIBRARIES PRESS
PLAINVIEW, NEW YORK

20772

First published 1951.
All rights reserved.
Reprinted 1972 by arrangement with
New Directions Publishing Corporation

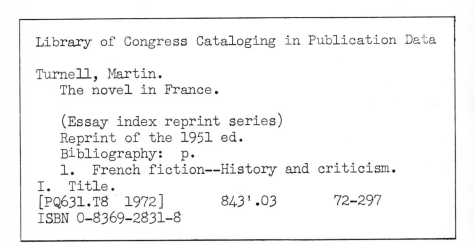
Library of Congress Cataloging in Publication Data

Turnell, Martin.
   The novel in France.

   (Essay index reprint series)
   Reprint of the 1951 ed.
   Bibliography: p.
   1. French fiction--History and criticism.
I. Title.
[PQ631.T8 1972]   843'.03   72-297
ISBN 0-8369-2831-8

PRINTED IN THE UNITED STATES OF AMERICA

TO
MY MOTHER
AND TO
THE MEMORY OF
MY FATHER

PREFACE

In the year 1913 a French newspaper indulged in an agreeable game which has been played in different forms in most European countries. It invited a number of distinguished writers to name their ten favourite French novels. When M. André Gide received his invitation he was slightly perplexed. He had no doubt about the identity of his favourite novelist, but it was more difficult to choose his favourite novel. The finest French novel was bound to be one of Stendhal's, but which was it to be? 'I hesitated', he said, 'for a long time between *Le Rouge et le noir* and *La Chartreuse de Parme*. In my state of doubt I almost wrote down *Lucien Leuwen*. . . . No: the *Chartreuse* remains the unique book.'

He gave second place, this time without the slightest hesitation, to the *Liaisons dangereuses*. Then he paused again. He preferred the *Chartreuse* and the *Liaisons* to any other novels written in any other languages, but he did not consider that France was really a country of novelists. The French moralists were unsurpassed, but the French novelists were not in his opinion the equals of the great English and Russian novelists. If he had not been confined by the rules of the game to Frenchmen, he said, the other eight places on his list would all have gone to foreigners.

The remaining eight, presumably in order of merit, were: *La Princesse de Clèves, Le Roman bourgeois, Manon Lescaut, Dominique, La Cousine Bette, Madame Bovary, Germinal*, and *La Vie de Marianne* 'which I blush to confess I have not yet read'.[1]

The essay in which M. Gide tells the story of his choice is one of the most polished and entertaining of his occasional writings.[2] He has something fresh and stimulating to say about nearly all the novels that he discusses which makes us feel like sitting down and re-reading each

---

[1] It is only fair to remind ourselves that this list was compiled nearly forty years ago. The essay originally appeared in the *Nouvelle Revue Française* seven months before the publication of the first two volumes of *A la Recherche du temps perdu* by Grasset, after Gallimard had turned the book down on Gide's advice. He has since admitted the mistake and we may assume that if the list were revised Proust would certainly find a place. The same is probably true of *Adolphe*, which appears from the *Journal* to have been one of Gide's blind spots until he reached middle life.

[2] It is reprinted in *Incidences* (Paris, 1924), pp. 143-9.

of them. To anyone who reads the essay for the first time in the course
of a study of the French novel, it must seem as though the examination
candidate's dream has come true, and that a set of model answers has
been handed out, inadvertently, with the questions.

Model answers, however, are not always the only answers, and this
is a test in which 'the reasons for your answers' are at least as important
as the answers themselves. My purpose is naturally very different from
M. Gide's. I have not tried to select the seven best French novels or,
necessarily, the seven best French novelists. Still less have I tried to write
a history of the French novel. I have simply examined the principal
works of some of the most celebrated French novelists in an attempt to
show where their excellence lies or, in cases where I feel unable to
share the customary enthusiasm for the writer, I have tried to show
where his work seems to me to fail.

It is a matter of some difficulty to decide where to begin. An American scholar has recorded that some 600 French novels were published
between 1600 and 1660, and a further 650 between 1660 and 1699.
In spite of their number and size very few of them have survived and
even fewer are still worth reading. We only need to glance at one
of the twenty volumes of *Le Grand Cyrus*—Madeleine de Scudéry's
famous best-seller which swept polite society off its feet in 1649—to see
that it is completely unreadable. Scarron's *Roman comique*, which was
published two years later, is sometimes amusing, but it is almost impossible to read it all through to-day. Furetière's *Roman bourgeois*, which
appeared in 1666, is a vivid and entertaining picture of middle-class
society in the seventeenth century—the author's sharp pen got him into
serious trouble—but as a novel it can only be described as primitive.

In spite of M. Gide's slightly disparaging comments, the *Princesse de
Clèves* seems to me to be the first French novel which was written
entirely for grown-ups and which we are entitled to call a 'modern'
novel. M. Gide himself has spoken of the great contribution of the
French moralists and it is right to emphasize that Mme de La Fayette's
novel was written in close collaboration with La Rochefoucauld. For it
is surely the gifts that have made the French a nation of moralists which
have contributed so largely to the impression of poise and maturity
that we have in reading the greatest French novelists. That is why Mme
de La Fayette appears to be the founder of a tradition which runs in a
direct line through Laclos, Constant and Stendhal to Proust.

I do not put the *Liaisons dangereuses* quite so high as M. Gide, but no
study of the major French novelists could omit that very great, very
unedifying and in England very neglected masterpiece.

The other five novelists chose themselves, and their inclusion does not call for comment or justification. It seems necessary, however, to say rather more about the omissions. I had hoped to include a short chapter on Marivaux which would have helped to bridge the gap between the *Princesse de Clèves* and the *Liaisons dangereuses*. He was a distinguished writer who has never had his due in this country either as a dramatist or as a novelist; but it is evident that he was not a novelist of the same calibre as the other seven, and I reluctantly decided to omit him in order to give more space to them. Rousseau's influence was immense, but he was only doubtfully a novelist and I cannot think that the intrinsic value of his works of fiction justified a separate study. I have therefore only discussed them incidentally. *Manon Lescaut* strikes me as a tiresome example of eighteenth-century pathos—I am glad to find that M. Gide is decidedly lukewarm about it—and I entirely agree with Stendhal over Voltaire. *Dominique*, which finds a place on M. Gide's list, is an engaging period piece, but surely nothing more. Recent attempts to present Guy de Maupassant as a great novelist seem to be somewhat misguided. We naturally expect accomplishment from a pupil of Flaubert's, and we certainly get it. In his way Maupassant is unique. He is an example of the supreme technician who appears to have been almost entirely devoid of the moral and intellectual qualities which are essential to a great writer. That, perhaps, is why he was virtually the inventor of the commerical short story.

I hesitated over Zola, but in spite of his bulk and his competence, I do not think that it can seriously be argued that he was a great novelist or that he was of the same order as the other nineteenth-century novelists with whom I have dealt. Artistically, naturalism (as the nineteenth century understood it) was never anything more than a blind alley, and for the most part Zola's novels belong to the study of political and social propaganda rather than to the study of fiction.

Criticism must be honest. It must also be critical. The critic is expected to tell his readers what he thinks of an author's books. He should approach the work of a great writer with humility; where he is unable to subscribe to current estimates he should at least read with respect what his predecessors in the same field have said, and should give due weight to their opinions. No writer's reputation, however, is or ought to be sacrosanct. The critic does not pretend to be infallible. Absolute impartiality is impossible and even the examples of a writer's work which he quotes are necessarily affected by subjective considerations; but provided that he produces his *pièces justificatives* and provided that he has tried to be fair in his selection of them, the critic is entitled to say what he likes and is, indeed, paid to do so. No criticism of a great writer can ever be final. All the critic can hope to do is to give his opinions and show how he arrived at them. He is justified in expecting collaboration from his readers, and dissent is not necessarily a less valuable form of collaboration than assent. There is plenty of room for controversy, but literary criticism ought not to degenerate into unseemly squabbles between contending factions. That is another reason why the critic should aim as far as possible at detachment.

I have emphasized these considerations in view of what I shall have to say about Balzac and Flaubert. Balzac was a genius. Without him, as a French friend put it to me not long ago, there would have been a gap in French literature which no other writer could have filled. Yet I cannot help feeling that it is Balzac's uniqueness rather than his achievement which has led to an exaggerated estimate of his work, that he is 'the greatest French novelist' in much the same sense that Hugo is 'the greatest French poet'. His work as social historian, 'visionary' and story-teller has been praised by many other writers. I have therefore confined my own study very largely to developing theories put forward by a recent French critic who describes his book on Balzac's language as 'the least Balzacian study to be written by a Balzacian'. Flaubert was a great writer; I never re-read any of his finest work without finding in it something which had escaped me in previous readings; but he was nevertheless a great writer whose technical equipment was vastly superior to his matter. That, I think, is the basis on which discussion of both writers should take place; and it is singularly unfortunate that in the case of Flaubert the issues should have been confused by the gratuitous introduction of political sectarianism.

It is, perhaps, right to conclude by laying the remainder of my own cards on the table. For me Stendhal is the greatest French novelist, and I can think of no one who has a better claim to second place than Proust. We feel a natural sympathy for novelists who manage to say what they have to say in half a dozen books, but it is a matter of great difficulty to 'place' a Laclos who produced a single novel of moderate length or a Constant whose solitary masterpiece is less than a hundred pages long. Their books appear at first to be superb flukes and we feel doubtful whether a man can be properly described as a great *novelist* on the strength of one book. Happily there is no doubt about their quality. The *Liaisons dangereuses* is the greatest French novel of the eighteenth century; and among French novels of the nineteenth century *Adolphe* seems to me to rank, as a finished work of art, immediately after the *Chartreuse de Parme* and *Le Rouge et le noir*.

·   ·   ·   ·   ·

Parts of this book have appeared in *The Times Literary Supplement,*
The Nineteenth Century and After, Scrutiny, Horizon and *The Month.* I am
indebted to the editors and publishers of those journals for permission
to reproduce them here. Acknowledgments are also due to the follow-
ing publishers for kindly allowing me to quote from English transla-
tions published by them: Messrs. Chatto & Windus for C. K. Scott
Moncrieff's *Remembrance of Things Past, Scarlet and Black* and *The*
Charterhouse of Parma, and Stephen Hudson's *Time Regained*; J. M.
Dent & Sons Ltd. for Anthony Goldsmith's *Sentimental Education*;
Hamish Hamilton Ltd. for Mr. Gerard Hopkins' *Madame Bovary,*
Mr. Carl Wildman's *Adolphe* and Miss Kathleen Raine's *Cousin Bette.*

February 1950   M.T.

CONTENTS

ILLUSTRATIONS

THE LANGUAGE OF FICTION

THE LANGUAGE OF FICTION

I

THE critic of fiction has a more difficult task than the critic of poetry or the drama. We all know or think we know what constitutes a poem or a play, but the critic of the novel has to begin by defining his elusive subject. A good many writers have adopted the historical approach and have tried to show that the contemporary novel is a direct development of the novel of classical times. They have selected a single concept—'character', 'plot', 'structure' and 'form' are among the best known—and have argued that it has always been the novelist's main concern and is the clue to his art. The result is that criticism of fiction tends to be too abstract and schematic to offer the reader much assistance in the appreciation of a particular novel.

The novel is perhaps the most unwieldy of all literary forms because the novelist's experience is much less compact than the poet's or even the dramatist's. The critic is bound to rely on a comparatively small number of quotations instead of being able to quote a complete work, and this naturally increases the danger of misinterpretation. He cannot easily dispense with abstractions like character, plot, structure and form which provide him with a convenient system of reference. When properly used, they have a certain utility value and they will appear frequently in the pages that follow. It must be recognized, however, that they belong to the presentation of experience and not to the substance of the novel. The mistake lies in imagining that when we speak of a novelist's 'convincing characterization', the excellence of his 'plots' or his 'narrative gift' we are pronouncing critical judgments, whereas in fact we are doing no more than commend the skill with which he displays his wares.

'Character' has naturally been by far the most popular of the definitions that I have mentioned, as it has been the most mischievous; and it is only during the past thirty years that critics have seriously challenged the widely accepted view that a novel or a play is no more than a biography of an imaginary person.

Now there are strong historical reasons for this belief in the supre-

3

macy of character and they are worth examining. It is sometimes said that character was an invention of the Romantic Movement, but in reality it is much older than that. It is a reflection of changing conceptions of man's nature and goes back to the emergence of the individual at the Renaissance. The Renaissance humanists diverted attention from man in society to the individual who dominates the community. The change was, perhaps, more marked in Protestant than in Catholic countries. The link between the Cornelian hero and the élite which produced him is much closer than that between the Shakespearean hero and Elizabethan society. We find an Englishman like Dryden expatiating on Shakespeare's characterization while a Frenchman like Saint-Évremond—a critic who was very much in advance of his time—was far more concerned with Corneille's impact on his audience.

The heroic age did not last long. Mr. Santayana has argued in *Winds of Doctrine* that the Copernican astronomy—Donne's 'new philosophy' —struck a mortal blow at the belief that man was the centre of the universe; and more recently M. Paul Bénichou has described the part played by Pascal and La Rochefoucauld in what he calls 'the demolition of the hero'.[1] It always takes some time for the full effect of philosophical changes to make themselves felt on art and the life of the people. Shakespeare's 'What a piece of work is man!' is echoed, mockingly, in the eighteenth century by Pope's 'The glory, jest, and riddle of the world!'

'Glory' has not entirely departed, but it has become slightly ridiculous and the focus is shifting to man's enigmatic qualities. This tendency received a powerful if indirect impetus from Rousseau's *Confessions*. Man might have become less glorious, but to the eighteenth and nineteenth centuries he appeared much more interesting. The last quarter of the eighteenth century saw the publication of a number of studies of Shakespeare's characters of which the most representative was Morgann's *Essay on the Dramatic Character of Sir John Falstaff*, and this approach culminated in the next century with its speculations about Hamlet's student life and the number of Lady Macbeth's children.[2]

The disruptive tendencies of the seventeenth and eighteenth centuries were reinforced by the rise of the scientific philosophies in the nineteenth century and their influence on the novel was very marked. Balzac's monomaniacs can be traced back through Molière to Corneille and, as we shall see, they represent the final dissolution of the hero in a commercial society. Flaubert's *ratés* seem to possess a similar historical importance; they point to the demolition not merely of the hero, but

[1] In *Morales du grand siècle* ('Bibliothèque des Idées'), (Paris, 1948), pp. 97–111.
[2] See Professor L. C. Knights's *Explorations* (London, 1946), pp. 1–39.

of man himself. When we compare Mme de La Fayette's portrait of
the Duc de Nemours with a passage from Zola's *Germinal* we can see
the extent of the changes which have taken place in the short space of
two hundred years:

> Mais ce prince était un chef-d'œuvre de la nature. . . . Ce qui le mettait
> au-dessus des autres était une valeur incomparable et un agrément dans son
> esprit, dans son visage et dans ses actions que l'on n'a jamais vu qu'à lui
> seul.

> Il y avait là des herscheurs, des moulineurs, jusqu'à des galibots de
> quatorze ans, toute la jeunesse des fosses, buvant plus de genièvre que de
> bière.

> [But this prince was nature's masterpiece. . . . What placed him above
> others was an incomparable valour and an attractiveness of mind, face and
> carriage which has never been seen except in him.

> There were putters, trammers, down to pit-lads of fourteen there, the
> whole of the youth of the pits, drinking more gin than beer.]

'I do not know', said Lanson of the second passage, 'what he meant
by *herscheurs, moulineurs, galibots,* but I have a vague picture of a cohort
of miners. . . .'[1] The implication is plain. The novelist no longer sees
man as an individual; he simply sees him in the mass, as part of a
'cohort' of workers.

The modern novel, indeed, divides into two main schools. One
concentrates on the sensitive individual who has become the prisoner
of his own sensibility. The other describes the cohorts of the 'party'—
for naturalism led almost inevitably to the contemporary political
novel—trying to destroy the last strongholds of individualism.[2]

It therefore appears that the attempt to break down the nineteenth-
century idea of character was not due entirely to critical acumen; it
was forced on the critic by the changes which had taken place in the
conception of man's nature. The development of the inner monologue,
the subtleties of Henry James and the unending meditations of Proust's
narrator showed that character had lost the finality which had been
claimed for it. The late C. H. Rickword drew attention to the ' "subjective" novelists' increasing tendency to rely for their effect not on set

[1] *L'Art de la prose* (Paris, 1908), p. 233.
[2] See Edwin Muir's 'The Natural Man and the Political Man' in *Essays on Literature
and Society* (London, 1949), pp. 151–65.

pieces of character drawing, but directly on the poetic properties of words';[1] and in a striking essay in the second volume of his *Stilstudien* Leo Spitzer remarked that Proust's syntax was 'the expression of the complexity of all being'.[2] It is evident that the conventional idea of character was a hindrance rather than a help in interpreting this 'complexity'. On the other hand, the exploits of the party member could only be measured by a non-literary criterion which made character equally irrelevant.

It is appropriate that a more suitable standard should already have been suggested by one of the first of the great nineteenth-century masters:

> Un roman [said Stendhal] est comme un archet, la caisse du violon *qui rend les sons*, c'est l'âme du lecteur.[3]

> [A novel is like a bow, the case which makes the sounds is the reader's soul.]

The novelist seeks to communicate an imaginative experience to his reader. He does so by imposing the pattern of his own sensibility on him and the medium which he uses is language. The critic of the novel no less than the critic of poetry is concerned first and foremost with 'arrangements of words on a page'. For, said Rickword, 'character is merely the term by which the reader alludes to the pseudo-objective image he composes of his responses to an author's verbal arrangements'.[4] This is an extreme statement of the new attitude, but it is evident that a character is a verbal construction which has no existence outside the book. It is a vehicle for the novelist's sensibility and its significance lies in its relations with the author's other constructions. A novel is essentially a verbal pattern in which the different 'characters' are strands, and the reader's experience is the impact of the complete pattern on his sensibility. The fact that we tend to consider certain characters from fiction in isolation means either that we are seeking to enlarge or add to the novelist's experience, or that he has chosen to incorporate what is most vital in his experience in one or two of his principal characters. It remains true therefore that 'character' belongs to the organization and presentation of experience rather than to its substance, and when it is used as a substitute for the detailed elucidation of the text it becomes a nuisance. The study of the novels which have been written during the last two centuries can tell us a great deal about moral, social and

---

[1] In *Towards Standards of Criticism* (London, 1933), p. 32. [2] Munich, 1928, p. 396.
[3] *La Vie de Henri Brulard* (Divan Edition), I, p. 227. [4] *Op. cit.*, p. 31.

political changes, but it is only by first submitting ourselves to the violinist's bow and listening to our own sensibility that we can say anything of value about the novelist's art.

It follows from this that the study of the French novel is primarily a study of the alterations which have taken place in the French language and of the novelists' use of their resources.

2

When we read the *Princesse de Clèves* for the first time, it seems to have something of the elusiveness of the French classical drama. The formal, elevated prose appears as remote as the alexandrine, and we are conscious of the same lack of sensuous appeal. It is only later that we perceive the delicate emotional overtones that Mme de La Fayette conveys with her abstract words and the skilful changes of tone.

Mais, ce qui rendait cette Cour belle et majestueuse, était le nombre infini de princes et de grands seigneurs d'un mérite extraordinaire. Ceux que je vais nommer étaient, en des manières différentes, l'ornement et l'admiration de leur siècle.

Le Roi de Navarre attirait le respect de tout le monde par la grandeur de son rang et par celle qui paraissait en sa personne. Il excellait dans la guerre, et le duc de Guise lui donnait une émulation qui l'avait porté plusieurs fois à quitter sa place de général pour aller combattre auprès de lui, comme un simple soldat, dans les lieux les plus périlleux. Il est vrai aussi que ce duc avait donné des marques d'une valeur si admirable, et avait eu de si heureux succès, qu'il n'y avait point de grand capitaine qui ne dût le regarder avec envie. Sa valeur était soutenue de toutes les autres grandes qualités: il avait un esprit vaste et profond, une âme noble et élevée, et une égale capacité pour la guerre et pour les affaires.

[But what made the Court fair and stately was the infinite number of princes and nobles of outstanding merit. Those whom I am about to name were, in different ways, the ornament and the admiration of their age.

The King of Navarre earned the respect of all by the greatness of his state and of his bearing. He excelled in war, and the Duke of Guise so stirred his emulation that he had been led on several occasions to leave his post as general in order to fight alongside him, as a private soldier, in the most perilous places. It is also true that the duke had given proof of such admirable valour and had enjoyed such great success that there was no great captain who could help envying him. His valour was reinforced by all the other great qualities: he had a vast and profound intelligence, a noble and lofty mind, and an equal capacity for war and for the affairs of state.]

It is evident from these passages that the *Princesse de Clèves* is a novel in the grand manner. Mme de La Fayette's prose, as surely as the alexandrine, is the product of a stable or an apparently stable society.

The first paragraph makes a general statement about the life of the Court. In the paragraphs which follow, the writer turns to individual examples of greatness and valour. The style is, intentionally, pitched in the same key; the words *grand* and *grandeur* echo and reinforce one another.

In an essay on the *Princesse de Clèves*, M. Albert Camus has defined the style of the classic artist as *une sorte de monotonie passionnée.*[1] It is an arresting phrase, but there is perhaps a danger of obscuring the variety of Mme de La Fayette's style. Its effect depends not on a *blend*, but on a *contrast* between 'monotony' and 'passion'. The straightforward syntax, which is the expression of a profound belief in order and in the diverse qualities which contribute to that order, is functional. It provides a norm by which personal experience and personal feelings are tested and judged. Later in the book we read:

'Venez, venez,' me dit-il, 'venez voir l'homme du monde le plus désespéré; je suis plus malheureux mille fois que je n'étais tantôt, et ce que je viens d'apprendre de Madame de Tournon est pire que sa mort.'

Je crus que la douleur le troublait entièrement, et je ne pouvais m'imaginer qu'il y eût quelque chose de pire que la mort d'une maîtresse que l'on aime et dont on est aimé. Je lui dis que, tant que son affliction avait eu des bornes, je l'avais approuvée, et que j'y étais entré; mais que je ne le plaindrais plus s'il s'abandonnait au désespoir et s'il perdait la raison.

'Je serais trop heureux de l'avoir perdue, et la vie aussi,' s'écria-t-il: 'Madame de Tournon m'était infidèle. . . .'

['Come here, come here,' he said to me, 'come and see the most despairing man in the world; I am a thousand times more unhappy than I was a few hours ago, and what I have heard about Madame de Tournon is worse than her death.'

I thought that he was completely deranged by his grief, and I could not imagine that there was anything worse than the death of a woman whom one loves and by whom one is loved in return. I told him that as long as his affliction had had limits, I had approved of it; but that I should no longer sympathize with him if he gave way to despair and lost his reason.

[1] *Problèmes du roman* (Brussels, 1945), p. 193.

'I should be only too happy to lose it, and life as well,' he cried. 'Madame de Tournon was unfaithful to me. . . .']

This dialogue between Sancerre, who speaks first, and the Prince de Clèves illustrates the sense in which syntax is functional. For we distinguish three voices in the novel. There is the voice of the novelist which sets the tone of the book; and there are the voices of the individuals which alternately blend in with the general tone and come into conflict with it. When the Prince de Clèves asserts his belief that grief must have limits which are absolute he contributes to the preservation of order, while Sancerre's threat to abandon himself to despair is also a threat to that order. We can go on to say that the dialogue is a ceremonial which deliberately seeks to impose a check on personal emotion in the interests of the community and to preserve a balance which is already felt to be precarious. The individual speakers do not play the same parts all the time. In this passage the Prince is on the side of order, but in an exchange with his wife later in the book he says:

'Comment pouviez-vous espérer que je conservasse de la raison? Vous aviez donc oublié que je vous aimais éperdument, et que j'étais votre mari? L'un des deux peut porter aux extrémités; que ne peuvent point les deux ensemble! . . . Je n'ai que des sentiments violents et incertains dont je ne suis pas le maître: je ne me trouve plus digne de vous; vous ne me paraissez plus digne de moi; je vous adore, je vous hais; je vous offense, je vous demande pardon; je vous admire, j'ai honte de vous admirer; enfin, il n'y a plus en moi ni de calme ni de raison.'

['How could you expect me to preserve my reason? Had you forgotten that I was madly in love with you, and that I was your husband? Either is enough to drive me to extremes; what can't happen with the two together! . . . I have only violent and uncertain feelings of which I am no longer master. I find that I am no longer worthy of you. You no longer appear to be worthy of me. I adore you, I hate you; I'm offensive and I ask your forgiveness; I admire you, I'm ashamed of admiring you. In short, I'm incapable of calmness or reasonableness.']

When we read this, we perceive that nearly all the characters speak with two voices—the voices of the private individual and the public personage—which maintain a perpetual dialogue. We overhear the murmur of the tormented, uneasy conscience, floating up to us from the underworld of temptation and desire, trying desperately to come to

B*

terms with itself and conform to a standard of conduct prescribed by
the community.

3

When we come to the eighteenth century, we are at once aware of a
change. The prose of Marivaux, Voltaire, Diderot and Laclos seems at
first to be more subtle, more elegant and better designed to convey
shades of feeling than that of their predecessors.

> Never [wrote Giraudoux] have the words 'friend' or 'son' or 'seducer'
> been used more directly to designate a friend, a son, a seducer; or the word
> 'woman' a woman. . . . Laclos has the advantage over his predecessors of
> a vocabulary which owes nothing to indignation or to the digestion and—
> we shall always return to the point—which is as carefully delimited and as
> fundamentally pure as Racine's.[1]

It was certainly a marvellous instrument for the analysis and dis-
semination of ideas. Sorel reminds us that in the eighteenth century
French took the place of Latin as the international language of philosophy and diplomacy, and he shows that it played an immense part in
the political upheavals of the age.[2] Its characteristics, said Lanson, were
'intellectualité, politesse, polissonnerie, esprit'.[3] The *philosophes*, as we
know, launched a full-scale attack on traditional religious and philosophical views and it was in order to prevent open scandal that they
developed and perfected the qualities described by Lanson. These
qualities, however, should not blind us to what was lost.

> When it is seen as it really was [said Lanson] and not according to the
> image which it was pleased to present of itself, the seventeenth century is
> overflowing with life—with energetic, fiery, brutal and even crude life. It
> was no doubt refined and not delicate; it submitted its fieriness and its
> brutality to complicated ceremonials whose very extravagance had some-
> thing violent about them.[4]

That is the measure of the eighteenth century's sacrifice. Its writers
possessed an instrument of extraordinary clarity. They were able, perhaps for the first time, to say exactly what they wanted; but the latent
vigour, the overtones of seventeenth-century prose, the phrases which

[1] *Littérature* (Paris, 1941), p. 71.
[2] *L'Europe et la Révolution Française*, I (Paris, 1885), pp. 147–57.
[3] *Op. cit.*, p. 143.   [4] *Ibid.*, p. 55.

echo in the memory had disappeared. For all its elegance, Laclos' prose has a faintly tinny sound.

In a discussion of this nature there are certain reservations to be made. When we look back at the literature of an earlier century, it usually appears more uniform and more homogeneous than it really was. We are aware of a discrepancy between the reality and 'the image that it was pleased to present of itself'. This is due partly to the selectiveness of our reading and partly to a conspiracy between the leading writers. The *philosophes* were very clear-headed and very unscrupulous. They did their utmost to discredit the work of any writers whose views were opposed to their own, not out of a disinterested pursuit of truth but in order to capture the literary market. A number of its most prominent writers were profoundly rationalist and secularist, but there were other forces at work which are overlooked because they do not fit in with the official picture created by the *philosophes*. An attempt to redress the balance was made some years ago by M. Pierre Trahard. In his massive study of *Les Maîtres de la sensibilité française au dix-huitième siècle* he argues that 'sensibility' and not 'reason' was the keynote of the century, and he discovers 'sensibility'—a term which is never satisfactorily defined—in Laclos, whom he describes as a disciple of Rousseau, as well as in the tragedies of Voltaire.[1] His book is a useful corrective to the conventional view of the eighteenth century, but it is difficult not to feel that he spoils his case by overstatement. All good writers naturally possess sensibility, but M. Trahard seems to me to make the mistake of paying insufficient attention to the quality of eighteenth-century sensibility which is often indistinguishable from mere emotionalism or mere sentimentality. It remains true, however, that the century of the Duc de Richelieu and the Comte de Tilly was also the century in which the Princesse de Condé and Mlle de Lespinasse died of love. It was the century of Voltaire, but it was also the century in which fanaticism, 'illuminism' and madness were rife. Saint-Preux was probably no less representative than Valmont. The task of the literary critic is to discover the relations between these different tendencies.

Oh! mourons, ma douce amie! mourons, la bien-aimée de mon cœur! Que faire désormais d'une jeunesse insipide dont nous avons épuisé toutes les délices? Explique-moi, si tu le peux, ce que j'ai senti dans cette nuit inconcevable; donne-moi l'idée d'une vie ainsi passée, ou laisse-m'en quitter une qui n'a plus rien de ce que je viens d'éprouver avec toi. . . . O chef d'œuvre unique de la nature! divine Julie! possession délicieuse à laquelle tous les transports du plus ardent amour suffisent à peine! . . .

[1] Four volumes (Paris, 1931–3).

Rends-moi cette étroite union des âmes que tu m'avais annoncée et que tu m'as si bien fait goûter. . . . (*La Nouvelle Héloïse*.)

Comme je n'ai pas de vanité, je ne m'arrête pas aux détails de la nuit: mais vous me connaissez, et j'ai été content de moi. (*Les Liaisons dangereuses.*)

[Oh! let us die, my sweet friend, let us die, beloved of my heart! What is there left for us to do with a youth which has lost its savour and whose delights we have exhausted? Explain to me, if you can, what I felt during that inconceivable night. Make me understand what a lifetime spent like that would be like, or let me take leave of a life which no longer has anything of what I experienced with you. . . . O nature's unique masterpiece! Divine Julie! Delicious possession for which all the transports of the most ardent love are barely sufficient! . . . Give me back that close union of souls which you foretold and of which you gave me a taste. . . .

As I am not vain, I won't dwell on the details of the night: but you know me, and I was satisfied with myself.]

La Nouvelle Héloïse was published in 1761 and the *Liaisons dangereuses* made its appearance in 1782. It is not to be supposed that human nature had undergone a startling change in the twenty-one years which separated them. M. Trahard is no doubt right in saying that Rousseau's influence is predominant in Laclos' treatise on the education of women and in his letters to his wife, but we are not entitled to assume that the novelist and the private individual are identical. It seems to me, indeed, that these passages are the expression of two different modes of feeling which instead of combining either remained separate and distinct or undermined one another. Their existence created a dilemma for the writer which was well described by Constant at the turn of the century when he wrote in *Adolphe*:

Les sentiments de l'homme sont confus et mélangés; ils se composent d'une multitude d'impressions variées qui échappent à l'observation; et la parole, toujours trop grossière et trop générale, peut bien servir à les désigner, mais ne sert jamais à les définir.

[Men's feelings are obscure and confused; they are composed of a great number and variety of impressions which defy observation; and words, always too crude and too general, may well indicate them but can never define them.]

Constant was acutely aware of the complexity of experience and of the difficulty of finding a medium which would do justice to it. This passage is a criticism both of the French classical style and of Rousseau's experiment. The moralists and novelists of the seventeenth century shared a profound belief in the Rational Man. Their work was an attempt to control the disturbing impulses which Constant was later to describe as *impressions primitives et fougueuses*, and to help man to live a reasonable life by providing him with a series of well-tried maxims for his guidance. The writers of the Enlightenment also admired the Rational Man, but they made the mistake of trying first to eliminate the *impressions primitives et fougueuses*, then to replace *emotion* by *sensation*. Their scepticism led to an impoverishment of the novel. In the work of Laclos we feel that the novelist is operating in a gradually narrowing circle. His analysis reminds us of a mechanic taking a machine to pieces and putting it together again. For human behaviour is absolutely predictable; that his creatures should be swayed by the *transports* of Racine's or the sudden impulses described by Constant and Stendhal is practically unthinkable. When he writes of the sexual exploits of the ruling class he reveals a curious greatness; but the stiff conventional phrases of the letters of Mme de Rosemonde and the Présidente de Tourvel reflect not merely psychological but moral failure.

Rousseau undoubtedly realized that the characteristic style of both centuries was the product of a small civilized élite and was no longer an adequate vehicle for experience; but though his novels provided a release for feelings which had been excluded, his attempt to create a balance was a failure. His Man of Feeling is just as partial and incomplete as the Rational Man. The prose of the *Nouvelle Héloïse*, as we can see from the example quoted above, is a curious hybrid. In his desire to give dignity and moral seriousness to the novel he moved away from the easy conversational style of his century back to the *style oratoire* of the seventeenth century. Unfortunately, he also sacrificed that clarity for which the eighteenth century is justly famous. He did not possess the insight necessary to disentangle the complexities of experience or the classic writer's power of translating obscure feelings into exact language. In his novels language is a barrier which is interposed between the artist and his experience, and the word becomes a substitute for the feeling that it purports to describe. The psychology of the *Nouvelle Héloïse* is pucrile. The characters remind us of a ventriloquist's dolls who maintain an unending stream of words and who always invoke 'virtue', 'chastity', 'honour' and 'purity' as they plunge into an adulterous couch.[1]

Paul Arbelet remarked in his admirable *Jeunesse de Stendhal* that both

---

[1] Contrast 'Le langage de Julie, dans la *Nouvelle Héloïse*, émeut comme celui de Bérénice . . .' (Trahard, *op. cit.*, IV, p. 277).

Constant and Stendhal were born in a barren period and he went on to argue that this accounted for what seemed to him the limitations of their work.[1] I find this view difficult to accept. It seems to me on the contrary to have been a period which was highly propitious for the great writer. It was an intermediate period—the neutral moment—which comes between the end of one age and the beginning of another. The classic virtues had not been finally lost, but there was no dominant mood, no decisive influence at work. The writer could therefore apply the whole of his talent to his books; he had no need to waste his energies trying to produce the conditions in which writing becomes possible or resisting hostile tendencies. He was free to use what seemed valuable in the classical tradition and to create new patterns of feeling. Constant and Stendhal were both influenced by Rousseau and the *philosophes*, but these influences were assimilated and transformed into something which was essentially their own.[2] Their novels exhibit those slight alterations in language which are an unmistakable sign of the great writer.

Ezra Pound once remarked that Flaubert wrote much better than Stendhal, but that in Stendhal there is 'a sort of solidity' which is lacking in Flaubert. He went on to define it as 'a trust in the thing more than the word, which is the solid basis.'[3] This 'solidity' is common to Stendhal and Constant, and they owe it to the discipline which they inherited from the previous century and which was beginning to disappear.

M. Émile Henriot, quoting Anatole France, speaks of a 'disaster of language which had begun under Mirabeau, extended during the Revolution and become aggravated during the Empire and the Restoration'.[4] The originality of the classic style lies in 'the choice and in the order of ideas'. The verb is the pivot of the sentence and gives it movement, balance and stability. The fall of the old order had an immediate impact on language. It is not easy to describe it in a few words. I think we can say that it disorganized the classical syntax, that the emotional upheaval and a sudden preoccupation with material reality led to a fresh emphasis on images and vocabulary.

In a confused situation Constant and Stendhal contrived to preserve

[1] Two volumes, Paris, 1919.

[2] Stendhal did not scruple to use the Romantic stock-in-trade of scaling ladders, lovers concealed in cupboards, log cabins and the rest, but the tone of his work is unromantic, and in the seduction of Mathilde de La Mole it becomes decidedly anti-Romantic.

[3] 'Letters to a Young Poet', written in 1916 and published in *The Changing World*, No. 7 (February–March–April, 1949), p. 27.

[4] *Stendhaliana* (Paris, 1924), p. 209.

the French classical syntax, the eighteenth-century gift for analysis as well as its clarity and good sense; but by a very subtle modification of the eighteenth-century vocabulary they came to express feelings which were undreamed of in the psychology of their predecessors. Constant was occasionally guilty of a Romantic flourish—the description of the death of Mme de Charrière in *Adolphe* is an example—but these lapses throw into relief the excellence of his instrument and the skill with which he normally used it. When he writes

Elle fixait avec une précision inquiète l'instant de mon retour.

[She anxiously fixed the exact moment of my return.]

the *inquiète* qualifies the *précision* and extends its meaning, but it is also controlled by it. When he remarks in another place:

Nous vécûmes ainsi quatre mois dans des rapports forcés, quelquefois doux, jamais complètement libres, y rencontrant encore du plaisir, mais n'y trouvant plus de charme.

[We lived thus for four months in a forced intimacy which was sometimes sweet, but never completely free. We found pleasure in it but no more charm.]

there is a complete correspondence between the words and the perceptions which they register; but though each of the key-words—*forcés*, *doux*, *libres*, *plaisir* and *charme*—has a separate and unmistakable identity, they are all closely interrelated and the final impression depends on these relations. In this way Constant constructs a complex network of feelings 'which is the solid basis'. His central experience—the experience of falling out of love—seems to be the reverse of Mme de La Fayette's in the *Princesse de Clèves*:

Mais l'amour, ce transport des sens, cette ivresse involontaire, cet oubli de tous les intérêts, de tous les devoirs, Ellénore, je ne l'ai plus.

[But, Ellénore, I no longer feel that ecstasy of the senses, that involuntary intoxication, that forgetting of all worldly interests, of all duties—I no longer feel love.]

Yet when it comes it is thrown into relief in very much the same way and the background of 'solidity' gives it its shattering reverberation.

Constant shared most of his positive qualities with Stendhal, but Stendhal's range was much wider and in spite of his apparent carelessness his style was a much more complex instrument. When he wrote of himself in *Une Position sociale*, which is 'a portrait of the artist as a middle-aged man':

> Du caractère en apparence le plus changeant, un mot parfois l'attendrissait jusqu'aux larmes. D'autres fois, ironique, dur par crainte d'être attendri et de se mépriser ensuite comme faible.

> [He appeared to be a person of the ficklest character and sometimes a word moved him to tears. At other times, he was ironical, harsh through fear of being moved and of later despising himself for being weak.]

he hints at that blend of 'tenderness' and 'irony' which gives the *Chartreuse* its strange resonance. *Changeant,* too, is an important word. A great deal of Stendhal's work was directed against both the Rational Man and the Man of Feeling of the eighteenth century. They had become conventions which no longer corresponded to any living experience. For this reason he was at pains to emphasize the contradictions of human nature. He set his personal stamp on the words *singulier* and *imprévu*. They occur again and again in the novels, and they express an attitude of opposition and revolt against convention. *Rêverie* was another favourite word; but Stendhal's *rêverie* was a sign of vitality which had nothing in common with Rousseau's and Flaubert's.

Stendhal's reliance on the verb and his extremely skilful use of short sentences give his prose its lightness and mobility. It is admirably designed to express sharp contrasts and sudden changes of mood, but here his practice differs from Constant's:

> Julien atteignit un tel degré de perfection dans ce genre d'éloquence, qui a remplacé la rapidité d'action de l'empire, qu'il finit par s'ennuyer lui-même par le son de ses paroles.

> [Julien reached such a pitch of perfection in this sort of eloquence, which replaced the rapidity of action of the Empire, that he ended by boring himself with the sound of his own words.]

Instead of relying like Constant on the eighteenth-century antithesis, Stendhal prefers the sudden, violent juxtaposition. The process is organic and interior. When he writes:

Dès qu'on déplaisait à Mlle de La Mole, elle savait punir par une plaisanterie si mesurée, si bien choisie, si convenable en apparence, lancée si à propos, que la blessure croissait à chaque instant, plus on y réfléchissait.

[Whenever anyone earned Mademoiselle de La Mole's displeasure, she knew how to punish him by a witticism so calculated, so well chosen, apparently so harmless, so aptly launched, that the wound it left deepened the more he thought of it]

there is a contrast between the quietness and measure of the means used and the damage done. The wound is an internal one. We have a sense of the blood slowly seeping through the victim's clothing, and when we come to 'plus on y réfléchissait' we feel him suddenly crumple up. I think that we can say that the effect of sentences like these is that of an underwater explosion.

4

With the nineteenth century proper we are on debatable ground. Admirers of Flaubert in this country are inclined to grow warm if anyone lays hands on the Master. The value of criticism naturally depends on the grounds on which it is made. I can see no excuse for the sort of attack which M. Sartre makes in *Situations II*, but there are undoubtedly grounds on which Flaubert can be legitimately criticized. A start was made nearly thirty years ago when Jacques Rivière wrote in the *Nouvelle Revue Française*:

From Stendhal onwards, there sets in a continuous degradation of our ancient, inveterate faculty of understanding and rendering feeling. Flaubert represents the moment at which the evil becomes sensible and alarming. I do not mean that *Madame Bovary* and *L'Éducation sentimentale* show no knowledge of the human heart; but neither of them reveals the slightest sign of a direct view into its complexity; neither carries us a step further in our knowledge of it or gives us a frontal view of fresh aspects. There is in the writer a certain heaviness of intelligence in relation to sensibility; it follows his sensibility badly; it no longer unravels it; and it can no longer penetrate into its caprices or its nuances.[1]

[1] 'Marcel Proust et la Tradition Classique' (February 1920), p. 194. Reprinted in *Nouvelles études* (Paris, 1947), pp. 149–56.

This essay has, unfortunately, only recently been reprinted and it has not had the impact which it should have done. Whether we agree entirely with Rivière or not, it must be recognized that his criticism of Flaubert is a serious one which cannot be disregarded by admirers of that novelist. The strength of Rivière's case lies in the fact that he begins in the right place. For if we believe that after Stendhal something went wrong with the French novel, it is not sufficient to point out weaknesses in the work of individual novelists. We must try to show that, as Rivière and M. Henriot suggest, the French language itself had begun to decay. The implications of this view are very far-reaching and they are by no means confined to Flaubert. Now it does seem to me that compared with Constant and Stendhal, the language of Balzac and Flaubert reveals a fatal imprecision which can easily be illustrated:

> La longue habitude que nous avions l'un de l'autre, les circonstances variées que nous avions parcourues ensemble avaient attaché à chaque parole, presque à chaque geste, des souvenirs qui nous replaçaient tout à coup dans le passé, et nous remplissaient d'un attendrissement involontaire, comme les éclairs traversent la nuit sans la dissiper. (*Adolphe.*)
> . . . mais l'envie resta cachée dans le fond du cœur comme un germe de peste qui peut éclore et ravager une ville, si l'on ouvre le fatal ballot de laine où il est comprimé. (*La Cousine Bette.*)
> Son voyage à la Vaubyessard avait fait un trou dans sa vie, à la manière de ces grandes crevasses qu'un orage, en une seule nuit, creuse quelquefois dans les montagnes. (*Madame Bovary.*)

> [Accustomed to each other as we were over a long period, the various vicissitudes we had experienced together, caused every word, almost every gesture, to arouse memories which translated us into the past and filled us with an involuntary emotion, like lightning flashing through the night but not dispersing the general darkness.
> . . . but envy remained hidden in her secret heart, like the germ of a disease that is liable to break out and ravage a city if the fatal bale of wool in which it is hidden is ever opened.
> Her journey to Vaubyessard had opened a yawning fissure in her life, a fissure that was like one of those great crevasses which a storm will sometimes make on a mountain-side in the course of one short night.]

There is nothing particularly arresting about Constant's image, but it has an obvious rightness. He is analysing the different factors in the attachment between Adolphe and Ellénore. The comparison between the 'flashes of lightning' and the sudden movements of *attendrissement involontaire*, between physical night and emotional 'night' has the effect of co-ordinating these different factors and fusing them into a single image. In Balzac and Flaubert the weaknesses are similar and spring from the same cause. The writers feel that the opening clause gives too faint an impression and needs reinforcing. Bette's 'envy' becomes a 'germ' which ravages her whole personality as though it were a town succumbing to a plague; and Emma's contact with the aristocratic world makes such a breach in her drab existence that it is compared with a huge natural cataclysm. In both cases there is a sense of strain as though the writers were using up their energies to overcome the weaknesses of their medium. In both cases the method used defeats their purpose; it disperses instead of concentrating emotion, blurs instead of clarifying the initial perception.

This is only part of a much larger problem. We are aware in Balzac of the same absence of 'solidity' that Ezra Pound detected in Flaubert, but we are in a better position to appreciate the causes. Constant and Stendhal were successful because they preserved an organic connection with traditional French prose style and moulded their instrument to their needs. In poetry Baudelaire achieved something of the same sort by his adaptation of the alexandrine, but he was less successful than the novelists and far too many of the poetic clichés of the day found their way into his verse. With the later prose-writers, one feels, there was a definite breach with tradition. Although Balzac and Flaubert are alike in their weaknesses, they approached their main problems from different angles.

> We must admit once for all [writes M. Gilbert Mayer] that Balzac was content to write French as it was spoken. His style was not apart from exceptions that of an artist.[1]

This draws attention to an important distinction. Balzac is an exponent of what may broadly be described as the 'natural' style and Flaubert of the 'artistic' style. In an age which was remarkable for the absence of an accepted style, Balzac tried to recover 'solidity' by basing his writing on the spoken word, while Flaubert's attempts to achieve the same end by artistry turned him into the greatest virtuoso of the century. I shall examine the language of both writers in greater detail in another place, but I want to comment briefly on Flaubert's virtuosity. Thibaudet has spoken of his debt to La Bruyère and to the eighteenth century. No one doubts that he learnt a great deal from both sources, but he does not seem to me to have assimilated and transformed

[1] *La Qualification affective dans les romans d'Honoré de Balzac* (Paris, 1940), p. 88.

these influences as Stendhal assimilated and transformed Rousseau and Laclos. On the contrary, what he learnt from them was a number of useful devices which he added to his repertoire. Proust once described his style as 'ce grand *Trottoir Roulant* . . . au défilement continu, monotone, indéfini'.[1] And he quoted a characteristic phrase from *L'Éducation sentimentale*:

> . . . la colline qui suivait à droite le cours de la Seine peu à peu s'abaissa, et il en surgit une autre, plus proche, sur la rive opposée.

> [. . . the hilly ridge which followed the course of the Seine on the right grew gradually lower, and gave place to a second hill, nearer the water, on the opposite bank.]

It is scarcely possible to read a couple of pages from any of Flaubert's novels without coming across this peculiar mechanical movement which Proust well compared to a *trottoir roulant*. The point that I want to make here is that this artificial movement was a substitute for the natural movement of French prose and that it is the key to Flaubert's curious greatness and his strange weaknesses.[2]

It has been suggested that some of the failings of the nineteenth-century novel were due to the 'decay' of the French language, but this needs some qualification. A language alternates between periods of growth and decay, but it must not be assumed that 'decay' is purely negative in its effects. Balzac was thrown back on the spoken word and was driven into strange places to find words to express his particular vision of French life, but he certainly made valuable discoveries in the process. 'A genuine artist like Flaubert', writes M. Charles Bruneau, 'received from the hands of Balzac an instrument which was richer in possibilities than the language of *Obermann*, *Adolphe* or *Ourika*, or even of the *Chartreuse de Parme*.'[3] For in spite of the disabling limitations of his own sensibility, Balzac was responsible for opening up horizons which transformed the French novel. He not only provided Flaubert

---

[1] *Chroniques* (Paris, 1927), p. 194. 'But we love those heavy materials that Flaubert's sentence lifts up and drops again with the intermittent noise of an excavator.' (*Ibid.*, p. 204.)

[2] One of the most striking examples of his virtuosity is the description of the forest of Fontainebleau in *l'Éducation sentimentale* where the verb changes its place in the sentence each time he mentions a different kind of tree. See Thibaudet's interesting analysis in his *Gustave Flaubert* (Paris, 1922), pp. 284-7.

[3] Ferdinand Brunot, *Histoire de la langue française des origines à nos jours*, T. XII, (*L'Époque romantique* par Charles Bruneau) (Paris, 1948), p. 384.

with an instrument which was richer in possibilities than that of any of his predecessors; he helped to forge the instrument which was used with incomparable effect by the greatest of his successors—Marcel Proust.

5

Flaubert's influence on later writers has been as potent and as pervasive as Baudelaire's. They have usually either borrowed and perfected his technical innovations or reacted strongly against his whole conception of the novel. In Proust, however, we find a combination of the two. His comment on the language of the Duchesse de Guermantes is a lucid statement of the problem which faced him as a novelist:

> . . . it is difficult, when one is disturbed by the ideas of Kant and the nostalgia of Baudelaire, to write the exquisite French of Henri IV, so that the very purity of the Duchess's language was a sign of limitation showing that in her both intelligence and sensibility had remained closed to all the novelties.[1]

His problem was twofold. He had to rid the novel of Flaubert's mechanical syntax and restore traditional prose rhythms; and he had to devise a vocabulary—it was here that Balzac, whom he greatly admired, was of immense assistance—which was sufficiently delicate to register the new complexity which came into being during the second half of the nineteenth century.[2] Proust's own syntax was very original and highly personal, but M. Mouton is surely right in describing him as 'un excellent disciple de l'ancienne rhétorique'.[3] It is the 'ancient rhetoric', as M. Mouton chooses to call it, which gives Proust's novel that 'solidity' which was temporarily lost after Stendhal.

> One of the commonest aspects of Proust's style [writes M. Mouton] is this constant effort to find the word which will be more and more precise.[4]

When we compare Balzac's

> Cet esprit rétif, capricieux, indépendant, l'inexplicable sauvagerie de cette fille . . .

[1] *Le Côté de Guermantes*, II, p. 171.
[2] Without Balzac he might possibly have found himself in a position not unlike the Duchesse de Guermantes with intelligence and sensibility 'closed to all the novelties'.
[3] *Le Style de Marcel Proust* (Collection 'Mises au Point'), (Paris, 1948), p. 151.
[4] *Ibid., loc. cit.*

[This stubborn, capricious, independent strain, and the inexplicable unsociableness of the girl . . .

with Proust's picture of the sick man waiting for day

. . . les yeux levés, l'oreille anxieuse, la narine rétive, le cœur battant . . .

[. . . my eyes staring upwards, my ears straining, my nostrils sniffing uneasily, and my heart beating . . .]

we perceive that Proust's language is capable of a far greater range of sense-perceptions than Balzac's and is at the same time far more precise. Instead of Balzac's heavy, muffled impression, Proust gives us a very sharp sensation of the *angoisse* of the patient lying in his bed at Combray. 'He begins', remarks M. Mouton, 'by what is most concrete, the eyes, then turns to the subtler senses, the hearing and the sense of smell. Finally, everything is summed up in a formula which symbolizes sensibility in general, *le cœur battant*, where this sensibility is entirely awakened for waiting.'[1]

In other places Proust speaks of Swann's old age as

. . . cette vieillesse anormale, excessive, honteuse et méritée des célibataires . . .

[. . . that abnormal, excessive, scandalous senescence, meet only in a celibate . . .]

of rooms as having

. . . toute une vie secrète, invisible, surabondante et morale que l'atmosphère y tient en suspens . . .

[. . . a whole secret system of life, invisible, superabundant and profoundly moral, which their atmosphere holds in solution . . .]

of the difference between the sound of bells

. . . non pas le grelot profus et criard qui arrosait, qui étourdissait au passage de son bruit ferrugineux, intarissable et glacé, toute personne de la maison qui le déclanchait en entrant 'sans sonner', mais le double tintement timide, ovale et doré de la clochette pour les étrangers.

---

[1] *Ibid.*, pp. 148–9.

[. . . not the large and noisy rattle which heralded and deafened as he approached with its ferruginous, interminable frozen sound any member of the household who had put it out of action by coming in 'without ringing', but the double peal—timid, oval, gilded—of the visitors' bell.]

There is no doubt that Proust used far too many adjectives in the early volumes of his novel, but in each of these examples we are aware of a constant effort to express highly complex impressions. His work is a reversal of the nineteenth-century novelists' use of words. Each of the epithets possesses a separate identity which relates it to what has gone before and what comes after it. In the description of Swann the first pair of adjectives conveys a psycho-physical impression and the second a moral judgment. In the second example *morale* gives us a shock of surprise. In the third he is extremely successful in distinguishing between the sound of the bells, and the influence of Symbolism is evident in the *ovale* which attempts, characteristically, to express one sense-perception in terms of another.

There has been a good deal of controversy about Proust's style. Rivière described it as a return to the French classical tradition,[1] while Mr. Edmund Wilson has called him 'the first important novelist to apply the principles of Symbolism in fiction'.[2] There is no conflict between the two views. Language can never stand still and there can be no such thing as a 'return' to the style of an earlier age. There are certain properties which are native to all good prose. Proust did not escape the preciosity which was one of the chief failings of the Symbolists, but he did restore some of the classic virtues which had been lost in the nineteenth century and at the same time he combined them with innovations which have made him the most original prose-writer of the age. The nature of his achievement was very well expressed by Benjamin Crémieux when he called him 'le fondateur du *classicisme impressionniste*'.[3]

[1] *Art. cit.*
[2] *Axel's Castle* (London, 1931), p. 132. See also L. A. Bisson, 'Marcel Proust in 1947', in *French Studies*, I, No. 3 (July 1947).
[3] *Du Côté de Marcel Proust* (Paris, 1929), p. 8.

MADAME DE LA FAYETTE AND
LA PRINCESSE DE CLÈVES

La passion ne peut être belle sans excès. Quand on n'aime pas trop, on n'aime pas assez.

PASCAL: Discours sur les Passions de l'Amour.

MADAME DE LA FAYETTE AND
LA PRINCESSE DE CLÈVES

I

'MONSIEUR DE LA ROCHEFOUCAULD,' wrote Mlle de Scudéry, pausing, perhaps, to wag a reproachful pen at the incorrigible Bussy-Rabutin, 'Monsieur de La Rochefoucauld vit fort honnêtement avec Madame de La Fayette. Il n'y paraît que de l'amitié. Enfin la crainte de Dieu, de part et d'autre, et peut-être la politique, ont coupé les ailes à l'amour.'

The spectacle of the disillusioned moralist, very gouty and rather blind, setting up house with the great lady of impeccable virtue who was twenty years his junior is a curious one, but it had a far-reaching influence on the development of the modern novel. Whether La Rochefoucauld and Mme de La Fayette slept in the same bed matters less to us to-day than the fact that they lived under the same roof at the time when *La Princesse de Clèves*—the finest novel of the seventeenth century—was written.[1]

They seem at first a strangely assorted couple, but though in many ways their fortunes had been different they had one thing in common. In 1665 the twenty-one-year-old Marie-Madeleine Pioche de la Vergne had married the Comte de La Fayette—'un homme discret et effacé', as one writer unkindly calls him—and had retired to the country. The marriage was not an unqualified success and after the birth of two children, Mme de La Fayette decided to leave her husband and return to Paris, where she became a prominent member of society. The husband spent most of his time managing his estates in Auvergne until his death in 1683. Mme de La Fayette's biographers do not give any reasons for

[1] 'M. de La Rochefoucauld et Mme de La Fayette ont fait un roman, qu'on dit être admirablement bien écrit. Ils ne sont pas en âge de faire autre chose ensemble.' (Mlle de Scudéry to Bussy-Rabutin.)

'Je serais bien fâché que ces auteurs fussent plus jeunes, car ils s'amuseraient à faire autre chose ensemble, qui ne nous divertirait pas tant que leur livre.' (Bussy-Rabutin to Mlle de Scudéry.)

her decision to leave her husband, but we may suppose that they were largely sexual. She was decidedly neurasthenic and though she was keenly interested in the study of passion, she herself was not passionate by nature. She may like the heroines of some of her own books have contracted a *mariage de raison*, found that it was repugnant to her and decided that the birth of an heir dispensed her from any further wifely duties. The parting appears to have been an amicable one. Whenever he went to Paris for those interminable lawsuits which afflicted so many seventeenth-century landowners, M. de La Fayette invariably stayed at his wife's town house.

La Rochefoucauld's life had been a stormy one. He had been the lover of the Duchesse de Chevreuse and the Duchesse de Longueville, had taken part in some of the most violent happenings of his time and been hopelessly implicated in the Fronde; but he too had been unfortunate in his marriage. In 1665—the year in which the *Maximes* were published—he and his wife parted company and he took the blow hardly. He sought and found consolation with Mme de La Fayette, but it was not until the death of his wife five years later that *la politique* permitted them to make the union public.

These events did not attract much attention in the seventeenth century, and they may not appear of much importance to us, but they were very important to the people concerned. In spite of her apparent lack of enthusiasm for marriage, Mme de La Fayette did not relish living alone. There is no doubt that she and La Rochefoucauld were drawn together by their common loneliness. Mme de La Fayette's unsatisfactory marriage certainly left its mark on her art. Her three principal works are all accounts of people who find out too late that they have married the wrong person and who try, not always successfully, to 'clip love's wings'. The note of sexual frustration which runs all through them bears the stamp of personal experience.

'C'était un misanthrope poli, insinuant, souriant, qui précédait de bien peu et préparait avec charme l'autre *Misanthrope*,' wrote Sainte-Beuve of La Rochefoucauld.[1] It is probable that La Rochefoucauld would have accepted this description of himself. 'Pour parler de mon humeur,' he said in one of those self-portraits in which the seventeenth-century artists delighted, 'je suis mélancolique.' The word *mélancolique* goes a long way towards explaining the limitations of his writings. It is one of the illusions of the Latin mind that truth can be reduced to a set of simple propositions and our unruly desires and emotions enclosed in a few neat formulas. The aim of the *Maximes* is to prove that selfish impulses are the motives of nearly all human actions and to reveal the

[1] *Portraits de femmes*, p. 300.

element of self-interest which lurks behind the most altruistic sentiments. La Rochefoucauld was an extraordinary artist in words, but we
may doubt whether he is altogether the master that he is usually said
to be; he was a very talented writer who had behind him the weight
of a great tradition. It is not surprising that he should have possessed
something of the psychological insight which distinguished the greatest
of his contemporaries or that this insight should have enabled him to
shed a brilliant but distorting light on the workings of the human mind.
We may suspect, however, that his art was not completely the product
of rational analysis as he liked to pretend. It was very largely the
systematization of a personal mood whose shortcomings were concealed by the classic perfection of form and are revealed by the word
mélancolique. His vision was partial and incomplete; he had grasped one
facet of the truth with great clarity and tried to erect it into a philosophy.
He needed a standard to sift and test his findings and a framework which
would set his discoveries in their proper perspective. It is curious to
think that his most balanced work was done at secondhand by colla-
borating in a work of fiction. For Mme de La Fayette possessed
precisely those qualities which La Rochefoucauld lacked. She had the
power of looking at life as a whole; she looked at it steadily and clearly;
and though she saw the impulses described by La Rochefoucauld, she
saw others which were beyond the horizon of his circumscribed vision.
'Monsieur de La Rochefoucauld m'a donné de l'esprit,' she once said,
'mais j'ai réformé son cœur.' It was no idle boast.

2

'While France was rent by civil war during the reign of Charles IX,'
runs the opening sentence of *La Princesse de Montpensier*, 'love was not
slow to find its place among so many disorders and to create plenty in
its own empire.'
   This is a good description of the theme of Mme de La Fayette's
work. In all her stories she is concerned with the disruptive effects of
sexual passion on the community. The *Princesse de Montpensier* was
written between 1660 and 1662 before she came under the direct
influence of La Rochefoucauld, and it lacks the maturity and insight of
the *Princesse de Clèves* and the *Comtesse de Tende*.[1] The difference is at
once apparent when we compare the frigid

[1] It was written in the years following La Rochefoucauld's death, but the actual
date of composition appears to be unknown.

Elle consentit donc à recevoir ses vœux, et lui permit de croire qu'elle n'était pas insensible à sa passion.

[She therefore consented to listen to his declarations, and allowed him to believe that she was not indifferent to his passion.]

with this passage from her last work:

'Je ne pense qu'à vous Madame: je ne suis occupé que de vous; et, dans les premiers moments de la possession légitime du plus grand parti de France, à peine le jour commence à paraître, que je quitte la chambre où j'ai passé la nuit, pour vous dire que je me suis déjà repenti mille fois de vous avoir obéi, et de n'avoir pas tout donné pour ne vivre que pour vous.'

['I think only of you Madame: I am taken up with you alone; and in the first moments of the lawful possession of the greatest match in France, when the day had scarcely begun to break, I left the room where I had spent the night in order to tell you that I have already repented a thousand-fold because I obeyed you and did not give up everything and live only for you.']

'This style and these sentiments are so remote from our own,' wrote Taine in his essay on the *Princesse de Clèves*, 'that we find it difficult to understand them. They are like perfumes which are too subtle; we no longer smell them; so much delicacy appears to us to be coldness or staleness.'[1]

The passage in the *Comtesse de Tende* comes from the letter written to the Comtesse de Tende by her lover, the Prince de Navarre, the day after the marriage that she had persuaded him to go through with the Princesse de Neufchâtel in the vain hope of putting an end to a relationship which was anything but *légitime*. Taine's comment reminds us we are much closer to the seventeenth-century writers than to some of the contemporary writers whom he admired. For the modern reader will scarcely find these sentiments *froids* or *fades*. It is not psychological insight alone which makes the passage remarkable. It is the fearlessness with which the speaker scrutinizes his feelings and his very clear sense of the outrage committed against accepted standards suggested by 'les premiers moments de la possession légitime', as well as the sense of a clear-cut social hierarchy in which the outraged bride is 'le plus grand parti de France'.

[1] *Essais de critique et d'histoire* (2nd edition, 1866), p. 347.

Nor will the modern reader find another passage in the same book *délicat* in the faintly derogatory sense implied by Taine. It is a description of the Comte de Tende's final attempt to regain his wife's affection:

> Il se joignit un nouveau tourment à ceux qu'elle avait déjà: le Comte de Tende devint aussi amoureux d'elle, que si elle n'eût point été sa femme; il ne la quittait plus, et voulait reprendre tous ses droits méprisés.
>
> La comtesse s'y opposa avec une force et une aigreur qui allaient jusqu'au mépris; prévenue pour le Prince de Navarre, elle était blessée et offensée de toute autre passion que de la sienne. Le Comte de Tende sentit son procédé dans toute sa dureté; et piqué jusqu'au vif, il l'assura qu'il ne l'importunerait de la vie; et, en effet, il la laissa avec beaucoup de sécheresse.

> [A new form of torment was added to those from which she already suffered: the Comte de Tende became as much in love with her as if she had not been his wife; he never left her and wanted to resume all his rights which he had treated with such disdain.
>
> The Comtesse resisted with a strength and bitterness which bordered on contempt; because she favoured the Prince de Navarre, she was wounded and offended by any passion except his. The Comte de Tende felt to the full the harshness of her behaviour; he was cut to the quick and assured her that he would never bother her again; and, in fact, he left her alone with considerable curtness.]

The social critic peeps out in the first sentence, but the point is only incidental here and the psychologist is more impressive than the social critic. It is the psychologist who anticipates the contemporary novelist in her presentation of that violent sexual passion which sometimes re-awakens in a husband on the threshold of middle age—that loveless, destructive passion described by Lawrence in *The Rainbow*. The reference to *droits* is characteristic of the seventeenth century; it is the knowledge that her unprepossessing husband's desires are *légitimes* which makes the Countess's feelings so complex and so bitter. Taine's essay helps to draw attention to the classic modesty with which the very intimate details of this violent story are 'put across'.

Mme de La Fayette's two brief *nouvelles* possess considerable merits, but the limitations imposed by the form help us to appreciate how necessary a novel was to give full scope to the writer's talent and to enable her to show the effects of *amour* not merely on a tiny group, but on the community as a whole.

She had, indeed, attempted to write a novel in 1670, but though *Zaïde* is the longest of her books, artistically it is the least successful.

The section called 'Histoire d'Alphonse et de Bélasire' contains a remarkable study of the effects of passion, but the book remains a series of 'episodes' rather than a novel, and it was not until she wrote *La Princesse de Clèves* that Mme de La Fayette found her true form.

3

La Princesse de Clèves was published anonymously in 1678 and was an immediate success. The story is a simple one. Mlle de Chartres comes with her widowed mother to the Court. She makes a highly suitable match with the worthy Prince de Clèves whom she respects but does not love. Almost at once she meets the Duc de Nemours, one of the handsomest and most distinguished men of his time, and falls in love with him. Her husband is overcome with grief at the turn of events and dies of a broken heart—a thing which was not uncommon in an age which believed that 'la passion ne peut être belle sans excès'. M. de Nemours waits for the Princess to recover from her grief and then renews his suit; but she is weighed down by remorse and refuses to marry the man whom she holds responsible for her husband's death. She retires to a convent which is renowned for its austerity, 'et sa vie, qui fut assez courte, laissa des exemples de vertu inimitables'.

The story, which is told with extraordinary charm and insight, could not fail to appeal to a highly civilized people who were acutely conscious of their deepest feelings. There were other reasons besides for its success. In this book the novelist gave her readers a full-length study of the life of the Court which was only lightly veiled by ascribing the events to the reign of Henri II.[1]

The particular qualities of the book are evident from the opening paragraphs:

> La magnificence et la galanterie n'ont jamais paru en France avec tant d'éclat que dans les dernières années du règne de Henri second. Ce prince était galant, bien fait, et amoureux: quoique sa passion pour Diane de Poitiers, duchesse de Valentinois, eût commencé il y avait plus de vingt ans, elle n'en était pas moins violente et il n'en donnait pas des témoignages moins éclatants. . . .
>
> Jamais Cour n'a eu tant de belles personnes et d'hommes admirablement bien faits; et il semblait que la nature eût pris plaisir à placer ce qu'elle donne de plus beau dans les plus grandes princesses et dans les plus grands princes.

[1] He reigned from 1547 to 1559.

[Magnificence and gallantry have never appeared in France with so much brilliance as in the last years of Henry II's reign. The prince was gallant, well-favoured and amorous: although his passion for Diane de Poitiers, Duchesse de Valentinois, had begun twenty years earlier it was no less violent and he gave no less striking evidence of its hold over him. . . .

Never had a Court had so many lovely women and so many strikingly handsome men: and it seemed as though Nature had taken pleasure in pouring forth all her bounties on the greatest princes and on the greatest princesses.]

The writer succeeds with classic economy in presenting a picture of the public life of the ruling class in the seventeenth century. There is immense conviction behind the words describing the particular qualities admired by the age—*magnificence, galanterie, bien faits*. This conviction gives the passage a solidity which makes us feel the *shape* of society. It is reinforced by the *éclat* and *éclatant* with their suggestion of hard brilliance.

What is, perhaps, most admirable is that while the novelist is keenly aware of the value of 'magnificence', 'gallantry' and 'good looks', her critical sense enables her to see that the absence of other virtues makes the society a precarious one. There is already a suggestion of brittleness as well as of splendour in the *éclat–éclatant*.

A few pages later she writes:

L'ambition et la galanterie étaient l'âme de cette Cour, et occupaient également les hommes et les femmes. Il y avait tant d'intérêts et tant de cabales différentes, et les dames y avaient tant de part, que l'amour était toujours mêlé aux affaires, et les affaires à l'amour. Personne n'était tranquille ni indifférent: on songeait à s'élever, à plaire, à servir ou à nuire; on ne connaissait ni l'ennui ni l'oisiveté, et on était toujours occupé des plaisirs ou des intrigues.

[Ambition and gallantry were the soul of the Court, and occupied the minds of men and women alike. There were so many interests and so many cliques and women played such a large part in them, that love was always mixed up with affairs of state and affairs of state with love. No one was calm or indifferent: people thought of improving their position, of making themselves agreeable, of rendering service or of doing ill: they knew neither boredom nor idleness, and were always taken up with pleasure or intrigues.]

C

The movement of the second passage differs sensibly from that of the first. The opening strikes the same note, but the tempo of the passage quickens until the slow urbane movement seems to merge in the sharp staccato

> Personne n'était tranquille ni indifférent: on songeait à s'élever, à plaire, à servir ou à nuire . . .

which reflects a feverish underground activity going on beneath the tranquil polished surface of society. It is not, as it seems at first, a simple change from one movement to another; it is one movement going on inside another. We have a vivid sensation of life moving simultaneously at two different tempos, of a subversive activity taking place within the framework of society.

There is a change, too, in the terms used. In the seventeenth century the French language was already a very precise instrument for the analysis of states of mind and was capable of conveying subtle shades of meaning. *Galanterie* stands for something that is public and open, for the degree of moral licence which is tolerated and perhaps applauded. It is associated with martial valour, but has no connection with *affaires*. *Amour* has the same sinister meaning as in Racine; it is inseparably bound up with *affaires*; it permeates the whole of society with its corrosive influence 'creating disorders of its own'.

On the next page the novelist is more explicit:

> Toutes ces différentes cabales avaient de l'émulation et de l'envie les unes contre les autres. Les dames qui les composaient avaient aussi de la jalousie entre elles, ou pour la faveur, ou pour les amants; les intérêts de grandeur et d'élévation se trouvaient souvent joints à ces autres intérêts moins importants, mais qui n'étaient pas moins sensibles. Ainsi il y avait une sorte d'agitation sans désordre dans cette Cour, qui la rendait très agréable, mais aussi très dangereuse pour une jeune personne.

> [All these different cliques emulated and envied one another. The ladies who composed them were also jealous of one another, and competed either for favour or for lovers; the interests of greatness and advancement were often connected with these other interests which were less important, but to which they were not less sensible. Thus there was a kind of agitation without disorder at the Court which made it highly agreeable, but also highly dangerous for a girl.]

Cabales is one of the focal words not only of this passage, but of the whole book. We sometimes become a little impatient with Mme de La

Fayette's digressions, but the accounts of amorous intrigue which are related with such wealth of detail are an essential part of the novel. They help to underline the main theme and they also give the book its restless movement, its sense of ceaseless friction not simply between groups of people or interests, but between groups of feelings which gradually wear themselves away. *Sensible* is another word that is familiar in Racine, and it stands for that extreme sensitiveness which makes members of a highly civilized community so vulnerable for one another.

One of the central themes of the book is well described by the words 'une sorte d'agitation sans désordre'. It is impossible not to be struck by the way in which words like *agitation, inquiétude, tranquillité* and *repos* seem, mockingly, to echo and answer one another all through the novel:

'Vous n'avez pour moi qu'une sorte de bonté qui ne me peut satisfaire [says the Prince de Clèves to his fiancée]; vous n'avez ni impatience, ni ni *inquiétude*, ni chagrin; vous n'êtes pas plus touchée de ma passion que vous le seriez d'un attachement qui ne serait fondé que sur les avantages de votre fortune, et non pas sur les charmes de votre personne. . . . Je ne touche ni votre inclination ni votre cœur, et ma présence ne vous donne ni plaisir ni *trouble*.'[1]

['You only feel a sort of kindness towards me which cannot satisfy me. You are neither impatient, restless nor fretful; you are no more affected by my passion than you would be by an attachment that was only founded on the advantages of your wealth and not on the charms of your person . . . I do not touch your affections or your heart, and my presence causes you neither pleasure nor emotion.']

In another place:

'Je n'ai rien de fâcheux dans l'esprit,' répondit-elle avec un air embarrassé; 'mais le *tumulte* de la Cour est si grand, et il y a toujours un si grand monde chez vous, qu'il est impossible que le corps et l'esprit ne se lassent, et que l'on ne cherche du *repos*.' 'Le *repos*,' répliqua-t-il, 'n'est guère propre pour une personne de votre âge.'

['I have nothing on my mind,' she replied with an air of embarrassment, 'but the noise and bustle of the Court are so great and there are always so

---

[1] Italics in this and all other quotations mine.

many people with you that it is impossible for body and mind not to grow weary and for me not to seek rest.' 'Rest,' he replied, 'is scarcely suited to a woman of your age.']

Agitation stands for an activity which may be good or bad, which may drive people 'à servir ou à nuire', and this is the crux of the problem. There is no *public* 'disorder' to begin with, but the subterranean *agitation* gradually undermines order.

The world of the *Princesse de Clèves* is a world in which the existence of absolute values is taken for granted, in which it is natural to speak of measure and proportion. Thus we read of 'un personnage si *éloigné* de la vérité', 'une opinion si *opposée* à la vérité', 'une fidélité *exacte*', 'un éclat *proportionné* à son dessein', 'une qualité *proportionnée* à sa beauté' and—most striking of all in its suggestion of controlled passion—'la plus *violente* et la plus *respectueuse* passion'. Yet this intense desire for measure and proportion, this emphasis on purpose (*dessein*) is accompanied by an intense fear that measure and proportion will be exceeded with disastrous results. The prevalence of words like *opposé*, *violence*, *combat* and *effort* betray a sense of strain of which all the characters are aware. They feel that their poise is extremely precarious and are very nervous of the outcome of the conflict between their rules of conduct and *agitation*.

There is every reason for their nervousness. The book itself is a criticism of the standards which are a bulwark against 'disorder', and one of the most important passages describes the moral education of the heroine:

After the loss of her husband, she [Mme de Chartres] had spent several years without returning to the Court. During her absence, she had applied herself to the education of her daughter; but she set to work not only to cultivate her beauty and her mind, she tried to inculcate virtue and to make it attractive to her. Most mothers imagine that it is sufficient never to speak of gallantry in front of young people to keep them away from it. Mme de Chartres adopted the opposite view. She often described love to her daughter, showing her what was agreeable in it so that it would be easier to convince her of what was dangerous in it. She told her about men's insincerity, their deceptions and their infidelity, and about the domestic misfortunes caused by liaisons. On the other hand, she showed her the tranquillity which belonged to an upright woman and what splendour and elevation virtue bestowed on a person who possessed beauty and birth. But she also explained to her how difficult it was to preserve this virtue except by an extreme mistrust of oneself and by taking great care to attach oneself to the only thing that can bring happiness to a woman, which is to love her husband and to be loved by him.

'Les *Maximes* de La Rochefoucauld', wrote Sainte-Beuve, 'ne contredisent en rien le Christianisme, bien qu'elles s'en passent.'[1] Some critics have declared that La Rochefoucauld and Mme de La Fayette were among the first apostles of what has since become known as the *morale laïque*. This description of the 'progressive mother' in the seventeenth century certainly appears to lend colour to the theory, but it seems to me that the novelist is concerned to show the inadequacy of contemporary moral values and that there is no evidence that she herself accepted the code. For here we find a woman attempting to instil the common virtues from which traditional sanctions have been removed. The precariousness of 'virtue' is apparent from the remarkable statement that Mme de Chartres 'tried . . . to make it attractive to her'. When we ask: What is virtue? the answer seems to be: conforming to the standards accepted by society. When we ask: Why should people conform? the answer is: because men are faithless and failure to do so brings *malheurs domestiques*. When we press for something more definite, we are told that the reward of virtue is that people will think well of you and you will possess that 'tranquillity' which graces the home of the *honnête femme*. And if one is beset by temptation, if one is inclined to plunge into 'agitation' and risk 'disorder'? Then one must cling to the only things that can bring happiness to a woman— 'to love one's husband and be loved by him.' In other words, when you look into it, you find that there are no absolutes in her world and that 'virtue' means little more than 'keeping up appearances'.

This then is the slender moral armament with which Mlle de Chartres is launched into the pleasant but very dangerous atmosphere of the Court, and it is not surprising that it proves inadequate.

[1] *Op. cit.*, p. 303.

[2] The shallowness of Mme de Chartres' views is evident from her comments on the relations between Henri II and Mme de Valentinois: ' "It is true", she replied, "that it is neither the merit nor the fidelity of Mme de Valentinois which gave birth to the King's passion or which has maintained it; and that is why it is not excusable. For if this woman had possessed youth and beauty in addition to her birth; if she had loved the King with complete fidelity, had loved him solely for himself without any concern for greatness or fortune and without making use of his power except for things which were proper or agreeable to the King himself, it must be confessed that it would be difficult not to praise the prince for the great attachment that he has for her." ' The implication of the passage is that youth and perseverance in an irregular union not only excuse it, but give it a sort of moral value which is held up to admiration.

The central fact in the book is a *mariage de raison*. When Mme de Chartres tells her daughter of the Prince's proposal, this is the reply:

> Mademoiselle de Chartres répondit qu'elle lui remarquait les mêmes bonnes qualités, qu'elle l'épouserait même avec moins de répugnance qu'un autre; mais qu'elle n'avait aucune inclination particulière pour sa personne.

> [Mademoiselle de Chartres replied that she had noticed the same good qualities in him, that she would even marry him with less repugnance than anyone else, but that she did not feel any particular attraction for him.]

The discussion between the Prince and his fiancée in which he reproaches her with not feeling *inquiétude* or *trouble* in his presence, closes with these words:

> Mademoiselle de Chartres ne savait que répondre, et ces distinctions étaient au-dessus de ses connaissances. M. de Clèves ne voyait que trop combien elle était éloignée d'avoir pour lui des sentiments qui le pouvaient satisfaire, puisqu'il lui paraissait même qu'elle ne les entendait pas.

> [Mademoiselle de Chartres did not know how to answer, and these distinctions were beyond her. M. de Clèves saw only too well that she was far from having for him the sort of feelings which would satisfy him because it appeared to him that she did not even comprehend them.]

This means that in spite of the 'peintures de l'amour', which had formed part of her moral education, Mlle de Chartres was protected for a time by her own innocence. Her mother reflects on the position with some satisfaction:

> Madame de Chartres admirait la sincérité de sa fille, et elle l'admirait avec raison, car jamais personne n'en a eu une si grande et si naturelle; mais elle n'admirait pas moins que son cœur ne fût point touché, et d'autant plus qu'elle voyait bien que le prince de Clèves ne l'avait pas touchée non plus que les autres.

> [Madame de Chartres marvelled at her daughter's sincerity, and she had good reason to do so, for never had anyone possessed greater sincerity or possessed it more naturally; but she marvelled no less that her heart had not been touched, the more so because she saw that the Prince de Clèves had not affected her any more than the others.]

Her husband could scarcely be expected to feel the same satisfaction:

M. de Clèves ne trouva pas que mademoiselle de Chartres eût changé de sentiment en changeant de nom. La qualité de mari lui donna de plus grands privilèges, mais elle ne lui donna pas une autre place dans le cœur de sa femme. Cela fit aussi que, pour être son mari, il ne laissa pas d'être son amant, parce qu'il avait toujours quelque chose à souhaiter au delà de sa possession; et quoi qu'elle vécût parfaitement bien avec lui, il n'était pas entièrement heureux. Il conservait pour elle une passion violente et inquiète qui troublait sa joie.

[M. de Clèves did not find that her change of name had altered Mademoiselle de Chartres' feeling towards him. His position as husband gave him greater privileges, but it did not give him a different position in his wife's heart. The outcome was that though he was her husband, he did not cease to be her lover because there was always something which he still wanted in addition to possessing her; and in spite of the fact that her conduct towards him was perfect he was not completely happy. He still had a violent uneasy passion for her which disturbed his happiness.]

The thesis which is implicit in all Mme de La Fayette's work is that passion, whether 'legitimate' or not, is deadly and it kills. Her characters are faced with the problem of working out the proper relationship between *passion* and *existence* on which not merely their happiness, but in the last resort their lives depend. Her distinction as a novelist lies in the remarkable skill with which she handles language and her use of apparently simple abstract words to convey a subtle and deeply felt moral experience. Her admirable control of her medium enables her to state her problem, to create her situation by balancing *agitation, inquiétude* and *trouble* against *vertu, tranquillité* and *repos*.

At the time of her marriage the Princess's attitude is purely negative:

Mademoiselle de Chartres replied . . . that she would even marry him with less repugnance than anyone else, but that she did not feel any particular attraction for him.

Her mother realizes that this negative attitude is due to lack of experience. That is why she is highly gratified to discover that marriage has done nothing to rouse her daughter's senses, that her heart remains 'untouched'. She is clearly the symbol of a bankrupt system of morality. The 'tranquillity' which she preaches is a neutral state; it can only be preserved by the exclusion of passion; and so far from being a solution of the problem of passion and existence, it simply evades it.

In the opening chapters of the novel the Princess gives the impression of a sleep-walker. The book is a record not merely of her awakening, but of a progress in self-knowledge which is purely destructive and which leads from the theoretical and unreal 'peintures de l'amour' to the very real torment caused by her *inclination* for M. de Nemours.

The unfortunate Princess is exposed to attack on all sides. I think we can assume that in this novel the *mariage de raison* is intended as a symbol of a negative attitude towards passion and as a protection against it. In practice it is no protection. What for the Princess was a *mariage de raison* was for her husband a *mariage d'amour*. The attack on her 'tranquillity' therefore begins inside the citadel where her husband clamours for the satisfaction of his 'legitimate' desires. She is also assailed by M. de Nemours who is to some extent helped by the subversive atmosphere of the Court. When she writes

> Il [M. de Nemours] fit *en peu de temps* une grande impression dans son cœur.

> [In a short time he made a strong impression on her feelings.]

the novelist seems to emphasize the uselessness of Mme de Chartres' 'system'. The mother is quick to perceive her own failure, but when she says to her daughter: 'Vous avez de l'inclination pour M. de Nemours' she only makes matters worse. She gives a name to the vague unrest which the Princess feels and assists in the destructive process. In another place she declares:

> 'Vous êtes sur le bord du précipice, il faut de grands efforts et de grandes violences pour vous retenir.'

> ['You are on the edge of the precipice. It will require a great effort and great strength to save yourself.']

We are told of the husband:

> Il ne trouvait de tous côtés que des précipices et des abîmes.

> [On all sides he saw nothing but precipices and abysses.]

The damage is done, and it is irreparable. Passion is involuntary and instantaneous, a *coup de foudre*, which carries everything before it. It is a sign of the novelist's artistry that she has only to mention the words *précipice* and *abîme* for maxims, slogans and rules of conduct to collapse, and for vast chasms to open in the ordered society which sne describes. The problem of passion and existence is insoluble. For Mme de La Fayette, as for Racine, passion is destiny. 'Tranquillity'—the condition in which there is 'ni impatience, ni inquiétude, ni chagrin'—is sterile and unnatural; but once passion makes its appearance the victim is doomed.

The whole book hinges on the scene in which the Princess tells her husband that she is in love, but refuses to disclose M. de Nemours' name. The *aveu*, which caused a great deal of discussion in the seventeenth century, is really an appeal for help, an attempt to convince the Prince that she must leave the Court in order to be saved from her own passion. The effects are disastrous. From that moment the Prince begins to go to pieces. Once again it is knowledge—the knowledge that another has discovered the secret which eludes him—which does the damage. The passion of the seventeenth-century masters is irresistible, but it has nothing in common with the blind urge of the Romantics. It is accompanied by an astonishing clairvoyance on the part of the victim. He cannot stop himself, but he sees exactly where he is going. For passion is disruptive not merely in the sense that it puts an end to 'tranquillity', but in the sense that it substitutes continual change for the monotony of 'repose'. The victim is constantly making fresh and disturbing discoveries about himself; the *trouble* augments all the time:

> Elle regarda avec étonnement la prodigieuse différence de l'état ou elle était le soir, d'avec celui où elle se trouvait alors. . . . Elle ne se reconnaissait plus elle-même.

> [She observed with astonishment the immense difference between her state of mind in the evening and the state of mind she was in then. . . . She no longer recognized herself.]

The fact that she is trying to 'resist' does not prevent her from becoming jealous:

> . . . elle avait ignoré jusqu'alors les inquiétudes mortelles de la défiance et de la jalousie; elle n'avait pensé qu'à se défendre d'aimer M. de Nemours, et elle n'avait point encore commencé à craindre qu'il en aimât une autre.

> [. . . until then she had known nothing of the deadly disturbance caused by mistrust and jealousy; she had thought only of ways of preventing her-

c*

self from loving M. de Nemours, and she had not yet begun to fear that
he might be in love with some other woman.]

The *morale laïque* is successful in the sense that the Princess is not unfaithful to her husband in deed, but her passion for M. de Nemours
causes 'disorders' of another kind which hasten the death of her
mother, who is broken by the failure of her 'system', and destroy the
Prince. It is only then that the moral drama reaches its climax. The
Princess passes from a state of 'violent affliction', of revulsion against
the man whom she holds responsible for the death of a model husband,
to a state of 'tristesse et langueur'. At this point the Duke decides to
renew his advances:

> Elle alla vers les fenêtres pour voir où elles donnaient; elle trouva qu'elle
> voyait tout son jardin et la face de son appartement; et, lorsqu'elle fut
> dans sa chambre, elle remarqua aisément cette même fenêtre où l'on lui
> avait dit que venait cet homme. La pensée que c'était M. de Nemours
> changea entièrement la situation de son esprit; elle ne se trouva plus dans
> un certain triste repos qu'elle commençait à goûter; elle se sentit inquiète
> et agitée. . . .

> [She went across to the windows to see what they overlooked; she
> found that she could see the whole of her garden and the front of her
> living-rooms; and, when she was in her bedroom, she at once saw this
> same window to which she had been told that the man came. The idea
> that it was M. de Nemours produced a complete change of outlook; she
> was no longer in a state of sad repose which she had begun to enjoy; she
> felt restless and agitated. . . .]

The *triste repos* of this passage is not the same as the *repos* which
precedes passion. It is a transitory state which is the result of exhaustion;
but passion, once it has entered the heart, is ineradicable; it either
switches to a different object or it kills the victim. The 'inquiète et
agitée' in the second sentence shows that the conflict is beginning again.
A page or two later we read:

> Mais cette persuasion, qui était un effet de sa raison et de sa vertu,
> n'entraînait pas son cœur. Il demeurait attaché à M. de Nemours avec une
> violence qui la mettait dans un état digne de compassion et qui ne lui
> laissa plus de repos. Elle passa une des plus cruelles nuits qu'elle eût jamais
> passées.

[But this conviction, which was the outcome of reason and virtue, had no effect on her heart. It remained attached to M. de Nemours with a violence which threw her into a state of mind that deserved pity and gave her no more rest. She spent one of the cruelest nights she had ever known.]

It is in these closing pages that the influence of La Rochefoucauld is most in evidence:

'Je vous avoue [she says to M. de Nemours] que vous m'avez inspiré des sentiments qui m'étaient inconnus devant que de vous avoir vu, et dont j'avais même si peu d'idée qu'ils me donnèrent d'abord une surprise qui augmentait encore le trouble qui les suit toujours.'

['I confess that you have aroused feelings which were unknown to me before I met you and of which I had so little idea that they gave me a shock which increased still further the disturbance which always follows them.']

But, she hastens to add:

'Cet aveu n'aura point de suite, et je suivrai les règles austères que mon devoir m'impose.'

['This confession will lead to nothing, and I shall be guided by the stern rules which duty imposes on me.']

The *règles austères* and the *devoir* have, to be sure, a solid, reassuring ring; but it is precisely the hollowness of these concepts that the novelist sets out to reveal. When M. de Nemours points out that there is no longer any conflict between her 'sentiments' and her 'virtue', she makes a very surprising answer:

'Je sais bien qu'il n'y a rien de plus difficile que ce que j'entreprends,' répliqua Mme de Clèves; 'je me défie de mes forces, au milieu de mes raisons; *ce que je crois devoir à la mémoire de M. de Clèves serait faible, s'il n'était soutenu par l'intérêt de mon repos*; et les raisons de mon repos ont besoin d'être soutenues de celles de mon devoir; mais, quoique je me défie de moi-même, je crois que je ne vaincrai jamais mes scrupules, et je n'espère pas aussi de surmonter l'inclination que j'ai pour vous. Elle me rendra malheureuse, et je me priverai de votre vue, quelque violence qu'il m'en coûte.'

['I know very well that there is nothing more difficult than what I am
going to do,' answered Mme de Clèves. 'In spite of the reasons I have
given, I distrust my own strength. What I think I owe to the memory of
M. de Clèves would have little power over me if it were not supported by
the interests of my own peace of mind; and the claims of my peace of
mind need the support of those of duty; but though I distrust myself, I do
not think that I shall ever overcome my scruples, nor have I any hope of
overcoming my affection for you. It will make me unhappy, and I shall
avoid seeing you however painful it is for me.']

'Duty' is far from being the disinterested affair that it is in Corneille
or that the Princess would like to believe that it is. Her primary concern is for her own *repos* and, as she remarks in another passage, she is
convinced that with his natural inclination for gallantry, M. de
Nemours' passion for her would hardly survive marriage; he would
disturb her peace with other adventures.[1] She would like to return to
the state of 'repose' which preceded passion, but she seems to recognize that this is impossible, that she is condemned to unhappiness. Now
it is of the essence of passion that it must be in a perpetual state of
eruption, and (whether or not she really believes that M. de Nemours
would abandon her) it is this that she simply cannot face. In other
words, 'duty' is little more than a mental fiction which is used to justify
an attitude of complete negation, a refusal to take any further part in
life. It is a sign of the miraculous clairvoyance of the seventeenth century that the Princess admits it:

'Il n'y a point d'obstacle, Madame,' reprit M. de Nemours: 'vous seule
vous opposez à mon bonheur; vous seule vous imposez une loi que la
vertu et la raison ne vous sauraient imposer.'

'Il est vrai,' répliqua-t-elle, 'que je sacrifie beaucoup à un devoir qui ne
subsiste que dans mon imagination.'

['There is no obstacle, Madame,' answered M. de Nemours. 'You
alone stand in the way of my happiness. You alone impose a law which
virtue and reason could not impose on you.'

'It is true,' she replied, 'that I am sacrificing much to a duty which only
subsists in my imagination.']

Her final reference to *devoir* recalls some words used earlier by M. de
Nemours:

[1] Compare: 'Les raisons qu'elle avait de ne point épouser M. de Nemours lui
paraissaient fortes du côté de son devoir, et insurmontables du côté de son repos.'

'Ah! Madame,' lui dit M. de Nemours, 'quel fantôme de devoir opposez-vous à mon bonheur!'

['Ah! Madame,' said M. de Nemours, 'what a phantom duty you put in the way of my happiness!']

In an admirable study of this novel, M. Poulet has pointed out that the 'phantom duty' is far more powerful than plain duty. While he was alive, her husband was impotent in the face of present passion; but once he is dead, once he belongs to the past, he is a far greater resource in helping the living woman to resist the man who has become for her the incarnation of Passion and all its ills.[1]

A final comment completes the picture:

Il se passa un assez grand combat en elle-même; enfin elle surmonta les restes de cette passion, qui était affaiblie pas les sentiments que sa maladie lui avait donnés. Les pensées de la mort lui avaient reproché la mémoire de M. de Clèves. Ce souvenir, qui s'accordait à son devoir, s'imprima fortement dans son cœur.

[A great battle raged in her heart, but she finally overcame the remains of her passion which had been weakened by the feelings which had come to her during her illness. The thought of death had turned the memory of M. de Clèves into a reproach for her. This memory, which was in harmony with her duty, made a deep impression on her heart.]

Unsatisfied passion feeds upon itself and destroys itself as well as the person who suffers it. In the last sentence 'duty' and 'memory' are indissolubly linked; Mme de Clèves makes a symbolical exit from the present into the past, from life to death, which points to her actual departure to the convent.

It is necessary to remind ourselves that Mme de La Fayette was a novelist of the heroic age. It was an age in which all the passions were writ large, in which we are confronted on almost every page by the words *grand* and *grandeur* and in which the great *Christian* moralist could declare that there could be no love without 'excess'.[2] There could be no compromise, no middle course between heroic love and complete renunciation. Mme de La Fayette, however, lived at the end of the heroic age, at a moment when men had come to realize that they

---

[1] In *Études sur le temps humain* (Edinburgh, 1949), p. 161.

[2] It is right to point out that there is a considerable difference of opinion among scholars over the authorship of the treatise attributed to Pascal.

could no longer stand up to the *coup de foudre*. In *La Princesse de Clèves* the conflict does not strengthen and purify as it does in Corneille. It leads to an incapacity for life, to the disintegration and collapse of personality. For the religious ending of the novel must not be misunderstood. There is no conversion here; the widow turns her back on life and lingers on for a few years, a pathetic broken woman. The discovery that great love affairs simply peter out because one of the parties has reached the point at which he or she cannot go on any longer is, perhaps, Mme de La Fayette's chief contribution to psychology and stamps her as a modern novelist.

4

La Princesse de Clèves does not bulk large in Lytton Strachey's *Landmarks in French Literature*, yet it is undoubtedly a landmark not only in French literature, but in the history of the novel. The work of Mme de La Fayette marks a complete break with the gaudy pretentious romances of her time ; it is something which must be recognized at once as a modern psychological novel and which in spite of differences of method looks forward to Laclos, Constant and Stendhal.

Its importance is not merely historical. It is in itself a remarkable work of art which possesses in a large degree the virtues of the great masters of the century—their clarity, insight and economy. It is a searching criticism of a highly civilized and up to a point a homogeneous society which nevertheless contains within itself the germs of its own dissolution. The characters are in no sense abstractions; there is none of the fumbling and none of the uncertainty which we sometimes find in the work of even the greatest of the nineteenth-century novelists. They have their place in the community and they are drawn with a sureness which reveals a profound belief in life; but though they are also symbols of civilized values which are rightly held up to admiration, it is apparent that the sanctions which produced these values are beginning to disappear and their disappearance, at any rate for a time, was recorded a hundred years later by the great novelist of the eighteenth century—Choderlos de Laclos. For Mme de La Fayette belonged to an age of transition which was not without affinities with our own. Civilization seemed to have survived the beliefs that created it and the task of the artist was to sift and test all commonly accepted beliefs and assumptions, to separate the true from the false and to point out the weaknesses which threatened to undermine the whole social order. That is what Mme de La Fayette did in her finest work. She showed that political corruption and intrigue, ambition and licence were sapping the foundations of society and gradually infecting even its soundest members. They were too intelligent to be unaware of the danger; they might make heroic efforts to resist the disintegrating influences; but a fundamental uncertainty about all moral sanctions made them exceptionally vulnerable, so that when the test came they simply collapsed.

CHODERLOS DE LACLOS AND
THE *LIAISONS DANGEREUSES*

CHODERLOS DE LACLOS AND
THE *LIAISONS DANGEREUSES*

I

TOWARDS the end of March 1782, polite society in Paris received a considerable shock. The *Mercure de France* announced among the spring publications *Les Liaisons dangereuses, ou lettres recueillies dans une société et publiées pour l'instruction de quelques autres*. The book was signed only by the initials of the author and purported to have been published at Amsterdam, though it could be obtained from Durand *neveu*, a fashionable Parisian bookseller.

The public was not deceived either by the initials or by the high moral claims which the author made for the book in his preface. It was known to be the work of a forty-one-year-old artillery officer, Pierre-Ambroise-François Choderlos de Laclos. We do not know a great deal about Laclos the writer. His book has been called the most impersonal novel in the French language and certainly the author is not to be found in it. His biographers describe him, a little vaguely, as an 'homme vertueux, bon fils, bon père, excellent époux'. We catch a glimpse, in Tilly's fascinating memoirs, of a 'grand monsieur maigre et jaune, en habit noir'.[1] He seems to have been cold and reserved, more inclined to observe people than to talk to them; but in a burst of confidence he once told Tilly that Valmont was a portrait of one of his comrades-in-arms. His Mme de Merteuil, he added, was only 'a feeble copy' of a certain *marquise* whom he had met at Grenoble and whose amorous exploits were said to be 'worthy of the times of the most insatiable of the Roman empresses'.[2]

If we know little about the writer, we are rather better informed about the soldier-politician. Four years after the publication of the *Liaisons*, Laclos got into serious trouble with the military authorities

---

[1] *Mémoires du Comte Alexandre de Tilly pour servir à l'histoire des mœurs de la fin du XVIIIe siècle*, ed. Christian Melchior-Bonnet (Collection 'Jadis et Naguère', Paris, 1929), I, p. 202.
[2] *Ibid.*, pp. 224–5. The initials mentioned by Tilly are thought to refer to a certain Mme de la Tour du Pin de Montmort whom Stendhal claims to have known when he was a child at Grenoble.

when his entry for the essay competition on Vauban, which was nothing short of an *éreintement* of that celebrity, cost him his commission. He devoted some years to politics as secretary to the Duke of Orléans, returned to the army in 1792 and died at Taranto in 1803, a General in Napoleon's armies.

It is possible to make out a case for treating Laclos as a moralist and Baudelaire declared roundly, in his tantalizingly brilliant notes on the *Liaisons*, that it is 'un livre de moraliste aussi haut que les plus élevés, aussi profond que les plus profonds'.[1] Laclos may have been a reformer at heart and he may have been convinced that Vauban's theories of defence were mistaken, but he was not altogether the detached critic that he pretended. There can be little doubt that in publishing the *Liaisons* he intended to cause a commotion, as there is little doubt that the essay on Vauban was intended to set the military experts by the ears.

He must have succeeded better than he expected, and he seems to have been surprised by the violence of the reactions that he provoked. The *Liaisons* was read by everyone and discussed in all the salons, but the people who read him with most passion shut their doors in his face; and though Marie-Antoinette had a copy of the novel in her library, she took care to have the title and the author's name removed from the cover of the book. We may wonder why a society which had been brought up on the works of the *libertins*, had applauded the *Sopha* of Crébillon *fils* and the *Poésies érotiques* of the Chevalier de Parny should have reacted so violently against the *Liaisons* which is certainly neither erotic nor obscene.

> I am not surprised that a son of M. Choderlos writes well [said Mme Riccoboni in a letter to the author]. Wit is hereditary in his family; but I cannot congratulate him on using his talents, his facility and the graces of his style to give foreigners such a revolting idea of the morals of his country and of the taste of his compatriots.[2]

The answer is that Laclos let the cat out of the bag. His novel is, as Baudelaire said, 'un livre d'histoire', and because it was so it was also an immense *trahison* which told the world exactly how French society spent its time, shattered the illusion created by the salacious little fairy tales of contemporary erotic writers which were popular precisely

---

[1] *Juvenilia, Œuvres posthumes, Reliquiæ* (Conard Edition), I, pp. 328–38.

[2] Laclos, *Œuvres complètes* (Bibliothèque de la Pléiade, ed. Maurice Allem, 2nd edition, Paris, 1943), pp. 710–11. (This admirable edition contains, among much other valuable material, the whole of Baudelaire's notes on the *Liaisons* and Tilly's account of the author which is well worth reading.)

because they were a smoke-screen that concealed the exploits of the aristocracy from the rest of the world. Instead of the pastoral dream, 'in this new mirror dainty shepherds and tender shepherdesses appear with criminal faces, their features livid and hollow, their eyes filled with hatred, their lips hissing and serpents twined round their crooks. Yet people recognized their portraits in them and the likeness was so good that they could not turn their horrified gaze from this new image of themselves.'[1]

This explains the consternation of Laclos' contemporaries, and the preoccupation with sexual intrigue may also explain why certain critics of the French novel are inclined to pay a timid and embarrassed tribute to this *beau livre* before hurrying on with obvious relief to some milder and more genteel writer. It does not explain why 'even to-day, the *Liaisons* remains the only French novel which gives you the impression of danger and on whose cover it seems necessary to have a label stating that it is for external use only. A hundred and fifty years after its appearance, its internal use attacks, gnaws [into us]. . . .'[2] It is like many great works a 'betrayal' not simply of an age, but of human nature itself.

2

In one of his letters Laclos describes *Clarissa* as a 'chef d'œuvre des hommes', and it was from Richardson that he borrowed his method. The novel written in the form of letters was one of the literary conventions of the time, but it was a convention which was peculiarly suited to his purpose. For, leaving aside the moralists, Laclos was one of the first great analysts of the human heart. In saying this I am not forgetting Baudelaire's observation on 'la puissance de l'analyse racinienne' or the *Princesse de Clèves*; but analysis is a term which can only be applied to the imaginative writers of the seventeenth century with the greatest circumspection. 'C'est à la poésie, à elle seule que seront toujours réservées la navigation et la découverte.'[3] Giraudoux's comment is an overstatement of an important truth. There is, properly speaking, no such thing as analysis in the seventeenth-century dramatists. Their discoveries are the product of intuition, of sudden insight into the workings of the human mind which enables them to reveal feelings which are still inarticulate:

> Déjà même je crois entendre la réponse
> Qu'en secret contre moi votre haine prononce.

---

[1] Émile Dard, *Le Général Choderlos de Laclos auteur des 'Liaisons dangereuses', 1741–1803* (nouvelle éd., Paris, 1936), p. 2.

[2] Jean Giraudoux, *Littérature*, p. 60.   [3] Giraudoux, *op. cit.*, p. 65.

There is, to be sure, something to which we can scarcely deny the name of psychological analysis in the elucidation of the moral problem at the end of the *Princesse de Clèves*, but for the most part the novelist uses the method of the dramatists and the novel of psychological analysis is the invention of the eighteenth century. For it is not until the eighteenth century that the novelist sits back and deliberately takes his mind to pieces. Now there are important differences between a novel like the *Liaisons dangereuses* and a nineteenth-century novel like *Adolphe*. The *solitary* destructive analysis of *Adolphe* is the nineteenth century's distinctive contribution. The seventeenth century had tried to answer the question: 'What is man?' The nineteenth century tried to answer the question: 'What sort of a man am *I*?' The novelist explained the causes of his feelings and passed judgment on them, provoking a conflict which ended by paralysing action and destroying him. Laclos' aim and method are different. He is interested not in thought, but in action, in answering the question: 'How must I *act* in order to . . . ?' The letter-writer supposes an audience and at once we have the normative influence of society. He only discusses those feelings which interest other people as well as himself. There is no analysis for its own sake; all analysis issues in action, for the writer only takes his mind to pieces in order to fit himself for living. The letters of which the novel is constructed are a series of monologues which makes it very easy to mark the contrast between the different characters, to weave the pattern which consists of contacts between different points of view, reactions to different situations.

The theme of the *Liaisons dangereuses* is sexual intrigue in the eighteenth century, or rather sexual intrigue is chosen as the means of revealing the fundamental antagonisms underlying society. Sexual relations are examined in all their subtle ramifications so that we close the book with the feeling that we have a document of singular completeness and veracity on this particular aspect of society.

At the beginning of the book Mme de Volanges is making preparations for the marriage of her daughter Cécile—'type parfait de la détestable jeune fille, niaise et sensuelle', observes Baudelaire bitterly—to the Comte de Gercourt. Now Gercourt has had the misfortune, or the *maladresse*, to wound the sexual vanity of the two principal characters, the Vicomte de Valmont and the Marquise de Merteuil (who were themselves formerly lovers) by abandoning the Marquise for the Intendante de —— who leaves the Vicomte to become his mistress. They plan revenge. Valmont sets to work not simply to seduce, but to debauch Cécile, who after a miscarriage retires to a convent. Mme de Merteuil seduces Cécile's young man, the Chevalier de Danceny, who retires to celibacy and the Knights of Malta. A large part of the book is devoted to Valmont's assault on the chaste and pious Présidente de Tourvel whom he first seduces, then destroys as a sacrifice to Mme de Merteuil's jealousy. The only human feeling that the pair possess is their affection for one another which survives their theories and their other *amours*. But they are both so determined to dominate, so impatient of any restraint, that Mme de Merteuil cannot make up her mind to return permanently to Valmont. They quarrel and she provokes a duel between Valmont and Danceny in which Valmont is killed. The heaviest doom, however, is reserved for her. She not only loses all her possessions in a lawsuit and is exposed publicly for what she is, she is struck down by smallpox and, hideously disfigured, flies to Holland with such jewels as she has been able to lay hands on.

3

The description in Letter X of an encounter between Mme de Merteuil and what she is pleased to term 'le chevalier régnant' is a good illustration of Laclos' interests and his method. The Marquise has been a little abrupt with the Chevalier:

> Aussitôt, pour le dédommager, peut-être pour me dédommager moi-même, je me décide à lui faire connaître ma petite maison dont il ne se doutait pas. . . . Arrivée dans ce temple de l'amour, je choisis le déshabillé le plus galant. Celui-ci est délicieux; il est de mon invention: il ne laisse rien voir, et pourtant fait tout deviner. . . .
>
> Après ces préparatifs, pendant que Victoire s'occupe des autres détails, je lis un chapitre du *Sopha*, une letter d'*Héloïse* et deux *Contes* de La Fontaine, pour recorder les différents tons que je voulais prendre.
>
> Il [le chevalier] voit d'abord deux couverts mis; ensuite un lit fait. Nous passons jusqu'au boudoir, qui était dans toute sa parure. . . .
>
> L'heureux Chevalier me releva, et mon pardon fut scellé sur cette même ottomane où vous et moi scellâmes si gaiement et de la même manière notre éternelle rupture.
>
> . . . je modérai ses transports, et l'aimable coquetterie vint remplacer la tendresse. Je ne crois pas avoir jamais mis tant de soin à plaire, ni avoir été jamais aussi contente de moi. Après le souper, tour à tour enfant et raisonnable, folâtre et sensible, quelquefois même libertine, je me plaisais à le considérer comme un Sultan au milieu de son Sérail, dont j'étais tour à tour les Favorites différentes. En effet, ses hommages réitérés, quoique toujours reçus par la même femme, le furent toujours par une Maîtresse nouvelle.

[In order to make amends to him and perhaps to myself, I at once decided to show him my little house whose existence he had never suspected. . . . When I reached this temple of love, I selected my most daring déshabillé. It's delicious. It's an invention of my own. It shows nothing and yet it suggests everything.

After these preparations, while Victoire was occupied with various other details, I read a chapter of the *Sopha*, a letter from *Héloïse* and two of La Fontaine's *Contes* in order to practise the different tones I intended to assume.

The happy Chevalier raised me to my feet, and my forgiveness was sealed on that same ottoman where you and I once sealed, with such gaiety and in the same manner, our eternal rupture.

. . . I calmed his raptures and a friendly coquettishness took the place of tenderness. I do not think that I have ever taken such pains to please or have ever been so satisfied with myself. After supper I was in turn childish and reasonable, playful and responsive, and sometimes even licentious; it amused me to treat him as a Sultan in his seraglio where I was in turn his different favourites. In fact, his repeated homage, though always received by the same woman, was always accepted by a fresh mistress.]

Baudelaire speaks disparagingly of 'la fouterie et la gloire de la fouterie', and at first one might pardonably suppose that the book is no more than a superior example of the *roman érotique*. The scene is certainly a phallic rite with *l'accouplement*, however elaborate and exciting, as its end and object. The 'temple de l'amour', the 'boudoir dans toute sa parure' and the uncomfortable *ottomane* are parts of the décor, the sultan in his seraglio is the last refinement of the rite. We might go on to conclude that Laclos does not make any contribution to the study of sexual relations, but simply describes in greater detail and with greater sophistication a *libertinage* which is as old as civilization.

There are, however, a number of things which distinguish this passage from the work of writers who are merely licentious. The first is the almost excessive elegance of the style—we remember the Goncourts' *gentille ordure*—and the complete absence of the hot, stuffy erotic mist which usually envelops a performance of this sort. The next is the gaiety and wit, the comedy of 'cette même ottomane où vous et moi scellâmes si gaiement et de la même façon notre éternelle rupture' and of 'ses hommages réitérés, quoique toujours reçus par la même femme, le furent toujours par une Maîtresse nouvelle'. Lastly, there is the supreme degree of sophistication revealed in the study of the 'authorities' and the preparation of 'les différents tons que je voulais prendre'.

This encounter is described objectively and needs to be completed by an earlier and more intimate passage from the same letter:

Dites-moi donc, amant langoureux, ces femmes que vous avez eues, croyez-vous les avoir violées? Mais, quelque envie qu'on ait de se donner, quelque pressée que l'on en soit, encore faut-il un prétexte; et y en a-t-il de plus commode pour nous, que celui qui nous donne l'air de céder à la force? Pour moi, je l'avoue, une des choses qui me flattent le plus, est une attaque vive et bien faite, où tout se succède avec ordre quoique avec rapidité; qui ne nous met jamais dans ce pénible embarras de réparer nous-mêmes une gaucherie dont au contraire nous aurions dû profiter; qui sait garder l'air de la violence jusque dans les choses que nous accordons, et flatter avec adresse nos deux passions favorites, la gloire de la défense et le plaisir de la défaite. Je conviens que ce talent, plus rare que l'on ne croit, m'a toujours fait plaisir, même alors qu'il ne m'a pas séduite, et que quelquefois il m'est arrivé de me rendre, uniquement comme récompense. Telle dans nos anciens Tournois, la Beauté donnait le prix de la valeur et de l'adresse.

[Come now, languishing lover, those women you've had, do you really imagine that you took them by force? However anxious, however impatient a woman may be to give herself, there must still be an excuse. And what excuse is there which is more convenient from our point of view than the one which gives the impression that we are yielding to force? Speaking for myself, I confess that one of the things which flatters me most is a vigorous, well-conducted attack in which events follow one another in an orderly manner but with speed; which never places us in the highly embarrassing position of having to make good ourselves some clumsiness of which on the contrary we ought to have taken advantage; which preserves the appearance of violence down to the very things which we grant, and skilfully flatters our two favourite passions—the glory of defence and the pleasure of defeat. I admit that this gift, which is rarer than people think, has always been a pleasure to me even when I was not carried away by it; and it has sometimes happened that I have given in solely to reward it. It was on such grounds that Beauty awarded the prize for valour and skill at our ancient tournaments.]

The prose, as good imaginative prose so often is, is a pantomime which performs the actions it describes. The passage opens in a mood of gentle raillery and the *amant langoureux* creates a slow, dreamy atmosphere. The reflection that however impatient a woman is to give in, there must be at least a show of force, creates the impression of desire stirring lazily beneath the polished surface and prepares the way for the changes in tempo. When we reach the 'Pour moi, je l'avoue . . .' the movement quickens, action succeeds action, terminating with *défaite*; but in spite of the sensuous pleasure, intellect remains in control. The whole scene is watched with the critical eye of a connoisseur who speaks approvingly of 'une attaque vive et bien faite, où tout se succède avec ordre quoique avec rapidité'. It is a very superior game in which a *gaucherie* would cause *both* parties the same embarrassment as a double fault on the centre court at Wimbledon. The illusion of violence must be maintained in order to preserve the reputation of the players. The use of images borrowed from military strategy is an interesting characteristic of Laclos' style of which there will be more to say later on. Love is a miniature battle, a sham fight in which generals take up their positions, advance or retreat with the same seriousness, the same skill as a general in the field. The military phrase links up with another, with the 'gloire de la défense et le plaisir de la défaite'. For this time the battle is a friendly one. Ostensibly the role of the female is to be 'defeated' by the predatory male; she derives her *gloire* from a spirited 'defence' which in the nature of things is 'hopeless'.[1] Yet the defeated woman is not so much a *victim* as an *accomplice*; the success of the performance depends on what a witness in a highly amusing case, which was recently before the English courts, described as 'willing co-operation' The engagement does not end in 'victory' for one party and 'defeat' for the other. It is a combination of the two, victory-and-defeat, which gives both the ambivalent feeling of *gloire-plaisir*.

> Comme je n'ai pas de vanité [writes Valmont of one of his exploits], je ne m'arrête pas aux détails de la nuit: mais vous me connaissez, et j'ai été content de moi.

[1] Mme de Merteuil remarks of the Présidente: 'Saviez-vous que cette femme a plus de force que je ne croyais? *Sa défense est bonne.* Tandis que nous nous occuperions à former cette petite fille pour l'intrigue nous n'en ferions qu'une femme facile. Or, je ne connais rien de si plat que cette facilité de bêtise, qui se rend sans savoir ni comment ni pourquoi, uniquement parce que l'on attaque et qu'elle ne sait pas résister. Ces sortes de femmes ne sont absolument que des *machines à plaisir*.'
[Did you know that this woman is stronger than I thought? *Her defence is good.* If we applied ourselves to the task of educating this little girl for a life of intrigue, we should only make her into a woman who was easy game. Now, I know of nothing so dull as the sort of facility which is due to stupidity and which drives a woman to give in without knowing how or why, simply because she is attacked and does not know how to resist. Women of that kind are absolutely nothing but pleasure-machines.]

It is a curious and revealing sentence which reinforces what has been said about sport and sham fights. In Laclos' society sexual exploits played the same part as sport in our own. The performers paced their rooms alone, working out new methods of bringing about the downfall of the friendly enemy as an English cricket captain once devised 'body-line'. They appraise one another's 'technique' with expert eye, discussing 'preliminaries', 'penetration' and 'potency' as cricketers might discuss 'flight', 'spin' and 'stroke play'. In this remarkable work the smoke-room story is raised to the level of art.[1]

A few moments' reflection enables us to see that this book expresses a view of life which is very different from that of the previous century. Moral sanctions have been replaced by the new strategy or what Valmont and Mme de Merteuil call their 'principles'. Letter LXXXI, in which she gives some account of her moral education, deserves particular attention:

> Mais moi, qu'ai-je de commun avec ces femmes inconsidérées? quand m'avez-vous vue m'écarter des règles que je me suis prescrites et manquer à mes principes? je dis mes principes, et je le dis à dessein: car ils ne sont pas, comme ceux des autres femmes, donnés au hasard, reçus sans examen et suivis par habitude, ils sont le fruit de mes profondes réflexions; je les ai créés, et je puis dire que je suis mon ouvrage. . . .
>
> Je n'avais pas quinze ans, je possédais déjà les talents auxquels la plus grande partie de nos Politiques doivent leur réputation, et je ne me trouvais encore qu'aux premiers éléments de la science que je voulais acquérir. . . .
>
> Ma tête seule fermentait; je ne désirais pas de jouir, je voulais savoir. . . .
>
> . . . j'arrivai vierge entre les bras de M. de Merteuil.—J'attendais avec sécurité le moment qui devait m'instruire, et j'eus besoin de réflexion pour montrer de l'embarras et de la crainte. Cette première nuit, dont on se fait pour l'ordinaire une idée si cruelle ou si douce, ne me présentait qu'une occasion d'expérience: douleur et plaisir, j'observai tout exactement, et je ne voyais dans ces diverses sensations, que des faits à receuillir et à méditer.
>
> J'étudiai nos mœurs dans les Romans; nos opinions dans les Philosophes; je cherchai même dans les Moralistes les plus sévères ce qu'ils exigeaient de nous, et je m'assurai ainsi de ce qu'on pouvait faire, de ce qu'on devait penser, et de ce qu'il fallait paraître.

[1] The perfect example is the story of the indomitable Prévan's seduction of the *trois inséparables*. According to Tilly, Laclos maintained that the story was founded on fact. (*Op. cit.*, I, p. 225.)

[But I, what have I in common with these rash women? When have you seen me depart from the rules which I laid down for myself or fall short of my principles? I say my principles, and I mean what I say. For they are not like those of other women adopted by chance, accepted without scrutiny and followed by habit. They are the fruit of deep thought. I created them and I can say that I am my own handiwork.

I was not yet fifteen, but I already possessed the gifts to which the majority of our politicians owe their reputations, and I was still occupied with the merest rudiments of the science that I wished to acquire.

My head alone was seething with excitement. I had no desire for pleasure. I wanted to know.

. . . I was a virgin when I found myself in M. de Merteuil's arms.—I waited for the moment which was to explain everything with a sense of security, and I had to apply my mind in order to display the proper degree of embarrassment and fear. This first night, which people usually imagine will be so unpleasant or so sweet, simply provided me with an opportunity for experience. I observed everything—pain and pleasure—with precision, and I simply regarded these different sensations as so many facts to be noted so that I could think them over.]

A few characteristic phrases leap to the eye: 'Je ne désirais pas de *jouir*, je voulais *savoir*'; 'la *science* que je voulais acquérir'; 'douleur et plaisir, *j'observais tout exactement*'; 'le fruit de mes *profondes réflexions*'; 'des faits . . . à *méditer*'. One of the greatest merits of this book is the absolute clairvoyance of the characters in examining their mental processes, in describing their conduct. They are not restrained by any inhibition, by any feeling of guilt or shame. They are completely untroubled by the modern *angoisse* and Constant's preoccupation with his *malheureuse maladie morale* would have been incomprehensible to them. Nor is this all. When Mme de Merteuil declares: 'Je puis dire que je suis mon ouvrage', the boast certainly is no idle one. For the letter is a perfect illustration of the *constructive* analysis of the eighteenth century in which, as I have already said, the writer only takes his mind to pieces in order to fit himself for living. It explains, too, why, when compared with the great novels of the next century, the *Liaisons* leaves us with the impression of sanity and poise, recalling forcibly Gide's dictum: 'The real secret of classicism is modesty.'

A similar revolution has taken place in the emotional life. 'Car enfin', writes Valmont

Car enfin si j'ai eu quelquefois, auprès de cette femme étonnante, des moments de faiblesse qui ressemblent à cette passion pusillanime, j'ai toujours su les vaincre et revenir à mes principes.

[In short, if I have sometimes had moments of weakness, which resembled this pusillanimous emotion, when I was with this astonishing woman, I have always managed to overcome them and return to my principles.]

Love is usually regarded as an emotional experience in which sexual passion is one of the factors. Now the thought that they can for a single moment be at the mercy of their emotions, or of what Valmont acrimoniously calls *cette passion pusillanime*, is intolerable both to him and to Mme de Merteuil. Their aim is to eliminate the emotional factor altogether. Love comes to mean the intellectual satisfaction they get from the pursuit and defeat of the 'enemy', and the sensual pleasure which accompanies it.

The consequences of these changes are far reaching. The drama of the seventeenth century is the conflict between sexual passion and duty, whether the characters emerge strengthened and unified as they do in Corneille or are hurried down the dizzy slope to destruction as they are in Racine. The drama of the nineteenth century is the conflict between love and worldly success, of the young man who ruins his career for women and its two most characteristic symbols are Adolphe and Frédéric Moreau.[1] In both cases the conflict is an *interior* one. It is this which makes or mars the characters. The eighteenth century presents a different picture. There is no interior conflict in the minds of Laclos' two principal characters because the elements of conflict—love as well as duty—have been removed. The real conflict is an *exterior* one—the conflict between individual men and women and ultimately, as we shall see, between Man and Woman. Their attitude is thrown into high and startling relief by the conflict in the mind of the Présidente. For it is because she stands for traditional principles and beliefs that she is hopelessly outmanœuvred by the 'new strategy' and is destroyed by a conflict which is identical with those of the characters of Mme de La Fayette.

It has been urged in criticism of the novel that the characters devote their immense gifts to frivolous ends, to seducing and being seduced.

---

[1] Cf. *Adolphe*, where one of Adolphe's advisors writes to him: 'Toutes les routes vous sont ouvertes . . . mais souvenez-vous bien qu'il y a entre vous et tous les genres de succès un obstacle insurmontable, et que cet obstacle est Ellénore.'

These words might serve as an epigraph not only for Constant's age but for the whole of the nineteenth century. For the alleged conflict between love and worldly success is the foundation on which a vast structure of false values was erected which ruined the lives of many unfortunate people.

This criticism needs to be examined by detailed reference to the text and particularly to Laclos' use of the word *gloire* and to his military images:

> Séduite par votre réputation, il me semblait que vous manquiez à ma *gloire*; je brûlais de vous combattre corps à corps. C'est le seul de mes goûts qui ait jamais pris un moment d'empire sur moi. (Merteuil to Valmont, Letter LXXXI.)

> Dépositaire de tous les secrets de mon cœur, je vais vous confier le plus grand projet que j'aie jamais formé [the seduction of the Présidente] . . . son succès m'assure autant de *gloire* que de *plaisir*. L'amour qui prépare ma couronne, hésite lui-même entre le myrte et le laurier, ou plutôt il les réunira pour honorer mon triomphe. (Valmont to Merteuil, Letter IV.)

> [I was carried away by your reputation. It seemed to me that you were necessary to my glory. I was burning to engage you in bodily combat. It is the only one of my fancies which has ever dominated me for a moment.
> You are the repository of all the secrets of my heart, and I am going to confide in you the greatest scheme that I have ever undertaken . . . success is certain to bring me as much glory as pleasure. Love itself, which prepares my crown, hesitates between the myrtle and the laurel, or rather it will unite the two in order to celebrate my triumph.]

The word *gloire* echoes and re-echoes throughout the literature of the seventeenth century. It is a word which more than any other the great writers of the time had made their own and on which they had set their personal stamp. It described the reputation and triumphs of the seventeenth-century heroes, but their triumphs were real ones and the esteem they enjoyed worth having. It described, too, the successes of the Cornelian hero on the battlefield as well as his triumphs in the moral sphere, and it signified the peculiar éclat of the Duc de Nemours in the *Princesse de Clèves*. It has a strange resonance, a glamour—I use the word in a favourable sense—for which we shall look in vain in the *Liaisons dangereuses*. With the passing of the century the scene changes too. The Court is replaced by the salon, the battlefield by the boudoir. When Laclos' characters speak of their *gloire*, they mean success in the chase followed by a good performance on the *ottomane*. It is impossible to escape the impression that civilization has suffered a drastic impoverishment, that the novelist, instead of consolidating and extending the conquests of his predecessors, has abandoned a good deal of the territory which they had won, that there has in short been a narrowing of the whole field of artistic experience.

In a sense this is true, but we must make some further distinctions. The criticism applies with most force to Laclos' *characters*, and we shall have to show that in choosing the approach he did, he has still been able to make a valuable criticism of man and society. He does not, however, altogether escape the implications. The limitations of the age that he was criticizing are reflected in his work. The style of the seventeenth-century writers would in th main have been useless for his purpose; but compared with theirs, his instrument, for all its grace and elegance, has comparatively few notes and these notes are singularly lacking in richness. The words have no overtones and no resonance; they say exactly what they mean and no more. They are admirably adapted for distinguishing between one sensation and another:

Tel est le charme de la confiante amitié [says Mme de Merteuil] : c'est elle qui fait que vous êtes toujours ce que j'*aime* le mieux; mais, en vérité, le chevalier est ce qui me *plaît* davantage.

[Such is the charm of a friendship in which we put our trust; it means that you are still the one of whom I am fondest, but to tell the truth the chevalier is the one who pleases me more.]

But as soon as the novelist tries to express emotions, the instrument fails him. When Valmont becomes serious over his pursuit of the Présidente, he also becomes crude and verbose; and even in the letters of the Présidente and Mme de Rosemonde—essential as they are to the pattern of the book—we feel that the stereotyped concepts are not adequate to the weight of the emotions they are intended to convey.

Laclos is, indeed, the chronicler of the decline of the civilization which the seventeenth-century writers had celebrated and his triumphs are of a different nature. French critics are fond of using words like *flétrir* and *dessécher* to describe the general impression made by the book, but we must go further than this. It is, paradoxically, one of the qualities of Laclos' style that it literally blights and withers the feelings which it presents, that human nature is made interesting by virtue of its degradation:

Si une fois vous formez cette petite fille [writes Mme de Merteuil], il y aura bien du malheur si le Gercourt ne devient pas, comme un autre, la fable de Paris.

[If you once mould the little girl, it will be very bad luck if Gercourt does not become the laughing-stock of Paris like anyone else.]

When Valmont suggests that they should renew their liaison, she replies:

> Je ne crois pas que mon Chevalier eût autant d'indulgence que moi; il serait homme à ne pas approuver notre renouvellement de bail.

[I do not think that my Chevalier would display as much indulgence as I; he is the sort of man who would not approve of the renewal of our lease.]

In another letter she observes:

> L'amour que l'on nous vante comme la cause de nos plaisirs, n'en est au plus que le prétexte.

[Love which is vaunted as the source of our pleasures is at most only a pretext for them.]

It is a triumph of Laclos' art that when he uses simple terms like *formez* or *renouvellement de bail* he can make us feel the sentiment wither beneath his touch. The last example illustrates his extraordinary power of deflation. It would be a mistake to assume that this style is purely negative and destructive. Only twenty years had passed since the publication of the *Nouvelle Héloïse*; there was room for astringency.

Laclos does not depend solely on the isolated word. He is master of a savage farce which is peculiarly his own. The best examples occur in Letters XLVII and XLVIII. In the second of these letters, which is written by Valmont to the Présidente and begins, 'C'est après une nuit orageuse et pendant laquelle je n'ai pas fermé l'œil', he goes on:

> Jamais je n'eus tant de plaisir en vous écrivant; jamais je ne ressentis, dans cette occupation, une émotion si douce et cependant si vive. Tout semble augmenter mes transports: l'air que je respire est plein de volupté; la table même sur laquelle je vous écris, consacrée pour la première fois à cet usage, devient pour moi l'autel sacré de l'amour; combien elle va s'embellir à mes yeux! j'aurai tracé sur elle le serment de vous aimer toujours! Pardonnez, je vous en supplie, au désordre de mes sens. Je devrais peut-être m'abandonner moins à des transports que vous ne partagez pas: il faut vous quitter un moment pour dissiper une ivresse qui s'augmente à chaque instant, et qui devient plus forte que moi.

[Never before did I enjoy writing to you so much; never before, while engaged in this occupation, did I experience a feeling which was so sweet and yet so vivid. Everything seems to add to my raptures. The air that I breathe is impregnated with a voluptuous feeling; the very table on which I am writing to you and which is being used for this purpose for the first time, has become for me the sacred altar of love. How it will gain in beauty in my eyes! I shall have written on it the vow to love you always! Forgive, I beg you, the disorder of my senses. I ought perhaps to be less ready to abandon myself to raptures which you do not share: I must leave you for a moment to get rid of an intoxication which increases with every moment and which has become too strong for me.]

The 'table' is the fetich in this passage and when we turn back to the previous letter to Mme de Merteuil we appreciate its significance. The scene is the *ottomane* of an old flame of Valmont's:

Cette complaisance de ma part est le prix de celle qu'elle vient d'avoir, de me servir de pupitre pour écrire à ma belle Dévote, à qui j'ai trouvé plaisant d'envoyer une lettre écrite du lit et presque d'entre les bras d'une fille, interrompue même pour une infidélité complète, et dans laquelle je lui rends un compte exact de ma situation et de ma conduite. Émilie, qui a lu l'Épitre, en a ri comme une folle, et j'espère que vous en rirez aussi.

[This piece of kindness on my side is the price paid for the kindness she has shown me by acting as a desk which I used to write to my fair *dévote*, to whom I found it amusing to send a letter written from the bed and almost from between the arms of a tart and even interrupted for an act of complete infidelity—a letter in which I have given her an exact account of my position and my behaviour. Émilie, who read the epistle, laughed like a lunatic over it, and I hope you'll laugh too.]

Compare these passages with almost any page from the *Princesse de Clèves* and you see where Laclos is leading us. The heroic age, with its spaciousness, its chivalry, its sense of the dignity of man, is a thing of the past. Continence did not always stand very high among its virtues, but there is a world of difference between what it called *l'amour* and what the eighteenth century called *la volupté*. A warmth and generosity have gone out of life, for there is nothing *généreux* about Laclos' characters. He paid a heavy price for that sanity and poise which we cannot deny him. His mind was primarily a critical one and his characters are intellectual creations. Their emotional poverty contrasts strangely with their complicated manœuvres. Mme de La Fayette's courtiers and the cloistered Adolphe drawing up a merciless indictment of his own weaknesses are far richer and more complex than the

D

exponents of the 'new strategy', hurrying from the salon to the boudoir, from the boudoir to the *petite maison* and back again; glancing up, from a preliminary encounter with an intended victim, at their reflection in one of the bright mirrors on the wall to ensure that their smile is right or that they are displaying the proper degree of gravity; trying hard to control that strident note which sometimes threatens to disturb the soft caressing tone which was so important a part of their 'technique'. Mme de La Fayette and Constant derived, from their contemplation of the human situation, a certain general wisdom which gives their books another dimension that we shall not find in Laclos'. Constant's wisdom in particular crystallizes in a series of maxims which are not unworthy of the greatest French moralists; but Laclos can offer us no more than a few pithy axioms which might have come from a military training manual.

4

I have suggested that sexual relations are used in this book to reveal the fundamental antagonisms underlying society. When we look into it, we see that Laclos is not really interested in conflicts between individuals. He is interested in conflicts between the representatives of the different parties into which society is divided and of the different sexes. There are two main parties. Mme de Volanges is the Virtuous Matron and the representative of conventional morality. Valmont and Mme de Merteuil are not precisely admirable figures, but the attack on conventional morality is not at bottom a frivolous one. Laclos sets out to show that it is ugly and ineffectual. He tries to strengthen his position by producing the Présidente and Mme de Rosemonde as the representatives of True Virtue and opposing them to conventional virtue. The fact that he failed completely with them seems to me to be the great weakness of his book.

The division of society into contending factions explains the existence of three different kinds of liaison. Valmont and Mme de Merteuil are the eighteenth-century couple who aim at a sexual pleasure which is entirely devoid of emotion. Cécile de Volanges and the Chevalier de Danceny apparently stand for the sentimental liaison which naturally develops inside the *parti des bonnes mœurs*. The motives behind the third kind—Valmont and Cécile, Valmont and the Présidente, Mme de Merteuil and Danceny—are more complex. Valmont and the Merteuil certainly seduce and debauch the young lovers to revenge themselves on Gercourt, but they are also trying to get at conventional morality at the same time.

Valmont's affair with the Présidente appears to be part of the attack on convention, but we shall see later that it introduces an interesting variation. This is how he speaks of it:

> Mon projet, au contraire, est qu'elle sente bien la valeur et l'étendue de chacun des sacrifices qu'elle me fera; de ne pas la conduire si vite, que le remords ne puisse la suivre; *de faire expirer sa vertu dans une lente agonie*; de la fixer sans cesse sur ce désolant spectacle; et de ne lui accorder le bonheur de m'avoir dans ses bras, qu'après l'avoir forcée à n'en plus dissimuler le désir.
>
> J'aurai cette femme; je l'enlèverai au mari qui la profane; *j'oserai la ravir au Dieu même qu'elle adore*. . . . Loin de moi l'idée de détruire les préjugés qui l'assiègent. Ils ajouteront à mon bonheur et à ma *gloire*.

> [I intend to see that she feels to the full the value and extent of each of the sacrifices she makes me; that she is not driven forward too fast for remorse to be able to follow; that her virtue is made to expire in a slow agony; that she is ceaselessly occupied with this distressing spectacle; and that she shall not be granted the happiness of holding me in her arms until I have compelled her to stop concealing her desire to do so.
>
> I shall have this woman; I will carry her off from the husband who profanes her; I shall even dare to snatch her away from the God whom she worships. . . . I am far from having any idea of destroying the prejudices which beset her. They will add to my happiness and my glory.]

Nothing could be more misleading than to describe Laclos' characters as sadists, to pretend that they have anything to do with the childish 'satanism' of the next century or to introduce confusing concepts like *le mal*.[1] Valmont and Mme de Merteuil are completely amoral and their unbelief is absolute. Whatever Laclos' own opinion of their conduct, his novel is essentially a *psychological* and not an *ethical* drama, and it represents a new phase in the French novel. The *Princesse de Clèves* is, among other things, a criticism of the *morale laïque*, of the inadequacy of moral concepts once traditional sanctions have been removed. The *Liaisons dangereuses* is a clear demonstration of the logical outcome of the 'new morality'. Laclos' characters have got rid of its concepts and are free to devote themselves to their particular ends without any interference from conscience. Their aims are something very different from the suffering of their rather feeble victims and they

---

[1] André Gide is, surprisingly, one of the worst offenders. See his Preface to the English translation (*Dangerous Acquaintances*, London, 1940). 'There is no doubt as to his [Valmont] being hand in glove with Satan.' (p. viii.)

become clear when we turn to the military imagery. This is Valmont's description of the fall of the Présidente:

> Jusque-là, la belle amie, vous me trouverez, je crois, une pureté de méthode qui vous fera plaisir; et vous verrez que je ne me suis écarté en rien des vrais principes de cette guerre, que nous avons remarquée souvent être si semblable à l'autre. Jugez-moi donc comme Turenne our Frédéric. J'ai forcé à combattre l'ennemi qui ve voulait que temporiser; je me suis donné, par de savantes manœuvres le choix du terrain et celui des dispositions. . . .

> [You will see, my fair friend, that up to this point I displayed a purity of method which will delight you; and you will see that I departed in no way from the true principles of this form of warfare which, as we have noticed, is often so like the other form of warfare. Judge me therefore as you would judge Frederick or Turenne. I brought to combat an enemy who only wanted to temporise; I was able by skilful manœuvring to choose the terrain and the position. . . .]

It is tempting to dismiss the claim to be judged 'like Turenne or Frederick' as an absurdity, as the fantasy of an excited seducer; but this explanation will not do. The concept of 'war' is an integral part of Laclos' view of life and the military imagery an organic part of his style. He is the chronicler not merely of the decline of civilization, but of a deliberate and successful attack on traditional values in which the intellect becomes purely destructive. Baudelaire has pointed out that the Présidente is the only character in the book 'appartenant à la bourgeoisie' and he adds that this observation is an important one. She is, indeed, a symbol of the solid middle class which had always been the moral backbone of France and for this reason she is the focus of the main attack.

There is, however, a difference between the attitudes of Mme de Merteuil and Valmont. Mme de Merteuil is far more incensed against the Présidente than Mme de Volanges because she perceives that she is genuine and therefore more dangerous. She is more dangerous because she makes Valmont forget his famous 'principles'. In spite of his protestations, the attraction is in a certain degree emotional. Mme de Merteuil sees what has happened and tricks Valmont into destroying the unhappy woman, tricks him into the destruction of True Virtue instead of the sham represented by Mme de Volanges.

It is surprising that Baudelaire should have described the Présidente as an 'admirable creation'. She is faintly drawn, and in spite of their dignity and virtuous sentiments her letters do not contain a single memorable phrase. That this should be so seems to me, as I have already suggested, a sign of moral failure on the part of the novelist.

We can begin to see now what is behind this attack on tradition, this unending pursuit of male and female. It is a desire to dominate, a lust for power which can only be satisfied by the submission and surrender of the 'enemy' and which creates, in the minds of Valmont and Mme de Merteuil, the sensation or better the illusion of *gloire*. Although there is nothing in the *Liaisons* which can be described as *angoisse* or *inquiétude*, the continual references to strategy and politics do betray a sense of frustration which may well reflect the personal frustration of the novelist and possibly the exasperation which led him to write the *Liaisons* and the essay on Vauban. It is because the characters have been unable to find a proper outlet for their talents that they devote them to such unworthy ends. Their 'wars' are substitutes for the real war— 'cette guerre . . . si semblable à l'autre' is a striking admission—in which they would be only too happy to engage, or for the large-scale dictatorship which would have given them empire over a whole people.[1]

The conflict between individual men and women is therefore a reflection of a deeper conflict, the conflict between Man and Woman, the sex war represented in its most ruthless form by Valmont and Mme de Merteuil. The famous Letter LXXXI contains an explicit statement of Mme de Merteuil's aims:

Née pour venger mon sexe et maîtriser le vôtre, j'avais su me créer des moyens inconnus jusqu'à moi.

[Born to revenge my own sex and to master yours, I was able to create means which were unknown before me.]

Again:

Dans cette partie si inégale, notre fortune est de ne pas perdre, et votre malheur de ne pas gagner. Quand je vous accorderais autant de talents qu'à nous, de combien encore ne devrions-nous pas vous surpasser, par la nécessité où nous sommes d'en faire un continuel usage!

[In this encounter, which is so unequal, our good fortune is not to lose and your misfortune is not to win. If I granted you as much talent as us,

---

[1] It is because a solution is impossible in modern society that the form of seduction practised by Valmont became, in Baudelaire's words, the 'source de la sensualité mystique et des sottises amoureuses du XIXe siècle'.

by how much more we should have to surpass you through the necessity
we are in of making continual use of our gifts!]

One detects in the second passage a feeling of dull resentment that
the odds against women are usually so heavy, that Mme de Merteuil
herself belongs to 'the weaker sex'.

The jealousy that they feel over one another's 'conquests' is not
merely a personal sexual jealousy; it is rather a *dépit* caused by the
success of the opposite sex and a limitation of their own ambition to
dominate:

> Tenez, ma belle amie [writes Valmont], tant que vous vous partagez
> entre plusieurs, je n'ai pas la moindre jalousie: je ne vois alors que les
> successeurs d'Alexandre, incapables de conserver entre eux tous cet empire
> où je régnais seul.

> [Look, my fair friend, as long as you share yourself out among several
> men, I am not in the slightest degree jealous. I see then that the successors
> of Alexander are incapable of preserving between them the empire over
> which I once ruled alone.]

The reference to Alexander's empire is another curious fantasy
where military and political ambitions once more come into play.

They are both equally determined to conquer: 'Conquérir est notre
destin,' cries Valmont. 'Il faut vaincre ou périr,' retorts Mme de
Merteuil. They are, unfortunately for Valmont, very unevenly
matched. Baudelaire speaks of 'un reste de sensibilité par quoi il est
inférieur à la Merteuil, chez qui tout ce qui est humain est calciné'. It
is a very penetrating comment which illuminates the novelist's intentions. What makes Mme de Merteuil an outstanding creation is first
her magnificent intelligence, and secondly her complete implacability.
Her boast that already at fifteen she possessed 'the talents to which the
majority of our politicians owe their reputations' and that this was
only a beginning, is the measure of her powers and of her tragedy. Her
ruthlessness is apparent not only in what she does, but in her slighting
references to the performances of others, to 'ces [femmes] incon-
sidérées, qui dans leur amant actuel ne savent pas voir leur ennemi
futur'. Valmont's 'reste de sensibilité' makes him extremely vulnerable for her. His uncertainty of himself slips out in his exaggerated
tone, in the angry reference to 'cette passion pusillanime', in

> Que nous sommes heureux que les femmes se défendent si mal! nous
> ne serions auprès d'elles que de timides esclaves.

[How lucky we are that women defend themselves so ill! Otherwise we should be no better than timid slaves in their hands.]

Now there is something more than irritation and uncertainty behind these passages. There is *fear*. Laclos knew very well what he was about in opposing Valmont and Mme de Merteuil. He uses Valmont as a symptom of a weakness which infected eighteenth-century life and literature. We cannot study eighteenth-century literature at all closely without noticing an ugly streak of sentimentality which runs all through it. There was, indeed, something exaggerated about the desperation with which the eighteenth century clung to its rationalism as though it were dimly aware of the sentimental flaw which made it so precarious and which led to the lacrymose flood that swamped the next century. Valmont's sentimentality was his undoing. That is why he is peculiarly a symptom of his age.[1]

It is not for nothing that Mme de Merteuil treats him as an *écolier* —the phrase is lifted from one of his own letters—as a blunderer in a field where she is an expert. A good deal of her criticism is caused by a jealousy which cannot admit that the other sex has any ability at all, but Valmont does not escape the irony of his creator. The fall of the Présidente is comedy of a different kind from the account of the letter written from Émilie's bed. After a prolonged siege the hero, who claims that his triumphs should be measured by those of Turenne and Frederick, only succeeds in seducing the woman when she has fainted from fright.

'As I have repeatedly told you,' writes Mme de Merteuil in another letter

> Vous n'en avez pas moins de l'amour pour votre Présidente; non pas, à la vérité, de l'amour bien pur ni bien tendre, mais celui que vous pouvez avoir.

> [You are nevertheless in love with your President. It is not, to be sure, a very pure or a very tender love, but the sort of love that you can feel.]

This analysis of Valmont's capacity for love is a striking illustration of Mme de Merteuil's understanding of other people and of her

[1] Only sentimentality can explain the immense admiration of Laclos' contemporaries for the colourless Présidente. Tilly's description of her is illuminating: 'The portrait of Mme de Tourvel is adorable and has caused the youth of both sexes to shed many a tear. How many girls would prefer to die like her rather than to live like her odious rival! There's homage to virtue. How many young men have dreamed of such a mistress, have bowed their knee to her shade! It is another tribute to true love!' (*Op. cit.*, I, p. 226.)

immense superiority over him. Although Valmont understands himself clearly up to a point, he is very limited and very often the dupe of his own sentimentality. His much vaunted 'principles' imply a serious limitation. He has none of the insight into other people's characters which distinguishes Mme de Merteuil. He can 'lay' the *femmes volages* of the day like anyone going, but as soon as he is faced with a woman, however ordinary, who is outside his experience he becomes a bungling amateur. Mme de Merteuil realizes, with genuine astonishment, that even after the dispatch of the diabolical letter which she composed for him to send to the Présidente, he is still thinking subconsciously of going back to her:

Quoi! vous aviez l'idée de renouer, et vous avez pu écrire ma lettre! Vous m'avez donc crue bien gauche à mon tour! Ah! croyez-moi, Vicomte, quand une femme frappe dans le cœur d'une autre, elle manque rarement de trouver l'endroit sensible, et la blessure est incurable.

[What! you imagine that you can make it up, and you dispatched my letter! So you thought that I in my turn was very clumsy! Ah! Vicomte, when a woman strikes at the heart of another, she seldom fails to discover the vulnerable spot, and the wound is incurable.]

She makes it clear, too, in the same letter that her victory over the Présidente is primarily a victory over Valmont:

Vous allez trouver peut-être que j'évalue bien haut cette femme, que naguère j'appréciais si peu; point du tout; mais c'est que ce n'est pas sur elle que j'ai remporté cet avantage; c'est sur vous: voilà le plaisant et ce qui est vraiment délicieux.

[You will think, perhaps, that I estimate very highly a woman of whom recently I thought so little. Not at all. It is because it is not she of whom I have got the better. It's you—that's the amusing thing and what's really delicious.]

When Valmont proposes that they should settle down together permanently, she replies:

J'ai pu avoir quelquefois la prétention de remplacer à moi seule tout un sérail; mais il ne m'a jamais convenu d'en faire partie. Je croyais que vous saviez cela. ... Qui, moi! je sacrifierais un goût ... et pour m'en occuper comment? en attendant à mon tour, et en esclave soumise, les sublimes faveurs de votre *Hautesse*.

[I may sometimes have claimed to take the place of a whole seraglio on my own; but it never suited me to be a member of one. I thought you knew that. . . . Who, I! I should sacrifice a fancy . . . and to spend my time doing what? Waiting in my turn, and as a submissive slave, for the sublime favours of your *Highness*.]

'J'ai accusé les individus,' wrote Benjamin Constant of women, in a memorable phrase in his diary, 'j'aurais dû m'en prendre à l'espèce'. The struggle between Valmont and Mme de Merteuil is the centuries-old antagonism between the sexes, the primitive impulse to dominate which is apparent in the coexistence of love and hate to which many writers have drawn attention. They both desire to rule in their own kingdoms and a serious preference for another member of their own sex is felt to be a threat to their position. But that Valmont can for a moment resist her demands or that she can refuse to accept his ultimatum to become in fact a member of his seraglio, is felt by both to be not merely a personal affront, but an affront to the whole sex.

Mme de Merteuil describes herself in one letter as a 'nouvelle Dalila' and goes on to explain the significance of the 'myth'. For the man each conquest is a victory for his sex; for the woman it is equally a victory for hers, because in allowing herself to be seduced, she dominates the male and deprives him of his strength—his strength to harm her sex—by transforming him into her 'slave'.

It is an ingenious explanation of the sex war from the woman's point of view, but it is not the whole story. If it were, there would be no conflict. The encounter would always be a 'friendly' one and would always end with honours even.

The battle only begins [said Giraudoux], when the woman is easy, when there is tacit agreement between the woman's virtue and the man's vice. There is no hostility when the man tries to take something which no one can have. . . . All our impregnable heroines are the friends of man; and the fact that she refuses to give herself to anyone at all, even to the man she loves, implies that a woman has a somewhat naïve faith in masculine greatness and the greatness of love. The battle begins the moment that each sex regards the other as its accomplice, and the woman who gives herself feels not so much that she is giving herself—a dubious and fragile gift—as that she is acting as her own procuress. . . . The man, by making her feel that it is less herself whom she is prostituting than her entire sex, makes use of her to inflict on the whole of the feminine sex a humiliation which at other periods the woman had simply experienced as an individual.[1]

[1] *Op. cit.*, pp. 72-3.

D*

The sense that the whole of her sex is being prostituted in her person is something which Mme de Merteuil cannot fail to perceive and which she can never forgive. It is this that produces the conflict.

The emergence of the dark forces which I have described gives the novel its vitality and its disturbing quality. Sexual pleasure, however refined, is an insufficient motive of action for people who are so monstrously 'enlightened', so *avertis*, so completely without illusions about themselves and the value of their pleasures as Laclos' characters. Mme de Merteuil shows that she realizes it very clearly when she remarks: 'L'amour que l'on nous vante comme la cause de nos plaisirs, n'en est au plus que le prétexte.' Sexual intrigue is only a means to an end, and this end is evident when she explains that she always wrests their personal 'secret' from her lovers. It is, she says, a safeguard which prevents betrayal and enables her to make the world believe that she is *un modèle de vertu*; but is not the real attraction that it gives her the power of life and death over another human being and a member of the other sex?[1]

'Je sacrifie beaucoup à un devoir qui ne subsiste que dans mon imagination,' says the Princesse de Clèves. She sacrifices both the Duke and herself to a sense of guilt for which there was no longer any rational justification. The eighteenth-century *philosophes* had no difficulty in continuing the work of the seventeenth century and in completing the destruction of moral sanctions on the rational plane; but the sense of guilt proved more difficult precisely because it was rooted in primitive, non-rational impulses. They chose a radical solution. Racine had removed 'honour' from the Cornelian formula; the eighteenth century removed 'love' and replaced it by something different. In the *Liaisons dangereuses* man—the Rational Man of the eighteenth century—is divided neatly into two. He possesses the intelligence of a highly civilized person and the body of a highly trained animal. The principal function of intelligence is to procure agreeable *sensations* for the body. In spite of Mme de Merteuil's disparaging description of easy women as *machines à plaisir*, her words would almost serve to describe Valmont and herself. 'Almost' because there comes a point at which the eighteenth-century system breaks down.

[1] In one of her letters, Mme de Merteuil writes: 'Cependant si j'avais moins de mœurs, je crois qu'il ["le chevalier régnant"] aurait dans ce moment un rival dangereux; c'est la petite Volanges. Je raffole de cette enfant: c'est une vraie passion. . . .' Her homosexual leanings for the child are not without significance. For the sex war—the desire to dominate and the fear of domination—is in part the psychological explanation of homosexuality and the dislike of homosexuals for the opposite sex.

Mme de Merteuil and Valmont admit that they were once 'in love' with one another.[1] This clearly infringed their most cherished 'principles', but in their anxiety to get rid of this very unseemly emotion *they overlooked the no less potent emotion of hate*. It is passionate hatred and a violent resentment against Valmont's pretence to be the dominant partner which lead Mme de Merteuil to make the mistake that shatters the alliance and causes the disaster. If she had not been carried away by a desire for vengeance, she would have seen that the death of Valmont must release her incriminating letters and destroy her legend.

The 'moral ending' has been a source of some perplexity to Laclos' readers. It was not, as it is sometimes assumed to be, a mere sop to the public which enabled the novelist to maintain that he had written a work of edification for *jeunes filles* on the threshold of marriage. It is really the final episode in the sex war. For in making the Female infinitely more brilliant and accomplished than the Male, the novelist created a dilemma for himself which could only be solved by his personal intervention in the world of his creatures. Valmont's death— the death of the Male—is deliberately invested with a certain glamour which atones for any lapses and perhaps for his inferiority to Mme de Merteuil. But it remains a victory for the other sex which must be expiated. The novelist's personal jealousy is aroused and he revenges himself on his greatest creation by covering her with shame and ignominy. She is deprived of wealth, reputation and looks—of all the things which enabled her to use her great intellectual powers to the detriment of Laclos' own sex—and she flies to Holland, a fugitive from *male* justice.[2]

5

What is to be our final estimate? We know Baudelaire's answer: 'Livre de moraliste aussi haut que les plus élevés, aussi profond que les plus profonds. . . . Livre essentiellement français.' 'Un traité d'anatomie

[1] She puts it a little differently: 'C'est le seul de mes goûts qui ait jamais pris un moment d'empire sur moi.'

[2] There are interesting ramifications. It is Mme de Volanges, the representative of conventional virtue, who warns the Présidente of Valmont's danger to the Sex, she who is among the first to console Mme de Merteuil after Prévan's supposed *tentative* against the Sex, she who is most assiduous in exposing Mme de Merteuil as the black sheep who has disgraced the Sex. She is an ironical figure who inevitably plays the Male game in leading the anti-Merteuil party. This applies in greater or lesser degree to all who take part in the 'battles'.

morale,' replies Suarès.[1] 'Les romans des autre peuples sont puérils près de celui-là.' 'Ce fut l'apparition,' answers a less friendly critic, 'la dernière apparition de notre littérature, apparition attardée, composée, froide, mais indéniable, de celui qui ne mélange pas, qui ne bégaye pas, qui ne transige et ne cille pas; de Racine. . . . Une grande voix parle par ce petit auteur.'[2]

We may not find Laclos' novel particularly enjoyable or particularly edifying, but that it is a masterpiece we cannot doubt. The appearance of a masterpiece and the artist's choice of his medium are not fortuitous; they depend on a number of different circumstances. The *Liaisons dangereuses* belongs to the great French tradition and it reveals the influence of the masters of the seventeenth century on every page, almost indeed in every line. Tradition is never static; it is constantly developing, and though the basic human emotions remain the same, feelings are perpetually shifting, changing. The accent never falls exactly in the same place in different ages. The Man of Honour and the Man of Passion had had their day and disappeared from the scene. Laclos' theme is the tragedy of the Rational Man, the man who was carefully conditioned through the removal of all moral scruples and the sense of guilt, but inevitably condemned to action in a very limited field. The novel is a masterpiece because it gives final expression to this phase of human experience.

It was because the grand manner was no longer a suitable vehicle for experience that the outstanding work of fiction of the eighteenth century was a novel in prose, and it reflects the novelist's experience as surely as the great *tirades* of the previous century. The encounters between Racine's characters take place in public. Their savage denunciation reverberates through vast appartments in lofty palaces, rises above the women's chatter in the seraglio of the 'Grand Seigneur' and drowns the childish singing in the Temple. The characteristic note of the eighteenth century is not publicity, is not the intimacy of the nineteenth century; it is *complicity*. It is the whispered confidence, the muttered confession of the letter-writer; the undertone which insinuates itself into your consciousness like a finger probing a secret wound. The murmur which rises from all these people bent industriously over their writing-tables is not less dramatic or less varied than the stormy entrances and exits of Racine's characters, and it is far more subversive. They all have their place in the pattern and each voice blends into the whole—the carefully modulated voices of Valmont and Mme de Merteuil, the anguished voice of the Présidente, the faltering voices of

[1] *Xénies* (Paris, 1923), p. 113.
[2] Giraudoux, *op. cit.*, pp. 64–5.

the young lovers, the chorus provided by Mme de Rosemonde and Mme de Volanges, the voices of servants and retainers.

More than any other great novel this is a book for grown-ups and the theme is treated with a clarity and integrity which have made the French novel supreme in Europe. It is, indeed, a 'livre essentiellement français' which makes not only its English counterpart, *Clarissa*, but also the much praised *Manon Lescaut* appear crude and immature by comparison. It is at once a portrait of an age whose tragedy lies in the waste of its great gifts, in a nihilism which drove it to expend its powers in defacing human nature, and a profound analysis of a perennial human situation. It matters little whether the writer was or was not a *petit auteur*: the *grande voix* is unmistakable.

BENJAMIN CONSTANT AND *ADOLPHE*

Je ne veux rien voir fleurir près de moi. Je veux que tout ce qui m'environne soit triste, languissant, fané. . . .

Letter to Mme de Charrière, 21 March 1788

I. PORTRAIT OF THE ARTIST

I

FEW great writers have left less flattering portraits of themselves than Benjamin Constant in his solitary novel. *Adolphe* is a masterpiece, but it possesses in a pre-eminent degree that peculiar unpleasantness which is sometimes said to be characteristic of nearly all great art; and most of those who have studied it at all attentively must recall occasions when, overcome by a physical malaise, they have had to lay the book aside, unable to continue their reading.

This feeling, which only disappears with long familiarity, is not confined to modern readers. The audiences of friends to whom Constant used to read his novel aloud in the nine years which passed between its composition in 1807 and its publication in 1816 were 'revolted' by the character of his hero.[1] The persistence of this feeling cannot be disregarded by the critic and the reasons for it are not difficult to discover. In this book the novelist, using the immense powers of analysis which he had inherited from a great tradition, gives a remorseless catalogue of his own failings. We may feel a secret envy for the vitality of Racine's characters, for the ferocity with which male and female rend one another and which speaks directly to primitive feelings that lie buried beneath layers of civilization in all of us. We feel nothing of the sort for the hesitations and vacillations of Adolphe which inflict appalling suffering on one unhappy woman. Yet honesty compels us to recognize that his findings are not less universal than Racine's. He makes articulate feelings which potentially at any rate are common to us all, but which we instinctively prefer to keep hidden. His revelations have nothing to do with the comfortably vague *mal du siècle* of the next generation; they are not blunted by that soothing mixture of sentiment and showmanship which made Rousseau so attractive to his contemporaries, and they are completely free from the melodramatic

---

[1] In 1807 he wrote in his diary: 'Soirée at Mme Récamier's with Fauriel. I read my novel to them which produced a peculiar effect. The character of the hero revolted them. They certainly do not understand me.' (*Journal Intime précédé du Cahier rouge et de Adolphe*, ed. Jean Mistler, Monaco, 1945, p. 245. This is the only reliable edition of the text of the diary.)

element which tainted the work of some of the greatest masters of the nineteenth century. They are presented with a nakedness which shatters complacency. Far from trying to excuse himself, Constant's hero sedulously pushes his virtues into the background and is at pains to underline and to condemn his weaknesses.

Paul Bourget has spoken of 'the coexistence in a single soul of the most ineffectual lucidity of mind and of the worst form of sensual or emotional disorder'.[1] It is difficult to understand or to forgive a man who is clearly endowed with immense intellectual gifts and who makes such ill use of them. The word 'forgive' illustrates the peculiar relationship between the reader and the book and the intensity of the experience. For there is a world of difference between the faintly remote princes and princesses of seventeenth-century tragedy and this man who seems at times to be altogether too close to us, as though his creator had succeeded too well in his task. It is the feeling of intimacy which disturbs. We seem to see the speaker bearing down on us, singling us out in a room full of people. He catches us by the lapel of the coat, peers at us with his weak eyes and begins to tell us the latest news about his relations with Mme de Staël or his senile affair with Mme Récamier. 'Cette furie qui me poursuit l'écume à la bouche et le poignard à la main,' he cries of Mme de Staël. 'Je suis las de *l'homme-femme*'—he plucks at our coat for emphasis—'dont la main de fer m'enchaîne depuis dix ans. . . .' And so the appalling stream of revelations continues.

We can only fully appreciate *Adolphe* when we know what manner of man the author was and something of the age in which he lived. Constant was not a dilettante, a mere man of letters who frittered away his life in drawing-rooms and happened almost by accident to write a great novel. He was not merely a gambler and duellist, the lover of Mme de Staël and the unsuccessful suitor to whom Mme Récamier refused what are politely termed *les dernières faveurs*. He was one of the most brilliant intellects of his time, a considerable scholar, an original thinker and a distinguished and ultimately successful liberal politician. He was a pioneer in the study of comparative religion and though his great book on the subject has long since been superseded, it can still tell us a good deal about the intellectual climate of the age. His political writings were among the ablest produced in his time and the best of them—the attacks on despotism and the pages on war in *De l'Esprit de conquête et de l'usurpation*—far from losing their freshness, read like a description of contemporary Europe. In a comparison between the conquests of antiquity and those of his own time he wrote:

[1] *Essais de psychologie contemporaine*, I (Éd. définitive, Paris, 1926), p. 27.

Picture Post Library

BENJAMIN CONSTANT

Nowadays therefore conquest has a further disadvantage which it did not have in ancient times. It pursues the vanquished into the innermost recesses of their being; it mutilates them in order to reduce them to uniform proportions. In the past the conquerors insisted on the representatives of the vanquished nations appearing in their presence on bended knees. To-day it is human morale that they wish to reduce to prostration.

His comment on the *arrondissement des frontières* in the same essay strikes a prophetic note which reminds us uncomfortably of our own problems of 'living space' and 'spheres of influence':

> The tyrant would argue the necessity of rounding off his frontiers as though, once it were admitted, this doctrine did not banish peace and equity from the earth. For it is always from outside that a government wishes to round off its frontiers. So far as one knows, no government has ever sacrificed a portion of its own territory in order to give the rest of it a greater degree of geometrical regularity.[1]

When we find a man writing in these terms it is tempting to try to establish parallels between his age and our own. Constant was born in 1767 and died in 1830. His life therefore covers one of the most troubled periods of modern history; but though it is a period which bears a superficial resemblance to our own, it is dangerous to press the comparison between the *events* of the two periods too far. The truth is that Constant lived at the beginning of a period which has not yet ended and he was, as the late Charles Du Bos suggested in an admirable study, one of the first 'modern men'.[2] His wide interests and insatiable curiosity brought him into close contact with the life of his time and his weaknesses made him a victim of its spiritual and intellectual upheavals. He was in the fullest sense of the term a child of his age and was perfectly endowed by mind, temper and upbringing to interpret it to a later generation.

[1] Compare the following passages from the same essay:
'The continent was nothing but a vast dungeon cut off from all communication with that noble England, the generous asylum of thought, the illustrious refuge of the dignity of the human race.'
'A few months ago each of us, looking round, wondered in what obscure asylum he would be able to write, speak, think, breathe, if England were subjugated.'
[2] *Grandeur et misère de Benjamin Constant* (Paris, 1946).

2

Benjamin Constant de Rebecque was born at Lausanne on 25 October 1767 of an old French Protestant family. His ancestors had settled in Switzerland at the time of the Revocation of the Edict of Nantes, but their ties with that country had been loose and many of them had spent their lives in the service of other states. Benjamin's father, Colonel Juste de Constant, was a soldier in the Dutch Army and Benjamin himself was educated in England, Germany and France, finally becoming a French subject to further his political ambitions.

His childhood was as restless and disturbed as the remainder of his life. His mother, Henriette de Chandieu, died at the time of his birth and as his father was garrisoned in Holland, he was brought up by his grandmother, Mme de Chandieu, and his aunt, Mme de Nassau, who spoiled him outrageously. When he was five, his father handed him over to Marianne Mangin, a girl whom he had abducted from her parents when she was nine and whom he later promoted to be Benjamin's stepmother. Two years afterwards, his father decided to take over Benjamin's education himself. This proved unsatisfactory and it was continued by a procession of rascally tutors—a German who beat him, a Frenchman who took him to live at a house of ill-fame to be near the scene of his pleasures and an unfrocked priest who made him copy out his writings.

It is evident from the family history that there was a marked strain of instability in the Constants which may have been caused in part by their reaction against the strong Calvinist discipline of an earlier generation. Benjamin's cousin, Charles de Constant, once observed in a letter to his sister Rosalie: 'Il y a dans notre sang une inquiétude qui a nui à plusieurs d'entre nous et n'a rien fait pour notre bonheur. La génération actuelle l'a bien moins, Benjamin toujours excepté.'[1] Benjamin echoed the thought when he said of his father: 'Mon père est bien, mais l'humeur qui a dévoré notre famille ne l'a malheureusement pas épargné.'[2] He inherited their *inquiétude* and it was certainly aggravated by his early upbringing. He was an exceptionally precocious child and two letters to his grandmother show that he was very much the son of his father. The first was written when he was ten:

I sometimes see a young English girl of my own age here whom I

[1] Quoted by G. Rudler, *La Jeunesse de Benjamin Constant, 1767–1794* (Paris, 1909), p. 39.
[2] *Ibid., loc. cit.*

prefer to Cicero, Seneca, etc. . . . She teaches me Ovid whom she's never read or heard of, but I find him completely in her eyes.[1]

Two years later he writes:

I wish I could give you some satisfactory news of myself, but I fear that everything is confined to my physical development, I am well and grow-ing fast. You will say that if this is all, it's hardly worth living. I think so too, but my *étourderies* upset all my plans. I wish there were some way of preventing my blood from circulating so fast and giving it a more cadenced movement. I have tried to see if music would produce this effect. I play *adagios* and *largos* which would send thirty cardinals to sleep. It's all right to start with, but by some magic, these slow airs always end by becoming *prestissimos*. It's the same with dancing. The minuets always end in gallops. I think, my dear grandmother, that the trouble is incurable and will be impervious to reason itself. . . . Do you know, my dear grand-mother, that I go into society twice a week. I have a fine suit, a sword, my hat under my arm, one hand on my chest and the other on my hip. I hold myself very straight and appear as grown up as I can. I look and I listen, but so far feel little desire for the pleasures of the smart world. All these people look as though they don't like each other very much. At the same time, the gambling tables and the gold I see spinning cause me some emotion. I would like to win some for a thousand needs I have, but other people treat my needs as fancies.[2]

When, many years later, this letter was shown after Constant's death to his second wife, Charlotte von Hardenberg, she remarked that it was Benjamin 'in miniature'. And the breathless *prestissimos*, the minuets which turn into gallops, do reflect the rhythm of his whole life.

When Constant was thirteen his father took him to England, intend-ing to send him to Oxford; but even the precocious Benjamin was too young to enter the university at that age. He stayed in England long enough to acquire a grasp of the language and was then sent to the University of Erlangen where he was placed in charge of the Mar-gravine of Anspach. At Erlangen he committed the first of his many *folies*. 'I wanted to be able to boast of having a mistress', he wrote in that fascinating autobiographical fragment, *Le Cahier rouge*, and, as one might expect, he fixed on 'a woman with a pretty bad reputa-

[1] J-H. Menos, *Lettres de Benjamin Constant à sa famille* (Paris, 1888), p. 82. Rudler, *op. cit.*, p. 74.
[2] Menos, p. 85. Rudler, p. 78.

tion'. The attempt was not a success. 'I am', he added, 'probably the only man whose advances she ever resisted.'[1]

He took his reverse lightly, but the Margravine was offended and he was removed from Erlangen and sent to Edinburgh. 'Hard work was the fashion among the young men at Edinburgh,' he tells us. According to his own account, this was one of the happiest years of his life and he distinguished himself at his studies. The stay at Edinburgh was certainly an event of capital importance in his career. For it was there that he came into contact with the ideas of British liberalism which had a great influence on the development of his own political thought. It was there, too, that he acquired his taste for gambling—already foreshadowed in the early letter to his grandmother—which was to prove a very expensive amusement.

He returned to Paris for a short time in 1787, committed more *folies* and came under the influence of the leading exponents of eighteenth-century materialism: La Harpe, Lacretelle and Marmontel.

The first woman to stand out in the procession of Constant's mistresses is Mme Johannot who seduced the eighteen-year-old Benjamin before he even had time to make his *déclaration*. She stands out for a very good reason. 'Madame Johannot . . .' he says in the *Cahier rouge*, 'has fixed herself in my memory in a different way from all the women I have known. My liaison with her was very short and amounted to very little. But she did not make me pay for the *sensations douces* that she provided by any mixture of agitation or suffering: and at the age of forty-four I still feel grateful to her for the happiness that she brought me when I was eighteen.'[2]

She is the only woman who did not provoke the conflict between 'head' and 'heart' of which there will be much to say, and this affair contrasts strongly with his other adventures. Professor Rudler points out that it marks a break in the equilibrium of the *Cahier rouge*.[3] Life becomes a feverish struggle to recapture the *sensations douces*, the sense of fulfilment which he had experienced for the first and last time.

Mme Johannot was followed by Mrs. Trevor, wife of the British Ambassador at Turin. 'Mais tout se borna à un chaste baiser sur des lèvres tant soit peu fanées.'[4]

The year 1787 marked a turning point in Constant's life. It was the year of his first meeting with Mme de Charrière when she was forty-seven and he was twenty. Sainte-Beuve has described this remarkable woman as 'the eighteenth century in person for Benjamin Constant',[5]

---

[1] Mistler, pp. 6–7.   [2] Mistler, p. 82.
[3] *Op. cit.*, p. 125.   [4] Mistler, p. 85.   [5] *Portraits littéraires*, III, p. 275.

and there is no doubt that she played a decisive part in the formation of his character. The exact nature of their relationship has been the source of the liveliest speculation among French critics. Was it purely an intellectual friendship or was it an *amitié amoureuse*, or something more? Sainte-Beuve thought that between 'un tout jeune homme et une femme mûre' there must have been 'une cérémonie d'initiation'. Why, he asks in mild surprise, why should two people who were completely free from all 'prejudices' not have made this 'petite expérience'?[1] Philippe Godet, the author of the standard life of Mme de Charrière, took the opposite view and was sure that a friendship between two people of such different ages must have been 'purely intellectual'.[2] Professor Rudler is more cautious. 'One thing is certain —that Benjamin was in love with Mme de Charrière. . . . One thing is more than uncertain—that Benjamin was ever the lover of Mme de Charrière.'[3]

Constant's family seem to have shared Sainte-Beuve's view. They were greatly concerned over his long visits to Mme de Charrière's home at Colombier and though he refers derisively in a letter to her to 'mes parents, alarmés sur ma chasteté',[4] we may wonder whether their fears were as groundless as he suggests. Whether they did or did not make the *petite expérience* does not, perhaps, much matter. There is no doubt that the connection was 'primarily', if not 'purely', intellectual. Her scepticism, her contempt for convention and the conversations between them, which used to go on all night, acted like an intoxicant on the young man. 'I am convinced', he said in the *Cahier rouge*, 'that without these conversations, my behaviour would have been much less foolish.'

Another passage from his account of the friendship takes us to the very heart of the problem of his character:

> For a partner in marriage I wanted only Mademoiselle Pourras. In point of looks, Mademoiselle Pourras was still my preference. In point of intelligence, I saw, heard and cherished only Madame de Charrière. This does not mean, however, that I failed to profit by the few hours during which we were separated, to indulge in still further follies.[5]

It is a classic statement of the conflict between 'head' and 'heart'. It was Constant's tragedy that the same woman never satisfied him

---

[1] Quoted by Rudler, *op. cit.*, p. 276.
[2] *Madame de Charrière et ses amis* (Geneva, 1906).   [3] *Op. cit.*, p. 275.
[4] Quoted, *Portraits littéraires*, III, p. 219.
[5] Mistler, pp. 22–3: *Adolphe* and *The Red Note-book* (tr. Norman Cameron, London, 1948), p. 120.

intellectually and emotionally, and in a revealing phrase in one of his letters he described his first wife as 'la femme que mon cœur avait choisie et dont ma tête s'est si mal trouvée'.[1] All through his life he was engaged with two women at the same time—the intellectual companion and the bedfellow. As soon as one of them dropped out, she was replaced and the curious pattern re-formed: Mme de Charrière and Mlle Pourras; Mme de Charrière and his first wife, the odious Wilhelmina von Cramm; Mme de Staël and Anna Lindsay; Mme de Staël and his second wife, Charlotte von Hardenberg.

His connection with Mme de Charrière lasted for seven years. There are signs in their correspondence that towards the end the liaison was becoming a strain on them both. Then, in October 1794, an event took place which made a breach inevitable. Constant met Mme de Staël. 'C'est la seconde femme', he wrote to Mme de Charrière with that extraordinary lack of feeling which he sometimes displayed, 'que j'ai trouvée qui m'aurait pu tenir lieu de tout l'univers, qui aurait pu être un monde à elle seule pour moi. Vous savez quelle a été la première.'[2]

The affair with Mme de Staël lasted from 1794 until 1811 and its effect on Constant, at any rate in its later stages, seems to have been wholly bad. 'I have never seen a woman', he said in his diary, 'who absorbs more of the life of those who surround her.'[3] She encouraged him to waste his time when he should have been writing his books; she played upon his brittle nerves and was certainly to blame for many of his *folies* which were more serious than the youthful escapades to which Mme de Charrière's conversation was supposed to have driven him.

Mme de Staël's husband died in 1802 and it was generally believed that she would marry Constant. The facts are obscure, but it is thought that she insisted on a secret marriage in order to retain a name which had become famous and that he refused to agree. Constant then turned his thoughts in another direction. He had met Charlotte von Hardenberg in 1793 while she was still the wife of Baron von Marenholz. She divorced Marenholz and married a Frenchman named Dutertre. Her second husband, who was a Catholic, developed scruples and was anxious to be rid of her for reasons of conscience, though his conscience was not too delicate to prevent him from exacting a substantial payment from the unfortunate Constant.

The sorry business lingered on for another six years and it was not until 8 June 1808 that Constant eventually married Charlotte after

---

[1] They married in 1789, separated in 1793 and two years later there was a final decree of divorce. She was, significantly, ten years older than he.

[2] Quoted, *Portraits littéraires*, III, p. 274.   [3] Mistler, p. 190.

hovering between her and Mme de Staël up to the last moment. He tried to put a brave complexion on the matter and pretended in his letters to his family that his marriage was a miracle of happiness. The diary, however, tells a different story. He was continually regretting Mme de Staël and in 1813 he observed: 'Le plus grand inconvénient de ma vie, c'est d'être marié!—Georges Dandin.'

Two factors seem to have been responsible for putting an end to the domination of Mme de Staël—political activities and a violent passion for Mme Récamier. There is something humiliating about the hysteria of the forty-six-year-old Constant and his attempts to approach Mme Récamier through the offices of Mme de Krüdner, the foundress of a curious religious sect; but the entries in his diary and his correspondence with her are of great psychological interest, and we must share Charles Du Bos's regret that he was obliged to abandon his plan to study them in his book.

'Fidelity in love', Constant once remarked, 'is a power like religious belief or an enthusiasm for liberty.' As he approached his fiftieth year, he seems to have become more reasonable. In 1811 he had declared in his diary that he would not care to wager that he and Charlotte would finish their lives together. But he was wrong. His passion for Mme Récamier died a natural death and she had no successor. The last fifteen years of his life were happy as well as successful. He devoted himself to politics, became the member for the Sarthe, then for the Bas-Rhin, and finally in 1829 Président du Conseil.

Constant speaks somewhere of his *malheureuse maladie morale* and the term is not too strong for his behaviour. The conflict between head and heart was genuine and symptomatic. It was caused, as he himself suggests in the Preface to the second edition of *Adolphe*, by 'cette analyse perpétuelle, qui place une arrière-pensée à côté de tous les sentiments, et qui les corrompt dès leur naissance'. But a man who was clear-sighted to the point of genius could not plead that he was unaware of what he was doing or of the unsuitability of his wives and mistresses or that he did not discover until it was too late. He may have been the victim of his age, but there was undoubtedly a good deal of wilfulness in the way in which he deliberately selected those women who were most likely to make him unhappy. He felt the need—it is, perhaps, his most representative trait—of living in a perpetual state of emotional crisis. He enjoyed abandoning himself to the violent passions which he describes; he enjoyed feeling that his life was being wasted and his work ruined by people who were unworthy of him. It is, indeed, the sensation that he was heading at break-neck speed for disaster that makes him a fascinating and dangerous example for our age which shares his weaknesses withou tpossessing the clear-sightedness and honesty that prevented him from harbouring any illusions about himself.

I do not want to be misunderstood. I yield to no one in my affection for Constant or in my admiration for his work, and what I have written above is not intended as censure. Great literature is not usually produced by social reformers or men of blameless lives: it is produced by men of unstable character living in periods in which social injustice is rampant. Constant is simply a classic example.

II. *ADOLPHE*

I

'TOUT ce livre de la Religion', wrote Sainte-Beuve in an illuminating aside, 'laisse lire à chaque page ce mot: *Je voudrais croire*—comme le petit livre d'*Adolphe* se résume en cet autre mot: *Je voudrais aimer.*'[1] It is a curious fact that though Constant's life appears so disorderly, so lacking in any centre, it yet possesses an odd consistency of its own. The connection between the man and his work is an unusually close one. In his writings disorder itself is woven into strange patterns, and we find that certain central themes are common to the novel and to his religious and political works.

The novel possesses at once the simplicity and the complexity of a seventeenth-century tragedy. A young man of twenty-two has just completed his studies with some distinction at the University of Göttingen. His father is the minister of one of the German Electors and intends his son to follow in his footsteps; but he feels that before settling down the son should see something of the world and the problems with which he will have to deal. Adolphe arrives at a little German principality to spend a few months at the Court. Soon after his arrival he becomes entangled with the mistress of a certain Comte de P——, who is ten years older than himself, who is already *une femme au déclin de l'âge* and the mother of the Count's two illegitimate children. Adolphe is not in love with Ellénore, never has been, is indeed incapable of loving anyone. He drifts into the liaison out of boredom and loneliness and a desperate need to fill a void which he feels within himself. But though his illusions about his feelings for Ellénore soon vanish, he cannot make up his mind to leave her. He postpones his return home for six months. There is a breach between Ellénore and the Count and to Adolphe's dismay she follows him to his native town. He discovers that his father is on the point of ordering her expulsion, and out of generosity and a mistaken sense of chivalry he runs away with her first to Bohemia, then to Warsaw. The bond becomes more and more wearisome, but he still hesitates to break it. The friction be-

[1] *Portraits littéraires*, III, p. 210.

tween them grows until finally Ellénore discovers that he is plotting to leave her and dies a broken woman.

Constant drew heavily on his personal experience for his materials. He was not content with making Adolphe a portrait of the artist or with allowing him to use practically the same words to describe his life at D—— that he himself had used twenty years earlier in the letters to Mme de Charrière describing his adventures at the Court of the Duke of Brunswick.[1] Family, friends, mistresses and rivals were all grist to his mill.[2] The portraits of his father and Mme de Charrière are barely disguised. Ellénore is a composite character. Mme de Staël, Anna Lindsay, Julie Talma and even Mrs. Trevor all seem to have played a part in her creation. There has been some controversy about the respective roles of Mme de Staël and Anna Lindsay, but Mr. Harold Nicolson is surely right in arguing that 'Constant disguised the emotional conflict between himself and Madame de Staël (which is the essential theme of *Adolphe*) by setting his story within the external framework of his affair with Anna Lindsay'.[3]

Critics have complained that some of the characters are unconvincing and others faintly drawn.[4] These criticisms are due perhaps to a failure to grasp the novelist's purpose, to an unconscious comparison between the presentation of his material in the novel and its presentation in the diary and letters. It is true that *Adolphe* is an autobiographical novel, but it is autobiographical in a very unusual way. Life and art are so closely interwoven that it is sometimes difficult to decide whether the novel followed life or whether life followed the novel, for some of the events of Constant's later life read like a repetition of scenes from *Adolphe*.[5] An autobiographical novel is not the same as an autobiography and *Adolphe* must not be judged as though it is. It must be

---

[1] Although he had written in his diary, 'I am going to start a novel which will be my own story', he hotly denied it in public. His friends, however, were not deceived.

[2] Adolphe takes Ellénore away from the Comte de P—— as Constant had taken Anna Lindsay away from Auguste de Lamoignon.

[3] *Benjamin Constant* (London, 1949), p. 177. According to Professor Rudler the novel describes the rupture with Mme de Staël. Professor F. Baldensperger will have none of it. When part of this chapter was published some years ago in a magazine, he wrote to the author to protest that far too little attention had been given to Anna Lindsay. He has since returned to the charge in an introduction to *Adolphe* in the 'Textes Littéraires Français' (Paris, 1946).

[4] Faguet is the chief culprit. See *Politiques et moralistes du dix-neuvième siècle*, I (4th edition, Paris, 1894), pp. 203-7.

[5] It is not possible to speak with certainty on this point as it is thought that the novel underwent a good deal of revision between 1807 and 1816. See Rudler's introductions to his editions (Manchester University Press, 1919 and 1941) and the same author's *Adolphe de Benjamin Constant* (Paris, 1935).

judged as a work of art. Our experience in reading it differs profoundly
from our experience in reading the *Journal intime* or the *Cahier rouge*.
The artist selects and rearranges his everyday experience until it is
transformed into a fresh pattern. This pattern is the novel. His characters
are in no sense 'contemporary portraits'; they are imaginative creations
which possess precisely as much or as little life as is necessary for his
purpose. Each of them represents a particular strand in the final pattern
and becomes the vehicle for the novelist's criticism of a concrete
situation.

These virtues can only be illustrated by a detailed examination of the
text.

> Je venais de finir à vingt-deux ans mes études à l'université de Göttingue.
> —L'intention de mon père, ministre de l'Électeur de ——, était que je
> parcourusse les pays les plus remarquables de l'Europe. Il voulait ensuite
> m'appeler auprès de lui, me faire entrer dans le département dont la direc-
> tion lui était confiée, et me préparer à le remplacer un jour. J'avais obtenu,
> par un travail assez opiniâtre, au milieu d'une vie très dissipée, des succès
> qui m'avaient distingué de mes compagnons d'étude, et qui avaient fait
> concevoir à mon père sur moi des espérances probablement fort exagérées.[1]

> [I was twenty-two and had just finished my studies at the University of
> Göttingen. My father, a minister of the Elector of ——, intended me to
> visit the most interesting countries of Europe, and then enter, at his side, the
> department of which he was the head, in order to prepare me for the day
> on which I should take his place. Though leading a dissipated life, I had
> worked rather doggedly and achieved some successes which distinguished
> me from my fellow students and caused my father to entertain hopes
> concerning my future which were probably much exaggerated.]

Göttingen carries us back to the Germany of the Romantic Movement, the Germany of a hundred tiny principalities and the easy-going
student life with its indulgences and its *folies*. This life is contrasted
with the dullness and respectability of the measured life of the bureau-
crat. There is an ominous inflection about the word *intention*. The
dream begins to fade; the life of dissipation must be put behind one;
unruly desires must be curbed and forced into the mould of conventional respectability, into the uniform life of the 'department', the position of 'trust'. The ironical 'espérances probablement fort exagérées'
marks the beginning of a conflict not merely between two different

[1] I have used Rudler's text, though in places I have modernized the spelling. All
italics in the quotations which follow are mine.

temperaments, but between two different ways of life. This becomes apparent in the third paragraph:

> Je ne demandais alors qu'à me livrer à ces impressions primitives et fougueuses qui jettent l'âme hors de la sphère commune, et lui inspirent le dédain de tous les objets qui l'environnent. Je trouvais dans mon père, non pas un censeur, mais un observateur froid et caustique, qui souriait d'abord de pitié, et qui finissait bientôt la conversation avec impatience.

> [My sole desire at that time was to give myself up to those primitive and passionate feelings which throw the mind out of harmony with the ordinary world and inspire contempt for all about one. In my father I found not a critic, but a cold and caustic observer who began by smiling out of pity but soon showed impatience to end the conversation.]

The words 'les pays les plus remarquables' in the first paragraph are intentionally conventional. It is possible to visit all the European countries in a spirit of correct admiration and even to sow one's wild oats before settling down to become an excellent administrator. It is far otherwise with the *impressions primitives et fougueuses*. For here the conflict between the rebellious individual and social convention is radical and dangerous. We can see already that the father is more than a personal portrait, is the symbol of certain accepted values. It is his voice that we shall hear at Caden and at Warsaw reminding his son of his abilities and begging him not to fritter away his life by sacrificing it to an attachment which had been prompted by his *impressions primitives et fougueuses*.

Although the father is a symbol of certain standards, these standards do not command unqualified respect:

> J'avais dans la maison de mon père adopté sur les femmes un système assez immoral. Mon père, bien qu'il observât strictement les convenances extérieures, se permettait assez fréquemment des propos légers sur les liaisons d'amour. Il les regardait comme des amusements, sinon permis, du moins excusables, et considérait le mariage seul sous un rapport sérieux. Il avait pour principe, qu'un jeune homme doit éviter avec soin de faire ce qu'on nomme une folie, c'est-à-dire, de contracter un engagement durable, avec une personne qui ne fût pas parfaitement son égale pour la fortune, la naissance et les avantages extérieurs. Mais du reste, toutes les femmes, aussi longtemps qu'il ne s'agissait pas de les épouser, lui paraissaient pouvoir, sans inconvénient, être prises, puis être quittées: et je l'avais vu sourire avec une sorte d'approbation à cette parodie d'un mot connu: Cela leur fait si peu de mal, et à nous tant de plaisir.

[In my father's house I had adopted, in regard to women, a rather immoral attitude. Although my father strictly observed the proprieties, he
frequently indulged in frivolous remarks concerning affairs of the heart: he
looked on them as excusable if not permissible amusements, and considered nothing in a serious light, save marriage. His one principle was that
a young man must studiously avoid what is called an act of folly, that is to
say, contracting a lasting engagement with a person who is not absolutely
his equal in regard to fortune, birth and outward advantages; he saw no
objection—provided there was no question of marriage—to taking any
woman and then leaving her; and I have seen him smile with a sort of
approbation at this parody of a well-known saying: It hurts them so little
and gives us so much pleasure!]

These are the views of the eighteenth-century libertine with their
shallow respect for 'les convenances extérieures', and their emphasis on
'fortune', 'naissance' and 'avantages extérieurs', the values of a society
which had lost its moral fibre.

Constant was too great a writer to be the dupe of such a society and
he goes on to point out that the expression of these opinions by parents
has a disastrous effect on the moral education of their children:

Ces règles [he says of the principles which are undermined] ne sont plus
à leurs yeux que des formules banales que leurs parents sont convenus de
leur répéter pour acquit de leur conscience, et les plaisanteries leur semblent
renfermer le véritable secret de la vie.

[In their eyes those rules cease to be anything but banal precepts which
their parents have agreed upon and which they repeat to children out of a
mere sense of duty, whilst the jokes appear to hold the real key to life.]

It must always be remembered that the Constants came of old
Calvinist stock, but the convictions which had once driven them into
exile had been undermined by their environment. They first weakened,
then turned into a revolt against traditional morality.[1] Juste de Constant's own life was far from blameless and in spite of his insistence on
the *convenances extérieures* its laxity had had a decisive influence on his
son's character. Now the puritan conscience is ineradicable and it may
well remain intact without exercising any practical influence on conduct. This is one of the clues to the tragedy of Adolphe and one of the

---

[1] Adolphe's voluntary 'exile' with Ellénore is a repetition of the exile of his Protestant ancestors, but the motives were very different.

secrets of Constant's greatness as a novelist. In the novelist the puritan
conscience was transformed into that sovereign honesty which stamps
a man as a great writer. The phrases, 'Je ne veux point ici me justifier',
'Certes, je ne veux point m'excuser', 'En relevant ainsi les défauts
d'Ellénore, c'est moi que j'accuse et que je condamne', which occur
so frequently in *Adolphe*, are not vain moralizing; they are a sign of the
writer's consciousness of his responsibility and of the sureness of his
apprehension of moral values which give his work its weight and place
it in a different class from the productions of the other novelists of the
Romantic period.[1]

The other decisive influence in Adolphe's life is the (anonymous)
Mme de Charrière:

> J'avais à l'âge de dix-sept ans vu mourir une femme âgée, dont l'esprit,
> d'une tournure remarquable et bizarre, avait commencé à développer le
> mien.[2] Cette femme, comme tant d'autres s'était, à l'entrée de sa carrière,
> lancée vers le monde qu'elle ne connaissait pas, avec le sentiment d'une
> grande force d'âme et de facultés vraiment puissantes. Comme tant d'autres
> aussi, faute de s'être pliée à des convenances factices, mais nécessaires, elle
> avait vu ses espérances trompées, sa jeunesse passer sans plaisir, et la
> vieillesse enfin l'avait atteinte sans la soumettre. Elle vivait dans un château
> voisin d'une de nos terres, mécontente et retirée, n'ayant que son esprit
> pour ressource, et analysant tout avec son esprit. Pendant près d'un an,
> dans nos conversations inépuisables, nous avions envisagé la vie sous toutes
> ses faces et la mort toujours pour terme de tout. Et après avoir tant causé
> de la mort avec elle, j'avais vu la mort la frapper à mes yeux.
>
> Cet événement m'avait rempli d'un sentiment d'incertitude sur la
> destinée, et d'une rêverie vague qui ne m'abandonnait pas. Je lisais de
> préférence dans les poètes ce qui rappelait la brièveté de la vie humaine. Je
> trouvais qu'aucun but ne valait la peine d'aucun effort. . . .
>
> [At the age of seventeen, I saw a woman die whose strange and remark-
> able cast of mind had begun to develop my mind. This woman, like so
> many others, had at the outset plunged into social life, of which she was

---

[1] Compare, for example, Goethe's view as reported in the *Journal intime*: 'Very
interesting supper with Goethe. . . . He's a man with plenty of wit, dash, depth, new
ideas. But he's the least good-natured man I know. When talking about *Werther* he
said: "What makes the book dangerous is that I described weakness as though it were
strength. But when I do something that suits me the consequences are nothing to do
with me. If there are lunatics who are harmed by reading it, *ma foi tant pis*."' (Mistler,
p. 161.)

[2] This is an example of the way in which Constant modified his facts. Mme de
Charrière died in 1805 when he was thirty-eight years old.

ignorant, with the feeling that she possessed great strength of character and really powerful faculties. As with so many others, also, her hopes were disappointed because she did not bow to arbitrary but necessary conventions; her youth passed without pleasure and, finally, old age overtook her without subduing her. She lived in a country house, neighbouring on one of our estates, dissatisfied and solitary, her only resource her mind with which she analysed everything. For nearly a year, during our inexhaustible conversations, we considered life in all its aspects and death always as the end of all things; and, after I had so often discussed death with her, death struck her down before my eyes.

This incident filled me with a feeling of uncertainty concerning fate and a vague dreaminess which never left me. In the poets, I read for preference whatever recalled the brevity of human life. I felt that no object was worth an effort. . . .]

A comparison between this passage and the description of Mme de Charrière in the *Cahier rouge*—too long to set out here—illustrates very well the difference between the methods of the novelist and the autobiographer. The passage from the *Cahier rouge* does not possess the *finality* of the passage from *Adolphe*. The writer confines himself to a particular incident—the escapade in England—which has no general significance. The portrait in *Adolphe* 'places' Mme de Charrière. She is here clearly 'the eighteenth century in person' for the hero. It is not merely that every word contributes something essential to her character, but that every trait assumes a larger significance and is essential to the novel. She encourages his revolt against the *convenances*, teaches him to rely only on his intellect and to analyse everything with it, until finally his belief in life is profoundly undermined. He perceives the dangers of this teaching, but it does not prevent him from adopting her habits of mind or from being deeply infected with her scepticism. He recognizes that the *convenances* though *factices* are 'necessary' and that disregard of them leads to frustration and disappointment. For excessive analysis without positive belief must work destructively and it was precisely positive belief that was singularly lacking in Mme de Charrière and her protégé.

It can now be seen that the characters divide into two groups—those who conform to accepted standards as Adolphe's father and the Baron de T—— ('vieux diplomate dont l'âme était usée') conform, and those who like Adolphe, Éllénore and Mme de Charrière revolt against them. The rebels are people with great gifts but unstable characters who could only have turned their gifts to good account in an ordered society.

E

The connection between the individual and society is a close one and is implied in every action, in every word that he speaks:

> Je me rendis, en quittant Göttingue, dans la petite ville de D——. Cette ville était la résidence d'un Prince, qui, comme la plupart de ceux de l'Allemagne, gouvernait avec douceur un pays de peu d'étendue, protégeait les hommes éclairés qui venaient s'y fixer, laissant à toutes les opinions une liberté parfaite, mais qui, borné par l'ancien usage à la société de ses courtisans, ne rassemblait par là même autour de lui que des hommes en grande partie insignifiants ou médiocres.

> [On leaving Göttingen, I went to the little town of D——. This town was the residence of a Prince who, like most of the princes of Germany, ruled in benign fashion over a State of small area, protecting enlightened men who came to settle there, and allowing complete freedom to all opinions; but having been restricted by ancient custom to the society of courtiers, he assembled about him, for that same reason, only men who were on the whole insignificant and mediocre.]

'Adolphe,' wrote the author of the first Russian translation of the book, 'Adolphe is neither a Frenchman, a German nor a Russian: he is the child of his age.' This comment goes a long way towards explaining the peculiar appeal of the novel. For *Adolphe* is among other things a modern morality. Only two of the characters are given names and we are only told their Christian names. The others are either anonymous or are designated by an initial—'le Comte de P——', 'le Baron de T——'. The same is true of the setting: 'la petite ville de D——', 'Caden, petite ville de la Bohême', the Polish plains 'not far from Warsaw'. Time and place disappear and we have a sense of beings without countries, without homes, without families, engaged in an endless drama 'somewhere in Europe'.

The description of D—— evokes again the Germany of the Romantic Movement, the liberal princes who protect enlightened men and guarantee freedom of opinion. Their excellent intentions, however, are frustrated by convention and they end by surrounding themselves with people who are for the most part *insignifiants ou médiocres*. The word *médiocres* is the basis of Constant's criticism of society. It is placed intentionally at the end of the passage—marking the decline from *éclairés*—and it occurs in other places where it is given the same force:

> Les maris étaient dépourvus de sentiments aussi bien que d'idées; les femmes ne différaient de leurs maris que par une *médiocrité* plus inquiète et

plus agitée, parce qu'elles n'avaient pas, comme eux, cette tranquillité d'esprit qui résulte de l'occupation et de la régularité des affaires.

[The husbands had as few feelings as they had ideas. The wives differed from their husbands only in that their mediocrity was of a more anxious and restless variety. They did not possess the calm of mind which comes from an occupation and the regularity it entails.]

The picture of the factions, jealousies and dubious morality, which are characteristic of a highly sophisticated society, emerges with striking clarity from his account of D——. It is a picture of intellectual and emotional bankruptcy. The women are vain, empty, restless; the men are potentially no better, but the external discipline imposed by *la régularité des affaires* provides a slender barrier against open anarchy.

In other places the criticism becomes specifically moral:

J'avais contracté, dans mes conversations avec la femme qui la première avait développé mes idées, une insurmontable aversion pour toutes les maximes communes et pour toutes les formules dogmatiques. Lors donc j'entendais la *médiocrité* disserter avec complaisance sur des principes bien établis, bien incontestables en fait de morale, de convenance ou de religion, *choses qu'elle met assez volontiers sur la même ligne*, je me sentais poussé à la contredire; non que j'eusse adopté des opinions opposées, mais parce que j'étais impatienté d'une conviction si ferme et si lourde.

[I had contracted, in my conversations with the woman who had first developed my ideas, an insurmountable aversion to all truisms and dogmatic sayings. Therefore, when I heard mediocrities holding forth with complacency on firmly established and undeniable principles of morality, behaviour or religion—things which they are only too apt to place on the same level—I felt obliged to contradict them; not that I had adopted contrary opinions but because I was irritated by so firm and weighty a conviction.]

The words that I have italicized emphasize the complete confusion of values which existed in society and the hollowness of the conventions.

On the next page he proceeds to give an interesting defence of the irritation that society arouses in him:

L'étonnement de la première jeunesse, à l'aspect d'une société si factice et si travaillée, annonce plutôt un cœur naturel qu'un esprit méchant. Cette société d'ailleurs n'a rien à en craindre; elle pèse tellement sur nous, son influence sourde est tellement puissante, qu'elle ne tarde pas à nous façonner d'après le moule universel. Nous ne sommes plus surpris alors que de notre ancienne surprise, et nous nous trouvons bien sous notre nouvelle forme, comme l'on finit par respirer librement dans un spectacle encombré par la foule, tandis qu'en entrant, on n'y respirait qu'avec effort.

[The astonishment of youth at the appearance of so artificial and laboured a society denotes an unspoiled heart rather than a malicious mind. Moreover, society has nothing to fear on that account. It weighs so heavily upon us, its blind influence is so powerful, that it soon shapes us in the universal mould. We are then merely surprised at our first astonishment, and we feel happy in our new shape, just as one finally manages to breathe freely in a congested theatre, whereas, on first entering, one breathed with difficulty.]

The contrast between the 'cœur naturel' and the 'société si factice et si travaillée' points to the dilemma of the sensitive person in a corrupt society. Revolt against the *convenances* leads to waste and disorder, but acceptance leads to the blunting of one's finer faculties and the impoverishment of one's emotional life. The homely image of a person becoming accustomed to the stale air in a theatre expresses very well both the degradation of the process of levelling down and the hopelessness of resistance.

The fate of the natural human being in an unnatural society is one of the central themes of *Adolphe*. Constant like all great writers sets his personal stamp on certain words which recur again and again. *Accoutumer* is one of them. For the characters become habituated to a certain kind of society, to a certain round of feelings and to certain knowledge of themselves. Among the others are *travestir, dénaturer, calculs, flétrir, déchirer, briser, factice, faiblesse*:

La *justesse* de son esprit était *dénaturée* par l'emportement de son caractère.

Ce n'est pas le plaisir, ce n'est pas la nature, ce ne sont pas les sens qui sont corrupteurs; ce sont les *calculs* auxquels la société nous *accoutume*, et les réflexions que l'expérience fait naître.

[The soundness of her judgment was perverted by her passionate nature.
It is not pleasure, it is not nature, it is not our senses which corrupt; it is the calculations to which society accustoms us, and the reflections to which experience gives rise.]

2

The originality of Constant's experience is inseparable from the originality of his method, and there is a sentence in Chapter II which throws a good deal of light on both:

> Presque toujours pour vivre en repos avec nous-mêmes, nous travestissons en calculs et en systèmes nos impuissances ou nos faiblesses. Cela satisfait cette portion de nous, qui est, pour ainsi dire, spectatrice de l'autre.

> [In order to live at peace with ourselves, we almost always disguise our impotence or weakness as calculated actions and systems, and so we satisfy that part of us which is observing the other.]

There are a number of ways in which Constant's art reminds us of that of the seventeenth century, but the analysis of emotion is not one of them. I have already suggested in discussing the *Liaisons dangereuses* that there is, properly speaking, no such thing as analysis in Racine and that the term only has a limited application to a novelist like Mme de La Fayette. There is instead the sudden spontaneous insight into the hidden places of the mind which disrupts personality. *Adolphe* is the perfect example of the solitary destructive analysis of the nineteenth-century novelists. The words, 'cette portion de nous, qui est, pour ainsi dire, spectatrice de l'autre', shows to what lengths the ravages of self-consciousness had already gone. Racine's characters are destroyed by a violent conflict, those of the nineteenth-century novelists by a process of gradual corrosion, a paralysis which spreads over their minds and reduces them to complete impotence.

'No one', said Rudler, 'would read *Adolphe* if it were a novel in three volumes.'[1] Its brevity is, indeed, an essential part of its greatness. Constant uses an ingenious adaptation of the method of Racine to present a nineteenth-century situation. The events which he describes extend over a period of four years, but by deliberately telescoping them, by compressing his story into a *récit* of less than a hundred pages, he achieves the same intense concentration of emotion, the same density that we find in Racine instead of the slow diffusion of emotion that we find in *L'Éducation sentimentale*. It is this which makes his experience so overwhelming, and sometimes so revolting.

[1] Introduction, 1941, p. xii.

The difficulties and dangers of the method are immense. It needs intellectual integrity and clear-sightedness amounting to genius. For one of the principal dangers is that the mind, speculating about its own processes in retrospect, will end by distorting and falsifying the *données*. It is the temptation to which Rousseau succumbed. The other great danger is that the novel will cease to be a work of art at all and will degenerate into a psychologist's case-book. This, it seems to me, is what sometimes happens in the later volumes of *A la Recherche du temps perdu* and in *Les Hommes de bonne volonté*.

Constant succeeded brilliantly where most of his successors failed. When we compare the opening of the *Confessions* with some of Adolphe's comments on his own experience, we have a very good idea of the quality of Constant's mind:

> Je forme une entreprise qui n'eut jamais d'exemple, et qui n'aura point d'imitateur. Je vais montrer à mes semblables un homme dans toute la vérité de la nature et cet homme sera moi. Je me suis montré tel que je suis; méprisable et vil quand je l'ai été, bon, généreux, sublime, quand je l'ai été: j'ai dévoilé mon intérieur, tel que tu l'as vu toi-même, Être éternel.

> [I am planning an undertaking which is without precedent and which will have no imitators. I am going to show my fellows a man in all the truth of nature and this man will be myself. I have shown myself as I am; contemptible and low when I was; good, generous, sublime when I was; I have unveiled my inner being just as you have seen it yourself, Eternal Being.]

The theatrical tone is at once suspect, and Rivière has pointed out that the adjectives *bon*, *généreux*, *sublime*, *vil*, *méprisable* actually prevent us from perceiving the feelings themselves; we see only Rousseau's interpretation of them. Constant's tone is very different:

> L'amour, qu'une heure auparavant je m'applaudissais de feindre, je *crus* tout-à-coup l'éprouver avec fureur.
> Je me sentais, *de la meilleure foi du monde*, véritablement amoureux.
> Offerte à mes regards dans un moment *où mon cœur avait besoin d'amour*, *ma vanité de succès*, Ellénore me parut une conquête digne de moi.

> [The love which, an hour earlier, I had congratulated myself on feigning I now thought I felt with frenzy.
> I was perfectly convinced that I was really in love.

Coming into my ken at a time when my heart needed love and my vanity success, Ellénore seemed to me a worthy conquest.]

'*Adolphe*', wrote Guy de Pourtalès, 'apportait la preuve que la partie la plus sérieuse et la plus riche de l'homme est intimement mêlée en lui à ses duperies et à sa littérature.'[1] Constant's attitude is one of extreme circumspection. He is determined to separate illusion from reality, false feelings from true, the feelings themselves from the interpretation which the mind automatically places on them to protect itself. It is not simply that he possessed that *vue directe*—that luminous glance—into the complexity of the human heart which Rivière declared to be singularly lacking in Flaubert; it is that we perceive the feeling and the moral judgment as separate and distinct. We do more than that. We perceive the simultaneous existence of different levels of feeling, the *partie la plus riche de l'homme* and his *duperies*, 'the need of his heart for love and of his vanity for success'. The *impuissances* and *faiblesses* are never converted into *calculs* and *systèmes*.

When this method is turned on Adolphe the results are impressive. He is not merely the pivot of the book; he is, strictly speaking, the only character in the book. Everything is rigorously subordinated to a single aim—to illuminating the deepest and unexplored places of the personality. In reading *Adolphe* I am sometimes reminded of an X-ray photograph, but an X-ray photograph in which one sees the blood flowing and the nerves throbbing.[2] There are four main factors in his make-up: an intense vitality, an extreme shyness derived from his father, a deep-seated pessimism and, most important of all, what he calls *un besoin de sensibilité*.

Je ne savais pas alors ce que c'était que la timidité [he says of his father in a passage which illustrates the trim precision of Constant's language], cette souffrance intérieure qui nous poursuit jusques dans l'âge le plus avancé, qui refoule sur notre cœur les impressions les plus profondes, qui glace nos paroles, qui dénature dans notre bouche tout ce que nous essayons de dire, et ne nous permet de nous exprimer que par des mots vagues ou une ironie plus ou moins amère, comme si nous voulions nous venger sur nos sentiments mêmes de la douleur que nous éprouvons à ne pouvoir les faire connaître. . . .

Ma contrainte avec lui eut une grande influence sur mon caractère. Aussi timide que lui, mais plus agité, parce que j'étais plus jeune, je

[1] *De Hamlet à Swann* (Paris, 1924), p. 177.
[2] 'His sentences have such a delicate skin that we see the blood flowing and the nerves vibrating.' (Pourtalès, *op. cit.*, p. 179.)

m'accoutumai à renfermer en moi-même tout ce que j'éprouvais, à ne former que des plans solitaires, à ne compter que sur moi pour leur exécution, à considérer les avis, l'intérêt, l'assistance et jusqu'à la seule présence des autres comme une gêne et comme un obstacle.

[I did not then know what timidity meant—that inner suffering which pursues you into old age, which forces the profoundest feelings back into the heart, chilling your words and deforming in your mouth whatever you try to say, allowing you to express yourself only in vague phrases or a somewhat bitter irony, as if you wanted to avenge yourself on your feelings for the pain you experienced at being unable to communicate them. . . . My feeling of constraint with him had a great influence on my character. I was as timid as he, but, being younger, I was more excitable. I kept to myself all that I felt, made all my plans on my own, and relied on myself to put them into effect. I considered the opinion, interest, assistance and even the mere presence of others as a hindrance and an obstacle.]

It must be recognized that the *impressions primitives et fougueuses* already referred to are the sign of a genuine vitality, but this vitality made intellectual discipline and direction essential, and it is here that intellect failed. The absence of discipline and direction meant that shyness and artificial social convention acted as a dam which inhibited the proper functioning of nervous energy. As a result, Adolphe's feelings are constantly wasting themselves in useless eruptions. 'Mon esprit', he said, 'm'entraînait au delà de toute mesure.' The reaction against this waste produced a no less dangerous lassitude which in turn undermined his vitality:

Je n'avais pas cependant la profondeur d'égoisme qu'un tel caractère paraît annoncer. Tout en ne m'intéressant qu'à moi, je m'intéressais faiblement à moi-même. Je portais au fond de mon cœur un besoin de sensibilité dont je ne m'apercevais pas; mais qui, ne trouvant point à se satisfaire, me détachait successivement de tous les objets qui tour-à-tour attiraient ma curiosité.

[However, I did not possess the depths of egoism which such a character would seem to indicate. Though only interested in myself, I was but faintly interested. Unconsciously I bore in my heart a need for sympathy which, not being satisfied, caused me to abandon, one after another, every object of my curiosity.]

'Constant', said Rudler in his great study, 'arrive en même temps . . . au dernier degré de la langueur vitale et de la lucidité intellectuelle.'[1] The weaknesses which are analysed with such skill in this passage are as different from the moral debility of the heroes of Chateaubriand and Musset as the method of Constant is from their wordy productions. The statement that Adolphe only took a feeble interest in himself points to a deep-seated despair which paralyses *action*, but not *thought*. A large part of the book is devoted to the elucidation and analysis of this *besoin de sensibilité* which was undreamed of in the psychology of the seventeenth-century writers and which bears no relation to the *froideur* and the *indifférence* that their characters display towards one another. What is disconcerting about Adolphe is that he is at once almost unbearably sensitive and insensible to the point of brutality, that he possesses great reserves of emotion but gives the impression of complete aridity. While it is true that his life is continually disrupted by gusts of violent feelings, these feelings are indeterminate and unattached. The intellect is incapable of directing them towards any useful end and they can never be *adequate* substitutes—I emphasize the word for reasons which will be apparent later—for other feelings that he does not possess. For the clue to the contradictions of Adolphe's character lies in the fact that he did not possess certain feelings which a normal person must be expected to possess. He is perpetually trying to create the missing feelings, to convince himself that he does possess them, that he is reacting normally to a particular situation. The strain gives the first part of the novel its restless, destructive movement—a movement which is reflected in phrases to which Constant has given a peculiar resonance: 'La fatigue d'une agitation sans but', 'Je me débattais intérieurement' and—most striking of all—'Une agitation qui ressemblait fort à l'amour'. But every time the intellect, which is so ineffectual in directing emotion into fruitful channels, shatters the illusion and reveals him to himself as he really is. Only his 'curiosity'—a sinister word in *Adolphe*—is engaged and it vanishes because the heart is empty.

The genesis of the love affair with Ellénore is of particular interest. A friend of Adolphe's at D—— has been paying court to a lady-in-waiting and after a long and arduous suit succeeds in seducing her. He is so overjoyed at his success that Adolphe jumps to the conclusion that a love affair is the proper solution of his own emotional problems. In other words, the connection with Ellénore does not originate in spontaneous attraction; it originates in an idea, in a *theory* of Adolphe's about his feelings:

[1] *La Jeunesse de Benjamin Constant*, p. 384.

E*

Tourmenté d'une émotion vague, je veux être aimé, me disais-je, et je regardais autour de moi; je ne voyais personne qui m'inspîrât de l'amour, personne qui me parût susceptible d'en prendre. J'interrogeais monc œur et mes goûts; je ne me sentais aucun mouvement de préférence.

[Some obscure emotion agitated me. I want to be loved, I thought to myself; and I looked around me but could see no one who inspired love in me, no one likely to want love. I examined my heart and my tastes; I could find no marked preference.]

The tragedy lies in the need of filling this interior void at all costs, of finding some means of stilling the devouring *agitation*. He naturally selects the person who can only stimulate and exasperate his own restlessness because she, too, is *en lutte constante contre sa destinée*:

Ellénore n'avait qu'un esprit ordinaire: mais ses idées étaient justes, et ses expressions, toujours simples, étaient quelquefois frappantes par la noblesse et l'élévation de ses sentiments. Elle avait beaucoup de préjugés, mais tous ses préjugés étaient en sens inverse de son intérêt. Elle attachait le plus grand prix à la régularité de la conduite, précisément parce que la sienne n'était pas régulière suivant les notions reçues. Elle était très religieuse, parce que la religion condamnait rigoureusement son genre de vie. . . . Ellénore, en un mot, était en lutte constante contre sa destinée. . . . Cette opposition entre ses sentiments et la place qu'elle occupait dans le monde avait rendu son humeur fort inégale. . . . Comme elle était tourmentée d'une idée particulière, au milieu de la conversation la plus générale, elle ne restait jamais parfaitement calme. Mais par cela même, il y avait dans sa manière quelque chose de fougueux et d'inattendu, qui la rendait plus piquante qu'elle n'aurait dû l'être naturellement. La bizarrerie de sa position suppléait en elle à la nouveauté des idées.

[Ellénore was not a woman of exceptional intelligence; but her ideas were sound and her way of expressing them, which was always simple, was sometimes made striking by the nobility and loftiness of her sentiments. She had many prejudices; but all of them ran counter to her interest. She attached the greatest importance to regularity of conduct, precisely because hers was not regular according to conventional notions. She was very religious, because religion severely condemned her kind of life. . . . In a word, Ellénore was for ever struggling against her destiny. . . . This opposition between her sentiments and her position in society caused her to be most changeable in mood. . . . As a single idea preoccupied her, she never remained perfectly calm, even in the midst of the most general conversation. For this very reason there was something spirited and unexpected in her manner which made her more striking than she would have been naturally. The strangeness of her position made up for the lack of novelty in her ideas.]

'Ce n'est elle [Mme de Staël] que sous le rapport de la tyrannie,' said Rosalie de Constant in a letter to her brother.[1] The way in which Constant modified her character—in so far as he did draw on her—is interesting. He may have felt that in real life Mme de Staël was the dominant partner in the relationship and that it was she who was responsible for the waste of his great gifts. In the novel he takes his revenge. Ellénore is endowed only with the 'esprit ordinaire' which belonged in life to Anna Lindsay, and after intolerable suffering on both sides it is Adolphe who destroys her though he ruins himself in the process. The passage closes with one of Constant's rare and lovely images:

On l'examinait avec intérêt et curiosité comme un bel orage.

[One observed her with interest and curiosity, like a magnificent thunderstorm.]

This image not only concentrates the diffused emotions of the whole scene; it marks a definite phase in the development of the novel. Adolphe is still the detached observer, but he will not remain so for long. The 'bel orage' looks forward ironically to another sort of storm.

Je pensais faire, en observateur froid et impartial, le tour de son caractère et de son esprit. Mais chaque mot qu'elle disait me semblait revêtu d'une grâce inexplicable.

[I thought I was going to size up her character and mind as a cool and impartial observer; but every word she spoke to me seemed to possess an inexplicable grace.]

The focus is shifting. The 'Je pensais faire . . .' shows that he is no longer altogether the detached observer, that he is becoming enveloped in the 'storm'. A few lines later and it has happened.

Je ne croyais pas aimer Ellénore; mais déjà je n'aurais pu me résigner à ne pas lui plaire.

[1] 12 July 1816. See *Adolphe* (ed. Rudler), p. 149.

[I did not believe that I loved Ellénore; but I could no longer entertain the idea of not pleasing her.]

He succeeds in making her fall in love with him and the blunt statement: 'Elle se donna enfin tout entière', is followed by the famous passage which begins, 'Charme de l'amour, qui pourrait vous peindre!' This passage is not, as it is sometimes said to be, a 'lyrical outburst' in the manner of Chateaubriand. It is a close piece of psychological analysis, but it has an immense élan which gives it a special importance. The movement of *Adolphe* is a twofold one. There are sudden élans, sudden expansions of feeling, but intimately connected with them is the reverse movement—the sudden contraction which deflates the feeling of fullness like a bubble and leaves only a desperate sense of emptiness and exhaustion. The 'Charme de l'amour' is followed almost immediately by

Ellénore était sans doute un vif plaisir dans ma vie: mais elle n'était plus un *but*; elle était devenue un *lien*.

[Ellénore was undoubtedly a source of keen pleasure in my life, but she no longer represented a goal: she had become a bond.]

The theory of the 'goal' and the 'bond' dominated Constant's personal life as it dominates the life of his hero. The intellect proposes the wrong 'goal', directs the violent but indeterminate feelings into the wrong channels, or at any rate allows them to flow into the wrong channels.[1] With a highly sensitive person this leads to a thoroughgoing emotional disorder:

Je souffrais deux heures loin d'elle de l'idée, qu'elle souffrait loin de moi. Je souffrais deux heures près d'elle, avant de pouvoir l'apaiser.
Je souffrais d'ignorer son sort, je souffrais même de ne pas la voir, et j'étais étonné de la peine que cette privation me causait.

[Away from her, I suffered for two hours at the idea that she was grieving through being away from me; and l suffered two hours more at her side before I was able to pacify her.

[1] It is significant that the only happy period of Constant's life came after the last love affair with Mme Récamier when he settled down to humdrum married life with Charlotte von Hardenberg and devoted the whole of his energies to their proper 'goal' which was politics.

I suffered at not knowing what her fate could be; I suffered even at not seeing her, and I was astonished at the pain which this privation caused in me.]

The feelings are described with Constant's customary lucidity, but it is clear that they are *substitute* feelings—substitutes for the feelings which were lacking in his make-up and which he was perpetually trying to create. This means that all his nervous energy is converted into 'suffering', into that personal and highly original suffering which springs from the perception of his own incompleteness and which inhibits action. Nor should we overlook the speaker's 'astonishment' —it is mentioned more than once in the book—at his sufferings, astonishment that he is capable of such depths of feeling at all. The explanation is given by Adolphe himself in the next chapter:

Je n'étais qu'un homme faible, reconnaissant et dominé; *je n'étais soutenu par aucune impulsion qui partît du cœur.*

[I was only a weak, grateful and dominated man; I was sustained by no impulse from the heart.]

The 'charm of love' may be unpaintable, but the disenchantment which follows the disappearance of an illusion is not and produces some of Constant's most striking pages. The eighteenth-century antithesis, often so clumsy, is moulded to his purpose and becomes an exact instrument for measuring the fluctuations of feeling, for registering the stages of his disenchantment. The contrast between the *but* and the *lien* is one example and there are others:

Je me reposais, pour ainsi dire, dans l'indifférence des autres, de la fatigue de son amour.
Nous vécûmes ainsi quatre mois, dans des rapports forcés, quelquefois doux, jamais complètement libres, y recontrant encore du *plaisir*, mais n'y trouvant plus de *charme*.
Avide de se tromper elle-même, elle cherchait un *fait* où il n'y avait qu'un *sentiment*.

[Tired by her love, I was, so to speak, basking in the indifference of others.
We lived thus for four months in a forced intimacy which was sometimes sweet, but never completely free. We found pleasure in it but no more charm.

Eager to deceive herself, she sought a fact where there was only a feeling.]

One of the most remarkable expressions of his emotional instability, of the ceaseless friction of feeling, occurs when he writes (under pressure from Ellénore) to ask his father's permission to spend another six months at D——:

La réponse de mon père ne se fit pas attendre. Je tremblais, en ouvrant sa lettre, de la douleur qu'un refus causerait à Ellénore. . . . Mais en lisant le consentement qu'il m'accordait, tous les inconvénients d'une prolongation de séjour se présentèrent, tout-à-coup à mon esprit. Encore six mois de gêne et de contrainte, m'écriai-je. . . .

[My father's reply was not long in coming. I opened his letter, trembling at the thought of the pain a refusal would cause Ellénore. . . . But on reading the consent my father granted me, all the drawbacks in prolonging my stay suddenly occurred to me. Another six months of torture and constraint, I cried. . . .]

When the time comes for his departure he describes his emotions in some sentences which are one of the glories of this sombre masterpiece:

Il y a dans les liaisons qui se prolongent quelque chose de si profond! Elles deviennent à notre insu une partie si intime de notre existence! Nous formons de loin, avec calme, la résolution de les rompre, nous croyons attendre avec impatience l'époque de l'exécuter; mais quand ce moment arrive il nous remplit de terreur; et telle est la bizarrerie de notre cœur misérable, que nous quittons avec un déchirement horrible, ceux près de qui nous demeurions sans plaisir.

[There is something so profound in prolonged affairs! They become unconsciously so intimate a part of our existence! A long while ahead, we calmly plan to break them off; we fancy we are waiting impatiently for the time to put this plan into effect: but when the moment arrives, it fills us with terror; and such is the strangeness of our miserable heart that it is with horrible anguish we leave those by whose side we lived without pleasure.]

The first sentence sounds like a nostalgic but faintly guilty sigh. *Profond* defines the quality of the liaisons, but it is qualified by *se prolongent* which is purely quantitative; it is not genuine feeling, but a habit which depends on the length of the connection. The second sentence shows the extent to which the habit can become part of the very fibres of one's being. 'Nous formons de loin, avec calme . . .' states the cynical attitude of the adventurer; but this attitude cannot be maintained. We think that we can sit back and decide, coldly, to break with a mistress; but we underrate the power of habit and the *bizarrerie de notre cœur misérable*; when the moment comes our resolution evaporates in the turmoil of feeling. *Déchirer* and its derivatives had been popular in descriptions of lacerated feelings ever since the seventeenth century, but Constant made the word his own and the direct impact of *déchirement horrible* in this passage is tremendous. It refers back to 'une partie si intime de notre existence'—stressing the closeness of the texture of the writing—and we have a really horrifying sensation of emotional disruption, of people being torn apart. Once again the eighteenth-century antithesis is organic. The realization that the liaison had been without 'pleasure' intensifies the disenchantment of the parting.

3

Paul Bourget once declared that the whole drama of *Adolphe* lies in 'the continued destruction of love in the young man's heart by the action of his mind, and his mistress's continual effort to rebuild by passion and tenderness the feeling which she sees crumbling away'.[1]

This view cannot be accepted without reservations. I have tried to show that the role of the intellect is other than Bourget suggests, but it is true that both Adolphe and Ellénore up to a point mistake the shadow for the substance, and in the last part of the book she tries ironically to reconstruct an illusion.[2] For *Adolphe* has three phases. The first is the pursuit of the 'goal'—the conquest and seduction of Ellénore. The second is the period of disenchantment—the discovery that there is no 'goal'. In the third, the 'goal' is the rupture with Ellénore.

In the last phase there is a new alignment of forces and Adolphe, in spite of himself, makes common cause with his father and the Baron de T—— in the destruction of his mistress. When his father writes:

> Votre naissance, vos talents, votre fortune, vous assignaient dans le monde une autre place que celle de compagnon d'une femme sans patrie et sans aveu. Votre lettre me prouve déjà que vous n'êtes pas content de

[1] *Op. cit.*, p. 23.
[2] Cf., 'Elle me crut: elle s'enivra de *son* amour, qu'elle prenait pour le *nôtre* . . .'. [She believed me: she was intoxicated by her own love which she took for ours.]

vous. Songez que l'on ne gagne rien à prolonger une situation dont on rougit. Vous consumez inutilement les plus belles années de votre jeunesse, et cette perte est irréparable.

[Your place in the world, by your birth, talents and fortune, should be a very different one from that of companion to a homeless woman without a country. Your letter proves to me already that you are not pleased with yourself. Reflect, then, that nothing is gained by prolonging a situation of which you are ashamed. You are uselessly wasting the best years of your youth and that loss is irreparable.]

he is voicing thoughts which have already occurred to Adolphe himself:

Je me plaignis de ma vive contrainte, de ma jeunesse consumée dans l'inaction, du despotisme qu'elle exerçait sur toutes mes démarches.

[I complained of the severe constraints imposed on me, of my youth wasted in inaction, of her despotic ruling over my every action.]

The father's voice is heard again as Adolphe prepares to leave for Poland, and in Poland it is echoed by the Baron de T—— who becomes, as it were, an extension of the father's role:

Toutes les routes vous sont ouvertes . . . mais souvenez-vous bien qu'il y a entre vous et tous les genres de succès un obstacle insurmontable, et que cet obstacle est Ellénore.

[Every road is open to you . . . but you must remember that, between you and all forms of success, there is one insurmountable obstacle—and that obstacle is Ellénore.]

These words reverberate in Adolphe's mind and they do not fail to make an impression:

Ces mots funestes, entre tous les genres de succès et vous, il existe un obstacle insurmontable, et cet obstacle, c'est Ellénore, retentissaient autour de moi.

[Those baleful words: 'Between you and all forms of success, there is one insurmountable obstacle—and that obstacle is Ellénore' echoed around me.]

The drama is more complex than at first appeared. The outer conflict between father and son, between the individual and society is reflected in the inner conflict in Adolphe's mind. The voices of the father and the Baron are like the chorus in a Greek tragedy. Whatever their short-comings, they represent a norm. The *convenances*, we remember, are *factices mais nécessaires*. Convention is beginning to assert itself:

Chère amie, lui dis-je, on lutte quelque temps contre sa destinée, mais on finit toujours par céder. Les lois de la société sont plus fortes que les volontés des hommes. Les sentiments les plus impérieux se brisent contre la fatalité des circonstances. En vain l'on s'obstine à ne consulter que son *cœur*: on est condamné tôt ou tard à écouter la *raison*. . . . Je serai toujours votre ami. J'aurai toujours pour vous l'affection la plus profonde. Les deux années de notre liaison ne s'effaceront pas de ma mémoire: elles seront à jamais l'époque la plus belle de ma vie.

['My dear,' I said to her, 'we struggle for a time against our destiny, but we always end by giving way. The laws of society are stronger than the will of men; the most powerful sentiments can be shattered on the fatality of circumstances. It is vain to persist in consulting only one's heart; sooner or later, one is bound to listen to reason. . . . I shall always be your friend; I shall always have the profoundest affection for you. The two years we have been together will never fade from my memory; they will always be the happiest years of my life.']

In another passage he reflects:

Ah! si le ciel m'eût accordé une femme que les *convenances sociales* me permissent d'avouer, que mon père ne rougît pas d'accepter pour fille, j'aurais été mille fois plus heureux de la rendre heureuse.

[Ah, had heaven granted me a woman whom social conventions per-mitted me to acknowledge and whom my father would not have been ashamed to admit as his daughter, then, making her happy would have been a source of infinite happiness to me.]

These passages reveal the extent to which Adolphe has compromised with society. The attitude that he displays is not held up to admiration. His father's disapproval of the connection with Ellénore is understand-able, but there is no genuine *moral conviction* behind this disapproval. The intentional vulgarity of the first passage and the *convenances sociales*, which always have a derogatory meaning, in the second provide all the comment that is necessary.

It is in other places that we must look for that peculiar wisdom which the book distils. It has not been sufficiently remarked that it contains a number of general statements which read for all the world like maxims lifted from the pages of the seventeenth-century moralists:

> Il y a des choses qu'on est longtemps sans se dire, mais quand une fois elles sont dites, on ne cesse jamais de les répéter.
>
> C'est un affreux malheur de n'être pas aimé quand on aime. Mais c'en est un bien grand d'être aimé avec passion, quand on n'aime pas.
>
> L'emportement, l'injustice, la distraction même se réparent. Mais la dissimulation jette dans l'amour un élément étranger qui le dénature et le flétrit à ses propres yeux.
>
> Cette duplicité était fort éloignée de mon caractère naturel: mais l'homme se déprave, dès qu'il a dans le cœur une seule pensée qu'il est constamment forcé de dissimuler.

> [There are things one does not say for a long time, but, once they are said, one never stops repeating them.
>
> It is a fearful misfortune not to be loved when you love; but it is a very great misfortune to be loved passionately when you love no longer.
>
> Anger, injustice, even forgetfulness can be repaired, but dissimulation generates in love a foreign matter which changes its nature and appears to poison it.
>
> This duplicity was far from my natural character, but man becomes depraved as soon as he has in his heart a single thought which he is constantly obliged to dissimulate.]

They are not abstractions or conclusions which are imposed on experience from without. They are statements of general validity which emerge logically from his experience. They are always dramatically appropriate—the last quotation is a particularly good example—and fall into their appointed places, carrying in each case the revelation of Adolphe to himself a stage further. They provide a background of sanity which places Adolphe's disordered feelings and the shabby *convenances* in their true perspective. It is this that gives the whole book its incomparable poise and maturity which make it almost unique in nineteenth-century literature.

The more one studies the text of *Adolphe*, the more impressed one is by the skill with which it is constructed, with which the diverse strands are woven into the pattern. The inner and outer conflicts revolve like concentric circles. Phrases and words are constantly echoing and answering one another. The 'travail assez opiniâtre au milieu d'une vie très dissipée, which had distinguished Adolphe from his fellow-students, is recalled to show that while he had wasted his youth in idleness less gifted men 'par le seul effort d'un travail opiniâtre et d'une vie régulière, m'avaient laissé loin derrière eux dans la route de la fortune'. The *bel orage*, which he had complacently examined from without, becomes another kind of storm—'Notre vie ne fut qu'un perpétuel orage.' In the same way images dovetail neatly into one another, contributing to the strength and tautness of the book. Ellénore makes a desperate effort to break down the opposition to her which has grown up in Adolphe's mind:

Elle aurait voulu *pénétrer dans le sanctuaire intime* de ma pensée, pour y briser une opposition sourde qui la révoltait contre moi.

[She would have liked to penetrate the inner sanctuary of my mind to break down the secret opposition which enraged her against me.]

When she succeeds by the intermediary of a third person in breaking into the 'sanctuary', it is only to find it deserted:

C'est un grand pas, c'est un pas irréparable, lorsqu'on dévoile tout-à-coup aux yeux d'un tiers les replis cachés d'une relation intime. Le jour qui *pénètre dans ce sanctuaire* constate et achève les destructions que la nuit enveloppait de ses ombres; ainsi les corps renfermés dans les tombeaux conservent souvent leur première forme, jusqu'à ce que l'air extérieur vienne les frapper et les réduire en poudre.[1]

[It is a great step, an irreparable step, when one suddenly reveals to a third person the hidden intricacies of an intimate affair of the heart; the light which penetrates this sanctuary picks out and completes the work of destruction which darkness had enveloped in its shades. Thus it is that bodies shut in tombs often preserve their original shape until the outside air reaches them and reduces them to dust.]

[1] I have already remarked that in spite of its disorder, Constant's life possessed an odd consistency of its own. In his philosophical and political writings, as well as in his novel, he is haunted by the necessity of preserving 'the inner sanctuary' against the encroachments of every form of despotism. It is interesting to note that the inner sanctuary appears in *De l'Esprit de conquête*: 'In short, despotism rules by silence and allows a man the right to be silent: usurpation condemns him to speak; it pursues him into the sanctuary of his thought (*le sanctuaire de sa pensée*) and, by compelling him to lie to his own conscience, takes from him the last consolation which still remains to the oppressed.'

There is something stuffy and unnatural about the connection between Adolphe and this woman who is ten years his senior which gives
us the sensation of two people living in an airless, overheated boudoir
without any contact with the outside world. As soon as it is brought
out into the open for a moment and discussed with other people, it
begins to crumble away.[1]

I have said that the images dovetail into one another, but the connection between them is so close that it would be more exact to call
them sections of a single expanded image. Ellénore's attempt to break
down Adolphe's opposition to her provokes a contrary movement
which is expressed in the third or final section of the image:

'Que je n'entende de vous,' dit-elle, 'aucun mot cruel. Je ne réclame
plus, je ne m'oppose à rien: mais que cette voix que j'ai tant aimée, que
cette voix, qui retentissait au fond de mon cœur, *n'y pénètre pour le
déchirer.*'

['Let me hear no cruel word from you,' she said. 'I make no further
demands. I oppose nothing; but that voice I loved so much, that voice
which moved my heart, do not, I pray, let it penetrate to my heart to
rend it.']

Although the 'storms' described in the closing chapters remind us of
the bitter encounters between Racine's characters, the resemblance is a
superficial one. They are the signs of nervous exasperation and their
function is to reveal an interior, subterranean process of dissolution.[2]

Nous vivions, pour ainsi dire, d'une espèce de mémoire du cœur, assez
puissante pour que l'idée de nous séparer fût douloureuse, trop faible pour
que nous trouvassions du bonheur à être unis. . . . J'aurais voulu donner à
Ellénore des témoignages de tendresse qui la contentassent. Je reprenais
quelquefois avec elle le langage de l'amour: mais ces émotions et ce
langage ressemblaient à ces feuilles pâles et décolorées, qui, par un reste de
végétation funèbre, croissent languissamment sur les branches d'un arbre
déraciné.

---

[1] As an example of the extent to which they were cut off from the normative
influence of society, he remarks of his conversation with the 'intermediary':
'Ellénore's reproaches had convinced me that I was guilty; I learned from the person
who was defending her that I was merely unhappy.'

[2] Cf., 'The truth broke in from every direction, and I employed, to make myself
understood, the harshest and most pitiless expressions.'

[We were living, so to speak, on memories of our hearts which were sufficiently strong to make the idea of separation painful to us, but too weak to permit us to find happiness in being united. . . . I should have liked to give Ellénore proof of my feelings which would make her happy; sometimes, I used afresh the language of love; but these emotions and this language resembled those pale and faded leaves which, amongst some remaining funereal vegetation, grow languidly on the branches of an uprooted tree.]

This passage is constructed out of simple materials which seem at first to give it a literary flavour; but when we look into it, we see how effective the first sentence is in describing the atmosphere of gradual dissolution. The 'reste de végétation funèbre', the 'feuilles pâles et décolorées' and the dying fall of 'croissent languissamment sur les branches d'un arbre déraciné' convey not merely the dissolution of an attachment, but the disappearance of all feeling. It is characteristic of Constant's images that they nearly all lead back to the speaker. It is Adolphe himself who is the 'arbre déraciné'.

These images are not numerous—it is this that makes them stand out with such power—but each one leads logically to the next and marks a further stage in the process of decay. The sections of the landscape image are as closely linked as those of the image of the *sanctuaire intime*, and the separate strands of the images winding in and out of one another give the book its rich complexity:

C'était une de ces journées d'hiver, où le soleil éclaire tristement la campagne grisâtre, comme s'il regardait en pitié la terre qu'il avait cessé de réchauffer. . . . Le ciel était serein: mais les arbres étaient sans feuilles: aucun souffle n'agitait l'air, aucun oiseau ne le traversait, tout était immobile, et le seul bruit qui se fît entendre était celui de l'herbe glacée, qui se brisait sous nos pas. Comme tout est calme, me dit Ellénore, comme la nature se résigne! Le cœur ne doit-il pas apprendre à se résigner?

[It was one of those winter days when the sun seems to light the greyish countryside with a melancholy light, as if it looked pityingly on the earth which it has ceased to warm. . . . The sky was calm; but the trees were leafless; no breeze stirred the air, no bird flew through it: everything was motionless and the only sound to be heard was that of the frozen grass crunching under our feet. 'How calm everything is!' Ellénore said. 'How resigned nature is! Should not the heart learn resignation too?']

Constant's experience is never merely personal. The autumnal imagery, with its emphasis on death and decay, faithfully reflects the mood of the age which produced it. The change from autumn to winter, too, has its point. It marks the beginning of the final phase in their relationship. The barren beauty of the scene, the pale sunshine which no longer warms the earth and the sigh of resignation leave an almost painful sensation of life running to waste. Adolphe's dilemma is not less painful. What feeling persists stiffens, becomes hard and brittle as a frozen immobility steals over it.

This imagery is interesting for another reason. In an earlier passage Constant had written:

L'amour supplée aux longs souvenirs, par une sorte de magie. Toutes les autres affections ont besoin du passé: l'amour crée, comme par enchantement, un passé dont il nous entoure. Il nous donne, pour ainsi dire, la conscience d'avoir vécu, durant des années, avec un être qui naguère nous était presque étranger. L'amour n'est qu'un point lumineux, et néanmoins il semble s'emparer du temps. Il y a peu de jours qu'il n'existait pas, bientôt il n'existera plus; mais, tant qu'il existe, il répand sa clarté sur l'époque qui l'a précédé, comme sur celle qui doit le suivre.

[Love makes up for the lack of long memories by a sort of magic. All other affections need a past; love creates a past which envelops us, as if by enchantment. It gives us, so to speak, a consciousness of having lived for years with a being who, not so long ago, was almost a stranger. Love is only a luminous point, and nevertheless it seems to take complete possession of time. A few days ago it did not exist, soon it will exist no more; but as long as it exists, it sheds light on the period which went before, just as it will on that which will follow.]

In spite of its brevity, *Adolphe* gives us an extraordinary, an oppressive sense of time passing. The young man whom we meet in Chapter I has no 'past'. The starting point is the *impressions primitives et fougueuses*, the spontaneous overflow of a genuine, unattached vitality. This vitality attaches itself to Ellénore, becomes the 'longs souvenirs', the past 'dont il nous entoure'. When we look back, we see that the whole book is a logical progression from the *impressions primitives et fougueuses* to the frozen winter scene, from youth to middle age, from middle age to death. Ellénore may seem, on account of her violence, to stand for life, but she is really a death-symbol. M. Poulet distinguishes, in an interesting essay, between a 'living past'—the past referred to in the passage I have just quoted—and a 'dead past'. 'Ellénore', he writes, 'demands from him something more than a memory and sacrifices; she demands fidelity to a stationary, petrified love which no longer belongs to a living past, but to a present constructed out of a dead past.'[1] That is his tragedy. He becomes chained to the 'stationary petrified love' which drags him down to destruction.

It has been said that Constant was lacking in imagination and unfavourable comparisons between his style and Chateaubriand's were sometimes made by nineteenth-century critics. Faguet, for example, called him 'un Chateaubriand qui n'est pas assez poète pour faire de son ennui une grande mélancolie lyrique'.[2] This judgment seems to rest on a misunderstanding of the nature of imagination. All that it means is that instead of writing a poetical prose in the manner of the Romantics with their large and blurred effects, Constant confines himself strictly to the prose use of language. His genius, like Racine's, is the genius of the French language. In English and German literature there is often an unanalysed residue in the feelings presented. We are conscious of intimate stresses and frustrations beating behind a wall of words, and this makes a whole poem or a whole novel vague and blurred. In Constant's prose there is no vagueness and no blur. He possessed the great French masters' power of seizing the obscurest feelings at the moment of their formation and translating them into exact language. Not a shade, not a tremor escapes him. This is not all. What is striking about his style is the number of different notes that he succeeded in extracting from his instrument. It ranges from passages of precise analysis and adaptions of the seventeenth-century moralists to passages like 'Charme de l'amour' and the autumnal imagery of the closing chapters which reveals his exceptional delicacy in rendering the shift and change of mood, his power of enclosing in a concrete image feelings which seem to lie just beyond language.

His clear-sightedness and restraint are seen at their best in the descriptions of Adolphe's state of mind at the time of Ellénore's death:

> Ce n'étaient pas les regrets de l'amour, c'était un sentiment plus sombre et plus triste. L'amour s'identifie tellement à l'objet aimé, que dans son désespoir même il y a quelque charme. Il lutte contre la réalité, contre la destinée; l'ardeur de son désir le trompe sur ses forces, et l'exalte au milieu de sa douleur. La mienne était morne et solitaire. Je n'espérais point mourir avec Ellénore. J'allais vivre sans elle dans ce désert du monde, que j'avais souhaité tant de fois de traverser indépendant. J'avais brisé l'être qui m'aimait: j'avais brisé ce cœur, compagnon du mien, qui avait persisté à se dévouer à moi, dans sa tendresse infatigable. Déjà l'isolement m'atteignait.

[1] *Op. cit.*, pp. 261-2.   [2] *Op. cit.*, p. 191.

[It was not that I was mourning my love, it was a darker, sadder feeling; love identifies itself so completely with the loved one that there is some charm even in despair. It struggles against reality, against destiny; the fervour of desire misleads it as to its strength and exalts it in the midst of suffering. Mine was gloomy and solitary; I did not hope to die with Ellénore; I was going to live without her in this desert of a world which I had so often wished to cross independently. I had broken the being I loved; I had broken that companion heart to mine which, in its indefatigable tenderness, had persisted in devoting itself to me; I was already being immured in solitude.]

The speaker begins by defining the normal reactions to a situation, then he turns suddenly on himself and shows how his reactions differ from the normal. The movement of the passage is characteristic. Love may mistake its strength, but the vigour behind the 'lutte contre la réalité' and 'l'ardeur de son désir' is genuine and it is contrasted with the horrible sinking sensation that we feel in 'La mienne était morne et solitaire'. They were both popular words with the Romantics, but Constant's handling of them reveals the way in which he profited from the extension of vocabulary which occurred at this turn of the century. They are not clichés. They give us an uncomfortably precise sensation of his wretchedness and his loneliness. The short, broken phrases, 'J'avais brisé l'être qui m'aimait', 'J'avais brisé ce cœur compagnon du mien', fall like blows striking down the mistress and, at the same time, driving into Adolphe's mind the consciousness of his own isolation.

Je sentis le dernier lien se rompre, et l'affreuse réalité se placer à jamais entre elle et moi. Combien elle me pesait, cette liberté que j'avais tant regrettée! Combien elle manquait à mon cœur, cette dépendance qui m'avait révolté souvent! Naguère, toutes mes actions avaient un but. J'étais sûr, par chacune d'elles, d'épargner une peine ou de causer un plaisir. Je m'en plaignais alors. J'étais impatienté qu'un œil ami observât mes démarches, que le bonheur d'un autre y fût attaché. Personne maintenant ne les observait: elles n'intéressaient personne. Nul ne me disputait mon temps, ni mes heures: aucune voix ne me rappelait quand je sortais; j'étais libre en effet; je n'étais plus aimé: j'étais étranger pour tout le monde.

[I felt the last link break and hideous reality come for ever between us. How heavily this liberty weighed upon me which I had so often longed for! How much my heart missed that dependence against which I had so often rebelled! Formerly, all my actions had an aim; I was sure that each one would either spare a pain or cause a pleasure; of this I had complained; I had been irritated that a friendly eye should observe my movements, that the happiness of another should be attached to them. No one now observed them; they interested nobody; no one contended with me for my time nor my hours; no voice called me back when I went out. I was free indeed; I was no longer loved. I was a stranger to all the world.]

This is the final stage in the revelation of Adolphe to himself. He had been living in a world of illusion, carefully shielded from the uncomfortable realities of everyday life by his own self-centredness and by Ellénore's extraordinary though oppressive affection. Now the awakening, which he had dimly perceived like an uneasy dreamer, has come. The final link snaps and 'l'affreuse réalité' imposes itself upon him. He has reached his 'goal', he has rid himself of the 'bond' only to find that life has suddenly lost its meaning, that he has become an outcast in a world which he does not know. The problem lies in the 'besoin de sensibilité', and it is insoluble. Ellénore ministered to his need and for a time gave him the illusion of fulfilment. It is Adolphe's incapacity for certain feelings which makes her at once a tyrant and a necessity, so that her death dissolves the 'bond' without solving the problem. The aim of the passage is the definition of a particular state of mind. It moves with mathematical precision from one point to another, from the shock of awakening in 'Je sentis le dernier lien se rompre' to the feeling of complete helplessness in 'J'étais étranger pour tout le monde'. The perception that there is no longer any 'goal', that no one is interested in him any longer, are stages on the way. The short, staccato phrases perform a different function here. They express a powerful sensation of disintegration, as though the speaker were falling apart.

The passage is also an admirable analysis of Constant's own tragedy. His religious and political writings show that his need of liberty was absolute, but it was pushed to the point at which it became his only object in life. He did not, or could not, believe that liberty can only be a stage in the realization of the Good Life and that it is useless unless one is free for some ulterior purpose. The result was that once he had achieved liberty, life ceased to have any meaning for him and there was nothing for him to do except to start all over again. That is why Constant's life presents the appearance of a series of obstacle races or, more appropriately, of greyhound races in which he is continually breaking the only rule which is never, never to overtake the hare.

I think we can add that *Adolphe* is in a sense the allegory of the rootless cosmopolitan who belongs nowhere, can settle down nowhere.

He chooses Ellénore as a protection against a hostile world, as a shield which enables him to evade problems which he is unable to face. His life with her is unsatisfactory, but there is a masochistic element in the way in which she is struck down. He destroys the object of his affections, destroys the protector in response to an unconscious urge to continue his wanderings, to a torturing need to feel that he is in fact 'étranger pour tout le monde'. Yet this does not detract from the unique value of *Adolphe*. It is an account of a man who achieved emotional freedom which at the same time freed the novel from the domination of an outworn psychology.

'*Adolphe*', wrote Pourtalès, 'enriched the world with a new form of suffering.' The interior void, the feeling of life ebbing into the sand, which is at the heart of *Adolphe*, is something new in European literature. It is different from Pascal's *angoisse métaphysique* and from the sense of emptiness and waste that we feel in *l'Éducation sentimentale*.

When we compare Constant's novel with the productions of our own time, we may easily conclude that its direct influence has been considerable. This is almost certainly a mistake. It is rather that the way in which man and society have developed has imposed a certain method on the novelist. Constant was the first representative of a fresh situation and his novel is an eminent example of the new technique.

Constant's maturity and the way in which his moral experience is an integral part of his emotional experience give *Adolphe* its immense stature among modern novels, make it a standard by which other writers can be tested. Far from being merely a personal confession, it is a record, as all great art must be, of something that happened to human nature. It records the disintegration of the unity of the individual in a hostile environment. All Adolphe's best faculties—his magnificent intelligence, his nervous vitality—are at odds with one another and contribute to the work of destruction; and this makes him the ancestor of the heroes of innumerable modern novels. Constant's unerring sense of moral values is one of his outstanding merits, but it is clear that his hold on them is precarious, that humanity is turning its back on them and moving in the other direction.

STENDHAL

Plus on admire Stendhal et plus on est intelligent.
André Suarès

I. M. BEYLE'S PRESS CONFERENCE

STENDHAL has defeated his critics more completely than any other great novelist. It seems strange at first that this should be so. For no other writer has been more helpful and accommodating or has provided more information about himself than Stendhal has done in the pages of his voluminous *Journal* and in his many autobiographical and semi-autobiographical writings. He not only knows all the answers; he seems to have gone out of his way to anticipate the questions that an admiring posterity would most have wished to ask him.

When I turn over the pages of the books he wrote and of the books which have been written about him, I sometimes imagine that I am a spectator at a great Press conference. All the eminent European critics are there from Sainte-Beuve to M. André Gide. I see them with their heads bent seriously over their notebooks, glancing up from time to time to look at the fat little man on the platform or to ask him a question. 'What is the aim of life, M. Beyle?' asks one. The answer comes pat: 'The pursuit of happiness.' 'What is the function of the novelist?' 'The study of the human heart.' 'What is the most reliable guide to life?' '*La lo-gique*', and we catch the famous drawl as he carefully separates the syllables.

The speaker warms to his work. The answers swell into a continuous stream which almost submerges the audience as he tells them of his admiration for the prose style of Montesquieu, his love of Shakespeare, Mozart and Cimarosa, his recollections of the salon of Mme de Tracy, his campaigns and his voyages, and his views on divorce reform. When at last he pauses for breath, someone asks whether he knew the great La Fayette. 'Certainly. He was over sixty when I met him, but even at that age he was the most frightful old bottom-pincher in France.' One or two of the more respectable critics begin to shuffle uneasily in their seats. An impudent young man at the back asks what M. Beyle thought of Mme X. There is a pause and a malicious gleam comes into his eye. 'Je l'ai eue un an de suite, six fois par semaine, [celle-là].' A *frisson* goes round the assembly, and someone whispers: 'I told you this would happen. We really ought not to have come.' 'Will M. Beyle give us his views on impotence?' The speaker looks like the venerable figure of

125

M. André Gide. M. Beyle is only too delighted. He plunges into a long discourse on *le fiasco*, happily brandishing an annotated copy of *De l'Amour*. Naturally he cannot resist telling us once again the shocking story of his misadventure with Alexandrine Petit.

When we look over the shoulders of the famous critics, we have to admit that the results are curious. Senator Sainte-Beuve, with his saturnine leer, remarks that M. de Stendhal's mind was essentially a critical one, and goes on to add, with his usual perfidy, that his characters 'are not living beings, but ingeniously constructed automata'. Professor Taine is writing an enthusiastic discourse on the importance of *Le Rouge et le noir* for experimental psychology. Professor Valéry has come to the conclusion that, boring as all novels undoubtedly are, this particular *novelist* is not without charm. 'In my view,' he writes at the close of his highly stimulating essay, 'Henri Beyle is much more a type of mind than a man of letters. He is far too much himself to be reduced to a writer.' Ramon Fernandez, 'the philosophical critic', tells us that 'the immense, the incalculable interest of Stendhal's work lies less in its intrinsic value than in the information that it provides about the respective characteristics of the autobiography and the novel'. There are a number of serious studies of *le Beylisme* and *le cas Stendhal*, some painstaking reconstructions of the itinerary of his many voyages and a few elegant trifles on 'Stendhaliens et Beylistes'; but with the exception of a capital essay by Paul Bourget, a useful book by M. Maurice Bardèche and an admirable note on Stendhal's style by Charles Du Bos, there is comparatively little to help the reader to understand Stendhal's *novels*.

These essays, however, do help us to realize the nature of the difficulty. The reasons for Stendhal's elusiveness seem to me to be three: the personality of the man, his characters and his style. The immense amount of information that he has given us about himself has not always been the great advantage that it should have been. It has been a temptation to his critics to forget the novels and to concentrate on his psychology and the vagaries of his sexual life. We have the impression that Stendhal is at the centre of a charmed circle while his critics hover round and round, trying in vain to penetrate his secret.

Stendhal's characters are disconcerting because they reflect the personality of their creator. He was a highly unconventional person and he was very careful not to impose a specious unity on his characters. He displayed—and sometimes exaggerated—the contradictions of human nature because it was one of his aims to disturb his readers' complacency, to shock them out of conventional attitudes and encourage them to make a fresh approach to experience. It is for this reason that we often feel 'at sea', feel that there is nothing to hang on to in our reading.

Finally, there is his style. The day is long past when late Romantics like Pierre Louÿs could denounce Stendhal for writing like an *épicier* and stamp on his books in an outburst of childish fury. He is recognized to-day as a *prince du langage*, but he is a prince who is sometimes altogether too easy to read. His style seldom calls attention to itself. We never have the impression, as we so often do with Flaubert, that the novelist is standing at our elbow waiting to pluck our sleeve and make us stop to admire his carefully contrived effects. We glide happily from page to page, carried along by the sweep of the narrative or the tension of the drama, missing many of the shades and subtleties. It is only occasionally that a phrase stands out and compels us to pause and admire it:

> La demoiselle se pencha en dehors du comptoir, ce qui lui donna l'occasion de déployer une taille superbe. Julien la remarqua; toutes ses idées changèrent.

> [The young woman leaned over the counter, which gave her an opportunity to display a superb figure. Julien observed this; all his ideas altered.]

In two sentences Stendhal achieves what any other writer would have done far less well in two pages of description and analysis. His two sentences express a physiological as well as a psychological reaction. In the first sentence, the girl seems suddenly to move towards Julien and the twist of her hips fixes his attention on her figure. Then, at the word *remarqua*, where another writer would have embarked on an elaborate description, Stendhal simply puts a semicolon and leaves a blank. It is the only way of conveying the full violence of the physical impact which makes him catch his breath and produces a momentary black-out. The last four words are, as Charles Du Bos pointed out, the exact equivalent of the blood rushing to his head.

He uses the same method in another sentence:

> Julien atteignit un tel degré de perfection dans ce genre d'éloquence, qui a remplacé la rapidité d'action de l'empire, qu'il finit par s'ennuyer lui-même par le son de ses paroles.

> [Julien reached such a pitch of perfection in this kind of eloquence, which replaced the rapidity of action of the Empire, that he ended by boring himself with the sound of his own words.]

There is no analysis and no argument. Stendhal suppresses the inter-
mediaries. Two worlds are suddenly juxtaposed—the world of action
and the world of windbags—providing a very pertinent comment on
contemporary France. The skill with which the words, 'qui a remplacé
la rapidité d'action de l'empire', are slipped into the sentence shows
how completely integrated Stendhal's vision was.

The scarcity of such sentences draws attention to another problem.
It is very difficult to illustrate Stendhal's quality by short extracts. His
full flavour is only apparent in the longer scenes or, better, sequences,
like the love affair between Julien and Mathilde, Fabrice at Waterloo
or Fabrice in prison.

'We should never be finished with Stendhal,' said Valéry at the end
of his essay. 'I can think of no greater praise than that.'[1] The man and
his work possess an extraordinary charm and fascination for the contemporary reader, but his fascination is not confined to admirers of his
books. One of the longest single studies ever made of him also contains
some of the harshest and least perceptive criticism of his novels. That
in a sense is the greatest tribute of all.

---

[1] *Variété*, II (Paris, 1930), p. 139.

II. *LA VIE DE HENRI BRULARD*

ON the night of 16 October 1832, the French consul at Civita-Vecchia was walking slowly homewards. He had been to a dull reception at the Embassy and he was brooding a little sadly over memories of his past life and over the thought that he would soon be fifty years old. 'Qu'ai-je été, que suis-je?' he murmured to himself. 'Je serais bien embarrassé de le dire,' he answered. The only thing to do was to put it all down in a book, though the last entry in that other autobiographical fragment, *Souvenirs d'égotisme*, was as recent as 4 July of the same year.

It was not until over three years later on 23 November 1835 that Stendhal settled down to write the book. *La Vie de Henri Brulard*[1] is a bewildering, tantalizing, repetitive work and like its predecessor it remained unfinished; but it occupies a special place in the Stendhal canon. The reason is evident when we turn to the writer's description of his method of composition:

> Je ne vois la vérité nettement sur la plupart de ces choses qu'en les écrivant en 1835, tant elles ont été enveloppées jusqu'ici de l'auréole de la jeunesse, provenant de l'extrême vivacité des sensations.
>
> A force d'employer des méthodes philosophiques, par exemple à force de classer mes amis de jeunesse par *genres*, comme M. Adrien Jussieu fait pour ses plantes (en botanique), je cherche à atteindre cette vérité qui me fuit (I, pp. 29–30).
>
> Je n'ai que des images fort nettes, toutes mes explications me viennent en écrivant ceci, quarante-cinq ans après les événements (I, p. 65).
>
> A côté des images les plus claires, je trouve des *manques* dans ces souvenirs, c'est comme une fresque dont de grands morceaux seraient tombés (I, p. 163).

> [I only perceive the truth about most of these things clearly when writing them down in 1835, to such an extent have they been enveloped up till

[1] All my references are to M. Henri Martineau's edition, Le Divan, two volumes (Paris, 1927).

now in the aura of youth which resulted from the extreme vividness of
the sensations.

Through employing philosophical methods, for example through class-
ing the friends of my youth by *genres* as M. Adrien Jussieu does with his
plants (in botany), I attempt to reach that truth which escapes me.

I have only very sharp images, all my explanations come to me as I am
writing this, forty-five years after the events.

Beside the clearest images, I find *blanks* in these recollections, it is like a
fresco of which large pieces had fallen away.]

Stendhal is not attempting to write a straightforward narrative in the
manner of *Souvenirs d'égotisme* or noting down day-to-day impressions
and reflections as he did in the *Journal*. *The act of writing is a method of
psychological investigation.* He turns his mind towards the past and waits
for the images to present themselves. He is a child standing in one of
the rooms in his grandfather's house. He notices the position of the
different pieces of furniture, then of the people who were present on a
particular occasion. He cannot distinguish their features at first, but as
he watches them they gradually come to life and he recognizes the
members of his family or the family circle.[1] All these scenes are associated with some strong emotion—grief over his mother's death, anger
with his father or his aunt. At this point, the work of *evocation* is complete; the writer sets to work to *analyse* the emotion which has kept
the scene alive in his memory. It is only through analysis that he *appears*
—he is very circumspect—to discover the inner meaning of the images
and the significance of a particular scene for his own development.
Nor should we overlook his statement that he is unable to evoke certain
moments of his past life 'où j'ai senti trop vivement' because his very
unusual sensibility is the clue to an understanding of the novels.

This general account of his method is strikingly confirmed when he
comes to the members of his family. The family circle and the atmosphere of his early life at Grenoble are described with remarkable vividness, but it is not this alone which makes the book unusual. 'Voilà les
personnages du triste drame de ma jeunesse', he writes in Chapter VII.
Henri Brulard is much more like a novel than an autobiography. His
relatives are not simply family portraits; they resemble the characters
of a novel and they all have their special place in the pattern of Stendhal's
life which unfolds before us.

There is the old grandfather, Henri Gagnon, to whom Stendhal was
devoted, with his round, powdered periwig whose three rows of curls

[1] The diagrams which he drew on his manuscript were obviously a means of
stimulating his mental processes and enabling him to *fix* the images.

showed that the wearer was a doctor of medicine. Henri Gagnon is an eighteenth-century vignette and he represents the mellower side of the Enlightenment in Stendhal's own make-up. 'He was a sage in the manner of Fontenelle,' we are told, 'very polite about religion rather than a believer', and very anxious to keep out of the feuds and quarrels which divided his household.

The other characters include Stendhal's great-aunt Élisabeth whose *âme espagnole*, as we shall see, had a decisive influence on his development, the 'terrible Aunt Séraphie' whom he calls *ce diable femelle*; his father, Chérubin Beyle, and, most important of all, his mother who died when he was seven.

His description of his affection for his mother is a classic example of the 'Œdipus complex':

> My mother, Madame Henriette Gagnon,[1] was a charming woman and I was in love with my mother. . . . I was perhaps six years old when I was in love with her (1789), but my character was exactly the same as in 1828 when I was madly in love with Alberthe de Rubempré. . . . As far as the physical side of love was concerned, I was in the same position as Cæsar would be over the use of cannon and small arms if he returned to the world. I should soon have learnt and at bottom it would not have changed my tactics in any way.
>
> I wanted to cover my mother with kisses and for her to have no clothes on. She loved me passionately and often kissed me; I returned her kisses with such fire that she often had to leave me. I abhorred my father when he came and interrupted our embraces. I always wanted to kiss my mother on the bosom. . . .
>
> She died in 1790 in the flower of her youth and beauty. She might have been twenty-eight or thirty (I, pp. 41-2).

'Là commence ma vie morale', adds Stendhal, and the words reveal the significance of his love for his mother. It was the direct cause of his loathing for his father[2] and Tante Séraphie of whom he paints a devastating portrait in which he underlines 'l'aigreur d'une fille dévote qui n'a pas pu se marier' and who was afflicted with 'le diable au corps'. 'Chance has never, perhaps, brought together two beings who were

---

[1] She was the daughter of Henri Gagnon and the fact that he calls her by her maiden name is not without interest.

[2] In another place he records the satisfaction with which he learnt from his great-aunt that his mother had never been in love with his father. 'Ce mot fut pour moi d'une portée immense. J'étais encore, au fond de l'âme, jaloux de mon père.' (I, p. 174.)

more fundamentally antipathetic to one another than my father and I,' he said (I, p. 92). In the diaries he commonly refers to him as *le bâtard*, and in *Henri Brulard* he does not scruple to suggest on several occasions that he seduced or was seduced by his sister-in-law, Séraphie.

Stendhal's antipathy did not remain a purely personal one. It led to a revolt not only against the stuffy middle-class society of Grenoble, but also against the *convenances* and against contemporary society as a whole.[1] He himself was the first to realize the importance of his up-bringing for his later development.

> My family [he wrote], were the most aristocratic people in the town. This meant that I became a fanatical republican on the spot (I, p. 130).
>
> All the elements which compose the life of Chrysale[2] have been re-placed in my case by romance. I believe that this speck in my telescope has been useful to me as a novelist. There is a sort of *bassesse bourgeoise* to which my characters could never succumb (I, p. 134).
>
> I had, and still have, the most aristocratic of tastes [he goes on in a passage whose humanitarian feeling we must all applaud]; I would do everything in my power to ensure the happiness of the *peuple*; but I think that I would rather spend a fortnight of each month in prison than have to live with shopkeepers (II, p. 56).

Although Stendhal's revolt began as an emotional protest against his family, it developed into an atttiude which was both logical and coherent. In these passages he is not attacking merely the bourgeoisie like the majority of nineteenth-century writers. He is systematically reject-ing the aristocracy, the bourgeoisie and the proletariat whom he found equally intolerable. This makes his position a novel one and stamps him as a patrician of a new kind. In the seventeenth and eighteenth centuries the writer had detached himself from his own social class. He was not allowed to enter the class above, but his relation to it was clearly defined and he had a place of his own in the community. In the nine-teenth century he also detached himself from his own class; but owing to the disappearance of the aristocratic patron after the Revolution, there was no longer any other class or section of the community to which he could attach himself. He was socially and intellectually out of place. The only course was for him to found a new intellectual aristocracy, a minority which lived inside society but which was at odds with every section of it. This explains Stendhal's interest in 'the

---

[1] Cf., 'Les convenances sont, comme les lois, destinées pour les gens médiocres et par des gens médiocres'. (*Journal*, V, ed. Debraye et Royer, Paris, 1934, p. 64.)

[2] He was the *honnête homme* in *Les Femmes savantes*.

happy few' and Baudelaire's 'dandyism'. Stendhal's attitude bears a certain resemblance to Baudelaire's, but in reality it was much more extreme. He seems to have felt that he was not merely isolated, but practically unique. It meant that he could not expect his contemporaries to understand either himself or his books. He set to work to rationalize his position and to compensate himself for their neglect by turning his life into a private drama in which he played nearly all the parts:

> On this private stage [said Valéry] he presents without intermission the performance of Himself. He turns his life, his career, his love affairs and his very diverse ambitions into an unending play.[1]

This accounts for his use of pseudonyms—scholars claim to have counted 171—and the dedications of his books. Since he was unique, the only way of overcoming his isolation was to multiply his own personality, to create a number of fictitious selves who were bound to understand him, and to send out his books like letters in bottles in the hope that somewhere there might be a handful of people like himself who would appreciate them.

His attitude throws some light on the novels. All his principal characters—Octave de Malivert, Lucien Leuwen, Lamiel, Julien Sorel, Fabrice del Dongo—are people who like himself do not 'fit in'. In creating them, it seems to me that Stendhal was exploring the different reasons which prevented people from fitting in. It should be emphasized that he was concerned with *reasons* and not with *solutions*. He knew that there was no solution, and neither Julien's death nor Fabrice's withdrawal to his monastery is a solution.

A good deal has been written about Stendhal's philosophy, but it is easy to be misled by his omnivorous reading and wide interests. 'In general,' he said, 'my philosophy belongs to the day on which I happen to be writing.' The first thing to realize is that he was not a systematic thinker and that he never used the novel to propound or to illustrate philosophical theories. His mind was formed by the study of the *philosophes*, and Cabanis and Destutt de Tracy seem to have remained an inspiration all his life; but he was very far from being the intransigent materialist for which he is sometimes taken. His grandfather was an ardent admirer of Voltaire. He used to take the young Stendhal to see a tiny bust of the philosopher which he kept in his study, and when Stendhal was very good he was allowed to touch the precious bust. He did not share his grandfather's admiration:

[1] *Op. cit.*, p. 89.

Les écrits de Voltaire m'ont toujours souverainement déplu. Ils me semblaient un enfantillage. Je puis dire que rien de ce grand homme ne m'a jamais plu (I, pp. 36–7).

[Voltaire's writings have always been supremely displeasing to me. They seemed to me to be a piece of childishness. I can say that I have never liked anything of this great man's.]

There is still more striking criticism of the eighteenth-century thinkers in *Racine et Shakespeare*:

L'âme ardente et tendre de Platon a senti des choses qui resteront à jamais invisibles à Condillac et gens de son espèce.[1]

[The ardent and tender soul of Plato felt things which will for ever remain invisible to Condillac and people of his sort.]

I do not think that these criticisms are inconsistent with Stendhal's general outlook. Nor is it true that like Benjamin Constant he began with an uncritical admiration for the thinkers of the Enlightenment and turned against them in middle age. His attitude was consistent from the start and it can only be understood when we remember that he was essentially an *artist*. There are moments in the novels when his personal views—particularly his strong anti-clericalism—make his characters' behaviour unconvincing; but in his greatest work theory goes by the board and he surrenders himself completely to his sensibility.

Stendhal's character was dominated by two factors—the *logique* of the philosophers and the *espagnolisme* which he claimed to have inherited from the Gagnons. He always maintained that his family was of Italian origin and that he derived his passionate temperament from his Italian ancestors. It seems curious that *espagnolisme* should be attributed to his Italian descent and at one time his critics were inclined to dismiss the claim as fanciful. Modern scholars, however, are more circumspect. Paul Arbelet considers that the Gagnons probably did come from Italy and he emphasizes the importance of heredity and environment for an understanding of Stendhal. His nature, he thinks, was a *blend* of the warm, passionate South and an innate scepticism, a taste for 'les réalités précises et fines' which belong to the Provençal mind and which were certainly developed by a study of the philosophers.[2]

[1] Paris, 1854, p. 97.   [2] In *La Jeunesse de Stendhal*, I (Paris, 1919), pp. 40–5.

It is necessary to emphasize the word 'blend'. It is tempting, but misleading, to suppose that *logique* and *espagnolisme* were opposites and to imagine that there was a conflict between the two which resembled the conflict between *devoir* and *amour* in Corneille, particularly when we recall Stendhal's immense admiration for that master. Nothing could be further from the truth.

Ma cohabitation passionnée avec les mathématiques [he said] m'a laissé un amour fou pour les bonnes *définitions*, sans lesquelles il n'y a que des à peu près (II, p. 202).

[My passionate cohabitation with mathematics has left me with an insane love of good *definitions*, without which there can only be approximations.]

I think we can assume that in this passage 'mathematics' is the equivalent of 'logic', and it explains its function very clearly. There is nothing tyrannical about Stendhal's 'logic'; it does not seek like Corneille's *raison* to *impose* order on the unruly life of the senses. It is simply an instrument, a method of unravelling and registering the complex movements of his sensibility which might not unreasonably be compared to the pattern or even to the wall on which he paints his 'fresco'.

Espagnolisme is something far richer and more complex. It is a shorthand description of Stendhal's own sensibility. It includes his immense vitality, his admiration for the wild exuberance and the baroque extravagance of the sixteenth century, and finally his extremely sensitive reactions to experience. When he writes of the country where he was born:

J'apprends au lecteur que le Dauphiné a une manière de sentir à soi, vive, opiniâtre, raisonneuse, que je n'ai rencontrée en aucun pays (I, p. 46).

[I can tell the reader that the Dauphiné has a way of feeling of its own—vivid, obstinate, reasoning—which I have not met in any other part.]

his words seem to bear out Arbelet's contention; and the three adjectives, *vive, opiniâtre, raisonneuse*—particularly the last—are a good description of his own complexity.

The book also contains some illuminating examples of his personal mode of feeling:

'Sa sensibilité est devenue trop vive' [he said of himself]: *'ce qui ne fait qu'effleurer les autres, le blesse jusqua' usang.'*[1] Tel en vérité j'étais en 1789, tel je suis en 1836, mais j'ai appris à cacher tout cela sous l'iron imperceptible au vulgaire . . . (II, p. 194).

[*'His sensibility has become too vivid: what only grazes the others, wounds him to the quick.'* Such I was, in truth, in 1789, such I am in 1836, but I have learnt to hide all that under an irony which is imperceptible to the vulgar. . . .]

His sensibility is at the root of his avid search for delicate sensations:

J'ai recherché avec une sensibilité exquise la vue des beaux paysages; c'est pour cela uniquement que j'ai voyagé. Les paysages étaient comme un *archet* qui jouait sur mon âme, et des aspects que personne ne citait, (la ligne des rochers en approchant d'Arbois, je crois, et venant de Dôle par la grande route, fut pour moi une image sensible et évidente de l'âme de Méthilde) (I, p. 20).

[I have sought with an exquisite sensibility the view of lovely scenery; it is solely for that that I have travelled. The landscapes were like a *bow* which played on my soul, and the aspects which no one mentioned, (the line of rocks when approaching Arbois, I think, and coming from Dôle along the main route, was for me a perceptible and evident image of Méthilde's soul).]

A final example deserves particular attention because of its bearing on the novels:

Je vois que la rêverie a été ce que j'ai préféré à tout, même à passer pour un homme d'esprit (I, p. 20).

[I see that *rêverie* has been the thing I have preferred to everything else, even to passing for a wit.]

Stendhal was anything but a religious man, but the ideal described here is essentially a *contemplative* one. He sets his own stamp on the word *rêverie*. It has nothing in common with the quietism of the Romantics or with the mournful day-dreams of Flaubert's characters. It is, to use a theological distinction, an 'activity' and not a 'state'. It is as contemplatives, in a sense which has nothing to do with mysticism, that Stendhal's two most famous characters end their days.

[1] Italics in the text.

I do not want to suggest that there was never a conflict between *logique* and *espagnolisme*. There were certainly moments in Stendhal's life and in his books when *espagnolisme* carried everything before it, when great gusts of emotion stretched his characters senseless on the ground. The point which needs emphasis is that *logique* and *espagnolisme* were the twin poles of Stendhal's own nature and of the nature of his characters. They are all capable of cold calculation, but they are all like their creator *âmes sensibles*. It is the combination of the two—'un amour fou pour les bonnes *définitions*' is a tell-tale phrase—which is the source of their extraordinary vitality and which makes them so immensely fascinating. We remember that he once compared the novel to the violinist's bow which draws forth sounds from the violin which is the reader's soul. 'Logic' is a discipline in the same sense as the violinist's bow; neither more nor less.

No account of Stendhal's personality would be satisfactory without a brief reference to his *amours* and his admiration for the Code Napoléon. 'L'état habituel de ma vie" he said, 'a été celui d'amant malheureux'; and in a touching passage in *Henri Brulard* he describes himself tracing in the dust the names of the women with whom he had been in love. Most of them, he reflected sadly, had resisted his advances. I cannot think of any other great writer who was more concerned with love in his private life and who had less success. 'He was highly sexconscious, but not particularly sexual,' observes Mr. Somerset Maugham.[1] This is plausible, but possibly a simplification. Stendhal seems to have suffered from chronic amorousness combined with an almost invincible shyness. 'Si j'avais osé, je l'aurais eue.' 'Si j'osais oser! Plus je l'aime, plus je suis timide'—the words recur like a maddening refrain in the earlier volumes of the *Journal*. His inhibition seems to have been connected with a conflict between *logique* and *espagnolisme* which for once were mutually destructive. He planned his seductions with the care of an eighteenth-century *roué*, but when the moment came he either behaved like an embarrassed schoolboy or had a *fiasco*. I suspect that there were two different causes. One was his excessive delicacy of feeling, the other excessive cerebration. It is not possible to speak with any certainty, but one may have produced a romantic repugnance and the other physical inhibition.[2] His attempts to over-

[1] *Great Novelists and their Novels* (Philadelphia and Toronto, 1948), p. 98.
[2] Cf., 'S'il entre un grain de passion dans le cœur, il entre un grain de fiasco possible.' (*De l'Amour*, ch. lx, 'Des Fiasco'.) (Stendhal uses the term *fiasco* in the sense of temporary sexual impotence.) See also Krafft-Ebing, *Psychopathia Sexualis* (12th edition, New York, 1934), p. 50.

F*

come these difficulties and his extreme shyness probably account for another interesting characteristic of his writings. His characters are scarcely remarkable for their continence; but with the exception of the heroine who tips a peasant fifty francs to relieve her of her virginity and a charming conversation between an amorous bishop and the bored abbess whom he has seduced, there is scarcely an indecent word or a really scabrous incident in the whole of the novels.[1] It is far otherwise in the diaries and autobiographical writings. He seems like Baudelaire, who was another *grand timide*, to have tried to compensate for his shyness by an extraordinary crudity of expression and by a gleeful emphasis on *ordure*.[2]

The Code Napoléon was not, as Stendhal was inclined to suggest, merely a model of prose style; it had a psychological significance for him which relates it to 'logic'. The Code enshrined the common law and the rules of public conduct which were binding on all Frenchmen. This made it a symbol of stability in a troubled world, a norm to which the personal adventures and crises of Stendhal's characters were related through the mere fact that he modelled, or claimed to have modelled, his prose style on it. It is for this reason that his books always have a background of sanity and common sense, that they combine a high degree of life with a high degree of order, that they reveal a fundamental belief in the greatness of human nature which is not impaired by the chaos of human society as it existed in Stendhal's time.

Stendhal has been well served—sometimes too well served—by his biographers. In France, indeed, the study of his life has developed into a veritable industry. We know practically all that it is humanly possible to know about him. The smallest facts—the books that he read, or may be supposed to have read, as a child, the lessons he learnt at school and the careers of his schoolmasters—have been examined with meticulous care. There have, inevitably, been differences of opinion about some of the finer points which have led to scholarly and not infrequently to

[1] The first occurs in *Lamiel* and the second in *L'Abbesse de Castro* where the abbess addresses the bishop in these terms: 'Go back to your palace and leave me as quickly as you can. Good-bye, Monsignor, you fill me with horror. I feel as though I've given myself to a lackey.'

[2] The editor of the definitive edition of the *Journal* observes that it contains 'des passages entiers d'une ordurière pornographie'. He adds that he did not feel able to include them in the text, but that as his conscience as a scholar did not allow him to suppress them altogether he enclosed them in envelopes at the end of each volume. It was thus left to the reader to decide whether to have them bound into their proper place in the text or destroy them! (*Journal*, I, ed. Debraye et Royer, Paris, 1923 pp. xxxviii–xxxix.)

acrimonious controversy. All through the two stout volumes which he devoted to Stendhal's first twenty years, Professor Arbelet carried on a relentless footnote warfare against Professor Chuquet, accusing him of mistaking the house in which the novelist was born, of confusing the 'concours de belles lettres' with the 'concours de grammaire générale' and of assigning that event to Year VI instead of to Year VII.

It is naturally of some interest to know whether Stendhal did or did not carry off the grammar prize at the École Centrale at Grenoble, but happily the literary critic is not obliged to take sides in these savage donnish battles. I shall therefore confine myself to the briefest outline of his career.

He left Grenoble for Paris in 1799, intending to enter the École Polytechnique. He found the preparation of the entrance examination too much trouble, fell ill and was taken charge of by his cousins the Darus. Noël Daru had two sons. The elder, Pierre, who was a high official at the War Office, did his utmost to help Stendhal in his career; the younger, Martial, taught him the art of seduction.

Stendhal became a clerk in the War Office and was posted to Milan during Napoleon's second Italian campaign. He enjoyed Milan very much and seems to have met Angela Pietragrua for the first time. While he was there, Pierre Daru secured him a commission as second lieutenant in the 6th Dragoons and he became A.D.C. to General Michaud. Chuquet thinks that with application Stendhal might well have risen to be a general. He may have been right, but the application was certainly lacking. Stendhal's enthusiasm for the army is famous, but in practice he found that army life was boring and disappointing. He soon became an expert in all the tricks of the 'old sweat', but the indefatigable Arbelet has proved beyond all reasonable doubt that the large claims that he made for himself as a soldier in his autobiographical works are pure fancy and that he was never a combatant.

Pierre Daru was not impressed by Stendhal's way of life and he was ordered, peremptorily, to join his unit. He avoided doing so for six months and when he eventually reported for duty, he at once succeeded in obtaining leave of absence. He returned home and a few months later resigned his commission.

He lived for a time in Paris on an allowance from his father, tried to write plays, attended a dramatic school and had the affair with Mélanie Guilbert. He followed her to Marseilles where he was in business for a time.[1] When this failed, he went back to the bureaucracy and repaid

[1] This episode is described in P. Arbelet's charming monograph, *Stendhal épicier ou les infortunes de Mélanie* (Paris, 1926).

Pierre Daru for his assistance by trying, unsuccessfully, to seduce his wife.

He returned to the army and took part in the Russian campaign as a non-combatant officer in the commissariat.

He lived in Italy from 1814 to 1821 when he was invited by the Austrian police to leave Milan on account of his relations with the Italian patriots. The next nine years were spent for the most part in Paris. In 1830 he was appointed French consul at Trieste, but the Austrian authorities refused to accept him and he was sent instead to Civita-Vecchia. It was not an exciting post, but he had to live and he succeeded in holding it until his death. He returned to France on sick leave in November 1841. On 22 March 1842, he went to a large official reception given by Guizot at the Ministry of Foreign Affairs. On the way home he had a stroke and died in the small hours the following day.

III. *LE ROUGE ET LE NOIR*

I

THE opening chapters of a novel by Stendhal must be read with the same care as the opening scenes of a comedy by Molière. They contain the essential clues to the understanding of the whole book. *Le Rouge et le noir* begins with a description of the little town of Verrières in which the novelist displays his admirable sensibility:

> La petite ville de Verrières peut passer pour l'une des plus jolies de la Franche-Comté. Ses maisons blanches avec leurs toits pointus de tuiles rouges s'étendent sur la pente d'une colline, dont les touffes de vigoureux châtaigniers marquent les moindres sinuosités. Le Doubs coule à quelques centaines de pieds au-dessous de ses fortifications, bâties jadis par les Espagnols, et maintenant ruinées.

> [The small town of Verrières may be regarded as one of the most attractive in the Franche-Comté. Its white houses with their high pitched roofs of red tiles are spread over the slope of a hill, the slightest contours of which are indicated by clumps of sturdy chestnuts. The Doubs runs some hundreds of feet below its fortifications, built in times past by the Spaniards and now in ruins.]

The little town nestling among the hills, with its 'habitants plus paysans que bourgeois' and its 'jeunes filles fraîches et jolies' who work in the mills, gives and is intended to give an impression of peacefulness. We must not overlook the 'fortifications'. In an earlier period, they had marked the limit reached by the invader. Nor is it without significance that they are 'ruined'. For Verrières will suffer from an 'invader' of another kind whose incursions will cause a considerable disturbance. The novelist goes on to describe the industries of the place: the sawmills, the manufacture of 'painted tiles' and nails. Then we are introduced to M. de Rênal, Mayor of Verrières:

> At the sight of him every hat is quickly raised. His hair is turning grey, and he is dressed in grey. He is a Companion of several Orders, has a high

141

forehead, an aquiline nose, and on the whole his face is not wanting in a certain regularity: indeed, the first impression formed of it may be that it combines with the dignity of a village mayor that sort of charm which may still be found in a man of forty-eight or fifty. But soon the visitor from Paris is annoyed by a certain air of self-satisfaction and self-sufficiency mingled with a suggestion of limitations and want of originality. One feels, finally, that this man's talent is confined to securing the exact payment of whatever is owed to him and to postponing payment till the last possible moment when he is the debtor.

It is not simply the portrait of an individual; it is the portrait of a class. For M. de Rênal is the symbol of the privileged classes—genteel on the surface, hard as nails underneath—in their ruthless struggle with the unprivileged.

No one who has read Stendhal's principal works will have failed to notice that he was obsessed with prisons, secret police and spies. The casual reference to 'fortifications' in the first paragraph of the book is caught up three pages later by a reference to 'walls':

> You must not for a moment expect to find in France those picturesque gardens which enclose the manufacturing towns of Germany; Leipsic, Frankfort, Nuremberg, and the rest. In the Franche-Comté, the more *walls* a man builds, the more he makes his property bristle with stones piled one above another, the greater title he acquires to the respect of his neighbours.

'Walls' is one of the focal words of the novel. They are in the first place the ramparts which separate the two worlds of the privileged and the unprivileged. They are also the 'fortifications' which preserve the bourgeois world from the incursions of peasants and workers. In spite of their gentility and respectability, the privileged are far from being idle behind their fortifications; they wage a ceaseless war against those outside and are constantly thrusting their ramparts further forward and acquiring fresh territory:

> M. de Rênal's gardens, honeycombed with *walls*, are still further ad-mired because he bought, for their weight in gold, certain minute scraps of ground which they cover. For example that sawmill, whose curious position on the bank of the Doubs struck you as you entered Verrières, and on which you noticed the name *Sorel* inscribed in huge letters on a board which overtops the roof, occupied, six years ago, the ground on which at this moment they are building the *wall* of the fourth terrace of M. de Rênal's gardens.

At this point the two worlds represented by M. de Rênal and Sorel —Julien's father—face one another directly. The Mayor's victory was hardly won. He had to pay Sorel a fat price to move his factory, but, adds Stendhal ironically, he also had to pull strings in Paris to have the *public* stream which fed the sawmill turned.

The theme is pursued in the second chapter:

> Fortunately for M. de Rênal's reputation as an administrator, a *huge retaining wall*[1] was required for the public avenue which skirts the hillside a hundred feet above the bed of the Doubs. To this admirable position it is indebted for one of the most picturesque views in France. But, every spring, torrents of rainwater made channels across the avenue, carved deep gullies in it and left it impassable. This nuisance, which affected everybody alike, placed M. de Rênal under the fortunate obligation to immortalize his administration by a *wall* twenty feet in height and seventy or eighty yards long.

Although the Mayor appears to be performing a public duty in constructing his 'huge retaining wall', it is not without substantial advantages to himself:

> The sun is extremely hot in these mountains; when it is directly overhead, the traveller's rest is sheltered on this terrace by a row of magnificent planes. Their rapid growth, and handsome foliage of a bluish tint are due to the artificial soil with which the Mayor has filled in the space behind his *immense retaining wall*, for, despite the opposition of the town council, he has widened the avenue by more than six feet. . . .

One of the central themes of *Le Rouge et le noir* is the 'class war'. Stendhal's conception of it was much wider than that of modern political theorists, but his book is the story of a parvenu who succeeds in penetrating the 'walls' which protect the privileged and in attaching himself to a class to which he does not belong. He penetrates not only the walls of M. de Rênal's estate, but the walls of the seminary and of the Hôtel de La Mole. In the end, society takes its revenge. With the same ease with which it casts the simple Abbé Chélan outside its walls, it finally shuts Julien behind prison walls and executes him not for slaying, or attempting to slay, one of its members, but for trying to usurp its privileges.

We must turn now to the character of the parvenu. Stendhal uses a number of different methods of creating character, but one of the most

[1] Italics in the text.

important is the description of his chief character's effect on other people. We are told of Julien at the seminary:

Julien avait beau se faire petit et sot, il ne pouvait plaire, il était trop différent.

[In vain might Julien make himself small and foolish, he could not give satisfaction, he was too different.]

The Abbé Pirard says to him:

Avec ce je ne sais quoi d'indéfinissable, du moins pour moi qu'il y a dans votre caractère, si vous ne faites pas fortune, vous serez persécuté; il n'y a pas de moyen terme pour vous.

[With this something indefinable that there is in your character, at any rate for me, if you do not make your fortune you will be persecuted. There is no middle way for you.]

He fares no better in his own family:

Objet des mépris de tous à la maison, il haïssait ses frères et son père; dans les jeux du dimanche, sur la place publique, il était toujours battu.

[An object of contempt to the rest of the household, he hated his brothers and father; in the games on Sundays, on the public square, he was invariably beaten.]

The Marquis de La Mole says of him:

Mais au fond de ce caractère je trouve quelque chose d'effrayant. C'est l'impression qu'il produit sur tout le monde, donc il y a là quelque chose de réel.

[But at the bottom of this character I find something frightening. It's the impression that he makes on everybody, so there must be something real about it.]

These observations reveal Julien from a number of different angles. We see him as he appeared to his proletarian family, to his fellow-seminarists, to his confessor and to aristocratic conservatives like M. de La Mole; but they have one thing in common. The *reader's* reactions are almost identical with those of the other *characters*. We, too, find Julien 'different', 'indefinable', 'difficult to place', 'frightening'. Stendhal certainly intended that we should, and he himself completes the evidence by describing him as 'un homme malheureux, en guerre avec toute la société'. For Julien is an *étranger* or 'outsider' in the society of his time.[1]

Now this conception of character is of capital importance in Stendhal's work and something must be said of the *étranger* type and of the age which produced him. It is commonly assumed that there are resemblances between the Napoleonic age and our own, but it is easy to exaggerate them. In spite of revolution, war and devastation, the Europe which emerged from the Napoleonic wars was on the threshold of a great age of peace and plenty. At the same time, to a contemporary observer, it must have presented an appearance of considerable confusion. The Revolution had petered out in dictatorship; and dictatorship led not simply to monarchy, but to an extremely sordid, conventional and repressive monarchy. In politics, France was divided between conservatives and liberals, but we often find it difficult to distinguish between their policies which appear equally confused.

A sensitive observer like Stendhal was struck by the muddle and lack of vitality of this society—it is the constant burden of his writings— and it is precisely in these conditions that the *étranger* makes his appearance. He is the Janus-face who emerges in periods when the sensitive individual cannot identify himself with any of the different groups of which society is composed. For the *étranger* has *no recognized mode of feeling*. In spite of his intelligence and his extraordinary calculations, he is continually swinging from one extreme of feeling to another and back again. 'Chez cet être singulier,' said Stendhal, 'c'était presque tous les jours tempête.'

The *étranger* is essentially an individualist at odds with society, but it must be recognized that he is an entirely new type in European fiction. He has little in common with the Romantic outcast or Flaubert's *ratés*, with Gide's *immoraliste* or Camus' 'outsider', who are all manifestations of a much more personal attitude. Stendhal's characters are the direct product of their age and are only comprehensible when seen in relation to it. They are left to work out their destiny in a chaotic society and their only supports are their own immense force of character and their own genius. In spite of their shortcomings, the way in which they set about their task stamps their attitude as an heroic one. I think that we can go further than this and say that Julien Sorel is 'the modern hero'.

[1] The word *étranger* is Stendhal's own.

Stendhal's conception of character is an example of the way in which he discarded philosophical theories when they came into conflict with his artistic vision. The materialism implicit in the work of the philosophers whom he admired led logically to determinism, to the belief that character is nothing but the product of environment. It would be an understatement to say that Stendhal did not accept this view. *Le Rouge et le noir* is based on the contrary view—on the view that genius is absolute and inexplicable. Stendhal took his 'plot' from a newspaper account of a peasant who was executed for shooting his mistress and proceeded to transform it in the light of his own experience.[1] There is nothing in Julien's upbringing or environment to account for his gifts. His instruction has been limited to a few Latin lessons with the *curé* and reading a life of Napoleon given to him by an old soldier. He has been bullied and obstructed in every possible way by his family, but when his chance comes he is ready to seize it with both hands. The lesson is obvious. The genius will either turn into Napoleon or be executed as a common criminal. The answer depends on the sort of society in which he finds himself and on the use he makes of his opportunities. In other words, environment does not determine a man's *character*, but it does determine his *fate*.

When this is grasped, it is easy to see what *Le Rouge et le noir* is 'about'. Julien's character is not, perhaps, drawn with the firmness of Fabrice's and there are moments when Stendhal slips into melodrama or reveals the unfortunate influence of Romanticism; but these are minor flaws in his great achievement. The book is a profound study of the impact of genius on a corrupt society.

When Sainte-Beuve said that Stendhal 'forms his characters with two or three ideas', he was certainly right; but when he added that 'they are not living beings but ingeniously constructed automata', he showed that he had failed to understand his aims. Julien has a good deal in common with his creator. He had lost his mother when a child and loathes his father and his family. All his actions are prompted by two feelings: anxiety at having no place in his own world and a consciousness of his genius. He is, as Taine remarked, *un esprit supérieur*, and he is determined to use his gifts to win a great position for himself. He has spent his youth brooding over the *Mémorial de Sainte-Hélène* and *Tartuffe*.[2] The first of these books is the story of a parvenu who,

[1] On the genesis of the novels, see M. Henri Martineau's admirable study, *L'Œuvre de Stendhal: Histoire de ses livres et de sa pensée* (Paris, 1945).

[2] 'In the provinces, a performance of *Tartuffe* had the same significance for the "left" as the setting up of a mission cross had for the "right". . . . *Tartuffe* had become to the same extent as *Athalie*, but in the opposite sense, a religious play.' (A. Thibaudet, *Stendhal*, Paris, 1931, p. 108.)

starting like Julien from nothing, had made himself master of Europe, and it represents the goal to be attained. The second is a handbook which explains the means which Julien must use in order to realize his ambitions. In this sense, and this sense only, Stendhal 'forms his characters with two or three ideas'.

It follows from this that the first step in Julien's career is to discover not merely what sort of a man he is, but what sort of a man he must become in order to succeed. When we read the novels, we find that all Stendhal's principal characters are tormented by the novelist's own question: 'Qu'ai-je été, que suis-je?' They are perpetually interrogating themselves about their own feelings, wondering what they really feel for this woman, why that woman leaves them cold or asking themselves whether or not some defect in their make-up renders them incapable of loving at all.

Il est dans l'essence de cette âme d'agir à la fois et de se regarder agir, de sentir et de se regarder sentir.[1]

Paul Bourget's comment draws attention to an important difference between Stendhal and all his predecessors. Self-knowledge is not destructive as it was for Mme de La Fayette and Constant; it is not merely a prelude to action as it was for Laclos; in Stendhal action and analysis are simultaneous. All his characters realize that they can only exploit their genius by becoming something, by discovering some principle of unity within themselves. They must first of all rid themselves of the gnawing sense of anxiety which dogs them and become integrated personalities, and they can only become integrated personalities by observing their feelings at the actual moment of action. *Logique* and *espagnolisme* play a big part in the drama. The function of *logique* is to integrate personality, to control and direct the blind forces of *espagnolisme*. It is *logique* which is continually pulling them up, making them pause and ask themselves what they feel and why they feel as they do.

Although *Le Rouge et le noir* deals with the class war, I think that it will be apparent that the term *étranger* is not primarily a *social*, but a *psychological* distinction. The 'walls' are barriers between the different classes, but they also stand for the psychological barriers which cut the 'outsider' off from the rest of humanity. For the book is much more than a conflict between two social classes. It is a conflict between two irreconcilable ways of life. Julien would have been an 'outsider' in any class of society, and he is equally out of place in the world of his

[1] *Essais de psychologie contemporaine*, I, p. 298.

father, of the Rênals and the La Moles. The fact that he belongs socially
to the proletariat simply provides a particular setting for the study of a
much wider problem and creates an additional obstacle to Julien's
success. There was not the slightest chance of his exercising his peculiar
talents in his father's world, and a rise in the social scale is necessary to
start him on his career.

He does not make the first breach in the 'walls' himself. M. de Rênal
is prompted by vanity to engage a tutor for his children in order to
score off his fellow-bourgeois. He approaches M. Sorel, knowing that
he has a son who enjoys a certain reputation for learning. The bourgeois
thus makes the first breach in his own walls which lets the outsider in.
From this moment Julien's fortunes depend on himself. His attack is
twofold. He has to impress the bourgeois, and he has to overcome his
own feeling of anxiety by a personal success. There could be no better
way than to persuade the bourgeois that he is a prodigy of learning and
to seduce his employer's wife. Everything goes according to plan. The
bourgeois, astonished by Julien's extraordinary verbal memory, treat
him as though he were a performing monkey; and Mme de Rênal,
whose maternal instincts are awakened by his youth and good looks,
allows her feelings to turn into something very different.

Julien's success with Mme de Rênal is a form of apprenticeship in
which for the first time he puts his theories into practice, and the
account of his feelings is instructive:

> Cette main se retira bien vite; mais Julian pensa qu'il était de son *devoir*
> d'obtenir que l'on ne retirât pas cette main quand il la touchait. L'idée
> d'un devoir à accomplir, et d'un ridicule ou plutôt d'un sentiment d'in-
> fériorité à encourir si l'on n'y parvenait pas, éloigna sur-le-champ tout
> plaisir de son cœur.

> [The hand was hurriedly withdrawn; but Julian decided that it was his
> *duty* to secure that the hand should not be withdrawn when he touched
> it. The idea of a duty to be performed, and of making himself ridiculous,
> or rather being left with a sense of inferiority if he did not succeed in per-
> forming it, at once took all the pleasure from his heart.]

In the French analysis of emotion, said Rivière, 'la morale même
devient un élément psychologique'.[1] Stendhal's use of the word *devoir*
is an excellent example. It is the focal word of the passage and he underlines it to make sure that its significance shall not escape us. It means
something very different from Corneille's *devoir*. It is not a disinterested

---

[1] *Le Français* (Paris, 1928), p. 27.

'duty'; the imperative comes from Julien's subjective need to bolster up his own inner morale or, as Stendhal, very much in advance of his time, suggests, to rid himself of a *sentiment d'infériorité*.

This is how Stendhal describes his feelings after he has made a conquest of Mme de Rênal:

Le lendemain on le réveilla à cinq heures; et, ce qui eût été cruel pour Mme de Rênal si elle l'eût su, à peine lui donna-t-il une pensée. Il avait fait *son devoir, et un devoir héroïque*. Rempli de bonheur par ce sentiment, il s'enferma à clef dans sa chambre, et se livra avec un plaisir nouveau à la lecture des exploits de son héros.

[Next morning he was called at five o'clock; and (what would have been a cruel blow to Madame de Rênal had she known of it) he barely gave her a thought. He had done *his duty, and a heroic duty*. Filled with joy by this sentiment, he turned the key in the door of his bedroom and gave himself up with an entirely new pleasure to reading about the exploits of his hero.]

The italics are again Stendhal's. Julien's feelings are no longer purely subjective and selfish. His experience has modified his whole outlook and the feelings which accompany his success are something entirely new for him. The *sentiment d'infériorité* has, at any rate for the time being, been exorcized and has been replaced by satisfaction over accomplishing 'son devoir, et un devoir héroïque'. There is an immense relief behind the words, a sense of release from something which was imprisoning him and preventing the development of his personality. Instead of being eaten up by a subjective feeling of inferiority, he has broken the vicious circle and identifies himself with the *public* figure of Napoleon.

2

'In contrast to the naturalness of the Rênal estate at Vergy,' writes Mr. Harry Levin of the love-affair with Mathilde de La Mole, 'her love has ripened in a library, nourished on the chronicles of Brantôme and Aubigné and the novels of Rousseau and Prévost.'[1]

It is a suggestive remark, but I find it difficult to accept Mr. Levin's conclusions. The contrast between the 'naturalness' of Vergy and the atmosphere of the 'library' in Paris is certainly intentional and the

[1] *Toward Stendhal* (Murray, Utah, 1945), p. 48.

meaning of the whole novel depends on a correct interpretation of it. Stendhal chose the Franche-Comté because it was on the outskirts of France and geographically remote from the sophisticated capital to which Julien will eventually graduate. It is the start of his career, the place at which the forward bastions of civilization are breached to admit the intruder.

Julien's career is a journey to the interior. When he leaves Verrières, we have the impression that he is entering a long, dark tunnel and that the 'fresh, deep valleys' which surround the 'little town' are the daylight receding behind him as he penetrates further and further into it. We are aware of a feeling of claustrophobia as the seminary doors close on him. Henceforth, the drama takes place not in the open air, but in the oppressive, airless seminary, in the library of M. de La Mole and at the secret session amid the candles and the sealing wax, the papers and the serious anonymous faces of the conspirators.

The physical journey is at the same time *a journey to the interior of the mind*. It is accompanied by a deepening of experience, a growing complexity of feeling. The outer world loses its importance; the 'action' shifts to the world within. The change is well illustrated by an encounter between Julien and Mathilde when she comes into the library and asks him to fetch a book for her:

> Julien avait approché l'échelle; il avait cherché le volume, il le lui avait remis, sans encore pouvoir songer à elle. En remportant l'échelle, dans sa précipitation, il donna un coup de coude dans une glace de la bibliothèque; les éclats, en tombant sur le parquet, le réveillèrent enfin.

> [He brought the ladder; he found the volume, he handed it to her, still without being able to think of her. As he carried back the ladder, in his preoccupation, his elbow struck one of the glass panes protecting the shelves; the sound of the splinters falling on the floor at length aroused him.]

The characters live in a dream world, entirely preoccupied with what is going on inside their own minds; and the movement of this passage reflects the mechanical movements of a sleep-walker. From time to time a violent incident in the external world—the breaking of the pane in the bookcase or the smashing of the Japanese vase—brings them back to earth with a shock. It is the striking of a clock which recalls the dreamer from the timeless world to the world of time and chance.[1]

[1] One of the most striking examples of this preoccupation is the occasion when Julien seizes an old sword from the wall of the library and is on the point of attacking

'Il a de l'imprévu,' remarks the Marquis in speaking to his daughter of Julien. It is his way of recognizing Julien's 'otherness', and it must be distinguished from the reactions of the bourgeois of Verrières who gape open-mouthed while he recites chapter after chapter of the New Testament from memory. The Marquis de La Mole is not interested in his looks or his parlour tricks, but in his intellectual attainments and his character. Julien's qualities are also recognized by Mathilde, but her reactions are quite different from her father's. For here like calls to like. Mathilde, too, is an *étrangère* in nineteenth-century society, and it is because she has failed to meet anyone like herself that, until Julien arrives, she spends her time in a private world of her own reading about the heroic exploits of her sixteenth-century ancestors. She is desperately bored and desperately out of place in a society of which she can say with some truth: 'Je ne vois que la condamnation à mort qui distingue un homme . . . c'est la seule chose qui ne s'achète pas.'

Her criticism is reinforced by an observation of the Comte Altamira's:

Il n'y a plus de passions véritables au XIXe siècle: c'est pour cela que l'on s'ennuie tant en France. On fait les plus grandes cruautés, mais sans cruauté.

[There are no longer any genuine passions in the nineteenth century; that is why people are so bored in France. We commit the greatest cruelties, but without cruelty.]

It used to be fashionable at one time to debate the respective merits of *Le Rouge et le noir* and *La Chartreuse de Parme*. The *Chartreuse de Parme* may be the greater novel, but I do not think that Stendhal ever surpassed the account of the love affair between Julien and Mathilde:

Rien [we are told] ne fut plaisant comme le dialogue de ces deux amants; sans s'en douter ils étaient animés l'un contre l'autre des sentiments de la haine la plus vive.

[Nothing could be more entertaining than the dialogue between these young lovers; unconsciously they were animated by a mutual sentiment of the keenest hatred.]

Mathilde who is delighted to think that she was almost killed by her lover. The sword is a talisman which transports them both to a different age, to the age to which spiritually they belong.

Their attraction-and-repulsion sounds at first like an episode in the sex war; but Stendhal's interpretation of this fundamental antipathy is much more profound than Laclos' in the *Liaisons dangereuses*. In the *Liaisons* it is inspired by a desire to dominate the opposite sex; in *Le Rouge et le noir* it is part of a larger war against society seen collectively. In spite of the violent conflict between them and the savage delight that they experience in humiliating one another's pride—always the vulnerable spot—Julien and Mathilde are allies against society and are united by a bond which goes far deeper than their antipathy. The words *singulier—singularité* must occur a hundred times in the second part of the novel, and they describe the link which unites Julien and Mathilde and separates them from everyone else.[1]

The forty-sixth chapter, which describes the seduction of Julien by Mathilde, illustrates some of Stendhal's most remarkable qualities— his insight into conflicting and contradictory feelings, his blend of tenderness and irony and also his use of the Romantics' stock-in-trade to express an anti-romantic attitude. Julien has just climbed into Mathilde's bedroom:

'Vous voilà, monsieur,' lui dit Mathilde avec beaucoup d'émotion; 'je suis vos mouvements depuis une heure.'
Julien était fort embarrassé, il ne savait comment se conduire, il n'avait pas d'amour du tout. Dans son embarras, il pensa qu'il fallait oser, il essaya d'embrasser Mathilde.
'Fi donc!' lui dit-elle en le repoussant.

['Here you are, sir,' Mathilde said to him with deep emotion; 'I have been following your movements for the last hour.'
Julien was greatly embarrassed, he did not know how to behave, he did not feel the least vestige of love. In his embarrassment, he decided that he must show courage, he attempted to embrace Mathilde.
'Fie, sir!' she said, and thrust him from her.]

They are both extremely embarrassed, but for different reasons. Their mutual attraction is deeper than they realize, but Julien has

[1] It is a quality which is recognized by members of Mathilde's entourage even when they do not like it: 'Mathilde a de la singularité, pensa-t-il [M. de Croisenois]; c'est un inconvénient, mais elle donne une si belle position sociale à son mari . . . cette singularité de Mathilde peut passer pour du génie. Avec une haute naissance et beaucoup de fortune, le génie n'est point un ridicule, et alors quelle distinction!'
It is an example of the way in which Stendhal's criticism is dissolved into the novel. Her 'genius' is a threat to a precarious social order, but it can be neutralized, or so her admirer hopes, by a great position and great wealth.

engaged in the escapade largely out of bravado and because he is flattered by the invitation to visit the daughter of the house in the small hours. A Romantic hero would certainly have worked himself up into a fine frenzy by a torrent of words. Julien does his best, but Stendhal shows us with his customary lucidity that in reality he feels nothing and has no idea what to do.

Mathilde, too, is anxious for a 'big scene', but she is paralysed by the conflict between what is really admirable in her—her boldness and *singularité*—and the conventional feelings against which she rebels:

> Elle souffrait étrangement; tous les sentiments de retenue et de timidité, si naturels à une fille bien née, avaient repris leur empire, et la mettaient au supplice. . . .
> Si elle l'eût pu, elle eût anéanti elle et Julien. Quand par instants la force de sa volonté faisait taire les remords, des sentiments de timidité et de pudeur souffrante la rendaient fort malheureuse. Elle n'avait nullement prévu l'état affreux où elle se trouvait.

> [She was strangely ill at ease; all the feelings of reserve and timidity, so natural to a young girl of good family, had resumed their sway and were keeping her on tenter-hooks. . . .
> Had it been possible, she would have destroyed herself and Julien. Whenever, for an instant, the strength of her will made her remorse silent, feelings of shyness and outraged modesty made her extremely wretched. She had never for a moment anticipated the dreadful plight in which she now found herself.]

Stendhal is remorseless in his exposure of their embarrassment:

> Mathilde faisait effort pour le tutoyer, elle était évidemment plus attentive à cette étrange façon de parler qu'au fond des choses qu'elle disait. . . .
> 'Il faut cependant que je lui parle,' dit-elle à la fin, 'cela est dans les convenances, on parle à son amant.'

> [Mathilde made an effort to use the more intimate form; she was evidently more attentive to this unusual way of speaking than to what she was saying. . . .
> 'I must speak to him, though,' she said to herself, finally, 'that is laid down in the rules, one speaks to one's lover.']

Then comes the final criticism of the Romantic attitude:

Après de longues incertitudes, qui eussent pu paraître à un observateur superficiel l'effet de la haine la plus décidée . . . Mathilde finit par être pour lui une maîtresse aimable.

A la vérité, ces transports étaient un peu *voulus*. L'amour passionné était encore plutôt un modèle qu'on imitait qu'une réalité.

[After prolonged uncertainties, which might have appeared to a superficial observer to be due to the most decided hatred . . . Mathilde finally became his mistress.

To tell the truth their ardours were a little artificial. Passionate love was still more of a model to be imitated than a reality.]

And the final exposure:

Mlle de La Mole croyait remplir un devoir envers elle-même et envers son amant. 'Le pauvre garçon,' se disait-elle, 'a été d'une bravoure achevée, il doit être heureux, ou bien c'est moi qui manque de caractère. Mais elle eût voulu racheter au prix d'une éternité de malheur la nécessité cruelle où elle se trouvait.

[Mademoiselle de La Mole believed that she was performing a duty towards herself and towards her lover. 'The poor boy,' she told herself, 'has been the last word in daring, he deserves to be happy, or else I am wanting in character.' But she would gladly have redeemed at the cost of an eternity of suffering the cruel necessity to which she found herself committed.]

The whole incident is related in a tone of ironic comedy, but we continually have the impression that Stendhal's words are *doing* more than they *say*. The hot, prickly embarrassment of the lovers is contagious and communicates itself to us; but we are aware of the underlying seriousness and we see far more deeply into the real impulses of the characters than they do themselves.

Stendhal's prose is, indeed, seen at its most impressive in the encounters between Julien and Mathilde. The conflict goes on at two levels. It begins with their unspoken thoughts. Suddenly there is a violent eruption and they denounce one another with the ferocity of Racine's characters. One of them is temporarily 'knocked out', and with equal suddenness the tumult subsides, as they revert to a sort of silent, hostile dialogue:

Il lui semblerait qu'une chose apporterait à sa douleur un soulagement infini: ce serait de parler à Mathilde. Mais cependant qu'oserait-il lui dire?

C'est à quoi un matin, à sept heures, il rêvait profondément, lorsque tout à coup il la vit entrer dans la bibliothèque.

'Je sais, monsieur, que vous désirez me parler.'

'Grand Dieu! qui vous l'a dit?'

'Je sais, que vous importe?'

'Si vous manquez d'honneur, vous pouvez me perdre ou du moins le tenter; mais ce danger, que je ne crois pas réel, ne m'empêchera certainement pas d'être sincère. Je ne vous aime plus, monsieur, mon imagination folle m'a trompée.'

A ce coup terrible, éperdu d'amour et de malheur, Julien essaya de se justifier. Rien de plus absurde. Se justifie-t-on de déplaire? Mais la raison n'avait plus aucun empire sur ses actions. Un instinct aveugle le poussait à retarder la décision de son sort. Il lui semblait que tant qu'il parlait, tout n'était pas fini. Mathilde n'écoutait pas ses paroles, leur son l'irritait, elle ne concevait pas qu'il eût l'audace de l'interrompre.

[It seemed to him that one thing would supply boundless comfort to his grief: namely to speak to Mathilde. And yet what could he venture to say to her?

This was the question upon which one morning at seven o'clock he was pondering deeply, when suddenly he saw her enter the library.

'I know, sir, that you desire to speak to me.'

'Great God! Who told you that?'

'I know it, what more do you want? If you are lacking in honour, you may ruin me, or at least attempt to do so; but this danger, which I do not regard as real, will certainly not prevent me from being sincere. I no longer love you, sir; my wild imagination misled me.'

On receiving this terrible blow, desperate with love and misery, Julien tried to excuse himself. Nothing could be more absurd. Does one excuse oneself for failing to please? But reason no longer held sway over his actions. A blind instinct urged him to postpone the decision of his fate. It seemed to him that so long as he was still speaking, nothing was definitely settled. Mathilde did not listen to his words, the sound of them irritated her, she could not conceive how he had the audacity to interrupt her.]

Stendhal's prose bears a marked resemblance to eighteenth-century prose, but this resemblance is deceptive. It was certainly founded on the classic syntax, but though the structure of his sentences is often similar, the movement of his paragraphs is sometimes quite different. The difference has been well expressed by M. Gide. 'With Stendhal,' he writes, 'one sentence never calls the next into being, nor is it born of the one that went before. Each of them stands perpendicularly to the fact or idea.'[1] His prose does not move steadily forward from one fixed point to another. It has greater density and greater range. Each sentence or each clause in a sentence corresponds to what the French call a *fait psychique*, and their relation to one another forms the pattern of his style. A passage like this is not the direct expression of emotion; it is rather a geometrical construction, a configuration of feelings, which enables us to perceive with startling clarity what is happening inside the characters' minds and to follow the clash of contradictory impulses. For this reason, instead of being a logical progression, Stendhal's prose is continually twisting and turning, changing direction and producing startling juxtapositions between the 'perpendicular' sentences. The outcome is that it seems to be moving in several directions at once and to touch us simultaneously in different places. The first two sentences are a series of sorties and retreats which lead up to the final assault on the position. At each sortie, Mathilde strikes Julien in a different place—his honour, his pride, his belief in himself, his emotional stability—then withdraws in order to deliver a still heavier blow. The total effect is of an attack which is at once very widespread and very concentrated. Then, suddenly, Mathilde seems to gather the whole of her energy for the final smashing blow: 'I no longer love you, sir; my wild imagination misled me.'

The first paragraph reveals Mathilde's complete command of the situation, the second the effect of her onslaught on Julien. When Stendhal writes, 'A ce coup terrible', we hear the sickening thud as the blow lands. In the French classic writers, *éperdu* always stands for complete mental and emotional disorientation, and in this passage it registers the devastating effect of Mathilde's attack. Julien is dazed, but makes a feeble and belated attempt to justify himself. The two short sentences —'Rien de plus absurde. Se justifie-t-on de déplaire?'—are the mocking reverberation of her words in his stunned mind. Instead of recovering, his pain increases. The attempt to justify himself is the last glimmer of sense before he becomes incoherent. The words, 'La raison n'avait plus aucun empire sur ses actions', are a sign of disintegration and collapse; and the *plus* makes us feel the mechanism of personality falling apart. When reason fails, he is thrown back on 'un instinct *aveugle*'. He struggles blindly on, persuaded that if only he can keep going, if only he can keep on talking, something must happen to save him.

These and similar passages have won for Stendhal the reputation of being one of the greatest psychologists among modern novelists. Beneath its dry sparkle, his prose has tentacular roots which thrust downwards into the hidden places of the mind. He possessed the *vue*

[1] *Journal des Faux-monnayeurs* (Paris, 1927), pp. 28–9.

directe into the complexity of the human heart, the power of seizing feelings at the moment of their formation and translating them with an admirable lucidity:

> Ce tutoiement, dépouillé du ton de la tendresse, ne faisait aucun plaisir à Julien, il s'étonnait de l'absence du bonheur; enfin, pour le sentir, il eut recours à sa raison. Il se voyait estimé par cette jeune fille si fière, et qui n'accordait jamais de louanges sans restriction; avec ce raisonnement il parvint à un bonheur d'amour-propre.

> [This use of the singular form, stripped of the tone of affection, ceased, after a moment, to afford Julien any pleasure, he was astonished at the absence of happiness; finally, in order to feel it, he had recourse to his reason. He saw himself highly esteemed by this girl who was so proud, and never bestowed unrestricted praise; by this line of reasoning he arrived at a gratification of his self-esteem.]

Once again the prose performs the actions that it describes. The novelist suggests a feeling to us, then proceeds to peel away the outer layers in order to show us that it is not at all what it appears to be. The *tutoiement* should be a sign of *tendresse*, but is not. It gives Julien no 'pleasure', and he is 'astonished' at the absence of a *bonheur* which is normally a product of *tendresse* and *plaisir*. *Enfin* marks the characteristic change of direction. Julien sets to work to produce a substitute feeling of 'happiness' by the use of 'reason'. He tells himself that if there is no 'tenderness' in Mathilde's tone, at least this person who is proud and not given to overpraising anyone 'esteems' him. This argument, this manipulation of ideas, produces a fresh combination of feelings. We have watched the whole process from the beginning, have seen the feelings transformed. With the *bonheur d'amour-propre* everything suddenly falls neatly into place.

In other places Stendhal writes:

> Deux mois de combats et de sensations nouvelles renouvelèrent pour ainsi dire tout son être moral.

> Ce cruel soupçon changea toute la position morale de Julien. Cette idée trouva dans son cœur un commencement d'amour qu'elle n'eut pas de peine à détruire.

> Ces souvenirs de bonheur passé s'emparaient de Julien et détruisaient bientôt tout l'ouvrage de la raison.

> Son mot si franc, mais si stupide, vint tout changer en un instant: Mathilde, sûre d'être aimée, le méprisa parfaitement.

[Two months of struggle and of novel sensations had so to speak altered her whole moral nature.

This cruel suspicion completely changed Julien's moral attitude. The idea encountered in his heart a germ of love which it had no difficulty in destroying.

These memories of past happiness took possession of Julien, and rapidly undid all the work of reason.

This speech, so frank but so stupid, altered the whole situation in an instant: Mathilde, certain of being loved, despised him completely.]

In all these examples, the operative words are the verbs *changer*, *renouveller*, *détruire*. The verb—usually a transitive verb—is the pivot of Stendhal's most characteristic sentences because he is much more interested in mental *activity* than in mental *states*. These three verbs indicate the field of experience. His characters' feelings are constantly 'changing', are engaged in a continual process of 'renewal' and 'destruction'. They are not superficial changes of mood; they go to the roots of the 'moral being'. A sudden shock 'destroys' their moral stability; they set to work slowly and painfully to rebuild it. Another shock undoes the work of 'reason', and the whole process starts all over again. A final sentence completes the picture:

Mathilde était alors dans l'état où Julien se trouvait quelques jours auparavant.

[Mathilde was at that time in the state in which Julien had been a few days previously.]

Although they are bound to one another in the innermost depths of their being, Julien and Mathilde are practically never both in the same mood on the same day, and this produces the clash. It is a psychological obstacle race in which they take it in turns to be pursuer and pursued, executioner and victim.

One of the most interesting things about Stendhal's characters is the impression that they give that the whole of their lives, the whole of their being, is engaged in every action:

Le courage était la première qualité de son caractère [we are told of Mathilde]. Rien ne pouvait lui donner quelque agitation et la guérir d'un fond d'ennui sans cesse renaissant que l'idée *qu'elle jouait à croix ou à pile son existence entière.*[1]

[1] Italics mine.

[Courage was the fundamental quality in her character. Nothing was capable of giving her any excitement and of curing her of an ever present tendency to boredom but the idea that she was playing heads or tails with her whole existence.]

It is this that makes the encounters between Julien and Mathilde so dramatic and such a strain on their personalities. We may sometimes wonder why they could not go on indefinitely, but Stendhal gives the answer in a sentence:

Elle [Mathilde] tomba tout à fait évanouie.
'La voilà donc, cette orgueilleuse à mes pieds,' se dit Julien.

[She fell to the ground in a dead faint.
'There she is then, the proud thing, at my feet,' Julien said to himself.]

The life of Stendhal's characters is a process of *extension* which finally reaches the point at which not merely something, but *everything* gives way. It is because they are 'outsiders' that they can find no proper outlet for their great gifts. Their incredible calculations and their immensely sharpened sensibility, which result from this position, subject their personalities to an intolerable strain until they are driven to abandon the world of action and to withdraw completely into the world of contemplation.

Julien's imprisonment and death have been variously interpreted. One writer, comparing him with Meursault, the hero of M. Camus' *L'Étranger*, suggests that he is a 'social' rather than a 'metaphysical martyr'.[1] An American critic speaks of 'the alienated libido and the expiating martyr "in love with death" '.[2] For reasons that I have already given, I think that it is easy to misinterpret the 'social' factor; and though the desire for 'martyrdom' and 'the death-wish' are present, I do not believe that they are decisive. When Julien reaches the prison at Besançon his sensibility is exhausted. The extended personality has reached the point at which it can no longer carry on, when there is nothing left for it in life. This explains Julien's attitude to Mathilde and Mme de Rênal. He cannot face the prospect of life together with Mathilde and he turns to the more restful figure of Mme de Rênal. She is of course the mother-image and the prison itself a

[1] H. A. Mason, 'M. Camus and the Tragic Hero' in *Scrutiny*, Vol. XIV, No. 2, p. 83.
[2] Matthew Josephson, *Stendhal or The Pursuit of Happiness* (New York, 1946), p. 346.

symbol of the womb to which he wishes to return. Once in prison, he can give himself up to *rêverie*. The last thing he wants is to be acquitted or to escape or even to return to the world of action after a term of imprisonment. Mathilde's attempts to save him are simply exasperating and he takes good care that they fail.

I think we must add that the prison episode is also a profound study of the psychology of heroism. Julien appears to stick to his ideals, to go heroically to his death. In fact, he commits suicide; but he does not do so for the reasons suggested by his critics. The 'hero' lives at a far greater pitch of intensity than the general run of men, and what appears to be an heroic death in battle is probably in many instances a case of suicide dictated by an unconscious realization that he is 'finished'.

The account of the execution is a masterly example of Stendhal's power of understatement:

> Tout se passa simplement, convenablement, et de sa part sans aucune affectation.

> [Everything passed simply, decorously, and without affectation on his part.]

The last scene, in which Mathilde follows the funeral cortège with Julien's severed head on her knees, has perplexed Stendhal's critics. It seems to me to be a deliberately macabre piece of comedy. His admiration for the sixteenth century was deep-rooted, and he certainly approved this final display of Mathilde's *singularité*, which could only have appeared odd to an effete age. It was Stendhal's parting shot at the men of 1830.

IV. *LUCIEN LEUWEN*
OR THE NOVELIST IN POLITICS

Dégouvernons—*French political maxim*

I

THE legend that classic art is impersonal and that the classic artist never puts himself into his books dies hard. Yet when we look into it, we find that it is little more than a legend and that it is based on a conception of art whose validity is extremely dubious. A novelist's or a dramatist's characters are nearly always symbols—sometimes unconscious symbols—of his personal interests. His work must to some extent be judged by the breadth and universality of his symbols or, to put it in another way, by the degree of correspondence between his personal sensibility and the sensibility of his age. The artist of the classic ages thought of himself as a member of the community and his work was the product of a social experience, but this does not mean that he never put himself into his books. There is a good deal of Molière in *L'École des femmes*, in *Le Misanthorpe* and in *Le Malade imaginaire*, and one sometimes feels that Racine might have anticipated Flaubert by declaring 'Phèdre, c'est moi'. It was not merely the *bienséances* which prevented him from doing so. For there is one very important difference between the French writers of the seventeenth century and their successors. In the seventeenth century there were no autobiographical novels and no 'confessions' in the manner of *Adolphe*. Molière and Racine put themselves into their plays, but they never put the whole of themselves into any one play. What they did was to dramatize different aspects of their personality or different phases of their experience in different plays. On the whole, Racine went further than Molière. The dialogue between Phèdre and Hippolyte, as I have shown in another place,[1] is a dialogue between the 'old' and the 'new' Racine; and in his last play Abner and Athalie are both partial portraits of the artist.

I hesitate to attach labels like 'classic' and 'romantic' to Stendhal because he does not belong wholly to either category; but in so far as he put himself into his novels he certainly followed the classical tradition. He was, as we know, extremely fond of women and extremely

---

[1] *The Classical Moment*, pp. 213–14.

shy. He admired Napoleon, had a taste for soldiering and a contempt for politicians, was at once an aristocrat and in theory a strong republican. The heroes of his three greatest novels all share his tastes and views, but there are other resemblances which go much deeper than any of these. 'The central problem', writes Mr. Josephson, 'is always the same: the education of youth for life; the formation of his mind and character under the blows of experience; his début in society.'[1] The books are all variations on the 'outsider' theme. They record an experience and an experiment. The heroes are all born into one of the three main classes; the novelist projects himself, or a part of himself, into them and watches to see what will happen. *Le Rouge et le noir, La Chartreuse de Parme* and *Lucien Leuwen* are really a triptych. Julien Sorel is the 'lower-class' outsider who determines to create a great position for himself in the France of 1830; Fabrice del Dongo is the aristocratic outsider who disrupts the pattern of the eighteenth-century police state which still survives in Parma; and Lucien Leuwen is the upper-middle-class outsider who cannot accept the subterfuges and corruption of the France of Louis-Philippe.[2]

There is one other important trait which is common to Stendhal's heroes. It is a curious dreaminess, a lack of awareness of what is going on in the world around them and of their own extraordinary assets. Julien does not realize the immense advantages of his good looks, Fabrice of his aristocratic birth and Lucien of his father's wealth until someone takes the trouble to explain it to them. Their dreaminess—their carefully cultivated dreaminess—certainly came from their creator, but he himself possessed none of the physical, social or material advantages with which he endowed them. Sometimes he is furious with them for missing an opportunity which he feels sure that he himself would have grasped; at others he apologizes to the reader for their 'silliness'. '*C'est un niais,*' he remarks, 'but you must make allowances for him. He's very young and very inexperienced.' Yet he also regarded them with affection and admiration. For they all possess what he liked to call *de l'imprévu*. At the critical moment they suddenly abandon the dream world and become men of action. Their reactions to a situation are extraordinarily rapid and totally unexpected. You can never tell exactly

---

[1] *Op. cit.*, pp. 391–2.

[2] The theme is less pronounced in the remaining novels. In his first novel, *Armance*, Octave de Malivert is cut off from a normal life by a disability which is purely physical in origin. The heroine of *Lamiel* is a survivor not from the sixteenth century like Mathilde, but from the eighteenth century and has obvious affinities with Laclos' Mme de Merteuil. Thibaudet remarked of *Lucien Leuwen* that 'It is the story of the lieutenant who died young and whom the consul survived in order to tell his story and re-live his romance'. (*Stendhal*, pp. 159–60.)

what they are going to do or say. It is this which makes them so immensely fascinating for us, and so disturbing.

'Politics in a work of literature', said Stendhal in the *Chartreuse de Parme*, 'is like a pistol shot at a concert. It is something crude from which it is nevertheless impossible to withhold our attention.' In spite of this somewhat ambiguous statement, all Stendhal's novels are criticisms of the social-political scene as he knew it. *Lucien Leuwen*, however, is the only one in which he made a frontal assault on contemporary political institutions.

> This novel [wrote Jean Mélia] lays bare the crookedest side of politics and reveals all its taints. *Lucien Leuwen* is the story of electoral campaigns where everything is thrown into the game—calumnies and lies, strikes which are deliberately fomented, consciences which are sold by auction, parliamentary machinations with their misuse of money, the incompetence of ministers. In short, it is an account of everything that happened in Stendhal's time, but Stendhal's novel possesses such breadth of psychology and such a degree of truth that the reader of *Lucien Leuwen* can apply its findings to many other periods.[1]

Lucien Leuwen is widely regarded in France as one of Stendhal's major achievements, but for reasons which are difficult to divine it has never been translated into English. A brief account of its genesis may therefore be of interest.

In the late autumn of 1833 Stendhal returned to his consulate at Civita-Vecchia after spending his leave in Paris. He took with him the manuscript of a novel called *Le Lieutenant* by his friend Mme Jules Gaulthier who had asked him to read and criticize it. On 4 May 1834, he wrote her a letter which provides an interesting commentary on his own practice:

> I have read *Le Lieutenant*, dear and kind friend [he said]. You must copy the whole thing out again and imagine that you are translating a German book. To my mind, the language is horribly noble and emphatic. I have been very cruel and scrawled all over it. . . . You must leave at least fifty superlatives out of the first chapter. Never talk about 'Olivier's burning passion for Hélène'. The poor novelist must try to make us believe in the *burning passion*, but he must never name it. That is contrary to modesty.[2]

[1] *Les Idées de Stendhal* (Paris, 1910), p. 376.
[2] Quoted, Henri Martineau, *L'Œuvre de Stendhal*, p. 387, and in the same writer's edition of *Lucien Leuwen* in the 'Collection Grands et Petits Chefs-d'Œuvre' (2nd edition, Monaco, 1945), pp. x-xi.

Mme Gaulthier's novel was never published and no one has succeeded in discovering the manuscript. We do not know to what extent Stendhal borrowed from her, but we do know that within a day or two of sending this letter he suddenly made up his mind to write a novel himself on a similar subject. He set to work at once and for the next eighteen months seems to have written little else. His work was interrupted by an attack of gout from 16 May to 22 June 1835, but as soon as he was better he went on with his novel. He broke off again on 23 November of the same year when he began to write *La Vie de Henri Brulard*. He seems to have felt that *Lucien Leuwen* could only be finished in Paris. He did a little more work on it while he was there in September and October 1836, but for reasons that are unknown to us he finally abandoned it and it remains unfinished.

He left the manuscript by will to his sister with the request to have it corrected and printed by 'some reasonable man'. Romain Colomb published a few chapters of it under the title of *Le Chasseur vert* in a volume of *Nouvelles inédites* in 1855. The bulk of the work appeared for the first time, in a very inaccurate and incomplete edition, in 1894; and it was not until 1926–7 that the *texte intégral* of *Lucien Leuwen*, as it was eventually called, became available to the public.[1]

It is the only one of the three principal novels of which the manuscript has survived. It is enlivened by a large number of the author's marginal notes which throw considerable light on his method of composition and the models which he used for his characters; and there are some extremely amusing comments on the characters themselves.[2]

2

The year is 1832. Politically, France is divided into three main parties: the 'moderates' or *juste-milieu* who support Louis-Philippe; the 'ultras' who conspire for the return of the exiled Charles X, and the republicans who assail them both. Lucien Leuwen, the twenty-three-year-old son of a wealthy Paris banker, has been expelled from the École Polytechnique. The official reason for his expulsion is that he went out during the political riots on a day when he was confined to barracks; but the real reason is that he was suspected of republican leanings.

[1] Stendhal found it difficult to decide on a suitable title. He toyed with the idea of *Leuwen*—a title he had suggested for the *Lieutenant* in his letter to Mme Gaulthier—*L'Orange de Malte*, *Le Télégraphe*, *Lucien Leuwen*, *L'Amarante et le noir*, *Les Bois de Prémol*, *Le Chasseur vert* and *Le Rouge et le blanc*.

[2] Most of them will be found in M. Martineau's edition in the 'Collection Grands et Petits Chefs-d'Œuvre'.

His father, a witty, cynical and very influential old man, disapproves of his son's seriousness and still more of his disreputable 'Saint-Simonism'. He tries to turn him into a *bon viveur* like himself and encourages him to have an affair with an Opera girl. When this comes to nothing, he uses his influence and secures him a commission as second lieutenant in the 27th Lancers. The regiment is ordered to the garrison town of Nancy. Stendhal describes the sad eastern provinces with his customary economy:

> . . . la plaine la plus triste du monde; le terrain sec et pierreux paraissait ne pouvoir rien produire . . . quelques vignes chétives . . . deux tristes rangées d'ormes rabougris. . . . Les paysans que l'on rencontrait avaient l'air misérable et étonné. 'Voilà donc la *belle France*!' se disait Lucien . . . le régiment passa devant ces grands établissements utiles, mais sales qui annoncent si tristement une civilisation perfectionnée, l'abattoir, la raffinerie d'huile etc.

> [. . . the saddest plain in the world; the dry stony ground appeared unable to produce anything . . . some puny vines . . . two sad rows of stunted elms. . . . The peasants that one met looked wretched and startled. 'So that's *la belle France*!' Lucien said to himself . . . the regiment passed those large, useful but ugly establishments which point so sadly to a perfected civilization—the slaughter-house, the oil-refinery etc.]

It is a prelude to the dreary society that Lucien will find at Nancy. For the main political divisions are repeated in a different setting in the garrison town. The regiment is naturally 'moderate'; the provincial nobility are 'ultras' to a man; and the republicans are an insignificant minority.

Lucien at once feels that he is an 'outsider':

> Certainement, pour plaire à ces messieurs, je ne prendrai pas ces manières rudes et grossières; je resterai un étranger parmi eux.

> [Certainly, to please these gentlemen, I shall not adopt uncouth coarse manners; I shall remain an outsider among them.]

His brother officers bore him; his superiors are jealous of his wealth; the ultra nobility are impossible; and his republican friend, Gauthier, is ineffectual. He begins to wonder whether he is after all a republican:

> Je ne puis vivre avec des hommes incapables d'idées fines, si vertueux qu'ils soient; je préférerais cent fois les mœurs élégantes d'une cour cor-

rompue. Washington m'eût ennuyé à la mort, et j'aime mieux me trouver dans le même salon que M. de Talleyrand. Donc, la sensation de l'estime n'est pas tout pour moi; j'ai besoin des plaisirs donnés par une ancienne civilisation.

[I cannot live with men who are incapable of acute perceptions, however virtuous they may be; I should prefer a hundred times the elegant manners of a corrupt court. Washington would have bored me to death, and I would much rather find myself in the same salon as M. de Talleyrand. Therefore, a feeling of esteem is not everything so far as I am concerned; I need the pleasures provided by an ancient civilization.]

All Stendhal's heroes feel that they have been born into the wrong age, but there is nothing 'escapist' about their admiration for the past; the accent falls squarely on 'une ancienne *civilisation*'. There is, how-ever, one difference between Lucien and the heroes of the other novels. Julien and Fabrice both look back to the passionate, heroic sixteenth century; but Lucien sighs—who shall blame him?—for a silver age, for the eighteenth century with its elegance, its entertaining conversation, its sensitive individuals, its notoriously lax moral code.[1]

Stendhal's political criticism is very subtle. He enjoyed 'laying bare the crookedest side' of the political game, but at heart he was not a reformer:

L'éloquence touchait Lucien, mais Gauthier ne parvenait nullement à détruire sa grande objection contre la République: la nécessité de faire la cour aux gens médiocres.

[His eloquence touched Lucien, but Gauthier did not in any way succeed in destroying his great objection to the Republic: the necessity of ingra-tiating himself with mediocrities.]

His real complaint was not that politics were corrupt, but that they destroyed people's sensibility and turned them into 'mediocrities'. He was quite prepared to put up with the corruption if he could have the 'elegance' as well:

Il me faut les mœurs élégantes, fruits du gouvernement corrompu de Louis XV. . . .

[1] This difference is an illustration of the experimental element to which I have referred above.

[I need the elegant manners which are the fruit of the corrupt rule of Louis XV. . . .]

Again:

Les temps sont maussades et tristes; sous Louis XIV, j'eusse été galant et aimable auprès d'une telle femme, j'eusse essayé du moins. En ce dix-neuvième siècle, je suis platement sentimental, c'est pour elle la seule consolation en mon pouvoir.[1]

[The times are sad and dreary; under Louis XIV I should have been gallant and made myself agreeable to such a woman, I should have tried at any rate. In this nineteenth century, I am drearily sentimental, for her it's the only consolation in my power.]

Stendhal gives a merciless picture of ultra society:

. . . Mme de Serpierre, grande femme sèche et dévote qui avait une fortune très bornée et six filles à marier.
Mais cet héroïque marquis avait des inconvénients; il n'entendait jamais nommer Louis-Philippe sans lancer d'une voix singulière et glapissante ce simple mot: *voleur*.
M. de Goéllo, grand jeune homme blond, sec et pincé, et déjà couvert des rides d'envie.

[. . . Mme de Serpierre, a large, dry, devout woman who possessed very limited means and six daughters to marry.
But this heroic marquess had drawbacks; he never heard the name of Louis-Philippe without uttering in a strange shrill tone this simple word: *thief*.
M. de Goéllo, a tall fair young man, dry and prim, whose face was already covered with wrinkles of envy.]

It is instructive to turn from these glimpses of the ultra nobility to Lucien's comparison between Dr. Du Poirier, the most astute of the royalist agents, and the republican Gauthier:

'Quelle différence d'esprit,' pensait-il, 'entre Du Poirier et Gauthier! et cependant ce dernier est probablement aussi honnête homme que l'autre est fripon. Malgré ma profonde estime pour lui, je meurs de sommeil. . . . Ceci me montre que je ne suis pas fait pour vivre sous une république; ce

[1] Cf., 'Il n'y a plus de passions véritables au XIXe siècle: c'est pour cela que l'on s'ennuie tant en France'. (*Le Rouge et le noir*.)

serait pour moi la tyrannie de toutes les médiocrités, et je ne puis supporter de sang-froid même les plus estimables. Il me faut un premier ministre coquin et amusant, comme Walpole ou M. de Talleyrand.'

['What a difference of mind,' he thought, 'between Du Poirier and Gauthier! And yet the latter is probably just as much a decent man as the other is a rogue. In spite of my profound esteem for him, I am dropping with fatigue. . . . This shows that I am not made to live under a republic; for me it would be the tyranny of all the mediocrities, and I can't even put up calmly with the most estimable among them. I need an amusing, rascally prime minister like Walpole or M. de Talleyrand.']

The implication is plain. There is nothing to choose between ultras and republicans or indeed any politicians. They are all bores and all mediocrities. At bottom Stendhal was essentially the non-party man; he simply entered into a temporary alliance with the republicans because they were the disruptive element in the State.

When we read *Lucien Leuwen* for the first time, we find it a little difficult to see the connection between love and politics. In the first volume the political conflicts seem to be used purely as a background for the love affair, and in the second love seems to fade out altogether. In reality, the connection between the two is a very close one. For Stendhal it was politics which made a man *platement sentimental* and love which provided an antidote. He was, as we know, a passionate student of love. He seems to have believed that man was only fully alive when he was in love and that it was the only bulwark against the disintegrating forces of the age. That is why his characters unhesitatingly sacrifice every other loyalty to love and are ready for every sort of political compromise if it will further their designs.

Love is therefore the most important factor in his characters' education. It is curious to observe that though they are immensely susceptible, they all fight bitterly against the surges of passion:

This republican [we are told of Lucien], this man of action, who regarded exercise on horseback as a preparation for battle, had never thought of love except as a dangerous and contemptible precipice into which he was certain not to fall. Besides, he·thought that this passion was extremely rare everywhere except on the stage.

Their education takes the form of an awakening to something which they are powerless to resist. Lucien's education begins the moment he enters Nancy. His horse throws him in one of the main streets. He catches a glimpse of a woman peeping at him through the shutters of a house. He learns that she is Mme Bathilde de Chasteller, a wealthy and beautiful young widow of twenty-four.[1] Although he has not been able to see her properly his interest is aroused. He is tormented at the thought that he may have ruined his chances by making himself ridiculous and spends hours every night gazing towards her window in the dark. The only way to meet her is to mix with ultra society. Political compromise follows. Lucien buys a large missal—the ultras are naturally *dévots*—and appears publicly at Mass. He at once becomes the darling of the ultra nobility who flatter themselves that a resounding conversion has taken place.

One of the most engaging things about Stendhal is the way in which he exposes the contradictions and inconsistencies of human nature. Although Lucien was blind to the charms of his father's nominee—the delightful Mlle Raimonde from the Opera—he is at bottom just as amorous as his creator:

Puisque Mme de Chasteller est une vertu [Lucien says to himself] pourquoi ne pas avoir une maîtresse en deux volumes? Mme de Chasteller pour les plaisirs du cœur, et Mme d'Hocquincourt pour les instants moins métaphysiques.[2]

[Since Mme de Chasteller is a woman of virtue, why not have a mistress in two volumes? Mme de Chasteller for the pleasures of the heart, and Mme d'Hocquincourt for less metaphysical moments.]

In Stendhal's three major novels the drama is always played out between a man and two women. I felt tempted to use the word 'triangle', but it gives a misleading impression of uniformity. The personnel may be the same, but the emotional pattern differs sensibly in each of the books. The motherless Julien sees in Mme de Rênal a mother-substitute and in Mathilde de La Mole a woman of action who shares his own enthusiasm for the sixteenth century: he seduces Mme de Rênal and is seduced by Mathilde. Fabrice has a mildly incestuous *inclination* for his aunt, the splendid Duchess of Sanseverina, but as Archbishop of Parma he beds the gentle Clélia. Lucien is the only one

[1] Bathilde de Chasteller is a portrait of Méthilde Dembowski, the wife of a general, to whom Stendhal had unsuccessfully paid court in Italy. She died in 1805. Stendhal considerably smooths the path of his timid hero by removing the husband!

[2] This seems to correspond to Stendhal's own distinction in the treatise on love between *l'amour-passion* and *l'amour-goût*.

G*

of the three who is on affectionate terms with both his parents; he flirts with Mme d'Hocquincourt and has his *grande passion* for Mme de Chasteller—a dreamer like himself—and except for the political connection with Mme Grandet towards the end of the book there are no seductions.

Rêver était son plaisir suprême [we are told of Mme de Chasteller]. On eût dit qu'elle ne faisait aucune attention aux petits événements qui l'environnaient; aucun ne lui échappait au contraire: elle les voyait fort bien, et c'étaient même ces petits événements qui servaient d'aliment à cette rêverie, qui passait pour de la hauteur. Aucun détail de la vie ne lui échappait, pourtant il était donné à très peu d'événements de l'émouvoir, et ce n'étaient pas les choses importantes qui la touchaient.

[Dreaming was her greatest pleasure. One would have said that she paid no attention to the little things which went on around her; not one of them escaped her on the contrary: she perceived them very clearly, and it was these same little things which provided the material for her dreaming which was taken for haughtiness. Not a single detail of life escaped her, yet very few events had the power to move her, and it was not the important things which affected her.]

Mme d'Hocquincourt is gay and easygoing with a string of conquests to her credit and a *mari complaisant*. Among the many gifts which make Stendhal a great novelist one seems to me to be supreme —his extraordinarily delicate sensibility. The passages in which he analyses emotion provide a striking contrast to the epigrammatic style of the political passages. This is the description of an encounter with Mme d'Hocquincourt:

'Vivre sans un ami de cœur,' disait M. de Sanréal plus qu'à demi-ivre de gloire et de punch, 'ce serait la plus grande des sottises, si ce n'était pas une impossibilité.'

'Il faut se hâter de choisir,' dit M. de Vassignies.

Mme d'Hocquincourt se pencha vers Leuwen, qui était devant elle.

'Et si celui qu'on a choisi,' lui dit-elle à voix basse, 'porte un cœur de marbre, que faut-il faire?'

Leuwen se retourna en riant, il fut bien surpris de voir qu'il y avait des larmes dans les yeux qui étaient fixés sur les siens. Ce miracle lui ôta l'esprit, il songea au miracle au lieu de songer à la réponse. Elle se borna à un sourire banal. . . .

Le soir, Leuwen, pour dire quelque chose, lui faisait compliment sur sa toilette:

'Quel admirable bouquet! Quelles jolies couleurs! Quelle fraîcheur! C'est l'emblème de la beauté qui le porte!'

'Vous croyez? Eh bien! soit! Il représente mon cœur, et je vous le donne.'

Le regard qui accompagna ce dernier mot n'avait plus rien de la gaieté qui avait régné jusque-là dans la conversation. Il ne manquait ni de profondeur ni de passion, et à un homme sensé ne pouvait laisser aucun doute sur le sens du don du bouquet. Leuwen le prit, ce bouquet, dit des choses plus ou moins dignes de Dorat sur ces jolies fleurs, mais ses yeux furent gais, légers. Il comprenait fort bien, et ne voulut pas comprendre.

['To go through life without a bosom friend,' said M. de Sanréal who was half drunk with glory and punch, 'would be the greatest of follies if it were not an impossibility.'

'One should hurry up and choose,' said M. de Vassignies.

Mme d'Hocquincourt leant towards Lucien who was in front of her.

'And if the person one's chosen,' she said in a low voice, 'has a heart of marble, what must one do?'

Leuwen turned round with a laugh, he was very surprised to see that there were tears in the eyes which were fixed on his own. This miracle robbed him of his wits, he thought about the miracle instead of thinking about his reply. It was confined to an empty smile. . . .

In the evening Leuwen, in order to say something, complimented her on her dress:

'What an admirable bouquet! What pretty colours! What freshness! It's the emblem of the lovely woman who's wearing it!'

'You think so? Very well! It represents my heart, and I make you a present of it.'

In the glance which accompanied the last word there was nothing left of the gaiety which up till then had animated the conversation. It was not lacking either in depth or in passion, and a sensible man would have been in no doubt about the significance of the gift of the bouquet. Leuwen took the bouquet, made some remarks which were more or less worthy of Dorat about the pretty flowers, but his eyes were gay, bright. He understood very well, and did not want to understand.]

It is the *petits événements* which produce the most striking exhibitions of Stendhal's sensibility. In this exquisite passage he achieves his effect precisely by avoiding (as he had advised Mme Gaulthier) 'emphatic' and 'noble' words. Mme d'Hocquincourt's quiet tones are in striking contrast to Lucien's fatuous compliments. The whole passage is as usual built up of *faits psychiques*. Sentences like 'Ce miracle lui ôta l'esprit' and 'Il représente mon cœur, et je vous le donne' show the extraordinary skill with which Stendhal's prose registers the constant twists and turns of feeling. Lucien is so absorbed by his passion for Mme de Chasteller that he is 'surprised' to discover Mme d'Hocquincourt's emotion, but though he remains indifferent—his 'eyes were gay, bright'—there is an answering vibration on the surface like a tuning fork. 'Il comprenait fort bien, et ne voulut pas comprendre' registers the double response.

The flirtation throws into strong relief the violent passions seeking an outlet in the affair with Mme de Chasteller and the almost super-human efforts to control or rather to stamp them out. Lucien and Bathilde are both in love and both horribly shy; but neither shyness nor respect for the *convenances* explains their resistance which appears surprising in a writer who believed so firmly in 'passion' as Stendhal. For there is something Cornelian about his characters' determination not to be carried completely away by passion. Yet the conflict is not identical with the Cornelian conflict. When Stendhal's characters congratulate themselves on being 'cured'—

'Je suis guéri,' s'écria-t-il après avoir fait quelques pas. 'Mon cœur n'est pas fait pour l'amour. Quoi! C'est là la première entrevue, le premier rendez-vous avec une femme que l'on aime!'

Ces reproches qu'il se faisait étaient sincères, mais il n'en sentait pas moins fort clairement qu'il n'aimait plus Mme de Chasteller. Penser à elle était ennuyeux. . . .

['I'm cured,' he said after walking a few steps. 'My heart isn't made for love. What! That's the first interview, the first rendez-vous with a woman with whom one's in love!'

He was sincere in reproaching himself, but he felt none the less very clearly that he no longer loved Mme de Chasteller. To think about her was boring. . . .]

—they are not celebrating the triumph of reason over passion or, to use Stendhal's own terms, of *logique* over *espagnolisme*. I can think of no other novelist who has described better than Stendhal the neutral moments in a love affair—the moments when the protagonists sud-denly feel nothing—before being caught up by still more violent feel-ings. He carries out to the letter the advice that he gave Mme Gaulthier: 'The poor novelist must try to make us believe in the *burning passion*, but he must never name it.' The subtle lucid prose registers the slightest movement. Its dry sparkle conceals a deliberate assault on our emotions. The last thing Stendhal wanted to do was to minimize the contradictions and inconsistencies of human nature. On the contrary, the continual shift of feeling calls for a continual readjustment on the part of the reader, compelling him to look at a situation from a fresh angle all the time. The movement of feeling is linked to physical movement and the characters are suddenly paralysed by what Corneille called a *surprise des sens*:

> Sans y songer, Lucien restait immobile, à trois pas de Mme de Chasteller, à la place où son regard l'avait surpris.

> [Without thinking what he was doing, Lucien remained motionless, three yards from Mme de Chasteller, on the spot where his eye had discovered her.]

The quiet tone and the neat punctuation make us feel Lucien pinned to the ground and suddenly becoming rigid all over.
Again:

> Leuwen se retourna vers Mme de Chasteller. Il appuya la main droite sur la rampe d'acajou; il chancelait évidemment. Mme de Chasteller eut pitié de lui, elle eut l'idée de lui prendre la main à l'anglaise, en signe de bonne amitié. Leuwen, voyant la main de Mme de Chasteller s'approcher de la sienne, la prit et la porta lentement à ses lèvres. En faisant ce mouvement, sa figure se trouva tout près de celle de Mme de Chasteller; il quitta sa main et la serra dans ses bras, en collant ses lèvres sur sa joue.

> [Leuwen turned towards Mme de Chasteller. He leant his right hand on the mahogany stair rail; he was tottering obviously. Mme de Chasteller was sorry for him, it came into her head to take his hand in the English fashion, as a sign of being good friends. Leuwen, seeing Mme de Chasteller's hand moving towards his own, took hold of it and raised it slowly to his lips. While he was doing this, he found that his face was very close to Mme de Chasteller's; he dropped her hand and folded her in his arms, pressing his lips against her cheek.]

It is a 'close-up', and a close-up in slow motion. We see Lucien turn slowly towards her, clasp the rail and stumble—the casual 'il chancelait évidemment' intensifies the effect—under the violence of his feelings. He notices the hand; an idea comes to him; he takes it and raises it 'slowly'—the adverb is the focal word—to his lips. Then everything goes.
The first volume of the novel comes to an abrupt end. Lucien falls

out with Du Poirier who determines to remove him from Nancy. He contrives by a pantomime, which is worthy of a minor Elizabethan dramatist, to make him think that Mme de Chasteller has had a child by a 'rival'. Lucien is taken in by this clumsy and improbable ruse, abandons the regiment and returns to his parents' home as fast as his horse can carry him.[1]

3

In his second volume Stendhal turns his attention to the political situation in Paris and gives us a remarkable picture of the machinery of government under Louis-Philippe. We are taken right behind the scenes, into the offices and homes of ministers, into the lobbies and the house of parliament and, finally, to the Palace. It is an astonishing chronicle of corruption and intrigue, of shady incidents, 'rigged' elections, and crooked, servile ministers. Neither party nor individuals are spared and even the king is described bitterly as 'le procureur de basse Normandie, qui occupe le trône'.

Lucien's father is naturally dismayed to see his son back with his solemn face, his prim morals, his republican reputation and an unhappy love affair on top of it all:

'What do you want me to be?' asked Lucien with an air of simplicity.
'A rogue,' answered his father, 'I mean a politician. A Martignac—I won't go so far as to say a Talleyrand. At your age and in the papers you read, they call that a *coquin*.'

And a *coquin* Lucien becomes. His father pulls the strings and he is appointed confidential assistant to the Comte de Vaize, Minister of the Interior.[2]

As soon as Stendhal has introduced his 'outsider' into the inner counsels, he gives free rein to his irony. This is the minister:

His Excellency continued in this strain for twenty minutes. During this time Lucien examined him. M. de Vaize was about fifty, tall and quite

---

[1] We can see from one of the many entertaining marginal notes that Stendhal felt that his 'plot' was a little weak. He congratulated himself on not making Mme de Chasteller Lucien's mistress because, as he put it with characteristic pungency, 's'il l'eût enfilée, il eût bien vu qu'elle n'était pas grosse: alors plus de brouille par l'enfant supposé'.

[2] His official title is Maître des Requêtes.

well built. Fine greying hair, very regular features and a head carried high predisposed people in his favour. But this impression did not last. A second glance revealed a low forehead covered with wrinkles and excluding all idea of thought. Lucien was thoroughly surprised and annoyed to find that the great administrator's appearance was more than common, that he looked like a valet. He had long arms and did not know what to do with them; and, what was worse, Lucien thought he detected that His Excellency was trying to give himself imposing airs. He spoke too loudly and listened to himself talking.

His Excellency continued:
'You know that we have the good fortune to live under five police forces. . . .'

It is not simply the portrait of a French politician who lived a hundred years ago. Stendhal has immortalized the typical cabinet minister who turns up again and again in the governments of all countries—stupid, futile, harassed and dishonest:

'Now, my friend,' added the minister, lowering his voice, 'the report of the Kortis affair, which was categorically denied in our papers yesterday morning, is only too true. . . .'

The Comte de Vaize is weak and vacillating, torn between the burden of the affairs of State and his anxiety to make money on the Stock Exchange which gives Lucien's father his hold over him.

Although Lucien appears to have compromised again by becoming a model public servant, he remains at heart an outsider—tormented by his position and still very much in love with Bathilde:

Le voilà qui souffre de son absurdité [observes one of his friends]: il prétend réunir les profits du ministériel avec la susceptibilité de l'homme d'honneur.

[Look at him upset by his absurdity: he thinks he can combine ministerial rewards with the susceptibility of a man of honour.]

M. Leuwen is far from being satisfied. The rumours of Lucien's republican sympathies persist; he is nearly involved in a duel with the Foreign Minister who has wounded his *susceptibilité délicate* and he is quite hopeless with the *demoiselles de l'Opéra*.

'Il est capital de te laver de la calomnie qui t'impute d'être saint-simonien [remarks M. Leuwen]. Ton air sérieux, et même imposant, peut lui donner cours.'

'Rien de plus simple: un bon coup d'épée. . . .'

'Oui, pour te donner la réputation de duelliste, presque aussi triste! Je t'en prie, plus de duel sous aucun prétexte.'

'Et que faut-il donc?'

'Un amour célèbre.'

Lucien pâlit.

'Rien de moins,' continua son père, 'il faut séduire Mme Grandet. . . .'

['It's of capital importance to put a stop to the slander which accuses you of being a Saint-Simonian. Your serious and even imposing expression helps to give it currency.'

'Nothing could be simpler: a good sword thrust. . . .'

'Yes, to give you a reputation as a duellist which is almost as bad! For heaven's sake, no more duels on any account.'

'What's needed then?'

'A celebrated love affair.'

Lucien turned pale.

'Nothing less,' his father went on, 'you must seduce Mme Grandet. . . .']

Lucien is genuinely fond of his father and is distressed to find that somehow there is a 'chasm' between them. The explanation is not difficult. M. Leuwen is the prototype of Mosca in the *Chartreuse de Parme*. He possesses immense ability and has no illusions about politicians, but he has compromised simply in order to have an amusing life. He does not possess the fundamental integrity of the 'outsider' which survives all the superficial changes of allegiance. Nor is that all. At bottom he is cynical and cynicism is instinctively felt to be the enemy of 'sensibility':

Tout ce qui, à tort ou à raison, paraissait sublime, généreux, tendre à Lucien, toutes les choses desquelles il pensait qu'il était noble de mourir pour elles, ou beau de vivre avec elles, étaient des sujets de bonne plaisanterie pour son père et une duperie à ses yeux.

[Everything which, rightly or wrongly, appeared sublime, generous, tender to Lucien, all the things for which he thought that it would be noble to die or with which he thought it would be fine to live, were subjects of good jokes for his father and a fraud in his eyes.]

When Stendhal adds:

Ils n'étaient peut-être d'accord que sur un seul sentiment: l'amitié intime consolidée par trente ans d'épreuves

[They were perhaps only in agreement on a single feeling: an intimate friendship strengthened by thirty years' trials]

he introduces a theme which is common to nearly all his novels. On the surface his characters appear to differ considerably, but at bottom there is an unbreakable link between them—the *amitié intime*—the belief in 'personal relationships' which is their supreme 'value' in a world of dissolving values and makes them the same sort of people.

Although Lucien is outwardly a *coquin* who serves his new masters loyally, he does so with an interior detachment. Like Fabrice he preserves the same strange innocence. He is not really involved in the political game and he is not contaminated by it.[1]

A large part of the second volume is devoted to the account of the two by-elections at Blois and Caen in which Lucien acts as the Government agent. He is mobbed by the crowd at Blois and has a violent quarrel with the Prefect at Caen who resents the Government's interference in his province:

'You will have money to distribute on the banks of the Loire [says Lucien's minister before he sets out] and, what is more, three tobacconists' shops. I think there are even two postmasters' jobs going. The Finance Minister hasn't replied to me yet on this point, but I'll send you a telegram. Moreover, you can dismiss practically anyone you like. . . .'

We see exactly how Louis-Philippe's minions go about their work with threats and bribes. There are lists of people who are to lose their jobs if they fail to support the Government and lists of those who are to be rewarded if they do. It is no use; the people are not deceived and, in spite of the intrigues and the buying and selling of votes, the Government candidate is beaten. It is not modesty which makes Lucien remove his name from the Minister's list of *gratifications* and substitute the name of his assistant whom he had rescued from a debtor's prison: it is the symbol of his inner detachment, the memory of the mud thrown at him at Blois and a determination not to lose his innocence. This is the final biting comment:

[1] 'Le matin avec des voleurs, et le soir avec des catins,' se disait-il amèrement.

Huit jours après, M. Coffe était sous-chef aux Finances avec six mille francs d'appointments et la condition expresse de ne jamais paraître au ministère.

[A week later M. Coffe was deputy chief-clerk at the Treasury with a salary of six thousand francs on the express condition never to show himself at the Ministry.]

The last part of the book is dominated not by Lucien but by M. Leuwen. It is curious to note that in his own way he plays the same role as Fabrice. His aim is to disrupt the whole political machine as Fabrice disrupts the political machine of Parma. M. Leuwen, more successful than his son, has managed to win a by-election by a very narrow majority in a rural constituency at Aveyron. It is a good thing for a republic, Stendhal once observed, to have in it *un esprit hargneux et inquiet*. They are not, perhaps, the adjectives which best describe the temper of the *homme de plaisir*, but they explain his role. He knows exactly what he is going to do. He is delighted at the chance of embarrassing the government out of a spirit of pure mischief, but he also intends to punish M. de Vaize for his treatment of his son. If he has to bring the Government down in the attempt to get rid of de Vaize, so much the better! The Comte de Vaize is astute enough to appreciate his qualities even though he does not like them:

'I see the argument on which his insolence is based,' said M. de Vaize to himself as he paced up and down his room with long strides. 'The king's decree makes a minister, but a decree cannot make a man like M. Leuwen. That's what we come to when the Government only leaves us in a post for a year or two. Would a banker have refused to call and see Colbert? . . .'

'Couldn't I do without this insolent person? But his integrity is famous, almost as famous as his malice. He's a pleasure-lover, a *bon viveur*, who for twenty years has jeered at everything respectable—the King, religion. . . . He's the Talleyrand of the Stock Exchange; his epigrams are the law of that world and since the July rising, *that world* has drawn closer every day to the great world. The people with money are on the spot and replace the great families of the Faubourg St. Germain. . . .'

He [M. de Vaize] combined a keen love of gain with the fantastic idea that the public believed that his integrity was unblemished. His main reason was that he had succeeded a thief in his present office.

Stendhal refers here to a change of great importance. The French Revolution was an attempt by the people to wrest power from the nobility. It did indeed break the nobility, but it did not give France a democratic régime. It led by devious ways to the emergence of the professional politician—M. de Vaize is an example—and to fresh forms of oppression. The July Revolution may have appeared to be a popular uprising, but it was the moment at which real power passed from the Government to the Stock Exchange and the banks. That is why later in the book M. Leuwen will reflect with satisfaction on the impregnability of the 'big bank'. In Stendhal's France ability alone is useless; but ability backed by wealth carries all before it.

M. Leuwen sets to work to form a little party of his own among the members of parliament and calls it the Légion du Midi. He grooms, feeds, clothes and drills the members, obtains 'eight little posts' from a friendly minister for their families, secures invitations to dinner at the Palace for them and the promise of a decoration:

> M. Leuwen had chosen the twenty members who were most completely without friends and connections, who were the most taken aback by their stay in Paris and who were the dullest witted, in order to explain this theory to them and invite them to dinner. They were almost all from the Midi. . . .

This is the 'theory':

> 'We are twenty friends. Very well. Each of us must think like the majority. . . . I shall always sacrifice my opinion to that of the majority of my friends because after all four eyes see better than two. . . . If, as I hope, we are twenty and eleven vote *for* a measure, the other nine must absolutely vote *for* it too even if they are passionately *against* it. That's the secret of our strength.'

We can see already where the argument is leading. M. Leuwen's 'theory' rests on the democratic view that 'four eyes see better than two', that the majority is always right. It can only succeed if the majority possesses a certain degree of common sense. Now it is precisely this that is lacking in the Légion du Midi and by implication in all political parties.

After dinner M. Leuwen's followers are carefully rehearsed for their performance in the House on the following day:

> . . . M. Leuwen made them deliberate. True to their instinct, out of the twenty-nine present, nineteen were in favour of the absurd side of the question. Next day M. Leuwen mounted the rostrum and the absurd side

was carried in the House by a majority of eight. The following day fresh diatribes in the Press against the Légion du Midi.

After this success, M. Leuwen spent a week in bed. A day's rest would have been sufficient, but he knew his country where, compared with merit, charlatanism is like a nought on the right-hand side of a figure and makes it ten times bigger.

Stendhal's most mischievous epigrams pour out. We are told that

M. Leuwen's speeches did not merit the name. They were not elevated, did not pretend to be solemn. They were simply quick, spicy social chatter, and he never indulged in parliamentary paraphrases.

Nevertheless, confusion reigns in the House. However reasonable the Government's proposals, there is often a majority for an absurd counter-proposal put up by M. Leuwen. The ministers bicker and squabble in private. The King intervenes. The Government rocks— and M. Leuwen has a waiting-list for his party! It is impossible to do justice to this part of the book in a short summary—it should be translated and made compulsory reading for all politicians. It is at once uproariously funny and immensely subversive. For the formation of M. Leuwen's little party and the theory of voting with the majority is the *reductio ad absurdum* of party politics and strikes at the heart of the political game. It will be seen that he makes no attempt to coerce his followers or to influence them in favour of a particular view. He knows that naturally and 'true to their instinct' they will vote for 'the absurd side of the question'. It seems childishly simple, but it was his great discovery. Opposition parties had brought governments down by proposing more reasonable, or apparently more reasonable solutions of political problems, but there was something new in the idea of bringing a government down by suggesting measures which were more idiotic than anything that even the ministers of the Crown could think of.

It sounds like comic opera politics, but Stendhal's criticism was extraordinarily acute and entirely serious; and in this, as in other ways, he was nearly a hundred years ahead of his time. M. Leuwen could not carry his policy to its logical conclusion, turn the Légion du Midi into a national party and 'go to the country' because even in the France of Louis-Philippe there was still some sort of reasonable political tradition *and there was no universal suffrage*. The absence of universal suffrage naturally meant that there was no chance of a parliamentary majority for the party which sponsored the silliest policy which anyone could

devise. All that has been changed by the advent of universal suffrage
and to-day there is nothing at all unusual in the spectacle of 'the absurd
side of the question' being carried not by a few votes (as it is in
Stendhal's novel) but by a vast, docile majority. Can one wonder if 'the
happy few'—the people who revolt against rigid political divisions
and find all existing parties excessively unsympathetic—regard M.
Leuwen with undisguised admiration and this novel as their political
breviary?

M. Leuwen's success far exceeds his hopes. All Paris realizes that
when the Government falls M. Leuwen will be able to make himself or
his friends ministers. The Comtesse de Vaize is in despair. 'You are
going to bring us down,' she says to Lucien, 'but you don't know what
to put in our place.'

She is wrong. 'You must have an *amour célèbre*,' M. Leuwen had said
to his son. 'You must seduce Mme Grandet.' Yet even he is surprised
when he learns that M. Grandet is hoping for a portfolio. 'I did not
think', he remarks, 'that the House would sink lower than the Comte
de Vaize.' But he is ready to play, and when Mme Grandet asks him
to call on her to discuss the matter he goes at once.

The scene in which he tells the beautiful and hitherto virtuous Mme
Grandet that her husband shall have the portfolio provided that she
admits his son to her bed is one of the most delightful and amusing in
the book. It also contains some shrewd criticism of the new situation
created by the July Revolution which emphasizes the similarity between M. Leuwen and Mosca:

> M. Grandet is like myself at the head of the bank and since July the bank
> is at the head of the State. The bourgeoisie has replaced the Faubourg St.
> Germain, and the bank is the nobility of the bourgeois class. Through
> imagining that men were angels, M. Laffitte was instrumental in his class
> losing office. The big bank is called by circumstances to recover its empire
> and return to office either itself or by its friends. . . . The House does not
> care for reasons and the king cares only for money. He needs plenty of
> soldiers to hold down the workers and the republicans. The Government
> has every interest in placating the Stock Exchange. A ministry can't bring
> down the Stock Exchange and the Stock Exchange can bring down a
> ministry.

The chapter follows its sutble sinuous argument. It is a model of
diplomatic tact on both sides. M. Grandet is a notoriously stupid man.
'His views are very sound,' observes M. Leuwen, 'but since you allow

me to speak as a friend, I must confess that without you I should never
have thought of M. Grandet.' 'I should be deeply grieved to hurt the
delicacy which belongs to your sex, but Mme de Chevreuse, the
Duchesse de Longueville, all the women whose names have become
famous in history or, more important, who established the fortunes of
their families, sometimes had a talk with their doctors. Very well, I am
a doctor of souls. . . .' The famous banker proceeds to barter the hypo-
thetical portfolio against her virtue which is discreetly called her
'stake'.[1]
A few days later:

> 'So I'm a happy man,' thought Lucien as he got into his carriage. He
> had not gone a hundred yards before he stopped. 'So I'm really a happy
> man', he said to himself, as he made his servant take the driver's seat. 'So
> that's all it is, the happiness that the world has to give? My father's going
> to form a ministry. He's got the best job in the House and the most bril-
> liant woman in Paris appears to yield to my pretended passion. . . .'

His reactions are identical with those of the fallen Lamiel and of
Julien after his first night with Mme de Rênal. He, too, is somehow
unsatisfied:

> Lucien's real character had not yet appeared. That is strange at the age
> of twenty-four. Beneath an exterior which possessed something singular
> and perfectly noble, his character was naturally gay and carefree. . . . His
> mind admired the vivacity and grace of Mlle Raimonde, but he only
> thought about her when he wanted to kill what was noblest in him.
> 'I am forgetting to live,' he said to himself. 'The follies of ambition
> distract me from the only thing in the world which is real to me. It's odd
> to sacrifice one's heart to ambition and yet not to be ambitious.'

M. Leuwen has a harder task than his son realizes. 'That man of yours
is nothing but a fool!' says the minister to whom he has presented M.
Grandet as a candidate for office. The dénouement is remarkable. Mme
Grandet falls violently in love with Lucien. Then M. Leuwen makes his
great mistake. He tells his son about the deal. Lucien's sexual vanity is
mortally wounded. 'I shall never have any success,' he reflects. 'If I do
it will . . . only be through what is vulgarly known as *la contagion de
l'amour*. I'm too ignorant to seduce anyone, even a tart.' Mme Grandet
is instantly dropped. There is an appalling scene at Lucien's ministry

[1] 'Moralité: les femmes honnêtes comme Mme Grandet ne sont que des catins qui
ne sont pas encore vendues, faute de *prix battant*.' (Author's marginal note.)

where Mme Grandet swoons through the violence of her feelings and then . . . And then, very suddenly, M. Leuwen dies.

He was not so wealthy as everybody thought. The staff of the house of Van Peters, Leuwen et Compagnie advise Lucien to go bankrupt in order to save sufficient money for his mother to keep her carriage and live comfortably. He refuses and insists on paying the creditors in full. There remains enough money to provide his mother with a small income and he is given a post at the French Embassy in Madrid. At this point the novel breaks off. We know from Stendhal's notes that there was to have been a reunion with Mme de Chasteller and something we do not find in any of the other novels—'a happy ending'.

'*Le Rouge et le noir*', writes M. Maurice Bardèche, 'shows us the political mechanism seen from below and from outside. We only perceive the results of its workings. *Lucien Leuwen* places the observer inside the political machinery; it is a conducted tour of the political works: but the complete political vision is lacking—we are too close. . . . With *La Chartreuse de Parme* we are above the spectacle; we have a sort of dizzy downward view which is total and terrifying. At Parma one *governs*.'[1]

It is an illuminating account of the different ways in which Stendhal approached the political theme. M. Bardèche seems to me to be very wide of the mark when he suggests, in another place, that *Lucien Leuwen* is a 'documentary', but he is surely right in saying that it does not possess 'the complete political vision' of the *Chartreuse de Parme*. When we compare *Lucien Leuwen* with the *Chartreuse*, we are not merely applying the highest possible standard, we are admitting that only Stendhal himself could provide a standard at all. *Lucien Leuwen* may not possess 'the complete political vision', but that it is a very great political novel we cannot doubt.

[1] *Stendhal romancier* (Paris, 1947), p. 417.

V. *LA CHARTREUSE DE PARME*

I

'Le vrai métier de l'animal', said Stendhal in a letter that he wrote to his cousin, Romain Colomb, in 1835, 'est d'écrire un roman dans un grenier, car je préfère le plaisir d'écrire des folies à celui de porter un habit brodé qui coûte 800 francs.' He was bored to death with his consulate at Civita-Vecchia. He did a great deal of writing there, but he never seemed to be able to finish anything and he badly wanted some more leave. The following year the leave was granted. He hurriedly packed his manuscripts and set out for Paris. This time he was lucky. Thanks to the good offices of his friend, Comte Molé, who had become a minister of the Crown, his leave lasted for over three years. He seems to have enjoyed himself. He saw old friends, dined at the Café Anglais or the Rocher de Cancale, went to the theatre, travelled widely in France, published the *Mémoires d'un touriste*, and only returned to Civita-Vecchia when his protector lost his portfolio.

He began to write the *Chartreuse de Parme* on 4 November 1838, and finished it on 26 December of the same year. It is an astonishing feat in which he seems to have surpassed Balzac on his own ground; but his motives and method were very different. He did not write in order to earn money or to keep importunate creditors at bay. Into this book he distilled the wisdom and experience of a lifetime. It was because he was a great master who knew exactly what he wanted to do that he was able to write the whole novel in less than eight weeks.[1]

Stendhal did not invent the 'plot' of the *Chartreuse de Parme* any more than he had invented the plots of *Le Rouge et le noir* and *Lucien Leuwen*. About 1833-4 he had discovered a collection of Italian chronicles belonging to the sixteenth and seventeenth centuries. He had been greatly impressed by these accounts of Italian life at the Renaissance and had drawn on them heavily for his own *Chroniques italiennes* which, after appearing in French reviews, were published in book form in 1839. One of the Italian *novelle* called the *Origine delle*

---

[1] There is one reservation to be made. He apparently intended to write a third volume dealing with Fabrice's life in the charterhouse, but was prevented from doing so by his publisher who insisted on his keeping the novel as short as possible.

grandezze della famiglia Farnese had given him particular pleasure. He proceeded in the manner of Shakespeare to borrow from it some of the principal characters and incidents for the *Chartreuse de Parme*; but like Shakespeare he transformed his material into something which was his own.

Scholars have spent a great deal of time discussing Stendhal's 'plagiarisms' and trying to decide whether the characters in the *Chartreuse de Parme* are Frenchmen or Italians. Croce declares that in this book we only see 'the Italy of Stendhal'. Mr. Josephson thinks that he may have overlooked the extent to which even in the 1820's Italy had become industrialized. He goes on to suggest that he 'reverses the procedure of Walter Scott' and that 'instead of writing really of modern people dressed in antique costumes, he writes of sixteenth-century characters and events as they appeared in his own time'.[1] It is difficult to resist the feeling that these observations are beside the point. Stendhal made no attempt to write an 'historical novel' or to give a 'realistic' picture of contemporary Italy. He simply used his material to convey a particular experience to the reader.

Although Stendhal's novels are all criticisms of the social-political scene as he knew it, he criticized it in different ways and at different levels. *Lucien Leuwen* is the only one in which he consistently relied on direct comment. This no doubt accounts for the impression that we are 'too close' to the political machine and that 'the complete political vision is lacking'; but it must be remembered that the book occupies a central position in Stendhal's *œuvre*. Without it, there would be a gap in his survey of the political scene; and I for one find it so fascinating that I cannot wish it different. It remains true, however, that as a rule Stendhal preferred the indirect approach. In his first novel, *Armance*, Octave de Malivert's sexual impotence is a symbol of the impotence of the ruling class. In spite of M. Gide's praise, the novel seems to me to be a failure because the principal character will not bear the weight of the symbolism attached to him and simply strikes the reader as a Romantic outcast who belongs to the same family as René and Obermann. But the method used in Stendhal's two greatest novels is a development of the one used in *Armance*. In *Le Rouge et le noir*, a peasant brooding over *Le Mémorial de Sainte-Hélène* in a remote corner of France suggests an embattled Europe and the distant tramp of marching armies. An angry father knocks the book into the mill stream and plop, as it strikes the water, is the faint echo of a falling empire and of a head falling on the guillotine. A citadel soaring above a miniature state marks the change from war to diplomacy, evokes the Europe of the

[1] *Op. cit.*, p. 420.

Holy Alliance and of a peace which is founded on the ruins of a liberalism whose representatives languish in the dungeons of the stately edifice.

Stendhal's use of a tiny stage, which only shows a small corner of society, has immense advantages. It enables him to study the individual characters with minute care and, at the same time, to reveal the significance of a drama which is being played out on a huge stage, to evoke the whole of contemporary Europe. It was the method used by Shakespeare in *Antony and Cleopatra*, where we are aware of a vast empire stretching out behind the characters who are the actors not in a small domestic tragedy, but in a world-drama and hold the fate of empires in their hands. I do not think that it is unduly fanciful to see resemblances between Shakespeare's Egypt and Stendhal's Parma which gives the same impression of vastness and depth that he so much admired in the sixteenth century.

The *Chartreuse de Parme* is not simply a political novel; it is one of the greatest of all political novels because the author was triumphantly successful in dissolving his politics into his novel. His refusal to paint a realistic picture of contemporary Italy and the deliberate creation of a state which appears, superficially, to be an anachronism were far from being a disadvantage. They enabled him to approach the political scene with a greater degree of detachment than in any of his other books, to give us the 'dizzy downward view' of it which makes his criticism so extraordinarily subtle. He turned from the French political game to an imaginary state where, by a process of selection and rearrangement, he was able to ridicule all the current political attitudes and slogans. The care with which the characters are subordinated to the main plan gives the novel its symmetry. Not the least important thing about his Parma is its *compactness*. We have the impression that we are looking at the world in a microcosm; the Europe of the post-Napoleonic era is reflected in the constantly changing colours of a bubble.

It is a brilliantly comic presentation of a miniature police state with its ridiculous, nervous dictator, his astute prime minister, the monstrous minister of justice, the time-serving governor of the Citadel haunted by nightmares of escaping prisoners, the brilliant duchess, the timid archbishop, the heir-apparent who cares only for mineralogy, the reactionary marquis professing 'une haine vigoureuse pour les lumières' and the sinister chorus with their grotesque names—Gonzo, Barbone, Grillo and Giletti. We see, too, the whole hierarchy of the duchy: the prince, the nobility, the courtiers, the bourgeois and the *peuple*, and their intricate relations with one another.

Stendhal's presentation of party politics provides an amusing comment on his time. Parma is divided between ultras and liberals who are engaged in incredible intrigues and fratricidal strife. Yet it is clear that a change of government would mean little more than a change of personalities, would be no more than a change 'inside the whale'. The liberals pay lip-service to freedom, but it is difficult to see any difference between their policy and the policy of the ultras who are in power. The only effective 'liberal' is a political outlaw who plies his trade as a highway robber—carefully keeping a note of the sums he 'borrows' from the rich—and who assassinates the prince and disappears discreetly into exile after an abortive revolution. The official head of the Liberal Party is the governor of the Citadel; but the Citadel is full of liberals who are imprisoned in cages which are too small for them to stand upright or even to lie down in comfort and which are the invention of the liberal governor who purchases in this way a weekly audience with his sovereign. When they learn that their tormentor has recovered from a supposed attempt to poison him, the prisoners subscribe to have a *Te Deum* sung in the chapel. Such is the weakness of human nature, remarks the novelist.

The details are filled in with a series of effortless touches. They float up to us, casually, in snatches of conversation overheard among the different characters:

> . . . Parme . . . ce pays de mesures secrètes [où] tout ce qui n'est pas noble ou dévot est en prison, ou fait ses paquets pour y entrer.
> . . . ce fameux prince de Parme, Ernest IV, si célèbre par ses sévérités, que les liberaux de Milan appelaient des cruautés.
>
> Or, entre autres idées enfantines, le prince prétend avoir un ministère *moral*.

> [. . . Parma . . . this land of secret measures [where] everyone who is not nobly born or devout is in prison, or is packing his bags ready to go there.
> . . . this famous Prince of Parma, Ernest IV, so famous for his severity which the Liberals of Milan called cruelty.
>
> Now, among other childish ideas, the prince claims to have a *moral* government.][1]

When Mosca shoots down sixty-odd people in the crowd who tried

---

[1] In his translation of the *Chartreuse de Parme*, Scott Moncrieff Italianized the Christian names and most of the titles. This seems to me to emphasize the Italian setting in a way that Stendhal had refrained from doing. I have therefore ventured to substitute the French Christian names and the English forms of titles in the quotations from Scott Moncrieff's translation used here.

to attack the statue of the prince in the uprising which follows his assassination, he remarks to his mistress:

Ils se portent fort bien, seulement ils sont en voyage. Le comte Zurla, ministre de l'intérieur, est allé lui-même à la demeure de chacun de ces héros malheureux, et a remis quinze sequins à leurs familles ou à leurs amis, avec ordre de dire que le défunt était en voyage, et menace très expresse de la prison, si l'on s'avisait de faire entendre qu'il avait été tué.

[They are in the best of health, only they are travelling abroad. Count Zurla, the Minister of the Interior, has gone in person to the house of each of these unfortunate heroes, and has handed fifteen sequins to his family or his friends, with the order to say that the deceased is abroad, and a very definite threat of imprisonment should they let it be understood that he is dead.]

Stendhal does not spare the values by which his characters live. 'Remarquez', says Mosca to the Duchess, when they are discussing Fabrice's career

. . . que je ne prétends pas faire de Fabrice un prêtre exemplaire comme vous en voyez tant. Non; c'est un grand seigneur avant tout; il pourra rester parfaitement ignorant si bon lui semble, et n'en deviendra pas moins évêque et archevêque, si le prince continue à me regarder comme un homme utile.

Crois ou ne crois pas à ce qu'on t'enseignera [says the Duchess to Fabrice] *mais ne fais jamais aucune objection.* Figure-toi qu'on t'enseigne les règles du jeu de whist; est-ce que tu ferais des objections aux règles du whist?

[Observe . . . that I do not pretend to turn Fabrice into an exemplary priest, like so many that you see. No, he is a great gentleman, first and foremost; he can remain perfectly ignorant if it seems good to him, and will none the less become Bishop and Archbishop, if the Prince continues to regard me as a useful person.

Believe or not, as you choose, what they teach you, *but never raise any objection.* Imagine that they are teaching you the rules of the game of whist; would you raise any objection to the rules of whist?]

When Fabrice is imprisoned for killing Giletti, everyone takes it for granted that he is guilty; but Clélia speaks for all his friends when she observes:

Qu'importe, après tout, qu'un homme de la naissance de Fabrice soit plus ou moins accusé d'avoir tué lui-même, et l'épée au poing, un histrion tel que Giletti.

[What does it matter, after all, that a man of Fabrice's birth should be more or less accused of having himself, sword in hand, killed an actor like Giletti?]

These passages are a perfect illustration of the view that Stendhal's strength was in a large measure an eighteenth-century strength. We know that he detested Voltaire's writings and his irony has nothing in common with the flashy vulgarity of *Candide*. It is a modification of what was best in the eighteenth century. His attitude is urbane, civilized and detached; and it gives the book its extraordinary poise and maturity. The passages are taken from different parts of the novel and they help to give it its particular resonance. Yet this irony is only one element in Stendhal's attitude, and its effectiveness depends to a considerable degree on being blended with a vein of poetry which also permeates the whole novel.

2

The novel opens with the arrival of Napoleon's armies in Italy and a picture of the country unfolds before us like a panorama:

Le 15 mai 1796, le général Bonaparte fit son entrée dans Milan à la tête de cette jeune armée qui venait de passer le pont de Lodi, et d'apprendre au monde qu'après tant de siècles César et Alexandre avaient un successeur.

[On the 15th of May, 1796, General Bonaparte made his entry into Milan at the head of that young army which had shortly before crossed the Bridge of Lodi and taught the world that after all these centuries Cæsar and Alexander had a successor.]

One critic has suggested that the first five chapters are a mock-heroic introduction, but this is perhaps a simplification. The novel derives its admirable poise in part from the constant variation of tone, and it is only by studying the tone of almost every sentence in the first chapter that we see how the book as a whole must be read. What is striking in this sentence is the mixture of levity and seriousness. Stendhal never lost his youthful admiration for Napoleon, but Napoleon's irruption into Italy is nevertheless the first episode in what is essentially a great comic novel. The attitude which informs his work is very different from that of the other great nineteenth-century novelists. The *Chartreuse de Parme* is a study of tragic individuals who find themselves in comic situations, and this explains the mixture of levity and seriousness.

Les miracles de hardiesse et de génie [he goes on] dont l'Italie fut témoin en quelques mois réveillèrent un peuple endormi. . . . Au moyen âge, les Milanais étaient braves comme les Français de la révolution, et méritèrent de voir leur ville entièrement rasée par les empereurs d'Allemagne. Depuis qu'ils étaient devenus de *fidèles sujets*, leur grande affaire était d'imprimer des sonnets sur de petits mouchoirs de taffetas rose quand arrivait le mariage d'une jeune fille appartenant à quelque famille noble ou riche. . . . Il y avait loin de ces mœurs efféminées aux émotions profondes que donna l'arrivée imprévue de l'armée française.

[The miracles of gallantry and genius of which Italy was a witness in the space of a few months aroused a slumbering people. . . . In the middle ages the Republicans of Lombardy had given proof of a valour equal to that of the French, and had deserved to see their city rased to the ground by the German Emperors. Since they had become *loyal subjects*, their great occupation was the printing of sonnets upon handkerchiefs of rose-coloured taffeta whenever the marriage occurred of a young lady belonging to some rich or noble family. . . . It was a far cry from these effeminate ways to the profound emotions aroused by the unexpected arrival of the French army.]

In this first chapter Stendhal is continually switching from positive to negative, from images of vitality to images of exhaustion and collapse. There is genuine feeling in his references to the heroic exploits of the French, and in the contrast between the Milanese of the Middle Ages and their successors in the eighteenth century. The arrival of the French appealed enormously to the martial Stendhal and provided the shock which set in motion the passions—the serious passions—that he studies in the comic setting. The *mouchoirs de taffetas rose* stand for the triviality of the Milanese and are an allusion to the miniature despotism. For the novel sometimes reminds one of a story told in coloured pictures on a handkerchief.

In a suggestive comment, Mr. Levin compares the *Chartreuse de Parme* to a comic opera, and points out that the dialogue between Fabrice and Clélia in the Citadel is 'recitative' and the reading of La

Fontaine's Fable towards the end of the book is a 'trio'. The analogy is a just one, but the book is more carefully orchestrated than he perhaps allows. The operatic motif runs all through it. It can be seen in the constant repetition of comments and scraps of gossip in which the characters echo one another's thoughts and words. Two of the most impressive examples are the scene between the Duchess and Ludovic before the opening of the reservoirs and the great *scène de jalousie* where the 'recitative' is transported inside Mosca's mind:

> ... elle l'aime comme un fils depuis quinze ans. Là gît tout mon espoir: *comme un fils* ... mais elle a cessé de le voir depuis sa fuite pour Waterloo; mais en revenant de Naples, surtout pour elle, c'est un autre homme. *Un autre homme!* répéta-t-il avec rage, et cet homme est charmant. ...

> [... she has loved him like a son for fifteen years. There lies all my hope: *like a son* ... but she had ceased to see him after his dash to Waterloo; now, on his return from Naples, especially for her, he is a different man. *A different man!* he repeated with fury, and that man is charming. ...]

The repetition reminds us of Molière's repetition of the words, *Le pauvre homme!* and *Sans dot!* in two famous scenes from *Tartuffe* and *L'Avare*; but the Count's obsession is nearer to tragedy than to comedy. The effect is heightened by the dumb show which follows:

> Il devenait fou; il lui sembla qu'en se penchant ils se donnaient des baisers, là, sous ses yeux. Cela est impossible en ma présence, se dit-il; ma raison s'égare.

> [He became quite mad; it seemed to him that, as they leaned their heads together, they were kissing each other, there, before his eyes. That is impossible in my presence, he told himself; my wits have gone astray.]

When Stendhal writes 'Ces soldats français riaient et chantaient toute la journée ...' and goes on to describe their efforts to learn the Italian dances, we can see that the opening chapter is also the opening scene of a comic opera with an immense chorus singing and dancing; but in the description of Napoleon's second entry into Milan after Marengo, the chorus suddenly changes into a *danse macabre*:

> Leurs figures pâles, leurs grands yeux étonnés, leurs membres amaigris, faisaient un étrange contraste avec la joie qui éclatait de toutes parts.

[Their pale faces, their great startled eyes, their shrunken limbs were in strange contrast to the joy that broke out on every side.]

In another place he strikes a burlesque note:

En 1796, l'armée milanaise se composait de vingt-quatre faquins habillés de rouge, lesquels gardaient la ville de concert avec quatre magnifiques régiments hongrois. La licence des mœurs était extrême, mais les passions fort rares.

[In 1796, the Milanese army was composed of four and twenty rapscallions dressed in scarlet, who guarded the town with the assistance of four magnificent regiments of Hungarian grenadiers. Freedom of morals was extreme, but passion very rare.]

The 'vingt-quatre faquins habillés de rouge' who, incongruously, form the front line defence of a great city are not, as they at first appear, comic opera soldiers. They are painted wooden soldiers, marionettes who might have come from an animated cartoon, marching jerkily up and down. There is a serious intention behind the parody. The 'four magnificent regiments of Hungarian grenadiers' are the symbol of an effete order—an order that is hollow and empty like the wooden soldiers —and the absence of passion is a sign of decadence. For in this book Stendhal sees life simultaneously under two aspects; he is at pains to emphasize the contrast between the elegant exterior and the inner moral decay, and the theme recurs all through the novel.

The dummy soldiers are followed at once by another sort of dummy —dummy 'dictator'. 'The Archduke,' we are told, 'who lived at Milan and governed in the name of the Emperor had the lucrative idea of entering the grain trade. In consequence, the peasants were forbidden to sell their corn until his Highness's granaries were full.' A young painter of miniatures named Gros arrives with the armies and hears the story. While sitting in a café, he does a cartoon of a fat archduke being bayoneted by a French soldier:

. . . au lieu de sang, il en sortait une quantité de blé incroyable. La chose nommée plaisanterie ou caricature n'était pas connue en ce pays de despotisme cauteleux.

[. . . instead of blood there gushed out an incredible quantity of corn. What we call a lampoon or caricature was unknown in this land of crafty despotism.]

The heroic monarchs of the past have been replaced by the petty dictator who is engaged in bourgeois commerce. The word 'miniature' reminds us that the despot is a miniature despot. For the effectiveness of Stendhal's criticism depends very largely on the fact that the *political* figures, but not the other characters in the book, are slightly less than life-size. In the caricature the fat archduke becomes a completely burlesque figure with grain pouring out of his belly, but the absence of 'blood' also emphasizes his inhumanity and his corruption. The last sentence but one draws attention to the humourlessness—the dangerous humourlessness—of the tyrant. The cartoonist, too, has a special significance. He has struck the first blow at despotism and laughter, which is unknown in his domains, is a more serious threat to his position than the bayonet which pricks the bubble. The passage looks forward to the strange figure of Ferrante Palla. For it is another 'artist' —a poet this time—who under the guidance of the duchess will explode the despotism from within.

The caricature of the Archduke reminds us of a crude portrait of a clown on the hoardings outside a music hall, and it prepares us for the 'personal appearance' of Ranuce-Ernest IV. We meet him in his study dressed not in uniform, but in the frock coat of a citizen-king. Over his desk hangs a portrait of Louis XIV—the despot on the grand scale— which provides the proper comment on his antics:

> Évidemment il cherchait le regard et la parole noble de Louis XIV, te il s'appuyait sur la table de *Scagliola*, de façon à se donner la tournure de Joseph II. . . . La duchesse trouva qu'en de certains moments l'imitation de Louis XIV était un peu trop marquée chez le prince; par exemple, dans sa façon de sourire avec bonté tout en renversant la tête.

> [Evidently he sought to copy the gaze and the noble utterance of Louis XIV, and he leaned upon the Scagliola table so as to give himself the pose of Joseph II. . . . The Duchesse found that at certain moments the imitation of Louis XIV was a little too strongly marked in the Prince; for instance, in his way of smiling good-naturedly and throwing back his head.]

Stendhal's irony is a process of inflation and deflation. His pompous little dictator swells with pride and importance as he struts up and down his study, but all the time he is wondering what people are saying about him and whether they are laughing at him. Then, suddenly, we overhear the damaging story which is recounted with polite laughter behind locked doors and which makes the prince a figure of fun to his loyal subjects:

H

Mais dans un moment d'ennui et de colère, et aussi un peu pour imiter Louis XIV faisant couper la tête à je ne sais quel heros de la Fronde que l'on découvrit vivant tranquillement et isolemment dans une terre à côté de Versailles, cinquante ans après la Fronde, Ernest IV a fait pendre un jour deux libéraux. . . . Croiriez-vous que le prince regarde sous les lits de son appartement avant de se coucher, et dépense un million, ce qui à Parme est comme quatre millions à Milan, pour avoir une bonne police, et vous voyez devant vous, madame la duchesse, le chef de cette terrible police.

[But in a moment of boredom and anger, and also a little in imitation of Louis XIV cutting off the head of some hero or other of the Fronde, who was discovered living in peaceful solitude on a plot of land near Versailles, fifty years after the Fronde, one fine day Ernest IV had two Liberals hanged. . . . Would you believe that the Prince looks under the beds in his room before going to sleep, and spends a million, which at Parma is the equivalent of four millions at Milan, to have a good police force; and you see before you, Duchess, the Chief of that terrible Police.]

The scene between the duchess and Ludovic which precedes the prince's death is, as I have already suggested, one of the most effective examples of Stendhal's use of the operatic motif. She is giving her retainer instructions to open the reservoir, which is the signal to Ferrante Palla to kill the prince, and also to provide wine for the tenants of her estate at Sacca:

'Enfin,' reprit la duchesse d'un air singulièrement dégagé, 'si je donne du vin à mes braves gens de Sacca, je veux inonder les habitants de Parme; le même soir où mon château sera illuminé, prends le meilleur cheval de mon écurie, cours à mon palais, à Parme, et ouvre le réservoir.'

'Ah! l'excellente idée qu'a madame!' s'écria Ludovic, riant comme un fou; 'du vin aux braves gens de Sacca, de l'eau aux bourgeois de Parme, qui étaient si sûrs, les misérables, que monsignore Fabrice allait être empoisonné comme le pauvre L——.'

La joie de Ludovic n'en finissait point; la duchesse regardait avec complaisance ses rires fous; il répétait sans cesse: 'Du vin aux gens de Sacca, et de l'eau à ceux de Parme. . . .' ·

'Et de l'eau aux gens de Parme,' répliqua la duchesse en riant. . . .

'*Et de l'eau pour les gens de Parme!*' reprit la duchesse en chantant. 'Comment exécuteras-tu cette plaisanterie?'

'Mon plan est tout fait: je pars de Sacca sur les neuf heures, à dix et demie mon cheval est à l'auberge des *Trois Ganaches*, sur la route de Casal-

Maggiore et de *ma* terre de Ricciarda; à onze heures, je suis dans ma chambre au palais, et à onze heures et un quart de l'eau pour les gens de Parme.'

['Finally,' went on the Duchess with a singularly detached air, 'if I give wine to my good people of Sacca, I wish to flood the inhabitants of Parma; the same evening on which my house is illuminated, take the best horse in my stable, dash to my palace in Parma, and open the reservoir.'

'Ah! What an excellent idea of the Signora!' cried Ludovic, laughing like a madman; 'wine for the good people of Sacca, water for the cits of Parma, who were so sure, the wretches, that Monsignor Fabrice was going to be poisoned like poor L——.'

Ludovic's joy knew no end; the Duchess complacently watched his wild laughter; he kept on repeating 'Wine for the people of Sacca and water for the people of Parma! . . .'

'And water for the people of Parma,' retorted the Duchess with a laugh. . . .

'*And water for the people of Parma!*' the Duchess went on chanting. 'How will you carry out this joke?'

'My plans are all made: I leave Sacca about nine o'clock, at half-past ten my horse is at the inn of the Tre Ganasce, on the road to Casalmaggiore and to my estate at La Ricciarda; at eleven, I am in my room in the palace and at a quarter past eleven water for the people of Parma.']

Stendhal strikes a new note here. The gaiety, the décors and the chorus belong to comic opera, but they are the heralds of murder; the servant riding towards the palace to open the reservoir is a character not from comic, but from grand opera, who is deliberately reduced to the proportions of a figure from musical comedy. The macabre comedy is heightened by the innocent reference—Ludovic knows nothing of the significance of the opening of the reservoir—to the attempts to poison Fabrice in the Citadel and by the contrast between wine and water. Stendhal may well have been conscious in writing this scene of the religious associations of wine and water. The drinking of wine by the *gens de Sacca* is transformed into a comic funeral celebration; and water, which is normally a symbol of purity, has a double meaning here. It is the signal for the administration of its opposite—poison—but, ironically, poison is the 'water' which cleanses Parma of the despot.

'Vous déplairez toujours aux hommes: vous avez trop de feux pour les âmes prosaïques,' observes the duchess to Fabrice, recalling the Abbé Pirard's words to Julien and reminding us of the connection between all Stendhal's greatest novels. In the *Chartreuse de Parme* Stendhal explores the problem of the 'outsider' in an aristocratic society. Fabrice is the born courtier who, far from being a 'have-not' like Julien, possesses all the worldly advantages—birth, wealth, intelligence, good looks and influence—which should have ensured him a triumphal career in Parma; but in spite of his apparent successes, his career ends as surely as Julien's in disaster. The answer seems to be that, whatever his material advantages, the *étranger* always meets with the same fate. His problem is a psychological one which makes material considerations irrelevant.

Stendhal refers ironically to Fabrice as *notre héros*, but his attitude towards him is, as usual, ambivalent; and the continual changes of tone recall Molière's attitude towards his Misanthrope. One of the clearest indications of it occurs in the description of his hero's exploits at Waterloo which is placed intentionally immediately after the account of the heroic exploits of Napoleon's armies in Italy. The description of the battle, as seen by a combatant, is one of Stendhal's greatest achievements. There is no staginess, no melodrama; the battle appears, as battles must to those actually taking part in them unless they are part of the high command, incredibly confused. Fabrice's role is a mixed one. Stendhal clearly admires the courage and spirit of adventure which take him to Belgium—his action was a protest against 'authority' and 'officialdom' as such—but Fabrice also plays the part of the proverbial *blanc bec*.[1] He scarcely knows which side he is fighting on, is incapable of loading his musket, is made drunk by the *vivandières*, runs after the soldier he has shot like a child dashing to pick up his first rabbit; and when the battle is over he is tormented by the problem of discovering whether he had really been at a battle at all and remarking like all Stendhal's heroes at the great moments of their life: 'So that's all it was.' In spite of his mockery, however, there are moments when Stendhal regards his hero with something very like tenderness. He certainly preferred his aristocrat to his *parvenu* and one has the impression that he never quite forgave Julien for being so 'lower class'. When, towards the end of the book, the new Prince of Parma writes to tell the duchess that he has been 'in action' in the absurd rising which followed his father's death, there is a reference back to Fabrice's adventures at Waterloo, but the laugh is not at Fabrice's expense.

Fabrice is in some ways a more complex figure than either Julien or Lucien and he has his roots in folklore. He plays a number of different

[1] Stendhal had personal reasons for admiring Fabrice and, indeed, for sending him to Belgium. He never quite forgave himself for spending the historic day in bed with Angela Pietragrua!

parts and the way in which they overlap, merge into one another, reflect the depth and richness of Stendhal's art. When he pursues la Fausta, disguised in an immense red wig, and ends by seducing her much more attractive maid, he is a parody of the Knight Errant; but this knight errant, who wears the purple stockings of a monsignor, is at the same time an ironical portrait of the eighteenth-century ecclesiastic. In other places he becomes the youthful hero of romance trying to win a bride who belongs to the world of fairy-tale.

His most characteristic part, however, is that of the young innocent who is almost unconscious of the events taking place about him in the outer world and of their significance. 'He had the faith', we are told on several occasions; but it does not prevent him from committing simony or adultery or from indulging in manœuvres which would have won the grudging admiration of Julien. It never seems to occur to him that they are inconsistent with his profession. We are inclined to attribute his conduct to Stendhal's irony, but this view is only partly correct. His decision to take Orders no doubt represents the same compromise as Julien's or Lucien's appointment at the Ministry of the Interior, but Fabrice is to a greater extent than either of the others a dual personality. His contacts with the life of the time are fewer, his withdrawal into another world more complete. The Fabrice who fights at Waterloo, who is in love with Clélia and whose first movement in a tavern brawl 'fut tout à fait du XVIe siècle' is the real Fabrice. The courtier who says 'all the right things' at his audience with the Prince, the Cleric who flatters the Archbishop and several of his other roles are *personæ*. He is simply 'going through the motions', is constructing artificial bridges between himself and everyday life, but his true self is not engaged. That is why the deepest impression that he makes on us is one of innocence, of being uncontaminated by the world.

The character of Fabrice is rich in other symbols—symbols 'surging up . . . from the dark of the unconscious mind'.[1] When he prowls round the outside of the family castle, its 'walls' have the same significance as the 'walls' in *Le Rouge et le noir*. They are the barrier which separates the outsider from the world into which he was born, and they stand for the tyranny of the father and brother whose betrayal has turned him into a fugitive from 'justice'.[2] The 'forests' and the 'lakes' where he wanders are both objective and subjective. They belong to the same inner world to which Julien withdraws after leaving Verrières.

[1] Josephson, *op. cit.*, p. 429.
[2] This scene is probably an allusion to the fact that Fabrice was the illegitimate son of the Marquise del Dongo and the French officer billeted at her house in 1796 whom Fabrice sees, but naturally does not recognize, at Waterloo.

The 'forests' are the labyrinth in which the outsider struggles with his psychological conflicts, the 'lakes' are symbols of 'peace' and of the solutions which, tantalizingly, elude him. His meditation on his feelings for the Duchess introduces the incest motif, and his doubts about his capacity for love reveal the hidden fear of impotence which is associated with it and which dogged his creator all his life.[1] One of the most remarkable symbols is the chestnut tree which Fabrice's mother had planted in his honour when he was a child and which he decides to inspect before leaving the forests:

En effet, au lieu de se retirer par la ligne la plus courte, et de gagner les bords du lac Majeur, où sa barque l'attendait, il faisait un énorme détour pour aller voir *son arbre*. . . .[2] Il serait digne de mon frère, se dit-il, d'avoir fait couper cet arbre. . . . Deux heures plus tard son regard fut consterné; des méchants ou un orage avaient rompu l'une des principales branches du jeune arbre, qui pendait desséchée; Fabrice la coupa avec respect, à l'aide de son poignard, et tailla bien net la coupure, afin que l'eau ne pût pas s'introduire dans le tronc. Ensuite, quoique le temps fût bien précieux pour lui . . . il passa une bonne heure à bêcher la terre autour de l'arbre chéri. Toutes ces folies accomplies, il reprit rapidement la route du lac Majeur. Au total, il n'était point triste, l'arbre était d'une belle venue, plus vigoureux que jamais, et, en cinq ans, il avait presque doublé. La branche n'était qu'un accident sans conséquence; une fois coupée, elle ne nuisait plus à l'arbre, et même il serait plus élancé, sa membrure commençant plus haut.

[For indeed, instead of retiring along the shortest line, and gaining the shore of Lake Maggiore, where his boat was awaiting him, he made an enormous circuit to go and visit *his tree*. . . . It would be quite worthy of my brother, he said to himself, to have had the tree cut down. . . . Two hours later he was shocked by what he saw; mischief-makers or a storm had broken one of the main branches of the young tree, which hung down withered; Fabrice cut it off reverently, using his dagger, and smoothed the cut carefully, so that the rain should not get inside the trunk. Then, although time was highly precious to him . . . he spent a good hour in turning the soil round his dear tree. All these acts of folly accomplished, he went rapidly on his way towards Lake Maggiore. All things considered, he was not at all sad; the tree was coming on well, was more vigorous than ever, and in five years had almost doubled in height. The branch was only

[1] It accounts for Stendhal's own preoccupation with *le fiasco* in his autobiographical writings and in *De l'Amour*.

[2] Italics in the text.

an accident of no consequence; once it had been cut off, it did no more harm to the tree, which indeed would grow all the better if its spread began higher from the ground.]

This passage like the imaginary descent into the labyrinth in *Phèdre* seems to me to be one of the very few passages in great literature where the Freudian symbols offer a complete explanation of the character's motives and where they contribute directly to the literary value of the writing. The 'tree' is a phallic symbol. *La ligne la plus courte* stands for Fabrice's temptation to leave the 'forests' without trying to solve his problems; but he resists it and the *énorme détour* is the struggle to re-assure himself about his virility. The fear that his brother, whom he always associates with his tyrannical father, may have cut down the tree is his fear of castration. When he sees that one of the principal branches has in fact been broken and is hanging down, dry and withered —a grisly symbol of the severed member—he believes for a horrible moment that they have succeeded. Then, by one of those immense efforts of the will which are characteristic of Stendhal's heroes at their greatest moments, he proceeds to identify the dead branch with his enemies and the tree, which becomes a symbol of 'life', with himself. This gives the passage its tension and its dramatic force. The pruning and tending of the tree is a ritual act. The lopping off of the dead branch stands for the death or castration of father and brother which will prevent any further interference in his life, and it may also refer to his decision not to yield to his incestuous *inclination* for the Duchess. When he secures the tree against water filtering into the trunk and spends an hour digging round it, he is carrying out a primitive fertility rite and protecting himself against the intrusion of corrosive elements which may undermine his virility. There is a feeling of great relief as he surveys his handiwork, observes the splendid foliage on the tree and realizes that his fears were groundless, that the dead branch like his enemies was only 'an accident of no consequence'. He turns with a clear conscience towards the 'lake' where the boat is waiting to carry him away from the 'forests' back to life in Parma.

Fabrice is flanked by the twin figures of Comte Mosca and the Duchess, and the relations between the three are vital to the pattern of the book. The Count and the Duchess are both people who unlike Fabrice are very firmly rooted in the society of their time which makes them appear the opposite of the *étranger* type:

En Espagne, sous le général Saint-Cyr [says the Count], j'affrontais des coups de fusil pour arriver à la croix, et ensuite à un peu de gloire; main-

tenant je m'habille comme un personnage de comédie pour gagner un
grand état de maison et quelques milliers de francs.

[In Spain, under General Saint-Cyr, I faced the enemy's fire to win a
cross and a little glory besides, now I dress myself up like an actor in a
farce to win a great social position and a few thousand francs a year.]

The Count's words are a frank admission that he has compromised
—compromised in a very different sense from Fabrice—with society
and with the demands of the police state. He has abandoned a career of
military glory to become a politician and the despot's pet—the irony
of *un personnage de comédie* and the powdered wig, which is the sign of
'political reliability', is not lost on us—preferring the chance of gaining
'a few thousand francs' to the *croix* which are awarded for 'valour'.
It is the victory of *logique* over *espagnolisme*. The Count has become a
raisonneur who sometimes reminds us of Molière's *honnêtes hommes*;
and it is 'logic' which prompts him to make the fatal omission from a
document which sends Fabrice to prison.

The Duchess is a magnificent creation. Her encounter with the despot
when she threatens to leave his domains and the reading of the La
Fontaine fable are among the highlights of the book. Her single-
mindedness throws Fabrice's rootlessness into high relief; but she too
has compromised. Although she is in a sense always 'in opposition',
she plays the political game and uses the methods of the police state to
revenge herself on the Prince. Her victory remains a hollow one, and
her incestuous passion for her nephew is never satisfied.

I have already suggested, in speaking of *Lucien Leuwen*, that in spite
of surface differences there is a link which binds all Stendhal's principal
characters and makes them 'the same sort of people'. The bond which
unites Fabrice, Clélia, the Duchess and Mosca is much closer, the relationship between them much more profound than that between Lucien
and his father. That it is so seems to me to be an unmistakable sign of the
deepening of the novelist's own experience between the writing of
Lucien Leuwen and the *Chartreuse de Parme*; and it is this that gives the
book a tragic ring.

His characters [writes M. Bardèche in a valuable comment] do not
believe in anything. The religion of politics which might have given them
a *mystique* has been vanquished. There remain only themselves. . . . Their
marvellous life, their Fortunate Isles are only an aristocratic copy of
hedonism. They perceive that their most precious possession, the only

spiritual possession which is left to them, is their disposition for happiness. They turn this happiness into the goal of their new life.[1]

That is the secret of their tragedy. They form an immensely civilized aristocratic élite and they stake everything on a single chance—happiness through personal relationships. Fabrice and Clélia may give the impression of gentleness and tenderness as the Duchess gives the impression of ruthlessness, but at bottom they are the same. They stop at nothing to gain their ends. The only difference lies in the choice of the means. The Duchess chooses regicide and the Count treachery, but Fabrice is at heart equally ruthless in using religion as the path to Clélia's bed. They are tragic figures precisely because 'they do not believe in anything'. For we cannot say that they 'believe in' personal relationships; they are passionately attached to them, but they are profoundly conscious of the absence of a *mystique* and of the precariousness of their way of life when it is pitted against despotism. The despot, to be sure, is 'liquidated', but no one supposes for a moment that his removal will produce a fundamental change or will even touch essentials. It is because their 'marvellous life' is so fragile, 'happiness' so elusive and its pursuit so certain to end in disaster that they appear infinitely desirable. That is why we continually have the impression in reading the book that when you look into things, you suddenly find there is nothing there.

3

The Citadel of Parma dominates the novel not merely because a large part of it is devoted to Fabrice's imprisonment there, but because of its symbolical importance. When Fabrice enters the Citadel, he stands at once for the sensitive individual, the unpolitical man, who is caught in the toils of the police state, and for the youthful hero escaping from a world in which he has no part.

Stendhal is at pains to emphasize the size of the prison, carefully noting down a bewildering string of measurements. For its physical size dominates the State of Parma, towering above its absurd intrigues, as it dominates the novelist's imagination. There is a deliberate contrast between the immense size of the building with its spacious rooms and the tiny corridor, the narrow corkscrew staircase *en filigrane*, by which the prisoner reaches his cell. The walls of the chapel which he passes, 'ornés d'une quantité de têtes de morts en marbre blanc, de proportions colossales, élégamment sculptées et placées sur deux os en sautoir' trans-

[1] *Op. cit.*, pp. 384–5.

H*

form the place into a fantastic charnel-house and are an allusion to the
'death-wish' which haunts Stendhal's characters. But this time Fabrice's
reaction is a positive one:

> Voilà bien une invention de la haine qui ne peut tuer, se dit Fabrice, et
> quelle diable d'idée de me montrer cela!

> [There is an invention of the hatred that cannot kill, thought Fabrice,
> and what a devilish idea to let me see it.]

He knows that his time had not come, that he is passing through the
chamber of death towards Clélia who stands for 'life'. The sombre
décors are merely the sign of the petty despot's hold over his country.
He hates and fears opposition; he spends a million on his secret police
and large sums on spies; but at bottom his hatred is feeble. It cannot kill,
or rather it cannot touch the *étranger* whose exploits have thrown the
political machine out of gear.

Fabrice's ascent to his cell is not a 'social climb' like Julien's ascent
to Mathilde's room. The devious winding staircases lead *out* of the
devious winding intrigues of the Court. His 'cell' is a cage suspended
in a room and only touches the wall on one side, apparently emphasizing his isolation and detachment. There seems to be a reference to
the cages where Clélia keeps her birds, for Fabrice becomes much more
her prisoner than the Prince's. In abandoning the world he has also
abandoned his ecclesiastical career which is part of the political game.
His breviary is only used to record the progress of his love affair with
Clélia; the prison chapel is a trysting place for the lovers. When he
escapes, another chapel is the scene of the Duchess's oath to go to bed
with the new Prince on condition that Fabrice is 'acquitted' and the
archbishopric is thrown in.

'In Stendhal,' said Proust, 'a certain feeling of altitude is linked with
the spiritual life.'[1] Fabrice's arrival at the summit is accompanied by an
immense sense of release. He looks down on Parma and its intrigues
(as he had looked down on the frivolous world from the Abbé Blanès'
tower) and on the mountains which appeared to be a hundred leagues
away:

> Ce ne fut qu'après avoir passé plus de deux heures à la fenêtre, admirant
> cet horizon qui parlait à son âme . . . que Fabrice s'écria tout à coup: Mais
> ceci est-il une prison? est-ce là ce que j'ai tant redouté?

---

[1] In *La Prisonnière*, II, p. 237.

[It was not until he had spent more than two hours at the window, admiring the horizon which spoke to his soul . . . that Fabrice suddenly exclaimed: But is this really a prison? Is this what I have so greatly dreaded?]

Mr. Levin speaks of the Citadel's 'chiaroscuro of spacious heights and claustrophobic depths'. Fabrice and Clélia are isolated in the same timeless world as Julien and Mathilde. For a moment they belong to 'the happy few'. Fabrice abandons himself to his *rêverie* and desires nothing better than to spend the rest of his days in the tower. But potent forces are working to destroy the idyll. The elegant superstructure of the Citadel is contrasted with the horrors of its depths where the appalling governor and his grotesque gaolers are planning to poison Fabrice; and the kitchens where the poison is prepared assume the sinister significance of a witches' cauldron.

There are other forces at work as well. Shortly after Fabrice reaches his 'cage' 'son attention fut violemment *rappelée à la réalité*'.[1] There is an immense commotion when the mongrel terrier dashes into the cage in pursuit of the rats which it kills. The rats are an emanation from the underworld, the dog a sign of vigilance—of the despot watching over his prisoner and the vigilance of Fabrice's friends protecting him from danger, killing the rats as they defeat the attempts to poison him.

Ironically, both are working for his doom. In his description of the Tour Farnèse, Stendhal remarks:

Cette seconde tour, comme le lecteur s'en souvient peut-être, fut élevée sur la plate-forme de la grosse tour, en l'honneur d'un prince héréditaire qui, fort différent de l'Hippolyte fils de Thésée, n'avait point repoussé les politesses d'une jeune belle-mère.

[This second tower, as the reader may perhaps remember, was built on the platform of the great tower in honour of a Crown Prince who, unlike Hippolytus the son of Theseus, had by no means repelled the advances of a young stepmother.]

It is a reference to the Duchess's love for her nephew, but the two stories ended differently. The Prince spent the seventeen best years of his life in the tower and only left when he succeeded his father on the throne. Fabrice's feelings towards the Duchess undergo a change:

[1] Italics mine.

Une nuit Fabrice vint à penser un peu sérieusement à sa tante: il fut
étonné, il eut peine à reconnaître son image; le souvenir qu'il conservait
d'elle avait totalement changé; pour lui, à cette heure, elle avait cinquante
ans.

[One night Fabrice began to think somewhat seriously of his aunt: he
was amazed, he found a difficulty in recognizing her image; the memory
that he kept of her had totally changed; for him, at this moment, she was
a woman of fifty.]

She becomes the 'mother' who can no longer penetrate *his* world,
but it is her skilful planning which procures his return to *her* world.
The immensely exciting escape is a *descent* into the world of political
intrigue; but, adds Stendhal, 'tout était anéanti chez notre héros'. He
looks back on his months in the Citadel as the happiest period of his life.
He returns to the world and to his ecclesiastical career only to find that
in losing Clélia he has lost everything. He is more of an *étranger* than
before, and the Duchess discovers with despair that he has also become
an *étranger* for her. She may have procured his physical return, but
spiritually he is further from her than when he was in prison.

Stendhal's attitude towards his 'hero' becomes extremely complex
in the closing chapters of the novel. The Knight Errant is replaced by
the medieval churchman, the famous preacher who empties the opera
house and fills the churches with weeping crowds, though his only aim
is to renew contact with Clélia. The novelist's attitude is certainly
ironic when he tells us that, though extremely scrupulous in keeping
her oath to the Madonna not to *see* Fabrice, the pious Clélia finally
bestows the *dernières faveurs* in the *dark*. Nor are the favours withdrawn
when Fabrice succeeds to the archiepiscopal see where 'his piety, his
exemplary morals and his eloquence' soon made people forget his
saintly predecessor. On the other hand, the note of tenderness seems to
break in which, after the death of Clélia, Fabrice finally abandons the
world:

Fabrice était trop amoureux et trop croyant pour avoir recours au
suicide; il espérait retrouver Clélia dans un meilleur monde, mais il avait
trop d'esprit pour ne pas sentir qu'il avait beaucoup à réparer.

[Fabrice was too much in love and too religious to have recourse to
suicide; he hoped to meet Clélia again in a better world, but he had too
much intelligence not to feel that he had first to atone for many faults.]

The fate of the principal characters resembles that of Julien and Mme de Rênal. Clélia is dead and Fabrice, his sensibility exhausted, only lasts a year in the charterhouse. The death of Fabrice removes the Duchess's only hold on life and she, too, dies. Ernest V and Mosca are left in possession of the stage, and the book closes with a final stroke of irony:

Les prisons de Parme étaient vides, le comte immensément riche, Ernest V adoré de ses sujets, qui comparaient son gouvernement à celui des grand-ducs de Toscane.

[The prisons of Parma were empty, the Count immensely rich, Ernest V adored by his subjects, who compared his rule to that of the Grand Dukes of Tuscany.]

The Count, who exchanged a military career for politics, has realized his ambition to 'gain a million'. That much is clear, but the rest of the sentence is characteristically ambiguous. The prisons are empty either because Ernest V is really a benevolent despot or because all the liberals are dead or in exile or because liberalism itself has died out. The Grand Dukes of Tuscany, to whom the Prince of Parma is compared, were notorious despots. It follows from this that his people worshipped him either because they really liked despotism or because they had become so downtrodden that they were not aware of it. The only other alternative is that Stendhal is pulling our leg and that his people secretly detested Ernest V. The novelist leaves us to work the answer out for ourselves. He was a liberal himself, but he had a poor opinion of other liberals and had no intention in this book of condemning one set of ideas and holding another set up to admiration. He is the urbane, cultured man-of-the-world, and the whole book is informed by a mellow wisdom. He obviously found life in Parma amusing and exciting and was not unappreciative of its grace. No doubt he felt that he could leave 'the happy few' to enjoy the performance.

Artistically it makes an admirable ending. The novel opens with an immense élan—an élan which reflects the joy of Stendhal's own discovery of Italy—but it closes on a muted note. We have witnessed the alternation of tenderness and irony, gaiety and sadness, but the dreams and hopes have faded. 'The paladin finishes as a monk', says one writer of Fabrice. But the paladin like the lieutenant in *Lucien Leuwen* died young, and once again the consul survives 'to tell his story and re-live his romance'. 'Logic' and compromise, in the person of the Count, have prevailed. Stendhal always identified himself a little enviously with the youthful dreams of his heroes, feeling that somehow they had got more out of life than himself. Now the elderly novelist seems to identify himself, a little ruefully, with the elderly politician who has secured the 'million' which in his own case had proved as elusive as happiness.

VI. 'A TICKET IN A LOTTERY'

'ET MOI,' wrote Stendhal, 'je mets un billet à une loterie, dont le gros lot se réduit à ceci: être lu en 1935.'[1] Critics have marvelled at the accuracy with which he foretold the dates at which his work would become popular. It was neither wishful thinking nor a lucky guess. He knew that he was a great novelist and that he was very much in advance of his time. He could not foresee the exact conditions which would make him popular or which would prompt one of the brighter cabinet ministers to re-read the *Chartreuse de Parme* at a critical moment in 1938: but he may well have realized that the conditions which turned Julien Sorel and Fabrice del Dongo into 'outsiders' were bound to be aggravated and grow more acute.

'Stendhal', writes M. Léon Blum, 'est l'homme des moments confus, des mélanges sociaux, des périodes désordonnées.'[2] The rise of the police state in Europe has no doubt given the *Chartreuse de Parme* a topical appeal which it did not possess between 1840 and 1920. War and revolution have hastened the disintegration of the community life which Stendhal perceived with such clarity and which caused the predicament of Julien and Fabrice. Their predicament is rapidly becoming that of every civilized man. For the growth of the omnicompetent state and what Baudelaire contemptuously called 'the rising tide of democracy' have transformed even 'the happy few' into submerged *étrangers*.

This may well explain why Stendhal has a particular appeal for our generation; but the reasons for his ultimate greatness have nothing to do with superficial resemblances between his age and our own; they lie much deeper. We expect a great novelist to interpret his age and to anticipate changes which are taking place in the life of the race; but his books must also record something that happened to human nature as a whole, and that is what Stendhal's finest work does.

A German critic has suggested that he belongs to the Cartesian tradition and is only interested in 'moral experience and the mechanics and dynamics of the heart'.[3] The traditional motifs of 'love' and 'ambition'

---

[1] *Henri Brulard*, II, p. 8. [2] *Stendhal et le Beylisme* (3rd edition, Paris, 1947), p. 244.
[3] Ernst Robert Curtius, *Französischer Geist im neuen Europa* (Berlin, n.d. *circa* 1925), p. 75.

certainly play a large part in the novels; but this is not the whole of the story. He wrote at a time when great changes were taking place in the emotional life of the people and when it was becoming increasingly difficult to explain the complexity of the human mind in terms of traditional psychology. He did not make the mistake of jettisoning the whole of it; he made a breach in what had become a closed system and opened up fresh fields for exploration. His characters like Constant's Adolphe transcend the categories of Cartesian psychology, and they are a triumphant success because their creator succeeded in integrating his vision into the framework of everyday life as he succeeded in fitting his books into the framework of the classic novel.

'Ce personnage', said Stendhal of Mathilde de La Mole, 'est . . . imaginé bien en dehors des habitudes sociales qui parmi les siècles assureront un rang si distingué à la civilisation du XIXe siècle.' His characters represent positive standards by which society is tested and condemned. It is because they stand outside the nineteenth century that they are closer to us than Flaubert's *ratés*. They impose themselves on their age; Flaubert's, one feels, are nothing but the product of their immediate environment. They are germ-carriers who are born with an incurable *maladie morale* and spend their aimless lives spreading the infection. Proust speaks of the narrator in his great work as being *entouré de son âme*. *Ame* is a word which occurs very frequently in Stendhal's writings, but it is a principle of vitality and not a veil which hangs between the writer and the world. Stendhal's ideal was the mixed life—the life of action and contemplation—which was becoming impossible in Europe. It is because the balance is held between the two until the moment comes for his characters' final retreat from the world that he made his discoveries about human nature without turning his characters into specimens who are studied on the dissecting table. His books are great psychological novels, but they are often as exciting to read as a *roman d'aventures*.

Stendhal was much more alive in his time, more conscious of its problems than his contemporaries and successors, and his vision has greater depth and greater breadth than theirs. He was a man of action and a contemplative, an intellectual who was also a born novelist. The originality of his vision and the discovery of a new psychological type have altered the whole perspective of European psychology and given him his immense stature. He is one of the most civilized of all French novelists and he seems to me to be the greatest.

BALZAC

I think Balzac is the greatest novelist the world has ever known.
W. Somerset Maugham
Il est bon de lire Balzac avant vingt-cinq ans; après cela devient trop difficile.
André Gide
Were I asked why I find fault with Balzac I should answer: Because he is a dauber.
... The longer we look at his work, the clearer it becomes that the object is not there.
Ortega y Gasset

I. THE NOVELIST AND HIS AGE

'I WISH,' I once said to a Frenchman, 'I wish someone would explain to me what the French see in Balzac.' 'I read him', came the reply, 'as I read Simenon.'

It is an amusing *boutade*, but it contains a hard core of truth. An interest in crime and a highly personal form of melodrama are two of Balzac's most striking characteristics. Melodrama is usually a matter of 'character' and 'situation'; but though there is plenty of this sort of melodrama in Balzac, his personal melodrama is a property of language:

> Son châle à franges maigres et pleurardes semblait couvrir un squelette, tant les formes qu'il cachait étaient anguleuses. Quel acide avait dépouillé cette créature de ses formes féminines . . . était-ce le vice, le chagrin, la cupidité? avait-elle été marchande à la toilette, ou seulement courtisane? Son regard blanc donnait froid, sa figure rabougrie menaçait. (*Le Père Goriot.*)

> Ce sinistre amas de crottes, ces vitrages encrassés par la pluie et par la poussière, ces huttes plates et couvertes de haillons au dehors, la saleté des murailles commencées . . . cette physionomie grimaçante allait admirablement aux différents commerces qui grouillaient sous ce hangar impudique, effronté, plein de gazouillements et d'une gaieté folle. . . . (*Les Illusions perdues.*)

> [Her shawl with its skimpy wistful fringes seemed to cover a skeleton, so angular was the figure it concealed. What acid had eaten away the feminine lines of this creature. . . . Was it vice, grief, cupidity? Had she been a wardrobe dealer or simply a courtesan? Her blank look gave you the shivers; her stunted face was threatening.

> The sinister heap of dirt, the windows clogged with rain and dust, the low shanties whose outside was covered with rags, the filth of walls which had been begun . . . the grinning physiognomy of the place was admirably suited to the different trades which swarmed in the shameless impudent shed which was filled with twittering sounds and a reckless gaiety. . . .]

The rhetorical tricks, the feverish tone and the lurid adjectives reveal a curious taste for violence and squalor for their own sake. The novelist does his utmost to dramatize experience, to turn people and places into a spectacle which is designed to take the reader's breath away. His characters lose their humanity and become monsters; a sordid street scene assumes an impossibly sinister air. It is difficult not to feel that there is something specious and unreal about the performance—particularly in the fanciful suggestion of the old maid's secret vices—but the melodramatic element belonged to the man and his age.

For Balzac was a novelist of the Romantic Movement or, to put it more accurately and less charitably, he was a product of the Romantic dissolution. As soon as we open one of his books, we are aware that there has been a break with the main French tradition, that the eighteenth-century virtues, which contributed largely to the success of Constant and Stendhal, have been lost and that nothing satisfactory has taken their place. French rationalism was not always the brilliant advantage that it is usually said to have been, particularly in the novels of Voltaire and Laclos, but it was vastly preferable to the cloudy theosophy on which the young Balzac was brought up. A certain measure of scepticism and a critical outlook in a novelist are salutary and necessary. They give him poise and enable him to sift and test his experience. They were singularly lacking in Balzac. Their absence meant that he had little protection against the disruptive tendencies of his age, that he was far too much the product of his environment and that far too much that was transitory and perishable went into his books. His vitality has been much admired, and it is right to say at the outset that it is his greatest single asset. We may doubt, however, whether it always sprang from the great novelist's need to create. It was diluted by less admirable elements which were characteristic of the age and it often degenerated into an urge to write, to use language for the discharge of violent, unrelated feelings which recalls Shelley's dangerous 'inspiration'.

The formative influences among contemporary writers seem to have been Scott, Fenimore Cooper and Mrs. Radcliffe. He has told us that his study of society in the *Comédie humaine* was based on Scott's regional novels; but Scott's analysis was elementary and it could not provide Balzac with the fresh start that he needed. He admired Fenimore Cooper as a story-teller and from Mrs. Radcliffe he derived an unfortunate taste for magic and sensationalism. He contrived to blend these influences into something that was his own, but the mixture was an uneasy one. We are conscious of the absence of a coherent vision of life that he was continually trying to conceal.

He began his career as the anonymous author of what are now called 'thrillers'—*Argow le pirate* is the best known of them—and the melo-

Picture Post Library

HONORÉ DE BALZAC

dramatic element persists all through his work. One critic has declared with some truth that the *Chouans* 'inaugurated the *roman policier*', and 'La Dernière Incarnation de Vautrin'[1] might well have been called 'La Dernière Incarnation d'Argow'. His world is a world of crime and fraud, a world where the Swindler and the Strumpet are supreme; but he often succeeds in hiding its crudities and improbabilities by his story-teller's gift of making us want to know 'what happens next'. We want to know what Mme Graslin's guilty secret was, whether Goriot's daughters will or will not come to their father's deathbed, what will be the end of Hulot, what will be the outcome of Birotteau's bank-ruptcy and whether Pons will succeed in defeating the criminals who are after his estate. We follow the admirable interrogation of Lucien de Rubempré in *Splendeurs et misères des courtisanes* and the duel in *La Rabouilleuse* with breathless interest; but it must be confessed that our experience in reading Balzac is not always very elevated and that his interests are by no means always those of an adult. His melodrama may at times have been highly personal, but there are undoubtedly occasions when his work reminds us not so much of Simenon or even of Mrs Christie as of the daily serial in the BBC's Light Programme.

Balzac's French admirers do not deny the existence of the melo-dramatic element, but they call it by other names. 'I have often been astonished', wrote Baudelaire, 'that the great glory of Balzac was to pass for an observer. It has always seemed to me that his principal merit was to be a visionary and a passionate visionary.' It was the beginning of a long debate between the realists and the anti-realists who both claimed that Balzac was one of them. Balzac liked to describe himself as an 'observer', but in the end Baudelaire's view prevailed.

> There is no need to insist at the present time [writes M. Maurice Blanchot] that Balzac has nothing in common with the realistic novelists who through an absurd misunderstanding claimed him as a model. It is clear that few writers have paid less attention than he to the taste for ob-servation or have shown less concern for verisimilitude and psychological analysis. . . . His work was created in order to achieve complete inde-pendence of the everyday world. It is neither a copy nor a caricature of reality. It claims to exist in its own right. Its aim is to attract and hold the reader, to make the real world uninhabitable for him and to close every outlet so that he becomes incapable of imagining any mode of life except that which belongs to the world of the *Comédie humaine*.
>
> This dialectic of composition [he remarks in the same essay] has assumed the most diverse forms. Language itself participates in it. The *idée fixe* takes

[1] Title of the last volume of *Splendeurs et misères des courtisanes*.

possession of words and extracts from them a series of images which lead
to a veritable hallucinatory dance. . . . It gives the great scenes to which
the paroxysmal unfolding of idea-characters and idea-situations leads a
significance and a power of evocation which is astonishing.[1]

It is an interesting account of the impression that Balzac makes on
one of his critics, but we may doubt whether such a degree of detachment from the world of common experience and the lack of control
which it implies is a merit in a novelist.[2] In reading Balzac, we often
have the impression that we are mere *spectators*. His world with its
violence, with its duchesses mixed up with the prostitutes, affords the
same vicarious satisfaction as a detective story. We enjoy the violence
because it is somehow never quite real, because we are shielded from
its direct impact. Instead of providing the reader with a genuine
experience which calls for an emotional reorientation, it fosters his
complacency, appealing to feelings and to standards which are only
valid in the closed world of the *Comédie humaine* and which cease to
matter as soon as he closes the book.

M. Blanchot's views, however, do help us to understand Balzac's
fascination for his English and French admirers. I think we can say that
the English admire him because he has certain affinities with the English
novelists of the eighteenth and nineteenth centuries, and the French
because he is so different from the French classic novelists. He possesses
something of the gusto and untidiness of the English tradition. He is
strong in that form of characterization for which the English have
always had a pronounced weakness, and he indulges in that minute
description of material reality which has always been popular in these
islands.[3] He has about him none of the intangibility which makes a
truly great French novelist like Stendhal so elusive for the Anglo-
Saxon mind, and he is strangely lacking in the French novelists'
psychological subtlety.

He certainly possessed genius, but we may doubt whether his gifts
are of the kind which justify the claims which have been made for him.

---

[1] *Faux pas* (Paris, 1943), pp. 212–13, 215–16.

[2] Two incidents related by his biographers illustrate his detachment from the world
of common experience. After commiserating in a very perfunctory manner with a
friend who had just lost his father, Balzac added: 'Let us return to reality. Whom will
Eugénie Grandet marry?' When he was on his deathbed, he constantly cried: 'Send
for Bianchon [the famous doctor of the *Comédie humaine*]. He can save me.'

[3] Compare Stendhal's view. 'I have forgotten to describe this salon. Sir Walter
Scott and his imitators would have begun with this; but I myself abhor material
descriptions. The boredom of doing them prevents me from writing novels.'
(*Souvenirs d'égotisme* (Paris, 1892), p. 41.)

He has been called 'the French Dickens' as Dickens has been called 'the English Balzac'. 'Of course,' retorted Henry James, 'if Dickens is an English Balzac, he is a very English Balzac.'[1] The warning is timely and necessary, and the comparison must not be pushed too far. Balzac's best work seems to me to be inferior in many respects to Dickens's, but the two novelists are not unlike in their strength and their weaknesses and M. Blanchot's words could, with comparatively little alteration, be applied to some of Dickens's work. They both inhabit the enclosed oppressive world of the nightmare; but while Dickens resorts to caricature as a protest against a hostile order, Balzac's caricatures seem designed to sever the connection between the actual world and a world which is very largely an emanation of his own personality. It might, perhaps, be said of Balzac, as it has been said of Dickens, that he was 'a great entertainer'; but there is a reservation to be made. We must, I think, say of both writers that they frequently create the illusion that we are enjoying 'literature' when we are really responding at a much lower level or, to put it in another way, in much of his work Balzac raises the detective story and the *roman d'aventures* to the level of a sort of art.

That is one explanation of his popularity and it needs to be kept in mind. He is, however, too large to be disposed of in a single formula. He was not, as M. Blanchot admits, a subtle psychologist and his claims to be considered 'an investigator of the human heart' will not bear examination. He was not a particularly sensitive writer and when we think of Constant and Stendhal we can hardly regard him as an outstandingly intelligent man. He was shrewd, but his intelligence was limited and his sensibility crude. He is seen at his best not in the studies of contemporary life like the fashionable *Père Goriot* or the excessively slick *Splendeurs et misères des courtisanes*, but in the novels with a provincial setting, in *Eugénie Grandet*, the *Curé de Tours*, *La Muse du département*, *La Vieille fille*, the *Illusions perdues*, parts of *La Rabouilleuse* and *Ursule Mirouët* and the opening of *Le Curé de village* where a simple mentality was in keeping with his own very real but undeniably limited talents.

---

[1] *French Poets and Novelists* (London, 1875), p. 147.

I

SOME French critics are alive to Balzac's shortcomings, though they maintain like Gide that he must be judged not by the individual volumes of the *Comédie humaine*, which are admittedly uneven, but by the undertaking as a whole. It cannot be denied that Balzac fashioned a world of his own, but his world is a very odd one. His real interests are three: money, lust and magic in that order. Everyone and everything comes to us with a ticket attached showing the price. He seldom introduces a character without telling us not merely what his or her income is, but where it came from, whether it is an absolute interest or only a life interest, how it is invested and what the prospects are of increasing it. Whenever a marriageable woman is named, we learn the precise amount of her *dot*, what her expectations are from parents, uncles and cousins. If a woman happens to be wearing a necklace, we hear how she came by it—not always a very creditable story—what it cost and what she would get for it if she took it to the pawnshop.

It is common knowledge that this obsession with money was partly the outcome of the financial difficulties which afflicted the novelist all his life, but Balzac did not write about money merely because he was always in debt. The problem of money is fundamental in the *Comédie humaine* because money was the great problem of Balzac's age as it is becoming the great problem of our own. It is one of his chief merits that he invests it with immense symbolical importance. No one can fail to notice the extraordinary interest that he displays in bankers, merchants, commercial travellers, misers and usurers, and it is easy to understand the reason. They are the most characteristic representatives not simply of a commercial society, but of a society obsessed by money.

'To go bankrupt,' says Grandet, 'is to commit the most dishonourable action among all those actions which can dishonour man.'

The warrior of classic literature has been replaced by the merchant, honour by commercial probity and the rules of the stock exchange. Money has to a large extent replaced passion as the destructive element;

and by making the honest merchant the hero and the usurer the villain of the piece, Balzac is able to define his own attitude towards the problem. The moral that emerges from the novels seems to be that in nineteenth-century society it is practically impossible to be honest and successful. César Birotteau is outwitted by unscrupulous business rivals while a usurer like Gobseck or a crooked banker like Nucingen carry off the prizes. The criticism that Balzac makes of society in *César Birotteau* is a valid one, but it clearly involves limitations. There is something very uninspiring about a man whose aim is merely to retain his probity in a corrupt society or to reinstate himself when he has gone bankrupt. We cannot escape the conclusion that Balzac's choice of heroes like Flaubert's was the reflection of something that was lacking in himself.

This, however, is only one side of Balzac's criticism. Although he excelled in portraits of misers—the people who love money for its own sake—money is very often regarded as a means to an end and it becomes the symbol of the deepest aspirations of a particular society. The idea that money is power is the dynamic behind many of the novels. Money means women, luxury and happiness—the realization of the dreams of the son of the ill-paid official which he projected into his characters. The transfer of wealth from the nobility to the middle and lower-middle classes explains the collapse of the old ruling class and the emergence of a new; it is at the bottom of that *déclassement* which permeates Balzac's world no less than Proust's. In this world nothing can compensate for the lack of money or for insufficient money; but if money is an obsession so is lust. Crevel, Hulot and Rubempré—young and old alike—want money because money can buy women. The less money they possess, the more violent, the more insatiable becomes the desire for rapacious and expensive women; and it is this that leads to disaster and collapse, to the loss of any and every form of moral integrity and finally, in the case of Hulot, to crime against the State. It is anything but a worthy ideal and though Balzac certainly condemns it, the extent to which he endorses his characters' view of the importance of wealth is a reflection on his work.

Magic may seem of less importance than avarice and lust and it certainly bulks less largely in the *Comédie humaine*, but in reality it is simply another aspect of the thirst for power, for material wealth and comfort. M. Maurice Bardèche has given an interesting analysis of *La Peau de chagrin* in his study of Balzac, but his careful elucidation of the symbolism of that work should not be allowed to conceal its literary defects or a certain childishness.[1] Yet as an explanation of the novelist's

[1] *Balzac romancier* (2nd (abridged) edition, Paris, 1947), pp. 211-21.

motives it is of considerable significance. It will be remembered that
where the book opens the principal character has lost his remaining
money and is about to commit suicide. He comes into possession of a
magic skin which fulfils his different wishes, but each wish causes the
skin to shrink until finally it shrinks to nothing and the owner falls into a
decline and dies. It is the incarnation of a simple wish-fulfilment which
has haunted nearly everybody at one time or another. Life without
wealth is inconceivable, but in Balzac the possession of wealth, whether
acquired by industry, fraud or magic, brings its own doom; and the
moral seems to be that it is the gratification of desires and ambitions
which leads to destruction.

It is naturally tempting to identify the novelist with his characters,
with his hopeful young men and his disillusioned old men; but in the
case of Balzac this temptation must be resisted. With the exception of
Louis Lambert and *Le Lys dans la vallée*, his novels are not autobiographical and he does not put himself into them in the same sense as
Stendhal and Flaubert. His characters certainly reflect his own interests
and he has his 'myth'. His books record the progress of the Romantic
misfit in an urban civilization. For behind all the excesses and exaggera-
tions—intellectual and material—of the *Comédie humaine* is the Romantic pursuit of the experience which transcends all other experiences, the
absolute of spiritual and material satisfaction which lures on his characters, usually with the voice of the 'sirens' of Restoration society, and
brings them to destruction. The myth which turns up again and again
in the novels is the myth of 'hidden treasure' which Balzac borrowed
from the adventure stories. His characters are divided not merely into
'good' and 'bad', but into 'haves' and 'have-nots'. The drama centres
round the efforts of the wicked 'have-nots' to obtain possession of the
'treasure' which simple, worthy men have amassed by industry and
ability. The Vautrins, Philippe Bridaus, Nucingens and Gobsecks are
simply different incarnations of the 'explorers', 'pirates' and 'buc-
caneers' of the treasure-trove stories.

2

Henry James once observed that Balzac's longest works are not
always his best. *L'Illustre Gaudissart* is not among his main achievements, but it has an almost Dickensian sense of fun and it illuminates
his method in a way that few of his other books do. This is an account
of the wiles of his commercial traveller:

He could call on the sub-prefect as an administrator, on the banker as a capitalist, on the royalist as a man of religious and monarchical principles, on the bourgeois as a bourgeois. In a word, everywhere he went he was as he should be; he left Gaudissart at the door and picked him up again when he left. . . .

He was full of gratitude towards hatters and said that it was by working on the outside of the head that he had come to understand the inside. . . .

In the famous Foreword to the *Comédie humaine*, Balzac claimed to have given a realistic account of the whole of French society. One of the difficulties of the undertaking has always seemed to me to be the gap between the setting and what the novelist was pleased to call the 'drama' in which the characters are involved. I now want to suggest that there are corresponding gaps inside the characters themselves. It must, I think, remain one of the most serious criticisms of Balzac that like Gaudissart all his characters have an 'envelope' which can be left at the door and 'picked up again on leaving'. There is a gap between the *personæ*, which are manipulated so surprisingly in the novels, and the humanity underneath, between 'Gaudissart' and the *commis-voyageur*. Nor is the apparently casual reference to hat shops less significant. For Balzac himself worked from outside and believed that once he had 'observed' externals he had arrived at a comprehension of the interior. This explains the technique of the novels which scarcely varies from one book to another. First we have the scene or décor, then the transition—not always very well managed—from bricks and mortar to the individual. Finally, an attempt is made to establish continuity between the man and the milieu.

We do not expect, nor do we want, a novel to be a biography of an imaginary person. We are not greatly concerned whether the characters are 'lifelike' and we do not care what becomes of them when we close the book. We do, however, expect them to be coherent. For it is only when they are coherent that they can assume a place in the pattern which the novelist is trying to create. It is here, it seems to me, that Balzac fails. When we look into it, we find that his characters only hold together by tricks which conceal or are intended to conceal their fundamental incoherence. We are very conscious—sometimes oppressively conscious—of the physical appearance of people and things. We see the ageing Hulot furtively putting on his corset and tinting his whiskers. We certainly hear, even if we do not understand, Nucingen's peculiar patois or Grandet's devastating stutter as he moves round the dark, cold house at Saumur. We appreciate the condition of the characters, the soldiers, bankers, merchants, poets and harlots. Nor can we fail to know about their supposed moral qualities. For Balzac is as explicit about their moral qualities as he is about their incomes. 'On est deux anges,' he writes of his modern lovers, 'et l'on se comporte comme deux démons si l'on peut.' Nearly all his characters are divided into 'angels' and 'demons', into black and white. Their moral qualities are recorded like mathematical signs. They make their entry with a plus or a minus—there is naturally no middle term—in front of them.

> Where do these beings come from? [asked Rivière of the characters of the Romantic novelists]. They are born [he answered] of a certain moral image: purity, greatness, innocence, sublime nobility or, on the contrary, infamy, bottomless perfidy, unspeakable baseness, unadulterated perversity, or again sadness, disgust with life, magnificent disdain, gloomy dis-interestedness. That is what their authors have in front of them before they have even begun to outline their characters. That is the scheme from which they are extracted.[1]

While I do not altogether share Rivière's view of the importance of character or his admiration for Balzac, his criticism of 'the romantic habit of imagining the qualities of the character before the character himself'[2] does illuminate not merely the incoherence of Balzac's characters, but a certain immaturity of outlook. It is one of his gravest weaknesses that like Flaubert he was far more successful with his minor characters than with his principals. The *mots* of certain of his principal characters—Hulot's 'Mais pourrai-je emmener la petite?', Grandet's 'Tu me rendras compte de ça là-bas', Marneffe's 'Il faut que je *fasse* le bon Dieu'—are rightly famous. It does not seem to have been pointed out, however, that they are words of limitation, that there must be something wrong with a novelist whose characters can be summed up as completely as Balzac's are in a death-bed epigram. The source of the weakness lies partly in the theory outlined in the Foreword, that just as there are 'zoological species', so there are 'social species'. He regards his characters' 'condition' as an absolute. They are all endowed with a charge of powerful anonymous 'passion' which must find an outlet and which is entirely uncontrollable. The form and the effects of this 'passion' are determined by the characters' 'condition'. This produces the famous 'monomania'—Balzac repeatedly uses this or some similar term—which is in itself a reflection of the limitations of his psychology. Goriot is completely absorbed by his obsession with his daughters, Grandet by money, Hulot by women. They cease, as one of the charac-ters in La Cousine Bette puts it, to be men and become 'a temperament'.

---

[1] *Moralisme et littérature* (Paris, 1932), p. 68.   [2] *Ibid.*, p. 77.

The trouble is that the characters only 'live' in so far as they have become 'a temperament' which means that they are only partly alive. Balzac cannot show us a man's personality being gradually corroded by an obsession. The 'monomania' is an intellectual concept which is 'imagined before the character himself' and imposed on the humanity which we never really see. When the monomania is not operating the characters turn into marionnettes because there is no correspondence between their actions and the inner man. But the virtual elimination or suppression of the whole range of 'normal' of emotions does give them their mobility and a misleading appearance of unity.

This method is less of a handicap in the provincial novels where Balzac is, for valid reasons, dealing with a simplified mentality; and in the minor characters it becomes the source of a positive strength. His picture of provincial life is less searching than Flaubert's, but he grasped the essentials and there is continuity between the characters and their milieu. We not only have the impression that the characters have been formed by the society in which they are living; we see that there is a relation of cause and effect between the gossip, intrigue, jealousies and petty spite of a provincial community and the desire of a sensitive woman to make her escape, of a wealthy spinster to find a husband or of an ignorant priest to become a canon. What is more, the setting had a moderating influence on the novelist and his creations. It must always be remembered that Balzac was born in the provinces and that at heart he remained a provincial all his life. That explains why he regarded Paris naively as 'the city of sin', indulged in the Paris novels in the absurd division into black and white and presented such an exaggerated picture of contemporary life. It would no doubt be going too far to use the term 'moral drama' of the *Vieille fille* and the *Curé de Tours*, but the books are a success largely because they are studies of weakness instead of vice and because the novelist does not apply the criterion of right and wrong to every action. Mlle Cormon's desperate hunt for a husband shows that she has lost her sense of proportion and Birotteau's covetousness is hardly in keeping with his calling, but they are not among the deadly sins. Their misfortunes spring from the fact that people with a particular failing happen to be living in a particular community where they prove fatal.

The minor characters are an essential part of the novels, but their role is similar to that of the *confidents* in seventeenth-century tragedy. They are there to pander to the weaknesses and vices of the principals, to set the machinery of the 'monomania' in motion. It is therefore only necessary for them to exhibit a limited range of impulses and they are drawn with a firmness and coherence which are lacking in the principals.

When the principals degenerate into 'a temperament' and sacrifice family and honour in order to buy 'love', we feel that too much is being left out; but it seems perfectly natural for the courtesan to sell herself to the highest bidder in order to obtain money, luxury and position or to throw over one 'protector' as soon as a richer one enters the scene. 'Ebouriffé, le chevalier de Valois n'existait plus', wrote Balzac of the middle-aged beau who 'let himself go' when his bourgeois rival stepped in and carried off the wealthy old maid. For there is something very precarious about the principal characters. We feel that if they deviated by a fraction of an inch from the rigid plan, made a false move, uttered a single word out of character or simply became 'ruffled', the whole apparatus would collapse. We feel nothing of the sort with the Joséphas, Jenny Cadines, the Florines and the Coralies. 'Ah! tu comprends maintenant, mon bonhomme,' says Josépha to Hulot as she turns him out. There is no hesitation, no blur. The incident is engraved on our minds.

3

In a letter to Mme Hanska Balzac once described style as a 'garment'. It is a revealing statement which explains the dissatisfaction that many of us must have felt in reading him. With the exception of the best of the provincial novels and the successful minor figures, we constantly have the impression that in Balzac's characters the person, the 'social species', the moral qualities and the language somehow remain separate and distinct.

> We must admit once for all [writes M. Mayer in a passage that I have already quoted], that Balzac was content to write French as it was spoken. His style was not apart from exceptions that of an artist.[1]
>
> Balzac [he observes in another place], seems to have been almost completely unaware of the resources which the Impressionists later derived from rare or recherché epithets and their curious application of some unexpected noun.[2]

The difficulty is a twofold one. The novelist regarded style as something that was added from outside, something that was saved up for the 'big scenes'. It is a conception which belongs pre-eminently to a period which does not possess a style in the assured sense of the classic ages. Now Balzac was no more capable than Flaubert of creating an organic style of his own and was obliged to rely on the spoken language of his

[1] *Op. cit.*, p. 88.   [2] *Ibid.*, p. 1.

time. This excessive addiction to the spoken word confirms the view that he was from the first far too much the product of his environment and failed to impose himself on his material.

The results were serious. There can be little doubt that Balzac was conscious that he was hampered by the lack of a sufficiently expressive vocabulary, and this explains his continual over-emphasis and his melodrama.

> We always notice [writes M. Mayer] that his choice of adjectives is the result of an effort to go one better which is dictated by the fear of being unable to express completely a subjective feeling. It is never the outcome of the stylist's attempt to achieve a particular form of oratorical beauty.[1]

He has done well to focus attention on Balzac's use of adjectives because it illuminates not only the shortcomings of Balzac's own novels, but the changes which took place in the French language after the disintegration of the classical tradition.

It has been said that French is the language of the epithet and English the language of the verb. Now this is only partly true. In the seventeenth and eighteenth centuries, as I have already suggested, French depended as much as English on the verb or on verb and substantive; it was not until the nineteenth century that the adjective became predominant and grammarians evolved 'the rule of the three adjectives'. We naturally expect the adjective to become more prominent as civilization grows more complex and man is increasingly conscious of his most intimate feelings. We must, however, make one further distinction. The clarity and elegance of the French classic style does depend to a remarkable degree on *le mot juste*, on the choice of a single adjective which is exactly right. We are not likely to forget the felicities of a moralist like La Bruyère or the extraordinary effects that Racine obtained with his *insensé, égaré, éperdu*. The great difference between the seventeenth and nineteenth centuries is that nineteenth-century prose achieved some of its most striking effects not by a single carefully placed adjective, but by concatenations of adjectives piled up at the ends of sentences. An historian like Michelet sometimes creates a startling sense of hallucination, and in spite of a good deal of preciosity there is no need to dwell on the brilliance with which the Symbolists used their epithets.

The weakness of many of the nineteenth-century prose-writers lies not in the number of adjectives they employ, but in the way they use them. It is clearly necessary to use several adjectives to express a number of different qualities and complex feelings or contrasting adjectives to

[1] *Ibid.*, p. 304.

express conflicting feelings. The seventeenth-century writers were sparing with their adjectives, but we sometimes come across accumulations of three or more. Saint-Simon describes Louis XIV as 'sage, modéré, secret'; and Mme de La Fayette tells us that the Vidame de Chartres was 'vaillant, hardi et libéral'. In the eighteenth century the practice becomes more common. Marivaux, Diderot and Voltaire all used it to produce an effect of comic exaggeration. In a well-known passage of *Candide* we are told, for example:

> Il s'en retournait, se soutenant à peine, prêché, fessé, absous et béni . . .

> [He went back, hardly able to stand, preached at, whipped, absolved and blessed . . .]

where the wit depends on the disrespectful contrast between *fessé* and words with a religious connotation.

An example of a rather different kind occurs in *Lucien Leuwen*:

> Tout en écoutant la parole lente, élégante et décolorée de M. d'Hocquincourt, Lucien examinait sa femme.

> [While listening to M. d'Hocquincourt's slow, elegant and colourless voice Lucien examined his wife.]

The word *lente* ironically qualifies *élégante*, and the slow faint voice seems to fade away altogether in *décolorée*. It qualifies *élégante* again, but it is also the perfect epithet for the *mari complaisant* that we know M. d'Hocquincourt to be. For when we reach the end of the sentence, we perceive that the sound of the voice faded because Lucien had ceased to listen and was glancing surreptitiously at the speaker's wife.

It seems evident that whether a writer uses one adjective or six, he should normally give a precise meaning to the individual word. That is the real difference between the writers of the first half of the nineteenth century and their predecessors. Saint-Simon sometimes indulges in fantastic accumulations of adjectives for purposes of invective as when he calls Harlay

> Superbe, vénimeux, malin, scélérat par nature, humble, bas, rampant devant ses besoins.

> [Proud, venomous, cunning, naturally criminal, humble, low, grovelling to his own needs. . . .]

In general, however, it is true to say that with the classic writers the
individual word rarely loses its separate identity and is seldom used
merely for emphasis. Now the spoken language tends to blur these nice
distinctions; and we find that, unlike the great masters of French prose,
Balzac nearly always uses his streams of adjectives for emphasis and
that he substitutes words for the qualities and feelings they ought to
signify. The description of the furniture at the Maison Vauquer is a
perfect instance:

> Pour expliquer combien ce mobilier est vieux, crevassé, pourri, trem-
> blant, rongé, manchot, borgne, invalide, expirant. . . .

> [In order to explain the extent to which the furniture is old, cracked,
> rotten, trembling, worm-eaten, one-armed, one-eyed, invalid, dying. . . .]

It is clearly an example of Balzac's attempt 'to go one better'. The
first five adjectives are the only ones which can properly be applied to
furniture and we feel already that they are too many. The last four
carry us further and further from the scene that the novelist purports to
be describing and the impression becomes progressively more blurred
and confused. It is perfectly legitimate to describe old furniture as
tremblant, but the word can also be used of a sick person, and it must
have been this association which led him to add 'manchot, borgne,
invalide, expirant'. In the same novel he writes:

> Les femmes avaient des robes passées, reteintes, déteintes.

> [The women wore dresses which were faded, redyed, faded again.]

Logically, it is a description of three different stages in the life of the
garments, but Balzac 'works' words in such a way that they become
practically synonymous. We have no sense of *succession* here; we simply
have a powerful impression of drabness and shabbiness, and we feel that
déteintes was added for no better reason than that it rhymes with
reteintes. When Crevel says in *La Cousine Bette*:

> Mais a-t-on jamais vu femme plus ignoble, plus infâme, plus scélérate
> que cette Valérie?

> [But have you ever known a woman who was more ignoble, more
> infamous, more criminal than that Valérie?]

I

we see how little difference there is between Balzac's descriptive prose
and his dialogue.

It is thus apparent that his handling of words is the reverse not merely
of the method employed by the writers of the seventeenth and eighteenth
centuries, but also of Proust's where we find once again the attempt to
give greater and greater precision to the notation of perceptions.[1]

Balzac's use of adjectives cannot be dismissed as a mere flaw in his
style. The weakness is central and radical. It is a sign not simply of lack
of analytical power and of that insight which is indispensable to the
great novelist, but of a tendency of all feelings to reduce themselves to
their simplest elements until they sometimes become practically indistinguishable from one another.

In fairness to Balzac, however, it must be emphasized that there is a
credit side to the account. His work is deficient in many of the qualities
which are native to all good prose, but his verbal inventiveness and even
the torrents of adjectives are the sign of an immense, though often ill-
directed, vitality. One example is the chanting of words ending in
-rama by the inmates of the Maison Vauquer in *Le Père Goriot* which
creates a strange sense of hallucination. Another is the play on Goriot's
name in the conversation between Mme de Beauséant and the Duchesse
de Langeais. From time to time a humdrum passage is lighted up by
one of those phrases which bear Balzac's personal stamp:

> Deux corruptions marchaient sur deux lignes parallèles, comme deux
> nappes qui, dans une inondation, veulent se rejoindre.

> [Two corruptions were walking along two parallel lines like two sheets
> of water trying to meet in a flood.]

The 'deux corruptions' are dancing girls and the effect depends on
the contrast between the sense of dissolution we get from *corruptions*
and the mathematical rigidity of *parallèles*.

Alain quotes a passage from *Le Père Goriot*:

> D'un côté . . . des figures jeunes, vives, encadrées par les merveilles de
> l'art et du luxe, des têtes passionnées pleines de poésie; de l'autre de sinistres
> tableaux bordés de fange, et des faces où les passions n'avaient laissé que
> leurs cordes et leur mécanisme.

> [On one side . . . young lively faces framed in the marvels of art and
> luxury, passionate expressions full of poetry; on the other sinister pictures

[1] See pp. 21-2 above.

edged with filth, and faces in which passion had left nothing except the cords and the mechanism.]

Alain points out that there is a definite attempt to write well in the opening clause of this passage with its *encadrées* and the commonplace abstraction of 'têtes passionnées pleines de poésie' which does not altogether come off; but he sees an immediate change when Balzac comes to the 'sinistres tableaux bordés de fange' and pronounces the final clause a stroke of genius.[1] He seems to me to be right. Balzac was, as surely as Flaubert, at his best when describing dissolution and collapse; and the sudden glimpses of 'cords' and 'mechanism', of a sinister background behind the crude melodrama are undoubtedly the most impressive things in *Le Père Goriot*.

[1] *Avec Balzac* (10ème éd., Paris, 1949), pp. 182-3.

III. FOUR NOVELS

1. *Le Père Goriot*

THE view that *Le Père Goriot* is Balzac's masterpiece seems to be common to his admirers and to hostile critics like Leslie Stephen and Henry James who both wrote damaging essays on him. This is a matter on which the critic has no right to temporize. I must therefore record my own opinion that far from being a masterpiece, it is as a whole one of the worst of Balzac's mature works, that it is mainly interesting as an illustration of his most characteristic vices as a novelist and that the chief reason for examining it in detail is to try to correct some of the exaggerated estimates of previous writers.

Nearly all Balzac's novels open with a factual statement which is apparently intended to prepare the way for the curious obsessions of which his characters are the victims:

> Madame Vauquer, née de Conflans, est une vieille femme qui, depuis quarante ans, tient à Paris une pension bourgeoise établie rue Neuve-Sainte-Geneviève, entre le quartier latin et le faubourg Saint-Marcel.

> [Madame Vauquer, *née* de Conflans, is an old woman who for forty years has run a middle-class Paris boarding-house which stands in the Rue Neuve-Sainte-Geneviève between the Latin Quarter and the Faubourg Saint-Marcel.]

On the next page we find the first attempt to link physical squalor and human misery:

> Les particularités de cette Scène pleine d'observation et de couleur locale ne peuvent être appréciées qu'entre les buttes Montmartre et les hauteurs de Montrouge, dans cette illustre vallée de plâtras incessamment près de tomber et de ruisseaux noirs de boue; vallée remplie de souffrances réelles, de joies souvent fausses, et si terriblement agitée, qu'il faut je ne sais quoi d'exorbitant pour y produire une sensation de quelque durée.

> The details of this Scene which is full of observation and local colour can only be appreciated between the rising ground of Montmartre and the

heights of Montrouge in the illustrious valley of broken bricks and mortar always on the verge of collapse and streams black with mud; a valley filled with real suffering and joy which is often false and so terribly agitated that it needs a suggestion of the extravagant to create any impression of permanency.]

Whatever his critics may think, Balzac liked to insist on the realism or supposed realism of his work, and it is no accident that the word *observation* turns up in the first sentence of this characteristically melodramatic passage. *Tomber* is a key word. The spectacle of buildings on the point of collapse looks forward to the moral collapse of Balzac's simple, worthy merchant. *Terriblement* and *exorbitant* are both tell-tale words. For here, as surely as in *L'Illustre Gaudissart*, the novelist seems without realizing it to point out exactly what he intends to do. A drama is about to unfold in which compared with normal standards the emotions will appear 'exorbitant' and which will (he hopes) strike the reader as 'terrible'.

A few pages later he switches from the exterior to the interior of the *pension*:

> Cette première pièce exhale une odeur sans nom dans la langue, et qu'il faudrait appeler l'*odeur de pension*. Elle sent le renfermé, le moisi, le rance; elle donne froid, elle est humide au nez, elle pénètre les vêtements; elle a le goût d'une salle où l'on a dîné; elle pue le service, l'office, l'hospice.

> [The first room exudes a nameless odour which should be called *the boarding-house smell*. It is an airless, mouldy, rancid smell; it gives you a chilly feeling; it is damp to the nostrils; it seeps into your clothes; it has the taste of a room where people have been eating; it stinks of meals, the pantry, the poor-house.]

The use of the present tense both in this and in the first passage that I quoted is intentional. The novelist's aims is to convince us that this *pension* still exists, that we have only to go as far as the Rue Neuve-Sainte-Geneviève to see the sign, 'MAISON VAUQUER: Pension Bourgeoise des deux sexes et autres', and arrive at the scene of the 'terrible drama' which he is about to relate. And the piling up of adjectives and images of physical decay does in the end give us a sickening sense of the stench of the building.

Balzac, we know, was convinced that once he had established the physical existence of the milieu—his preoccupation with 'atmosphere' is another link with the writers of 'detective fiction'—he could make its inhabitants seem equally real to us:

Aussi le spectacle désolant que présentait l'intérieur de cette maison se répétait-il dans le costume de ses habitués, également délabrés. Les hommes portaient des redingotes dont la couleur était devenue problématique, des chaussures comme il s'en jette au coin des bornes dans les quartiers élégants, du linge élimé, des vêtements qui n'avaient plus que l'âme. Les femmes avaient des robes passées, reteintes, déteintes, de vieilles dentelles raccommodées, des gants glacés par l'usage, des collerettes toujours rousses et des fichus éraillés.

[Thus the desolate spectacle presented by the interior of the house was reflected in the residents' clothes which were equally dilapidated. The men wore frock coats whose colour had become problematic, shoes of the kind that are thrown out in the fashionable quarters of the city, worn linen, garments of which there was nothing left but the soul. The women wore dresses which were faded, redyed, faded again, old lace which had been mended, gloves which were shiny with use, collars which were always brownish and frayed shawls.]

The most important word in the passage is *désolant*. It illustrates the novelist's habit of working certain words—particularly words suggesting decay—with the result that they attract other words with similar associations. *Désolant* leads to *délabrés* which somehow evokes the *couleur problématique*, the *linge élimé* and the 'robes passées, reteintes, déteintes . . . des fichus éraillés'. This is apparently what M. Blanchot means by 'the paroxysmal unfolding of idea-characters and idea-situations' or 'the hallucinatory dance' of words. No doubt there is an internal logic about the process, a progressive withdrawal into the spectral world of the *Comédie humaine*, but the value of this form of creation is less evident.

In another place we are told: 'M. Poiret était une espèce de mécanique.' *Mécanique* was a favourite word of Balzac's, and it explains why we so often have the sensation that his characters are marionettes whose gestures, repeated over and over again, have a hypnotic effect which reminds us of a nightmare. They are grotesque and somehow frightening, but you feel that at any moment the springs may give way and the whole apparatus collapse into a mass of metal, rag and sawdust.[1]

Balzac uses the same factual approach when he introduces Goriot himself:

[1] Cf., 'Semblables à de vieux époux, elles n'avaient plus rien à se dire. Il ne restait donc entre elles que les rapports *d'une vie mécanique, le jeu de rouages sans huile.*' (Italics mine.)

Le père Goriot, vieillard de soixante-neuf ans environ, s'était retiré chez madame Vauquer, en 1813, après avoir quitté les affaires.

[Old Goriot, an old man of about sixty-nine, had gone to live at Madame Vauquer's in 1813 after retiring from business.]

In another passage he strikes a familiar note:

Il devint progressivement maigre; ses mollets tombèrent; sa figure, bouffie par le contentement d'un bonheur bourgeois, se rida|démesurément; son front se plissa, sa mâchoire se dessina . . . le bourgeois gros et gras . . . semblait être un septuagénaire hébété, vacillant, blafard.

[He became steadily thinner; his calves fell; his face, puffy with the satisfaction of bourgeois happiness, became immeasurably wrinkled; his forehead furrowed; you could see the contours of his jaw . . . the big fat bourgeois looked like a man of seventy—dazed, shaky, wan.]

A few pages later we read:

Le commerce des grains semblait avoir absorbé toute son intelligence. S'agissait-il de blés, de farines, de grenailles, de reconnaître leur qualité . . . Goriot n'avait pas son second. . . . Sorti de sa spécialité, de sa simple et obscure boutique . . . il redevenait l'ouvrier stupide et grossier, l'homme incapable de comprendre un raisonnement, insensible à tous les plaisirs de l'esprit, l'homme qui s'endormait au spectacle, un de ces Dolibans parisiens, forts seulement en bêtise.

[The grain trade seemed to have absorbed the whole of his intelligence. When it came to judging the quality of corn, flour, tailings, Goriot had no equal. . . . Once he was off his special subject and away from his dark, simple shop he became the common stupid workman, the man who was incapable of following an argument or experiencing any of the pleasures of the mind, the man who fell asleep at the theatre, one of those Parisian Dolibans whose stupidity is their only endowment.]

There is no reason why a novelist should not put simple souls into his books, but his characters are after all the instruments which he uses to express a particular experience and we cannot be indifferent to the fact that the choice of a sentimentalized figure like Goriot is the sign of a defective view of life. For this account of his limitations is the prelude to the main theme of the book—the obsession with his daughters which

brings him to destruction. We learn that after the death of a wife 'who
was the object of a religious wonder to him, a boundless love'

> . . . le sentiment de la paternité se développa chez Goriot jusqu'à la
> *déraison.*

> [. . . with Goriot the sense of fatherhood was developed to the point of
> unreason.]

Again:

> L'éducation de ses deux filles fut naturellement *déraisonnable.*

> [The education of his daughters was naturally unreasonable.]

In order to be sure that we are well prepared for what is to come,
Balzac cannot resist the observation:

> Ice se termine l'exposition de cette obscure mais *effroyable* tragédie
> parisienne.

> [Here ends the prologue to this obscure, but appalling Parisian tragedy.]

Nor is the background of the book more impressive. The reflections
of Mme de Beauséant and Vautrin on 'life' are distressing in their
banality:

> Vous saurez alors ce qu'est le monde, une réunion de dupes et de
> fripons.
> Vous croyez à quelque chose de fixe dans ce monde-là! Méprisez donc
> les hommes et voyez les mailles par où l'on peut passer à travers le réseau
> du Code. Le secret des grandes fortunes sans cause apparente est un crime
> oublié, parce qu'il a été proprement fait.

> [You'll find out then what the world's like—a collection of gulls and
> rogues.
> You believe in something unchanging in that world! Come, despise
> men and look for the loopholes by which one can get round the law. The
> secret behind all the great fortunes which have no apparent cause is a crime
> which was forgotten because it was properly carried out.]

The arrest of Vautrin shows Balzac at his worst:

Le lendemain devait prendre place parmi les jours les plus extraordinaires de l'histoire de la maison Vauquer.

Le forçat évadé jeta sur Eugène le regard froidement fascinateur que certains hommes éminemment magnétiques ont le don de lancer, et qui, dit-on, calme les fous de dans les maisons d'aliénés. Eugène trembla furieux tous ses membres.

[The next day was destined to take its place among the most extraordinary in the history of the Maison Vauquer.

The escaped convict shot a coldly fascinating glance at Eugène—the sort of glance which belongs to certain men who are in a high degree magnetic and which is said to soothe raging lunatics in asylums. Eugène trembled in every limb.]

Then comes the actual arrest:

Le chef alla droit à lui, commença par lui donner sur la tête une tape si violemment appliquée, qu'il fit sauter la perruque et rendit à la tête de Collin toute son horreur. Accompagnées de cheveux rouge brique et courts qui leur donnaient un épouvantable caractère de force mêlée de ruse, cette tête et cette face, en harmonie avec le buste, furent intelligemment illuminées comme si les feux de l'enfer les eussent éclairées. . . . Collin devint un poète infernal où se peignirent tous les sentiments humains moins un seul, celui du repentir. Son regard était celui de l'archange déchu qui veut toujours la guerre.

[The chief of police went straight up to him and began by giving him such a violent blow on the head that it knocked off his wig and restored to Collin's head all its horror. Covered with short brick-red hair which gave them an appalling character of strength mixed with cunning, the head and face which matched the body were intelligently lighted up as though the fires of hell had shone on them. . . . Collin became a poet of the nether regions in whom one saw all human feelings with a single exception— repentance. His look was that of the fallen archangel who always wants war.]

There would be no point in dwelling on this curious exhibition if the passages were not taken from what is generally regarded as one of the great French novels and if Vautrin had not been described by some critics as 'a great creation'. It is a perfect example of Balzac's Light Programme manner. For this is crude melodrama as distinct from what I have called Balzac's highly personal melodrama. Vautrin is a borrowing from the *roman frénétique* which has been transported bodily into the novel.

I*

It is, perhaps, only fair to add that it is the story not so much of
Vautrin as of Goriot's insensate passion for his daughters which has
excited the admiration of critics on both sides of the Channel. Comparisons between Goriot and Lear have become commonplaces of criticism.
Nor are they always as favourable to Shakespeare as one might expect.
It was once claimed for *Eugénie Grandet* that it shows us a particular
miser in a particular French province in the nineteenth century while
in *L'Avare* Molière managed to give us no more than a picture of the
Miser in abstract terms. Something of the same sort has been said of
Le Père Goriot. In their comparisons, Balzac's critics have been at pains
to point out that Goriot is a 'modern' Lear—a Marxist critic has
recently called him a 'bourgeois' Lear—with the implication that he
knows more about the detailed workings of the human mind than
Shakespeare.

Turn to some characteristic passages and the comparison at once
ceases to be even credible:

'Mon Dieu! pleurer, elle a pleuré?'
'La tête sur mon gilet,' dit Eugène.
'Oh! donnez-le-moi,' dit le père Goriot. 'Comment! il y a eu là des
larmes de ma fille, de ma chère Delphine, qui ne pleurait jamais étant
petite! Oh! je vous en achèterai un autre, ne le portez plus, laissez-le-moi.'

'Mes filles, mes filles! Anastasie, Delphine! je veux les voir. Envoyez-les
chercher par la gendarmerie, de force! la justice est pour moi, tout est pour
moi, la nature, le Code civil. Je proteste! La patrie périra si les pères sont
foulés aux pieds. Cela est clair. La société, le monde, roulent sur la pater-
nité, tout croule si les enfants n'aiment pas leurs pères. Oh! les voir, les
entendre, n'importe ce qu'elles me diront, pourvu que j'entende leur voix,
ca calmera mes douleurs. . . .'

['God! cry, she cried?'
'With her head on my waistcoat,' said Eugene.
'Oh! give it to me,' said old Goriot. 'What! my daughter's tears were
there, my dear Delphine who never cried when she was little. Oh! I'll
buy you another one. Don't wear it any more. Let me have it.'

'My daughters, my daughters! Anastasie, Delphine! I want to see them.
Send the police to bring them by force! Justice is on my side. Everything
is on my side—nature and the law. I protest! The country will perish if
fathers are trampled underfoot. That's quite clear. Society and the world
are founded on fatherhood. Everything will collapse if children don't love
their fathers. Oh! just to see them, to hear them speak. It doesn't matter
what they say, if only I could hear their voices it would ease my pain.']

There are many more pages in the same strain. It scarcely seems necessary to evoke the name of the greatest poet to place this cataract of words or Balzac's curious sentimentality in their true perspective. One critic has suggested that Shelley's *Cenci* is a more suitable term of comparison; and in both works we find the same hysteria, the same lack of feeling for language and the same surrender to the most dubious form of inspiration.

2. *Eugénie Grandet*

'It does not seem to me to be one of the best of Balzac's novels or to deserve the extraordinary favour it has enjoyed,' remarks Gide of *Eugénie Grandet*. 'The style is extremely mediocre; the characters could scarcely be more summary; the dialogue is conventional and often inacceptable. . . . Alone the story of old Grandet's speculations seems to me to be masterly; but that is perhaps because I am not competent in such matters.'[1]

Eugénie Grandet was completed a year before Balzac began *Le Père Goriot*. The style is undoubtedly 'sticky' in places, but it does not seem to me that an occasional awkwardness in the writing is sufficient grounds on which to condemn the book. M. Gide's other criticisms apply to most of Balzac's novels. None of them is completely satisfactory even in its own genre. They are, in so far as they are successful, only good in parts. Nor does it seem to me that an understanding or lack of understanding of financial machinations ought to affect our judgment. I have probably less skill in this respect than M. Gide, but I, too, find the account of Grandet's activities 'masterly'; and the book as a whole seems to me to be one of Balzac's most successful works. For here there is no straining, as there is in the *Père Goriot*, to fit the characters into their background; the characters—the principals as well as the minor characters—are certainly there. They belong to their province, to their town, to their community. There is nothing forced or melodramatic about the description of the damp, cold, old-fashioned house at Saumur:

> . . . cette maison pâle, froide, silencieuse, située en haut de la ville, et abritée par les ruines des remparts.

> [. . . the pale, cold, silent house standing above the town and sheltered by the ruins of the ramparts.]

[1] *Journal, 1889-1939* (Second Edition, Paris, 1948), p. 1040.

For once the three adjectives are necessary and place the house before us. The house and its owner belong to one another:

Les manières de cet homme étaient fort simples. Il parlait peu. Généralement, il exprimait ses idées par de petites phrases sentencieuses et dites d'une voix douce. . . . Au physique, Grandet était un homme de cinq pieds, trapu, carré, ayant des mollets de douze pouces de circonférence, des rotules noueuses et de larges épaules; son visage était rond, tanné, marqué de petite vérole; son menton était droit, ses lèvres n'offraient aucune sinuosité, et ses dents étaient blanches; ses yeux avaient l'expression calme et dévoratrice que le peuple accorde au basilic. . . . Son nez, gros par le bout, supportait une loupe veinée que le vulgaire disait, non sans raison, pleine de malice. Cette figure annonçait une finesse dangereuse, une probité sans chaleur, l'égoïsme d'un homme habitué à concentrer ses sentiments dans la jouissance de l'avarice et sur le seul être qui lui fût réellement quelque chose, sa fille Eugénie, sa seule héritière. . . . Aussi, quoique de mœurs faciles et molles en apparence, M. Grandet avait-il un caractère de bronze. Toujours vêtu de la même manière, qui le voyait aujourd'hui le voyait tel qu'il était depuis 1791.

[The man's behaviour was simplicity itself. He spoke little. Usually he expressed himself in brief sententious phrases, delivered in a gentle tone. . . . Physically, Grandet was five feet in height, thick-set and squarely built, his calves over twelve inches in diameter, his knees bony and his shoulders broad. His face was round and marked by smallpox; his chin straight, his lips level, his teeth white; his eyes had the calm devouring expression which the people attribute to the basilisk. . . . His nose, which was fat at the end, had a veined knob on it which the common people alleged, not without reason, was full of malice. This face suggested a dangerous finesse, a probity devoid of any warmth of feeling, the selfishness of a man who concentrated all his feelings on the enjoyment of avarice and on the only being who meant anything to him—his daughter and sole heir, Eugénie. Thus, though his behaviour was easy and gentle, M. Grandet had a character of iron. He was always dressed in the same fashion: anyone who saw him to-day, saw him as he had been since 1791.]

The description of Grandet is free from all Balzac's usual faults. It has the economy and precision of a seventeenth-century 'character'. There is complete correspondence between the inner and the outer man. The grave, hard exterior reflects his preoccupation with a single dominating passion. Once Balzac has described the character of the miser, which clearly leaves no place for psychological development, he merely has to invent the actions and gestures which will bring him to life and, so to speak, set him in motion. He therefore concentrates like Dickens on a few tell-tale gestures which fix themselves in the mind— the maddening stutter, the horrible 'Ta ta ta ta', the daily distribution of 'rations', the meanness over fuel and candles which all lead back to the miser's absorbing passion:

'Ta ta ta ta!' dit Grandet, 'voilà les bêtises qui commencent. Je vois avec peine, mon neveu, vos jolies mains blanches.'

Il lui montra les espèces d'épaules de mouton que la nature lui avait mises au bout des bras.

'Voilà des mains faites pour ramasser des écus!'

['Ta, ta, ta, ta!' said Grandet. 'You're starting to be silly. It pains me to see your nice white hands, nephew.'

He showed him objects like shoulders of mutton which nature had attached to the ends of his arms.

'These are the sort of hands made to rake in the shekels!']

M. Gide, we know, has complained about the faintness of the other characters in the book. Their limitations are due partly to the nature of the undertaking and partly to Balzac's artistic shortcomings. The pic- ture of the old servant, of mother and daughter spending their days over their needlework in the dim house and of the factions between the des Grassins and the Cruchots seems to me to be admirable of its kind and at its particular level. They have on the whole sufficient life to throw into relief the activities of Grandet, and if we are not told a great deal about them it is largely because there is not much to tell.

Where, it seems to me, the novel is most open to criticism is in the account of the love affair between Eugénie and her cousin. This is the description of her emotional awakening:

Cette physionomie calme, colorée, bordée d'une lueur comme une jolie fleur éclose, reposait l'âme, communiquait le charme de la conscience qui s'y reflétait, et commandait le regard. Eugénie était encore sur la rive de la vie où fleurissent les illusions enfantines, où se cueillent les marguerites avec des délices plus tard inconnues.

[Her calm fresh-complexioned face, which was surrounded by a glow like a lovely flower in full bloom, was restful to the spirit; it made you feel the charm of the mind reflected in it and compelled attention. Eugénie was on the threshold of life where childish illusions still flourish and where you pick daisies with a delight which is unknown in later years.]

There is no real penetration into her feelings here. The repeated reference to flowers merely gives the passage a vague, facile charm For Eugénie and Charles are to a considerable degree conventional figures and like Vautrin represent the alien element which Balzac often incorporated uncritically into his work. Yet if Charles is not closely observed, he possesses sufficient life for Balzac's purpose. Balzac, as we know from his other books, is master of a certain form of social comedy. Without probing deeply into psychological motives, he is often admirable in his descriptions of the gaucheries of the young man making his début in society. Rastignac's clumsy efforts to ingratiate himself with the great seem to me to be much the best part of *Le Père Goriot*. In *Eugénie Grandet* we see the situation in reverse. Whatever the shortcomings of the portrait of Charles Grandet, we do feel the full impact of the dandy on the narrow provincial society of Saumur.

Still, we must agree with M. Gide that what is impressive about the novel is old Grandet and his speculations and that once he is dead the interest evaporates.

3. *Le Curé de Tours*

The *Curé de Tours* was written nearly eighteen months before *Eugénie Grandet*. It is not like the earlier book a short novel, but a *nouvelle*. It seems to me to be one of the most enjoyable of all Balzac's books and it reinforces the view that he was at his best on a tiny stage.

The approach is similar, but in this book the covetousness of an ignorant priest is substituted for the avarice of the miser as the ruling passion. For twelve years the Abbé Birotteau has desired the lodging of his old friend Canon Chapeloud. At last he has it and the only thing that he still needs to complete his happiness is a canon's stall at St. Gatien. In his blundering way he offends his landlady, Mlle Gamard, who makes up her mind to expel him and give his room to Canon Troubert. She not only succeeds, but a clause in the contract gives her the right to keep the Abbé's furniture which had been left to him by Chapeloud. The town is divided into two factions, but the political influence of Birotteau's ecclesiastical opponents induces his aristocratic friends to abandon him. Troubert sees to it that he is exiled to a parish on the outskirts of Tours which prevents him from enjoying the society of his former friends. We leave the old man dying in his presbytery garden as Troubert drives past on his way to take possession of his see, for he has become a bishop.

In the opening pages Balzac describes Birotteau's 'monomania':

Depuis le jour où le camarade du chanoine vit les rideaux de lampas rouge, les meubles d'acajou, le tapis d'Aubusson qui ornaient cette vaste pièce peinte à neuf, l'appartement de Chapeloud devint pour lui l'objet d'une monomanie secrète. .... Quand son ami tombait malade, il venait certes chez lui conduit par une sincère affection; mais, en apprenant l'indisposition du chanoine, ou en lui tenant compagnie, il s'élevait, malgré lui, dans le fond de son âme, mille pensées dont la formule la plus simple était toujours:

'Si Chapeloud mourait, je pourrais avoir son logement.'

[From the day on which the canon's friend saw the curtains of red lampas, the mahogany furniture and the Aubusson carpet that adorned the vast room which had recently been redecorated, Chapeloud's rooms became the object of a secret monomania. ... When his friend fell ill, he certainly came to see him out of genuine affection; but when he learnt of the canon's illness or while he was keeping him company, there arose in the bottom of his heart and in spite of himself a hundred different thoughts whose tenor, reduced to its simplest form, was always this:

'If Chapeloud died, I could have his rooms.']

Balzac's hand does not falter in displaying these simple, tenacious passions. Birotteau's covetousness attaches itself to concrete things—the flowered silk curtains, the Aubusson carpet, the mahogany furniture—and because he is ignorant and unspiritual, his preoccupation with his own comfort becomes more powerful than his feeling of friendship for Chapeloud. The same weakness places him at the mercy of the contending factions. If he had been less self-centred, he would not have offended the embittered Gamard; and if he had been more spiritual, he would not have been broken by the loss of his material possessions.

The account of the enmity between Birotteau and Mlle Gamard is no less good:

Entre personnes sans cesse en présence, la haine et l'amour vont toujours croissant; on trouve à tout moment des raisons pour s'aimer ou se haïr mieux. Aussi l'abbé Birotteau devint-il insupportable à mademoiselle Gamard . . . il fut pour elle l'objet d'une persécution sourde et d'une vengeance froidement calculée. Les quatre circonstances capitales de la porte fermée, des pantoufles oubliées, du manque de feu, du bougeoir porté chez lui, pouvaient seules lui révéler cette inimitié terrible dont les dernières conséquences ne devaient le frapper qu'au moment où elles seraient irréparables.

[Between people who are continually together, hate and love are always on the increase: you discover every moment reasons for loving or hating one another more. Thus the Abbé Birotteau became intolerable to Mlle Gamard . . . he was the victim of a silent persecution and a coldly calculated revenge. The four incidents of capital importance—the locked door, the forgotten bedroom slippers, the absence of fire and the candlestick which had been brought to his room—alone could reveal the terrible enmity whose final results were only to strike him at the moment when they would be irreparable.]

The very narrowness of the circle in which the Abbé lives intensifies the passions released and mere pinpricks—the closed door, the forgotten bedroom slippers and the absence of fire—assume tragic proportions. The tension developed in this hostile intimacy does invest circumstances with a sort of nightmare horror:

Il arriva dès lors rapidement au désespoir, en apercevant, à toute heure, les doigts crochus et effilés de mademoiselle Gamard prêts à s'enfoncer dans son cœur.

[From that moment onwards he quickly reached a state of despair when he saw all the time the thin crooked fingers of Mlle Gamard ready to bury themselves in his heart.]

The adjectives—*crochus et effilés*—are not put in from without. There is no gap between word and feeling; we are aware of the thin, crooked claws about to bury themselves in his heart.

It is the story of the eternal struggle between the simple soul and those who without actually transgressing the law are totally unscrupulous in dealing with their rivals and enemies. The shortness of the book is one of the secrets of its success. On the tiny stage we are shown the parties and rivalries which divide provincial society; and the rightness of the proportions, the suggestion of larger forces called into play by this provincial squabble give the book its economy and its shapeliness.

I felt tempted to describe both *Eugénie Grandet* and the *Curé de Tours* as 'small scale' works, but the term 'short range' is more accurate. They are clearly not books of the same calibre as *Adolphe*; they should rather be classed with Flaubert's *Un Cœur simple*. In each case we feel that the artist has produced a finished work of art; but we can scarcely avoid the suspicion that in a sense he has been too successful. The books are so complete that they suggest nothing beyond themselves. They do not possess the disturbing qualities of Constant's masterpiece or its universal appeal.

4. *La Cousine Bette*

'This story', wrote Balzac in the *Curé de Tours*, 'belongs to all times. It is sufficient to extend a little the narrow circle in the middle of which these people are about to play their parts to discover the efficient reason of the events which take place in the highest spheres of society.'

In theory he was perfectly right, but when he tried to describe 'the events which take place in the highest spheres of society' he encountered the same sort of difficulty as Flaubert when he turned in *L'Éducation sentimentale* from the sad Norman villages to the complexities of urban life. Novels like *Le Cousin Pons* and *La Cousine Bette*, which belong to Balzac's final period, are more accomplished and mature than the earlier works, but we cannot help feeling that the development of his sensibility failed to keep pace with the development of his craft as a novelist.

La Cousine Bette seems to me to be much the best of the novels of Paris life and its merits are fairly described by the term 'powerful'. The ground plan does not differ sensibly from that of many of the other novels. It is the story of an obsession and its deplorable consequences or rather it is the story of two obsessions—Bette's jealousy and vindictiveness, and the sexual mania of a retired general and a retired scent merchant. It has a greater firmness and solidity than most of the other novels of urban life, and as 'a social document' it is much more impressive; but it does not reveal an appreciably greater degree of psychological penetration and the absence of inner development, which is comparatively unimportant in the short books, is obviously a serious weakness in a novel of this length.

The opening is one of Balzac's most effective scenes. The retired perfumer—the Dickensian Crevel who is always 'striking an attitude' —tries to buy his way to the bed of the virtuous Mme Hulot by offering to replace her daughter's dowry which has been squandered by the Baron on a succession of expensive courtesans. It has its counterpart in another scene much later in the book when Mme Hulot tries, also unsuccessfully, to sell herself to Crevel in order to retrieve the family fortunes which have taken a still more disastrous turn on account of the Baron's infatuation for Mme Marneffe. For the book chronicles the rise of the commercial class and the downfall of an aristocracy which had come to power through its undeniable merits during the Napoleonic era. Balzac describes it as 'économe, sage, prévoyante, enfin

bourgeoise sans grandeur'. As he is being 'shown the door', Crevel
notices the state of Mme Hulot's salon:

> . . . une vieille lampe, un lustre dédoré, les cordes du tapis, enfin les
> haillons de l'opulence qui faisaient de ce grand salon blanc, rouge et or, un
> cadavre des fêtes impériales.

> [. . . an old lamp, a sconce with its gilt falling away, the threadbare
> carpet, the tatters of an opulence that conspired to make the great room
> in white, red and gold look like a corpse of Empire festivities.]

Balzac excels in the description of the shabby tawdriness of Restoration life and the unobtrusive image—'un cadavre des fêtes impériales'
—is very successful in conveying its loss of spirit.

He is equally successful in his own way in showing what has taken
the place of the 'corpse':

> Notre temps [observes one of the merchants] est le triomphe du com-
> merce, de l'industrie et de la sagesse bourgeoise qui ont créé la Hollande.

> [We live in times when trade, industry, and middle-class common sense
> are supreme, the virtues that made Holland what she was.]

Again:

> J'adore Louis-Philippe, c'est mon idole, il est la représentation auguste,
> exacte de la classe sur laquelle il a fondé sa dynastie, et je n'oublierai jamais
> ce qu'il a fait pour la passementerie en rétablissant la garde nationale.

> [I honour Louis-Philippe; he is my idol, he is the august representative
> of the class on which he has established his throne, and I shall never forget
> what he did for the trimming business by re-establishing the National
> Guard.]

The comment is effective because it is implicit. The National Guard,
which under Napoleon had been one of the glories of France, is interesting only in so far as it stimulates trade.

One of the principal merits of the novelist is to have reduced the gap
between the social background and his main figures. He sets out to
show that a society which is based entirely on commercial values and
in which everyone and everything has a price must lead to the destruc-

tion of *grandeur*. Hulot, who rose to fame on account of his exploits on the battlefield, can find no better outlet for his talents than the pursuit of the Jenny Cadines, the Joséphas and Mmes Marneffes of Restoration society and he becomes so hopelessly entangled in this form of 'commerce' that he finally uses his position as a public servant to rob the State.

The best part of the book is undoubtedly the account of the rise of the *poule de luxe*. 'Love' is a commodity which is sold to the highest bidder, and as soon as one victim has been squeezed dry he is given his *congé* and his successor installed. When Josépha hands over the house that Hulot has rented for her out of his daughter's dowry to one of her less brilliant colleagues and goes to live in a more splendid house provided by the wealthy Duc d'Hérouville, this is how she announces it:

Monsieur . . . j'ai cédé les guenilles de la rue Chauchat à la petite Héloïse Brisetout de Bixiou; si vous voulez réclamer votre bonnet de coton, votre tire-botte, votre ceinture et votre cire à favoris, j'ai stipulé qu'on vous les rendrait.

[Monsieur . . . I left the rubbish of the Rue Chauchat to little Héloïse Brisetout; if you wish to collect your cotton nightcap, your shoe-horn, your corset, and your moustache-wax, I have stipulated that they are to be returned to you.]

In spite of their ascent in the social scale, Balzac's courtesans retain the crude vigour of the proletariat from which they came and they are also the expression of the novelist's own innate vulgarity. This is Josépha on her good behaviour with Mme Hulot:

Eh bien, si vous aviez eu, voyez-vous, un peu de notre *chic*, vous l'auriez empêché de courailler; car vous auriez été ce que nous savons être; *toutes les femmes* pour un homme. Le gouvernement devrait créer une école de gymnastique pour les honnêtes femmes!

[But you know, if you had had some of our *chic*, you could have kept him from straying; because then you would have been what we know how to be—all kinds of woman at once to a man. The Government ought to start a school for training honest women!]

This is Mme Marneffe:

Lisbeth, mon amour, ce matin deux heures de Crevel à faire, c'est bien assommant.

[Lisbeth darling, two hours of Crevel this morning! Such a bore!]

Balzac himself describes Mme Marneffe as 'cette Merteuil bourgeoise' and this places her very neatly. She may protest to Crevel:

Toujours des marchés! les bourgeois n'apprendront jamais à donner! Vous voulez vous faire des relais d'amour dans la vie avec des inscriptions de rente? . . . Ah! boutiquier, marchand de pommade! tu étiquètes tout!

[More bargains! Shopkeepers never learn to give! You want to invest in love by instalments, all through your life, by means of security bonds. . . . Tradesman! Hair-oil seller! You put a price on everything!]

But the effectiveness of the picture depends precisely on the fact that she has exchanged the motives of a Mme de Merteuil for those of a commercial society, that she can only exist in a society in which love has become a mere commodity.

I have said that one of Balzac's principal merits in this book is to have reduced the gap between the social background and his main characters, but to reduce a gap is not the same thing as to abolish it completely. He is very far from doing that. He is successful at the documentary level in revealing certain aspects of Restoration society, but when we compare the novel with *Lucien Leuwen* we see how incomplete his picture was and how far he was from really grasping the complexities of the contemporary situation.[1] This is evident when we turn to the main characters. He describes Bette as 'cette ardente fille, passionnée à vide', and at the time of Hulot's disgrace the Prince de Wissembourg says to him:

Ces femmes-là vous ôtent donc le bon sens? elles vous mettent donc des coquilles de noix sur les yeux? ou vous êtes donc fait autrement que nous autres? Il fallait quitter l'administration, du moment que vous n'étiez plus un homme, mais un tempérament!

[Do these women rob you of your common sense? They must put blinkers over your eyes! Or are you made differently from the rest of us? The day you ceased to be a man and became only a temperament you should have retired from administration.]

[1] It is surprising to find M. Bardèche writing: 'De *Lucien Leuwen* aux romans de Balzac, il y a la différence d'un dessin à un tableau.' (*Stendhal romancier*, p. 261.)

For like nearly all Balzac's other novels *La Cousine Bette* is very largely a study of a passion which functions in the void, of a man who has ceased to be a man and degenerated into a 'temperament'. It is the familiar thesis that each human being is endowed with a dose of anonymous and uncontrollable 'passion' whose origin is unexplained and unmotivated and whose form is determined by circumstance and *métier*. All Balzac's characters are fanatics, but he cannot explain his facile division into good and bad, or why fanaticism should drive Mme Hulot into a sanctity which is as incredible as her husband's amorous exploits.

'L'amour du baron et celui de Crevel', we are told, 'étaient néanmoins une rude charge pour Valérie.' They are for us too. The trouble is that it is always the same story pitched in the same key. We can always foresee not merely what will happen next, but the precise impact of events on our exhausted sensibility. The method works well enough in short books like *Eugénie Grandet* and the *Curé de Tours* where the effect of the book depends on the maintenance of a uniform tone; but it is only too apparent that when Balzac tackles a larger and more ambitious theme there is insufficient material to fill his canvas and he is driven to that form of repetition which is peculiar to him, to the switch from the *roman* to the *récit*. For it becomes impossible to maintain our interest in a rake's progress which at the end of nearly six hundred pages leads a retired perfumer to a hideous death and a *beau de l'Empire* to his cook's bed.

IV. 'WHAT DOES IT PROVE?'

'QU'EST-CE que cela prouve?' the French scientist, Laplace, is reported to have remarked of *Phèdre*. It is a startling question. 'Naturally,' we answer, a little dazed, 'naturally *Phèdre* "proves" nothing. It is simply there. It is a supreme work of art and like all supreme works of art it does something to us, alters us, modifies our experience.' Yet one cannot help feeling that the same question would have appeared much less startling and much more difficult to answer if it had been asked of Balzac instead of Racine. For what in fact does the *Comédie humaine* 'prove' or, to put it in another way, what does it do to us? Does it alter us? Does it modify our experience?

I think the answer must be that it doesn't. It gives us an entertaining and informative account of France from the Revolution to the close of Louis-Philippe's reign at a documentary level. We can read Balzac in small doses and enjoy him as a story-teller, and he produced a number of 'short range' works of art. But the tiny impact of the *Comédie humaine* on the adult reader—on the reader who properly expects a novel like any other form of art to provide him with an important experience—seems to me to be out of all proportion to its vast bulk. We cannot escape the impression that Balzac's outlook was fundamentally immature and that it was this which led him to express himself through simple or deliberately simplified figures. Henry James, we remember, spoke of 'a certain heroic pressure which drives them home to our credence'; but he made a damaging reservation when he added, 'a contagious illusion on the author's part'. For the 'heroic pressure' remains ill-defined and unattached, and it is difficult to see that any pattern, any conception of the good life, emerges from the *Comédie humaine*. Balzac's monomaniacs are in the last analysis the disinherited and degerate offspring of Corneille. The impulse, which in more propitious times produced Rodrigue and Polyeucte, produces in a commercial society nothing better than Vautrin. Our abiding impression is, indeed, that 'there is something there', but something which because he was too much the product of his environment, Balzac failed to put across.

FLAUBERT

Tout ce que je demande, c'est à continuer de pouvoir admirer les maîtres avec cet enchantement intime pour lequel je donnerais tout, tout. Mais quant à en devenir un, jamais, j'en suis sûr. Il me manque énormément; l'innéité d'abord.

Flaubert in a letter to George Sand

I. THE POLITICS OF A NOVELIST

I

'THERE are two Flauberts', Mr. Middleton Murry once wrote. 'One was born on 12 December 1821, in the surgeon's house at Rouen hospital; the other in enthusiastic minds in the last quarter of the nineteenth century. One was a broad, big-boned, lovable, rather simple-minded man, with the look and the laugh of a farmer, who spent his life in agonies over the intensive culture of half a dozen curiously assorted volumes; the other was an incorporeal giant, a symbol, a war-cry, a banner under which a youthful army marched and marches still to the rout of the bourgeois and the revolution of literature.'[1]

Nearly thirty years have passed since these lines were written and Flaubert's work is still a battleground. Where Mr. Murry saw only two Flauberts, we can discern perhaps four or five. Flaubert is still bitterly attacked and warmly defended, but the focus has shifted. In the 'twenties Proust was discussing the poverty of his imagery and Rivière the thinness of his psychology: to-day it is his political convictions or lack of convictions which engage us. Mr. Edmund Wilson has dis-covered a socialist Flaubert 'who had observed something of which Marx was not aware'.[2] M. Sartre, on the other hand, produces a bour-geois Flaubert. 'I hold Flaubert and Goncourt responsible for the repres-sions which followed the Commune,' he remarks, 'because they wrote not a single line to prevent them.'[3]

While it is an encouraging sign that Flaubert's work still provokes such lively discussion, the change of emphasis is unfortunate. For a narrow, sectarian approach, which is unable to appreciate Flaubert's integrity and his single-minded devotion to his art, is scarcely a contri-bution to the formation of a 'responsible literature'. It can only add to the existing confusion of critical values. Nor is it easy to see in what way a greater infusion of politics would have improved Flaubert's novels.

[1] *Countries of the Mind*, I (revised edition, Oxford, 1931), p. 158. (The essay was originally written and published in 1921.)
[2] *The Triple Thinkers* (London, 1938), pp. 114-15.
[3] *Situations*, II (Paris, 1948), p. 13. Compare Flaubert's own comment on the wreck of the Tuileries in 1871: 'This need never have happened if they had only understood *L'Éducation sentimentale*.'

He was more keenly aware than many of his contemporaries of the
menace of political corruption and vested interests. Whatever his shortcomings, 'timidity' and 'irresponsibility' are hardly words that can be
fairly applied to the author of the prophetic comment on M. Dambreuse
and his circle in *L'Éducation sentimentale*:

> La plupart des hommes qui étaient là avaient servi, au moins, quatre
> gouvernements; et ils auraient vendu la France ou le genre humain, pour
> garantir leur fortune, s'épargner un malaise, un embarras, ou même par
> simple bassesse, adoration instinctive de la force.

> [Most of the men present had served at least four Governments; and
> they would have sold France, or the whole human race, to safeguard their
> fortune, to spare themselves a moment's uneasiness or embarrassment, or
> else out of sheer servility, through their instinctive reverence for brute
> strength.]

Later in the same book he describes the sacking of the Palais Royal
by the mob:

> La canaille s'affubla ironiquement de dentelles et de cachemires. Des
> crépines d'or s'enroulèrent aux manches des blouses, des chapeaux à plumes
> d'autruche ornaient la tête des forgerons, des rubans de la Légion d'hon-
> neur firent des ceintures aux prostituées.... Puis la fureur s'assombrit. Une
> curiosité obscène fit fouiller tous les cabinets, tous les recoins, ouvrir tous
> les tiroirs. Des galériens enfoncèrent leurs bras dans la couche des princesses,
> et se roulaient dessus par consolation de ne pouvoir les violer.

> [In mockery, the rabble draped themselves in lace and cashmere. Gold
> fringes were wound about the sleeves of blouses, hats with ostrich plumes
> decked the heads of blacksmiths, ribbons of the Legion of Honour made
> sashes for prostitutes.... Then their frenzy took a darker turn. In obscene
> curiosity they ransacked the cupboards and closets, and turned out all the
> drawers. Jailbirds thrust their arms into the princesses' bed and rolled on
> top of it, as a consolation for not being able to rape them.]

Flaubert was happily free from sentimental illusions about 'the
common man', from that narrow party spirit which has persuaded
itself that humble origins and a lack of instruction are necessarily qualifications for good government. He saw very clearly that big business was
ruining France; but though he perceived the weaknesses of the ruling
class, he was not unaware of the civilized standards for which the owners

of 'hats with ostrich plumes', 'ribbons of the Legion of Honour' and those who had lain in 'la couche des princesses' had stood. He was not a political novelist in the ordinary sense; he looked beyond politics to the moral situation which produced them and, because he was a distinguished artist, he saw that politics, so far from being the whole of life, was only one element in the 'mess' which he set out to describe.

2

Flaubert maintained that there had been three main stages in the evolution of humanity: *le paganisme, le Christianisme* and what he called *le muflisme*. In his study of 'Flaubert's Politics', Mr. Edmund Wilson has argued that each of his works illustrates one or other of these stages and has tried to give it a unity which it does not seem to me to possess. Among Flaubert's 'half a dozen curiously assorted volumes', there are only three that 'count: *Madame Bovary, L'Éducation sentimentale* and *Un Cœur simple*. Mr. Murry has well described *Salammbô* as 'the painful polishing of a hollow surface'. Its main interest lies in the fact that it illustrates most of Flaubert's principal faults and demonstrates the artistic impossibility of the historical novel. *La Tentation de saint Antoine* possesses the same faults and hardly deserves the compliment intended in the description of it as 'the French *Faust*'. Nor can I share the view of those who regard *Bouvard et Pécuchet* as a great comic novel. It seems to me to be a failure, and a glance at *Madame Bovary* helps us to understand why it failed. The most successful characters in that novel are not the principals, but the Abbé Bournisien and Homais. They are genuine creations and they are a success because there is complete identity between what is loosely called the 'character' and the 'symbol'. Bournisien stands for the inadequacy of the rural clergy in Normandy as Homais stands for the limitations of 'progressive' thought. The exchanges between the two are among the best comic scenes that Flaubert ever wrote and are an admirable comment on the *bêtise* which provoked him all his life. They are effective because they are subordinated to the plan of the book as a whole and are never allowed to get out of hand. In *Bouvard et Pécuchet* Flaubert tried to make middle-class stupidity the subject of a whole book, to elevate characters whose role could only be secondary into principals. 'L'effort des siècles', observes M. Mauriac sorrowfully, 'aboutit à ces profondes caricatures . . . il éliminait l'âme du composé humain, pour obtenir de la bêtise à l'état pur.'[1] Artistically, the result was disastrous—a book without point

[1] *Trois grands hommes devant Dieu* (Paris, 1930), pp. 144, 153.

or plan, a mere endless boring repetition of the author's personal dislikes with scarcely the ghost of a smile in its four hundred pages.[1]

This leads to a further conclusion. There are many grounds on which Flaubert can legitimately be criticized, but he remains a great writer. A great writer yes, but a great writer with whom there was something badly wrong. The trouble lay not in incidentals, but at the heart of his work. When he turns from his successful minor characters to his principals, his hand falters; there is a blur at the centre of these books.

[1] For an interesting statement of the contrary view, see M. Raymond Queneau's 'Introduction à *Bouvard et Pécuchet*' in *Fontaine* (Algiers), No. 31.

II. THE MAN AND THE WRITER

Je suis tout bonnement un bourgeois qui vis retiré à la campagne, m'occupant de littérature et sans rien demander aux autres. . . .

Letter to Maxime Du Camp

WHEN we read the lives of the Frenchmen who began to write about the middle of the last century, we cannot fail to notice how different they were from those of their predecessors. From a worldly point of view, the careers of Constant, Stendhal and Balzac were certainly not an unqualified success, but we are left with a strong feeling that all three of them had *lived*. Their unhappy love affairs, their travels, their political misfortunes and even their financial embarrassments were somehow part of their work as writers and provided them with the material out of which their books were constructed. They became writers because they had lived; they did not live in order to become writers, and they were untouched by the *mystique* of the Artist which became fashionable with Baudelaire and Flaubert.

M. Sartre had described Baudelaire's life as an experiment in a vacuum, but his words apply with much greater force to Flaubert.[1] With Flaubert there seems to have been a gap between the man and the writer, between the recluse of Croisset and the author of *Madame Bovary* which had a very bad effect on his art. His life was, indeed, the life of a typical nineteenth-century writer—uninteresting, uneventful and drab.

His early years were spent in the surgeon's house adjoining the hospital at Rouen in which he had been born. His biographers have told us that Gustave and his sister Caroline used to creep up to the windows of the theatre and peep through at the corpses lying there, surrounded by flies and waiting for dissection. They are undoubtedly right in emphasizing the importance of this childish experience for his work. It accounts for the grotesque, macabre element and for the delight with which he dwelt on the details of physical dissolution.

'I went to school when I was only ten,' Flaubert once wrote, 'and I very soon contracted a profound aversion for the human race.' His pessimism and his misanthropy have been a source of perplexity to his

---

[1] *Baudel aire* (Paris, 1947), p. 224. (English translation, London, 1949, p. 185.)

critics. They undoubtedly date back to his childhood, but they were not due to material causes. He came from a comfortable, well-to-do home; his parents were sympathetic and indulgent; and as a young man he was well-favoured besides being gifted. Nor can they be written off as Romantic melancholy. Their roots went deeper than that, and they were more lasting.

The Romantic Movement left a profound impress—I feel inclined to call it a deadly impress—on Flaubert's character. It was already causing havoc in boys' schools by the time he went there in 1831. One of his schoolfellows blew his brains out; another hanged himself with a necktie. It was certainly responsible, as we shall see, for Flaubert's curious devotion to Élisa Schlésinger which began when he was fifteen and lasted all his life.

He had begun to write at a very early age, but the *Mémoires d'un fou* —his first work of any interest—was not written until 1838, the year in which he left school.

As a reward for matriculating, he was sent on a voyage to Corsica and the Pyrenees. On his way home, he contrived to get himself seduced at Marseilles by a woman named Eulalie Foucaud de Lenglade who was waiting for a boat to join her husband in French Guiana. This incident seems to have been more than a passing fancy. It profoundly disturbed Flaubert and Eulalie, and it provided the material for his next work, *Novembre*.

After leaving school Flaubert went to Paris to study law and hated it.

When he was twenty-three he was suddenly struck down, while travelling from Rouen to Croisset, by the first attack of the mysterious illness which has intrigued his medically-minded biographers. It is unlikely that we shall ever know for certain whether it was epilepsy or some form of hysteria. Nor is its ultimate nature of great importance to the critic. For there is no evidence that it had any real effect on the writer.

Dr. Flaubert died in January 1845. His death was followed only two months later by what was for Flaubert a still heavier blow. His sister Caroline of whom he was passionately fond died in childbirth.

The year 1846 marked the beginning of the long-drawn-out affair with Louise Colet; but though the formal rupture did not come until 1854, Flaubert's real attachment only lasted some nine months.

In the autumn of 1849 he set out with Maxime Du Camp on his voyage to the Middle East and did not return to Croisset until May 1851.

The only documents which are of much assistance to the critic who wishes to understand the formative years are Flaubert's own letters, particularly those written during his twenty-fourth and twenty-fifth years. In April 1845 we find him writing to Alfred Le Poittevin:

> For a long time now my heart has had its shutters closed, its steps deserted. In the past it was a noisy, bustling hostelry, but now it's empty and sonorous like a vast sepulchre without a corpse.[1]

Two months later he wrote to the same correspondent:

> A love that was normal, regular, permanent and solid would take me out of myself too much, would worry me. I should return to active life, physical truth and, finally, to the common path. And it's precisely that which has proved harmful every time I've tried it.[2]

Writing of his family's grief over the death of Caroline, he remarks to Maxime Du Camp:

> It's strange. Sorrows in fiction make me expansive, flood me with facile emotions, but actual sorrows remain hard and bitter in my heart, crystallizing as soon as they come into being.[3]

> It's strange how little faith in happiness I was born with [he writes to the same correspondent]. When I was very young, I had a complete presentiment of life. It was like the stench from an evil-smelling kitchen escaping through the ventilator. You didn't need to eat anything from it to know that it would make you vomit.[4]

> *Ennui* has no cause [he said in another letter]. Any attempt to argue about it or try to overcome it with reasons shows that you haven't understood it.[5]

> Perhaps it's my heart which is impotent [he wrote to Louise Colet]. I'm exhausted by the deplorable mania for analysis. . . . You thought me young, and I'm old.[6]

It is possible to draw one or two conclusions from these revealing statements. There seems little doubt that by the time he was twenty-four Flaubert's emotional development had almost come to a stop. A detached reader will hardly feel inclined to challenge the truth of the observations that the shutters of his heart were closed or that it was his heart which was impotent. He was afflicted, too, with a curious emotional inhibition. He could suffer with Emma Bovary and taste the

[1] *Correspondance*, 1ère série (Conard Edition), p. 166. [2] *Ibid.*, p. 186.
[3] *Ibid.*, p. 195. [4] *Ibid.*, p. 201. [5] *Ibid.*, p. 204. [6] *Ibid.*, p. 230.

arsenic with which she killed herself, but when his sister died his feelings simply dried up. He was tormented by a disgust with life, a hatred of people and an *ennui* which appear to have been almost entirely unmotivated. There is little difference between the sentiments described here and those which he was later to describe in the novels. They are not the sign of a mature outlook; and the passionate conviction that they could not be explained or cured sprang surely from some lack in the man. For some reason he refused to explain them, and that makes the analysis of which he speaks sterile and destructive.

His relations with women and his travels support these conclusions. Élisa Schlésinger is the untouchable idol of Romantic myth, and the strength of his attachment to her shows how inhuman and destructive this myth could be. His life was divided, characteristically, between his devotion to Élisa and hurried connections with prostitutes. It is impossible not to regard his behaviour as a deliberate attempt to cut himself in two, to make an artificial distinction between the woman who satisfied him emotionally and the women who satisfied him sexually. This seems to be the real explanation of the affair with Louise Colet. For a brief period he was or imagined that he was passionately in love with her. Then he began to retreat. He told her, with unpardonable tactlessness, that she was dearer to him when he was back at Croisset than when they were together in Paris. We can only conclude that during this brief period she satisfied him emotionally and sexually, that he came to look on her not merely as a rival to Élisa, but as a threat to the Romantic myth. That is why she had to be sacrificed. His sudden retreat was a retreat from life, from a love which might have proved 'normal, regular, permanent and solid', but which would have taken him out of himself too much. For without the phantom of Trouville, he might very well have settled down and adapted himself to life, which was the last thing he wanted.

From the writer's point of view, the voyage to the Near East was a failure. It was a failure because it was already too late. The shutters of the heart were closed; sensibility had begun to atrophy; development had ceased. It produced nothing comparable to Stendhal's life in Italy, only the external décors of the empty, vacant *Salammbô*.

There is little more to tell. With the exception of the short visit to North Africa in 1858 to gather more material for *Salammbô*, which had as little effect on him as the voyage with Du Camp, Flaubert's active life had come to an end. He retired to Croisset where for many years he lived the life of a wealthy provincial bourgeois, devoting himself to his novels, to the care of his mother and the education of his niece until like Caroline she, too, married a worthy business man. He strongly

Picture Post Library

GUSTAVE FLAUBERT

resented any intrusion into his secluded existence. He had always refused to introduce Louise Colet to his mother or to have her at Croisset. When she succeeded in forcing an entry in 1854, she was brutally thrown out by Flaubert in spite of the protests of his horrified mother.

The spectacle of the recluse shut up in his study at Croisset wrestling with problems of syntax or declaiming his sentences on the balcony may give the impression of a sudden withdrawal from life. The truth is that Flaubert had barely come into contact with it, that his *physical* withdrawal was no more than the outward visible sign of a *psychological* withdrawal—a refusal of experience—which had taken place years earlier.

III. *MADAME BOVARY*

'MADAME BOVARY' is a study of the Romantic outlook. Its principal theme is the Romantic longing for a happiness which the world of common experience can never satisfy, the disillusionment which springs from the clash between the inner dream and an empty, hostile universe. Emma's misfortunes are caused by her inability to adapt herself to the world of everyday life. Her hunt for a Romantic passion leads to adultery which undermines her character, involves her in a life of subterfuge and deceit, and in the dubious financial transactions which ultimately drive her to suicide.

Flaubert's intentions in writing the book were exemplary. His early work—particularly the first version of *La Tentation de saint Antoine*—had been marred by the excesses and extravagances which are commonly associated with nineteenth-century Romanticism. His friends Louis Bouilhet and Maxime Du Camp had convinced him that he needed discipline. They persuaded him that this could be achieved by abandoning legend and writing a novel based on fact and using the society which he knew as a setting. Their advice was eminently sound. The strength of *Madame Bovary* lies largely in the fact that it is not merely a study of the Romantic outlook, but of the Romantic outlook in a realistic setting which effectively prevented it from degenerating into another extravaganza in the manner of *René* or from being no more than a superior version of *Novembre*. The setting was not only a discipline; it made the book into a novel. For Emma's disillusionment does not spring merely from her desire for an impossible happiness. It springs from the conflict between impulses and emotions which are often sound and the pervading middle-class *bêtise* which corrodes them.

The Romantic malady has become a permanent part of our consciousness. Emma has her counterparts to-day among the millions who crowd hungrily to the cinema to escape from a drab existence by battening on the impossible loves and the luxury palaces of American films. Now day-dreaming is not the monopoly or the vice of any one class. Emma appeals to those 'stock responses' from which not even the most sensitive readers are completely free. This leads them to assume that she is a symbol of universal validity without considering the value of the emotions which she symbolizes, and it explains their somewhat exaggerated estimate of the novel.

Madame Bovary is a remarkable book because of the subtlety with which Flaubert explored his theme, but it is not the flawless masterpiece for which it is usually taken. Its weaknesses lie partly in its execution and partly in the novelist's attitude towards his principal character. When Stendhal used the story of Berthet as his starting-point in *Le Rouge et le noir*, it became an *opportunity* for the display of his magnificent gifts and he created something which far transcended his original. Although the story of the Delamare family provided Flaubert with a discipline, it was also a *temptation*. We may suspect that he attempted a dispassionate analysis of the Romantic malady in the unconscious hope of curing himself of its ravages, but he was not really successful. It became an excuse, as we shall see, for exploiting all sorts of private manias.

Flaubert's relation to the Romantic Movement was a curious and an interesting one. Its impress is apparent on almost every page he wrote, but though it accounts for some of his most serious weaknesses, it also enabled him to make some of his most important discoveries. The French classic novel was the product of a small homogeneous society which possessed a common language. Its precision enabled the novelist to make a profound study of human nature, but he worked in a field which was necessarily restricted. He was confined in the main to the great primary emotions, to a settled round of feelings. The break-up of this society in the eighteenth century transformed the scene. Man became a problem to be explored and there were no longer any limits to the exploration, no longer any clear-cut outlines. The change did not come overnight. The process was a gradual one. Constant and Stendhal made discoveries about human nature, but they combined them with an eighteenth-century discipline. The 'outsider' may be unpredictable, but we are aware of the rational being underneath. He never becomes a welter of conflicting impulses or a mere succession of moods. We do not have this feeling with their contemporaries. For the break-up of society led in the end to the break-up of man. The Romantic Movement did far more than release emotions which had been repressed by eighteenth-century decorum. It blurred the division between man and nature, dream and reality, creating a new kind of awareness which could not be expressed in classic French prose. Its writers had moments of insight, but their work reveals a progressive movement away from the psychological realism of the seventeenth and eighteenth centuries, and it tends to dissolve into a flood of unrelated words and images. Flaubert attempted, with varying success, to create a style which was

capable of exact analysis and which would at the same time make use
of the colour and suggestiveness discovered by the Romantics.

There is a striking passage in Part I, chapter 7, which throws some
light on Flaubert's originality:

> Elle songeait quelquefois que c'étaient là pourtant les plus beaux jours
> de sa vie, la lune de miel, comme on disait. Pour en goûter la douceur, il
> eût fallu, sans doute, s'en aller vers ces pays à noms sonores où les lende-
> mains de mariage ont de plus suaves paresses! Dans des chaises de poste,
> sous des stores de soie bleue, on monte au pas des routes escarpées, écoutant
> la chanson du postillon qui se répète dans la montagne avec les clochettes
> des chèvres et le bruit sourd de la cascade. Quand le soleil se couche, on
> respire au bord des golfes le parfum des citronniers; puis, le soir, sur la
> terrasse des villas, seuls et les doigts confondus, on regarde les étoiles en
> faisant des projets. Il lui semblait que certains lieux sur la terre devaient
> produire du bonheur, comme une plante particulière au sol et qui pousse
> mal toute autre part. Que ne pouvait-elle s'accouder sur le balcon des
> chalets suisses ou enfermer sa tristesse dans un cottage écossais, avec un
> mari vêtu d'un habit de velours noir à longues basques, et qui porte des
> bottes molles, un chapeau pointu et des manchettes!

> [She thought, at times, that these days of what people called the honey-
> moon, were the most beautiful that she had ever known. To savour their
> sweetness to the full, she should, of course, have travelled to those lands
> with sounding names where newly wedded bliss is spent in exquisite
> languor. Seated in a post-chaise behind curtains of blue silk, she should
> have climbed, at a foot's pace, precipitous mountain roads, listening to the
> postillion's song echoing from the rocks to the accompaniment of goats'
> bells and the muted sound of falling water. She should have breathed at
> sunset, on the shores of sea bays in the South, the scent of lemon trees, and
> at night, alone with her husband on a villa terrace, have stood hand in
> hand, watching the stars and planning for the future. It seemed to her that
> happiness must flourish better in some special places than elsewhere, as
> some plants grow best in certain kinds of soil. Why was it not her fate to
> lean upon the balcony of a Swiss chalet or hide her melancholy in some
> Highland cottage, with a husband dressed in black, long-skirted velvet
> coat, soft leather boots, a pointed hat, and ruffles at his wrist?]

At a first reading one might pardonably suppose that this is no more
than an unusually well-written description of a Romantic day-dream,
but in reality it is far more than that. It is not only one of the central
passages in *Madame Bovary*, it is also a landmark in the development of

the European novel. The feelings are not in the nature of the under-taking very profound or very original, but in analysing the content of the Romantic *rêverie* Flaubert comes closer, perhaps, than any of his predecessors to the intimate workings of consciousness and his method clearly points the way to the inner monologue.

The passage, so far from being a straightforward description, is a deliberate piece of stylization which anticipates the method that was later used with conspicuous success by the Symbolists. For Flaubert translates feelings into *visual* images, enabling him to control expression by building each image into the final picture—in this case an imaginary voyage—and to register the transitions from one set of feelings to another with greater fidelity than had been possible before. The result seems to me to be a complete success and the passage an artistic whole. It is not, strictly speaking, a description at all, but the dramatic presenta-tion of a 'mental event'. There is complete identity between image and feeling. Every image is a particle of Emma's sensibility and a strand in the final pattern. The 'lune de miel' is the symbol of a vague feeling of happiness associated with Emma's childhood, but its function is com-plex. It is the first of a series of images—landscapes, sounds, perfumes—which lead naturally from one to the other, and it also marks the point at which Emma's contact with the actual world ends and the *rêverie* begins. Her feeling of happiness is the material out of which she con-structs an adventure in an imaginary world which has the sharpness and heightened reality of an hallucination. The *noms sonores*, the *douceur* and the *suaves paresses* build up a general impression of softness and languor, a lazy voluptuous happiness. As they echo and answer one another, so too do the sounds—the song which reverberates in the mountains is answered by the tinkle of the goats' bells, mingles with the muffled sound of the cascade and finally dies away in the silence of a summer night. When we come to 'Il lui semblait que certains lieux . . .' we notice a change in the tone of the passage. The note of exaltation symbolized by 'lune de miel', with which it opens, changes to a wistful-ness as she contemplates a *bonheur* which already belongs to the past, and this is followed by a sudden sinking as the *bonheur* is transformed into *tristesse*. The image which dominates the first part of the passage and gives the whole its particular flavour is the image of the blue silk blinds with their smooth vivid tactile suggestions. Flaubert had a par-ticular fondness for blue and we may suspect that here it was uncon-sciously suggested by statues of the Madonna which he had seen in churches. The blinds are drawn and are supposed to conceal strange depths of passion at play within the coach. So we have the impression of a blue mist radiating over the whole scene and enveloping it. The most striking thing about the passage, however, is the absence of the Romantic lover. The drawn blinds do not conceal an exotic passion, but an empty coach or a coach in which there is only a lonely woman. We catch a glimpse of 'les doigts confondus', but they are anonymous fingers—fingers without hands. There is, too, the 'mari vêtu d'un habit de velours noir', and we see the black velvet jacket with its long tails very clearly. We also see the 'chapeau pointu', but we never see the features of the man inside because there is no one there, only a tailor's dummy rigged out in extravagant garments.

The passage leaves us with a sense of absence and this is the crux of the book. The account of the *physical* absence of the lover here is completed by the account of his *psychological* absence in another place:

Elle se promettait continuellement, pour son prochain voyage, une félicité profonde, puis elle s'avouait ne rien sentir d'extraordinaire. Cette déception s'effaçait vite sous en espoir nouveau, et Emma revenait à lui plus enflammée, plus avide. Elle se déshabillait brutalement, arrachant le lacet mince de son corset, qui sifflait autour de ses hanches comme une couleuvre qui glisse. Elle allait sur la pointe de ses pieds nus regarder encore une fois si la porte était fermée, puis elle faisait d'un seul geste tomber ensemble tous ses vêtements;—et pâle, sans parler, sérieuse, elle s'abattait contre sa poitrine, avec un long frisson.

[On the eve of each of their meetings she told herself that *this* time their happiness would be unclouded, only to confess, after the event, that she felt no emotions out of the ordinary. Such recurrent disappointments were always swept away by a renewed surge of hope, and when she next saw him, she was more on fire, more exigent, than ever. She flung off her clothes with a sort of brutal violence, tearing at her thin stay-lace so that it hissed about her hips like a slithering snake. She tiptoed across the room on her bare feet to make sure that the door was really locked, and then, with a single gesture, let her things fall to the floor. Pale, speechless, solemn, she threw herself into his arms with a prolonged shudder.]

The first sentence describes with great insight the central experience of Flaubert's work. The sensation of 'falling out of love' is not, perhaps, an unusual one, but Flaubert invests it with immense significance. He is the great master of negation. Some of the most impressive pages in his books describe the sudden collapse of all feeling, the void which suddenly opens at the supreme moments of life and the realization that not simply one's emotional life, but one's whole world has fallen into ruin. There is no crash, no disaster—it is this that makes it so horrifying

—life simply comes to an end. When you look into it, you find that there is nothing there.

What I have called physical and psychological absence is combined in the *long frisson*. Emma's tragedy is twofold. It lies in her inability to adapt herself to the normal world and in her failure to construct a durable inner life which would compensate for its drabness. The *long frisson* reflects the tendency of the human mind to escape from the disenchantment of awakening and from the pressure of thought by deliberately submerging itself in primitive animal contacts, as Emma does here. It is a mental blackout, a voluptuous swoon in which the intelligence is completely suspended. The placing of the closing words and the punctuation—'et pâle, sans parler, sérieuse, elle s'abattait . . .' —convey the sensation of someone losing consciousness, falling into nothingness. The words are interesting for another reason. They mark the limit of Flaubert's power of analysis. His preoccupation with negative states almost certainly reflects his own inability to penetrate deeply into the content of experience. This makes the contrast between 'elle s'avouait ne rien sentir d'extraordinaire' and 'elle se déshabillait brutalement' of particular interest. For here the novelist intervenes in the life of his creature. It is his own starved sensibility, his own incapacity for deep feeling that he portrays in Emma. The violent actions which follow are an attempt to whip up the feelings that he is convinced he ought to experience, to obtain a vicarious satisfaction of feelings which life had refused him.

'Je me suis toujours défendu de rien mettre de moi dans mes œuvres,' Flaubert had said in a letter to Louise Colet, 'et pourtant j'en ai mis beaucoup.'[1] Although these words were written ten years before the publication of *Madame Bovary*, they suggest that he was already conscious of a divided purpose which later disturbed the unity of the book. *Madame Bovary* purports to be a study of the romantic outlook, but it is only partly that and partly an expression of the novelist's personal attitude which could not always be conveyed through the symbols that he chose and was sometimes in flagrant conflict with them. 'Madame Bovary, c'est moi,' he said on another occasion. She was, but she was also the narrator as well as the heroine of *Novembre*. The similarity of outlook between the autobiographical story written when he was twenty-one and *Madame Bovary* is striking, and it brings home forcibly how little Flaubert developed.

'En somme,' wrote M. André Maurois, 'Mme de La Fayette avait étudié l'amour en métaphysicienne, Rousseau en moraliste, Stendhal en amoureux, Flaubert en mécréant et en iconoclaste.'[2] This comment

[1] *Correspondance*, 1ère série, p. 254.   [2] *Sept visages de l'amour* (Paris, 1946), p. 219.

draws attention to interesting possibilities. There was nothing new in Flaubert's preoccupation with sexual passion, but his approach differs sensibly from that of his predecessors. The great dramatists and novelists of the past had concentrated on it because it is one of the profoundest of human instincts and enabled them to make some of the most search- ing studies of human nature that we possess. In Flaubert it had the reverse effect, narrowing instead of widening the scope of his work. He was aware of its importance, but he was only interested in its destruc- tive effect on personality, and he selected it because it was the most vulnerable point for his carefully planned attack on human nature. For when we look into the structure of *Madame Bovary*, we find that so far from being a detached study of sexual mania and in spite of its superfi- cial moral orthodoxy, it is an onslaught on the whole basis of human feeling and on all spiritual and moral values.

The first fifty pages, where he keeps his personal preoccupations severely under control, are amongst the best that Flaubert ever wrote. The main characters are introduced and their significance sketched. The narrative moves swiftly and economically forward. There is no padding and none of those disastrous descriptions of external reality which contribute so much to the ruin of *L'Éducation sentimentale*.

The book opens with the arrival of the absurd Charles Bovary as a new boy at his school. It is a delightful piece of comedy, but Flaubert's intention was serious. The description of his peculiar hat is a charac- teristic example of his symbolism which enables him to prepare the setting for Emma:

C'était une de ces coiffures d'ordre composite, où l'on retrouve les éléments du bonnet à poil, du chapska, du chapeau rond, de la casquette de loutre et du bonnet de coton, une de ces pauvres choses, enfin, dont la laideur muette a des profondeurs d'expression comme le visage d'un imbécile. Ovoïde et renflée de baleines, elle commençait par trois boudins circulaires; puis s'alternaient, séparés par une bande rouge, des losanges de velours et de poils de lapin; venait ensuite une façon de sac qui se terminait par un polygone cartonné, couvert d'une broderie en soutache com- pliquée, et d'où pendait, au bout d'un long cordon trop mince, un petit croisillon de fils d'or, en manière de gland. Elle était neuve; la visière brillait.

[It was a nondescript sort of object, combining a number of different features—part woollen comforter, part military headdress, part pillbox, part fur bonnet, part cotton nightcap; one of those shoddy affairs which, like the face of an idiot, seems to express a certain secretive significance.

Its general shape was that of an egg, and the upper part, stiffened with whalebone, rose from a base consisting of three bulging, circular, sausage-like protuberances. Above these was a pattern of alternating lozenges of rabbit-fur and velvet separated from one another by strips of some scarlet material. Higher still was a species of sack ending in a polygon of cardboard covered with a complicated design in braid, and finished off with a long, and excessively thin, cord from which depended a small cross of gold thread in place of a tassel. The whole contraption was brand new, and had a bright, shining peak.]

I felt inclined to assume at first that no special significance should be attached to the five different kinds of military and civilian headdress mentioned in the first sentence, but I think that this view was mistaken. The busby[1] and the lancer cap are almost certainly an allusion to Charles's father. For we learn, a page or two later, that he had been a professional soldier, had had to leave the army on account of some discreditable transaction, had married the daughter of a prosperous hosier and taken to heavy drinking. The catalogue, which begins with a busby and ends with a nightcap, is clearly arranged in descending order and points to the moral and material decline of father and son. The ironical *composite* is one of the operative words. Charles's hat may contain 'elements' of several different kinds of hat, but it does not belong completely to any recognizable category. It is a stupid, shapeless muddle like the wearer and the society in which he lives. The downward movement leads naturally to

une de ces pauvres choses . . . dont la laideur muette a des profondeurs d'expression comme le visage d'un imbécile.

The poor, silly, good-natured Charles becomes the incarnation of *la bêtise*, and Flaubert emphasizes the depth of his stupidity. The second sentence develops not merely the idea of shapelessness, but its nature and extent. The downward movement is succeeded by an unwinding movement whose importance will shortly become apparent. The grotesque, egg-shaped hat, with its tiers of ridiculous ornaments, suggests a society constructed in layers where each layer exemplifies its particular kind of stupidity. Nor should we overlook the point of the 'trois boudins circulaires'. For the novel is in a sense a widening 'circle'. Flaubert is concerned to explore stupidity at one level—the middle-class level. The cord with the cross on the end is probably intended to

[1] Mr. Hopkins translates *bonnet à poil* as 'woollen comforter', but it seems to me to mean 'busby'.

K*

suggest a clown's hat and looks forward to Charles's failure as a doctor. He thus becomes one of a 'circle' which includes Bournisien and Homais. In this circle he stands, as they do, for professional incompetence. When later on, his incompetence leads to the amputation of Hippolyte's leg, the unfortunate man becomes a projection of Bovary's stupidity, and the thud of his wooden leg on the paving drives home remorselessly the idea of professional failure.

I have spoken of the unwinding movement of the second sentence. The story which 'unfolds' in the novel appears to be no more than a development of something which is implicit in the image of Charles's hat. The wearer, you feel, is bound to come to grief. The stolid, unimaginative Charles is not merely a bad doctor; he stands for the ordinary man, for humdrum everyday reality, and the first phase closes with his disastrous alliance with the unbalanced over-imaginative Emma.

The rift between them begins shortly after their marriage. They are invited to stay with the Comte de Vaubyessard for the family ball. Emma finds herself for a moment in an aristocratic world, a world of luxury and romance which suddenly seems to offer everything for which she has unconsciously been longing:

Leurs habits, mieux faits, semblaient d'un drap plus souple, et leurs cheveux, ramenés en boucles vers les tempes, lustrés par des pommades plus fines. Ils avaient le teint de la richesse, ce teint blanc que rehaussent la pâleur des porcelaines, les moires du satin, le vernis des beaux meubles, et qu'entretient dans sa santé un régime discret de nourritures exquises. Leur cou tournait à l'aise sur des cravates basses; leurs favoris longs tombaient sur des cols rabattus; il s'essuyaient les lèvres à des mouchoirs brodés d'un large chiffre, d'où sortait une odeur suave. Ceux qui commençaient à vieillir avaient l'air jeune, tandis que quelque chose de mûr s'étendait sur le visage des jeunes. Dans leurs regards indifférents flottait la quiétude des passions journellement assouvies; et, à travers leurs manières douces, perçait cette brutalité particulière que communique la domination de choses à demi faciles, dans lesquelles la force s'exerce et où la vanité s'amuse, le maniement des chevaux de race et la société des femmes perdues.

[Their evening coats, better cut than those of their fellow guests, seemed to be made of a more elastic cloth; their hair, which they wore in clustered curls over their temples, and lustrous with pomade, of a silkier texture. They had the colouring which comes of wealth, that pallor which is enhanced by the white sheen of china, the iridescence of watered satin, the polish of fine furniture, and is maintained by a diet of exquisite food never indulged in to excess. Their necks moved freely above low cravats, their long whiskers fell over turned-down collars, and they wiped their lips with embroidered handkerchiefs marked with large monograms and diffusing a sweet perfume. Those on the threshold of middle age looked young, while the more youthful of their company had an air of maturity. Their indifferent glances told of passions dulled by daily satisfaction, and through their polished manners showed that peculiar aggressiveness which comes of easy conquests, the handling of thoroughbred horses and the society of loose women.]

I think we must admit that Flaubert achieves something here which his predecessors had not attempted, something of which classical French prose for all its merits was perhaps incapable. In a few lines, with a few deft touches, he *evokes* the life of a highly civilized society; the description of the cut of a coat, the turn of a head, is sufficient to reveal the essential gifts of the ruling class which had made France great. The final sentence, with its restrained irony, indicates both the strength and the weakness of this society. It would be difficult to improve on his description of its patrician dignity and pride: 'Dans leurs regards indifférents flottait la quiétude des passions journellement assouvies; et, à travers leurs manières douces, perçait cette brutalité particulière. . . .' Nor would it be easy to improve upon the way in which Flaubert hints at the weaknesses which had led to the ruin of the French nobility when he speaks of 'la domination de choses à demi faciles . . . le maniement des chevaux de race et la société des femmes perdues'. This sort of language—this combination of evocation and critical appraisal—is one of Flaubert's most effective and important innovations.

The damage done by Emma's experience to the Bovarys' married life is irreparable:

Son voyage à la Vaubyessard avait fait un trou dans sa vie, à la manière de ces grandes crevasses qu'un orage, en une seule nuit, creuse quelquefois dans les montagnes.

[Her journey to Vaubyessard had opened a yawning fissure in her life, a fissure that was like one of those great crevasses which a storm will sometimes make on a mountain-side in the course of one short night.]

It is a characteristic sentence. The fact of the rift is stated with Flaubert's customary forthrightness in the first clause; the common-place image which follows shows how he tried to force his sensibility, giving us a feeling of a vain and unrewarding hunt for the *mot juste* which always eludes him.

The third phase opens with the Bovarys' removal to Yonville-l'Abbaye and Emma's first encounter with Léon. The confused and excited feelings released by her visit to la Vaubyessard seek an outlet. She hovers on the verge of adultery and is only saved by Léon's departure for Paris. In her perplexity her mind turns to religion and Flaubert takes the opportunity of making a critique of religion:

Un soir que la fenêtre était ouverte, et que, assise au bord, elle venait de regarder Lestiboudois, le bedeau, qui taillait le buis, elle entendit tout à coup sonner l'*Angelus*.

On était au commencement d'avril, quand les primevères sont écloses; un vent tiède se roule sur les plates-bandes labourées, et les jardins, comme des femmes, semblent faire leur toilette pour les fêtes de l'été. . . . La vapeur du soir passait entres les peupliers sans feuilles, estompant leurs contours d'une teinte violette, plus pâle et plus transparente qu'une gaze subtile arrêtée sur leurs branchages. Au loin, des bestiaux marchaient, on n'entendait ni leurs pas ni leurs mugissements; et la cloche, sonnant toujours, continuait dans les airs sa lamentation pacifique.

A ce tintement répété, la pensée de la jeune femme s'égarait dans ses vieux souvenirs de jeunesse et de pension. Elle se rappela les grands chandeliers, qui dépassaient sur l'autel les vases pleins de fleurs et le tabernacle à colonnettes. Elle aurait voulu, comme autrefois, être encore confondue dans la longue ligne des voiles blancs, que marquaient de noir çà et là les capuchons raides des bonnes sœurs inclinées sur leur prie-Dieu; le dimanche à la messe, quand elle relevait sa tête, elle apercevait le doux visage de la Vierge, parmi les tourbillons bleuâtres de l'encens qui montait. Alors un attendrissement la saisit; elle se sentit molle et tout abandonnée . . . ce fut sans en avoir conscience qu'elle s'achemina vers l'église, disposée à n'importe quelle dévotion, pourvu qu'elle y absorbât son âme et que l'existence entière y disparût.

[One evening when she was sitting by the open window watching Lestiboudois, the sexton, trimming the box-hedge, she suddenly heard the sound of the Angelus bell.

It was the beginning of April, when the primroses are in bloom. A warm wind was blowing over the dug flower-beds, and the gardens, like women, seemed to be furbishing their finery for the gaieties of summer. . . . The mist of evening was drifting between the leafless poplars, blurring their outline with a violet haze, paler and more transparent than a fine gauze hung upon their branches. Cattle were moving in the distance, but her ear could catch neither the noise of their hooves nor the sound of their lowing. The bell, continuously ringing, struck upon the air with its note of peaceful lamentation.

The repeated tolling took the young woman's mind back to the memories of childhood and of her school. She remembered the branched candlesticks which used to stand upon the altar, overtopping the flower-filled vases and the tabernacle with its little columns. She would have liked, as then, to be an unnoticed unit in the long line of white veils in which, here and there, the stiff coifs of the good sisters kneeling at their desks, showed as accents of black. At Mass, on Sundays, whenever she raised her head, she could see the sweet face of the Virgin in a blue cloud of eddying incense. At such moments she had been conscious of deep emotion, had felt alone and immaterial. . . . It was almost without knowing what she was doing, that she set out towards the church, ready to enter into any act of devotion provided only that her feelings might be wholly absorbed, and the outer world forgotten.]

It is an admirable example of Flaubert's art at its finest. The insistent ringing of the church bell through a process of sensuous suggestion, which bears a striking resemblance to Proust's *mémoire involontaire*, sets the mechanism of memory in motion. The dying away of the sounds from the external world marks the beginning of the *rêverie*, so that the final stroke of the bell merges into the remembered sound of the bell at the convent. The images dovetail perfectly into one another. 'Les jardins, comme des femmes, semblent faire leur toilette pour les fêtes de l'été', suggests the flowers on the altar and the white veils of the schoolgirls on feast days. The 'vapeur du soir . . . d'une teinte violette' floats into the 'tourbillons bleuâtres de l'encens'. There is no direct comment, but Flaubert by employing the same method that he used in the account of the ball at la Vaubyessard shows that Emma's religion is of the same quality as her dreams of Romantic love. It is largely emotional, a desire to return to her childhood and be one of a row of little girls in white veils, or to plunge into 'n'importe quelle dévotion' provided that like the *long frisson* it brings oblivion, 'que l'existence entière y disparût'.

On her way to the church she meets the Abbé Bournisien to whom she turns for help, but he completely fails to understand her. The intention of this memorable scene is to show the inability of the Church to provide a solution. It reminds us to some extent of the Russian films with their hideous, bloated bourgeois; but while one is reading it, it is effective enough. This double criticism disposes of religion and Emma is now ripe for a fall.

The fourth phase is the liaison with Rodolphe. The outstanding scene, which from a technical point of view has had an immense influence, is the visit of Emma and Rodolphe to the Comices Agricoles. Flaubert was very proud of it, as he had every right to be, and compared it to a symphony. Thibaudet shrewdly suggested that it was arranged in three tiers like a mediæval mystery. The animals and peasants were at the bottom, the platform with the distinguished visitor and the local notabilities in the middle, and the lovers at the window above. He went on to point out that the animal noises, the speeches from the platform and the conversation between the lovers were all varieties of *la bêtise* which blended in the symphony.[1] The *conseiller de préfecture's* speech certainly alternates with the dialogue between the lovers; the platitudes about religion, duty, progress and patriotism and Rodolphe's platitudes about enduring passion and the new morality answer one another mockingly, cancel one another out, leaving the reader with the impression that love and duty are mere shams, that nothing has value. The effect is intensified when the speech is followed by the distribution of prizes to deserving farmers:

Et il saisit sa main; elle ne la retira pas.

'Ensemble de bonnes cultures!' cria le président.
—'Tantot, par exemple, quand je suis venu chez vous ..'
'A M. Bizet, de Quincampoix.'
—'Savais-je que je vous accompagnerais?'
'Soixante et dix francs!'
—'Cent fois même j'ai voulu partir, et je vous ai suivie, je suis resté.'
'Fumiers.'
'Comme je resterais ce soir, demain, les autres jours, toute ma vie!'
'A M. Caron, d'Argueil, une médaille d'or!'
— 'Car jamais je n'ai trouvé dans la société de personne un charme aussi complet.'
'A M. Bain, de Givry-Saint-Martin!'
—'Aussi, moi, j'emporterai votre souvenir.'
'Pour un bélier de mérinos. . . .'
—'Mais vous m'oublierez, j'aurai passé comme une ombre.'
'A M. Belot, de Notre-Dame. . . .'
— 'Oh! non, n'est-ce pas, je serai quelque chose dans votre pensée, dans votre vie?'
'Race porcine, prix *ex æquo*: à MM. Lehérissé et Cullembourg; soixante francs!'

[1] *Gustave Flaubert*, p. 117.

[He pounced upon her hand. She did not withdraw it.

'We must work together for the good of farming,' cried the President.

'Recently, for instance, when I came to your house . . .'

'. . . To Monsieur Bizet of Quincampoix . . .'

'Did I know that we should be together in this place?'

'. . . Seventy francs!'

'A hundred times I even strove to break from you, but ever followed, ever stayed . . .'

'. . . Manures. . . .'

'As I should so dearly love to stay this evening, to-morrow, all the days of my life!'

'. . . To Monsieur Caron of Argueil, a gold medal. . . .'

'For never have I found a charm so powerful in the companionship of anybody. . . .'

'. . . To Monsieur Bain of Givry-Saint-Martin . . .'

'This memory of you will be with me always . . .'

'. . . For a merino ram. . . .'

'But you will forget me: I shall be for you as a shadow that has passed. . . .'

'. . . To Monsieur Belot of Notre-Dame . . .'

'But no! Tell me I shall count for something in your thoughts and in your life!'

'Pig class—a prize of sixty francs, divided between Monsieur Lehérissé and Monsieur Cullembourg. . . .'

The opening announcement is an ironic comment on Emma and Rodolphe, standing furtively hand in hand. For we know that at bottom they are anything but 'bonnes cultures'. When Rodolphe cries: 'Savais-je que je vous accompagnerais?' the mocking voice, which chimes in with 'Soixante et dix francs', becomes the voice of the courtesan announcing the price of her favours or of the hard-boiled man of the world making an offer for those favours. When Rodolphe whispers that he stayed because he could not tear himself away, the strident voice answers jeeringly: 'Fumiers.' The promise to remain 'this evening, to-morrow, all the days of my life' is greeted derisively by: 'Une médaille d'or!' 'J'emporterai votre souvenir' is answered by 'Un bélier de mérinos'. In the final announcement the irony grows savage. 'I shall count for something in your thoughts and in your life shan't I?' asks Rodolphe. The voice retorts, brutally: 'Race porcine ex æquo—Pigs, the pair of you.'[1]

[1] The account of the Comices Agricoles is more than an attack on sexual passion. The ceremony, which closes with the presentation of a silver medal worth twenty-five

I think it will be agreed that this scene is a decidedly impressive performance, an ironical commentary not merely on Emma's assumed modesty and Rodolphe's vows of eternal fidelity, but on the whole basis of love. It ends by transforming the pair into a couple of pigs rolling over each other on the dung-heap. For the words which give it its particular tone are *fumiers* and *race porcine*. They sum up Rodolphe's views on love and there seems little doubt that Flaubert himself shared them, or that he used this slick, shallow adventurer as part of his general plan for bringing it into discredit. Later in the book we read of him:

> Ce qu'il ne comprenait pas, c'était tout ce trouble dans une chose aussi simple que l'amour.
> Il jugea toute pudeur incommode. Il la traita sans façon. Il en fit quelque chose de souple et de corrompu.

> [He could not see why she should make such a fuss about anything so simple as love.
> He had no use for modesty, and rode over it roughshod. He turned her into something supple and corrupt.]

When he comes to write his *lettre de rupture*, Emma already means so little to him that he has to turn up some of her old letters to him to provide inspiration. He comes across a mass of letters from different women:

> En effet, ces femmes, accourant à la fois dans sa pensée, s'y gênaient les unes les autres et s'y rapetissaient, comme sous un même niveau d'amour qui les égalisait. . . .
> 'Quel tas de blagues! . . .'
> Ce qui résumait son opinion; car les plaisirs, comme des écoliers dans la cour d'un collège, avaient tellement piétiné sur son cœur, que rien de vert n'y poussait, et ce qui passait par là, plus étourdi que les enfants, n'y laissait pas même, comme eux, son nom gravé sur la muraille.

> [All these women, crowding together in his thoughts, got in one another's way. They seemed to shrink in size, to assume an identity when reduced to the same level of love. . . .

---

francs to Catherine-Nicaise-Elisabeth Leroux for fifty-four years' service on the same farm, is also an attack on the whole life of the French agricultural community. For Flaubert shows no appreciation of agricultural life. It is reduced to the same boring monotony as everything else.

'Just a lot of nonsense!'

The phrase did, in fact, sum up what he felt, for the succession of his pleasures, like boys in a school playground, had so trodden his heart underfoot that now not a single shoot of green could show above the ground, and what passed over it, more scatterbrained than children, did not, as they might have done, leave even a name scribbled on the wall.]

The final phase of the novel opens with Léon's return and Emma's liaison with him. The prelude is their meeting in Rouen Cathedral which is followed by the celebrated drive in the cab with its drawn blinds. It is interesting to recall that when the novel was originally published in serial form in the *Revue de Paris* this was one of the first scenes which the editors insisted on cutting. It may seem strange that the people who had apparently passed the ride with Rodolphe and the seduction in the forest should have felt any scruples over the second scene. I think we must assume that they sensed obscurely what to-day is plain. It is possible to argue that the symbolism is sometimes a little obvious, but on the whole it is an impressive display of literary craftsmanship with the pompous, boring guide pursuing the distracted lovers round the cathedral, the cab travelling at breakneck speed, the wretched perspiring *cocher* and the furious voice bellowing at him from inside the cab every time he slows down.

The cathedral and the cab both possess a moral significance, but there is a contrast between them. When Léon compares the cathedral mentally to 'un boudoir gigantesque [qui] se disposait autour d'elle', the significance is clearly sexual and anticipates the highly Freudian 'cab'. For Emma the cathedral provides a momentary and inffectual moral support before she gives in. The drive 'sans parti pris ni direction, au hasard' stands for a loss of moral direction which can only have one end:

Une fois, au milieu du jour, en pleine campagne, au moment où le soleil dardait le plus fort contre les vieilles lanternes argentées, une main nue passa sous les petits rideaux de toile jaune et jeta des déchirures de papier qui se dispersèrent au vent et s'abattirent plus loin, comme des papillons blancs, sur un champ de trèfle rouge tout en fleurs.

[Once, about midday, out in the open country, with the sun striking full on the plated lamps, a bare hand emerged from behind the little curtains of yellow canvas, and scattered some scraps of paper which eddied in the wind and settled afar off, like so many white butterflies, on a field of red flowering clover.]

I suspect that there is an ironic contrast between this drive and Emma's youthful daydream of the romantic honeymoon drive in the 'pays à noms sonores'. The fragments of paper belong to the *lettre de rupture* which she had intended to hand to Léon in the cathedral; but, whether consciously or unconsciously, they also suggest clothes. For the 'naked' hand stretching out of the closed cab is a signal that 'marriage vows' have once more been 'torn up', that 'virtue has succumbed'.[1] The 'butterflies' stand for the transitoriness of the relationship with Léon. The 'red' clover is a symbol of adultery (contrasted with the 'white' pieces of paper) as the 'blue' blinds of the carriage in the imaginary honeymoon were a symbol—a traditional symbol—of innocence.

In a comment on the liaison with Rodolphe with novelist remarks:

Alors elle se rappela les héroïnes des livres qu'elle avait lus, et la légion de ces femmes adultères se mit à chanter dans sa mémoire avec des voix de sœurs qui la charmaient.

[Then she called to mind the heroines of the books that she had read; the lyrical legion of those adulterous ladies sang in her memory as sisters, enthralling her with the charm of their voices.]

We are told of the affair with Léon:

Emma retrouvait dans l'adultère toutes les platitudes du mariage.

[Emma found in adultery nothing but the old commonplaces of marriage.]

They are characteristic of the book. The sudden expansion signified by *lyrique* collapses inevitably from within into *platitude*; *mariage* and *adultère* cancel out. Marriage or adultery, it is always the same story of frustration and disappointment.

There is another passage which sums up not only Emma's experience, but the author's intention:

Les premiers mois de son mariage, ses promenades à cheval dans la forêt, le vicomte qui valsait, et Lagardy chantant, tout repassa devant ses yeux. . . . Et Léon lui parut soudain dans le même éloignement que les autres.

---

[1] There may be a reference to the opening of the shutters of the farm-house at the beginning of the book which was old Rouault's 'signal' to Bovary that his daughter accepted the proposal of marriage.

'Je l'aime pourtant!' se disait-elle.

N'importe! elle n'était pas heureuse, ne l'avait jamais été.

D'où venait donc cette insuffisance de la vie, cette pourriture instantanée des choses où elle s'appuyait?

[She saw in imagination the early months of her marriage, her days of riding through the woods; she saw the Vicomte waltzing and Lagardy singing . . . and suddenly, she saw Léon too, diminished in the same perspective of time.

'But I *do* love him!' she said to herself.

But what good did that do? She was not happy; she never had been happy. Why had her life been such a failure? Why did everything on which she leaned crumble immediately to dust?]

Fumiers, *race porcine*, *pourriture* and *corruption* reflect the novelist's own personal outlook, a mood which envelopes everything, undermining, dissolving feeling into nothingness. We read, for example, of Charles after Emma's death:

Il mettait du cosmétique à ses moustaches, il souscrivi tcomme elle des billets à ordre. Elle le *corrompait* par delà le tombeau.

[He put pomade on his moustache, and followed her example in the matter of signing bearer bills. Her power to corrupt him was still active from beyond the grave.]

The last fifty pages possess the same qualities as the first fifty. They are the traditional excellences of the finest European novels. In these pages, too, Flaubert displays all his technical mastery. Emma becomes a trapped animal trying desperately to escape from her enemies. All through the novel we are conscious of the dialogue which goes on ceaselessly—sometimes in an undertone, sometimes openly—between Bournisien and Homais, between the Ecclesiastic and the Progressive, between the religious and the secularist *bêtise*. In the final pages the other characters also become symbolic figures, and we see them crowding in on Emma with hostile faces. Lheureux is the Usurer demanding, insistently, his pound of flesh; the beggar, with his hideous deformity and his ghastly song, is Death or, possibly, as Thibaudet suggests, the Devil to whom she throws her last five-franc piece. Rodolphe and Léon are both variations of the Faithless Lover. The sense of her enemies closing in on Emma in a constantly narrowing circle gives the final chapters their dramatic force. The clandestine journeys to Rouen to see

Léon when she is supposed to be having music lessons are replaced by a different sort of journey. Emma rushes to and fro between Rouen and Yonville in a frantic attempt to borrow money to keep her creditors at bay and avoid being sold up. She fails. Her main outlet has been blocked and she is confined to Yonville. She moves hither and thither at Yonville, seeks refuge with the old nurse where, by an ominous association of ideas, the sound of the spinning-wheel recalls the sound of Binet's lathe on the day she nearly committed suicide after Rodolphe's defection. She is on the point of selling herself to the local solicitor, pays a visit to the tax-gatherer. As so often happens in Flaubert, these scenes remind us of a film in which we watch the action from different angles and different heights. We go with her into Rodolphe's château and into the solicitor's breakfast-room, but we watch her visit to Binet from above and through the eyes of spiteful neighbours:

'Viendrait-elle lui commander quelque chose?' dit Mme Tuvache.
'Mais il ne vend rien!' objecta sa voisine.
Le percepteur avait l'air d'écouter, tout en écarquillant les yeux, comme s'il ne comprenait pas. Elle continuait d'une manière tendre, suppliante. Elle se rapprocha; son sein haletait, ils ne parlaient plus.
'Est-ce qu'elle lui fait des avances?' dit Mme Tuvache.
Binet était rouge jusqu'aux oreilles. Elle lui prit les mains.
'Ah! c'est trop fort!'
Et sans doute qu'elle lui proposait une abomination, car le percepteur
... tout à coup, comme à la vue d'un serpent, se recula bien loin en criant:
'Madame! y pensez-vous?'
'On devrait fouetter ces femmes-là!' dit Mme Tuvache.
'Où est-elle donc?' reprit Mme Caron.
Car elle avait disparu durant ces mots. . . .

['Is she going to give him an order?' said Madame Tucavhe.
'But his things aren't for sale'—objected her neighbour.
The Collector seemed to be listening. He was blinking his eyes as though finding it difficult to grasp what was being said. Madame Bovary talked on in a gentle, supplicating manner. She went close to him, her breast rising and falling. Neither was saying anything now.
'D'you think she's making advances to him?' said Madame Tuvache.
Binet had flushed crimson to the tips of his ears. Emma took his hands.
'That really is too much!'
She must be making some abominable suggestion, because the Collector
... suddenly recoiled as though he had seen a snake, exclaiming:
'Madame, what can you be thinking of?'

'Women like that ought to be whipped!' said Madame Tuvache.
'Where has she gone now?' asked Madame Caron.
For during this brief exchange, Emma had disappeared. . . .]

We hear the old women's comments, but we do not hear the conversation between Emma and Binet. We simply suspect that she is trying to persuade him to lend her the tax-payers' money as she had tried to persuade Léon to 'borrow' money for her from the office where he worked. Suddenly, the horrified 'Madame! y pensez-vous?' reaches us. Then she disappears, to reappear in the main street. We go with her into Lheureux's shop, into Homais' store where she takes the arsenic, and into the room where she dies horribly to the sound of the beggar's song:

> Souvent la chaleur d'un beau jour
> Fait rêver fillette à l'amour. . . .

There is another important change in these closing pages. The novelist manages to forget himself and keep his eye on his principal figure. The morbid satisfaction with which he has recorded her misfortunes gives way to a pity which adds another dimension to the book. The scene in which she tries to obtain money from Rodolphe shows Flaubert at his best:

'Mais, lorsqu'on est si pauvre, on ne met pas d'argent à la crosse de son fusil! On n'achète pas une pendule avec des incrustations d'écailles!' continuait-elle en montrant l'horloge de Boulle; 'ni des sifflets de vermeil pour ses fouets'—elle les touchait!—'ni des breloques pour sa montre! . . . Eh! quand ce ne serait que cela,' s'écria-t-elle en prenant sur la cheminée ses boutons de manchettes, 'que la moindre de ces niaiseries! on en peut faire de l'argent! . . . Oh! je n'en veux pas! garde-les.'

Et elle lança bien loin les deux boutons, dont la chaîne d'or se rompit en cognant contre la muraille.

'Mais, moi, je t'aurais tout donné, j'aurais tout vendu, j'aurais travaillé de mes mains, j'aurais mendié sur les routes, pour un sourire, pour un regard, pour t'endendre dire: "Merci."'

['But a poor man like you doesn't lavish silver on the butt of a gun, or buy a clock inlaid with tortoiseshell'—she went on, pointing to a buhl timepiece—'or silver-gilt whistles for riding-crops'—she touched them as she spoke—'or trinkets for watch-chains. . . . Why, the smallest of these knick-knacks could be turned into money. . . . Not that *I* want them . . . you can keep the lot for all I care!'

She threw the links from her so violently that the gold chain broke against the wall.

'I would have given you everything, would have sold all I had. I would have worked with my hands, would have begged on the roads, just for a smile, a look, just to hear you say "thank you".']

This is a different Emma from the unbalanced romantic who is studied throughout the greater part of the book. Her voice, freed from the confusing undertones of her creator, has a different accent. There is no blur here. The simple, direct words contrast strangely with her muddled dreams. They come straight from the heart and appeal to something far deeper in us.

We cannot help noticing that Flaubert displayed a marked reluctance to give due weight to what was valid and genuine in Emma. She was not, as Henry James alleged, a woman who was 'naturally depraved'. She possessed a number of solid virtues which were deliberately played down by the novelist. It was after all to her credit that she possessed too much sensibility to fit comfortably into the appalling provincial society of Yonville l'Abbaye and it was her misfortune that she was not big enough to find a way out of the dilemma. We cannot withhold our approval from her attempts to improve her mind or from the pride that she took in her personal appearance and in the running of her house. The truth is that Flaubert sacrificed far too much to his *thèse*. These virtues express his instinctive appreciation of what was sane and well-balanced in the French middle classes. In sacrificing them to a doctrinaire pessimism, which was held intellectually instead of arising from his contemplation of his material, he destroyed the findings of his own sensibility and involved himself in a confusion of values. We may conclude, too, that it was this nihilism, this sense that nothing—neither religion, morals nor love—has value rather than a few lurid scenes which really upset French *mères de famille* in the year 1857 and led to Flaubert's prosecution for indecency.

The critic is faced with another problem. While *Madame Bovary* is admittedly only partly successful on account of conflicting attitudes, it still has to be decided what value should be attached to Flaubert's pessimism, whether it was a mature conception of life or an immature cynicism which is masquerading as mature vision.

Thibaudet was in no doubt about the answer:

The world described in *Madame Bovary* [he said] is a world which is falling apart. . . . But in every society when something is destroyed, another thing takes its place. When the Bovarys' fortune collapses,

Lheureux's rises. . . . The novel has two sides—the defeat of Emma and the triumph of Homais.[1]

The book does, indeed, end with a remarkable stroke of irony. 'Homais', we are told

> Homais inclina vers le pouvoir. Il rendit secrètement à M. le préfet de grands services dans les élections. Il se vendit, enfin, il se prostitua. . . .
> Depuis la mort de Bovary, trois médecins se sont succédé à Yonville sans pouvoir y réussir, tant M. Homais les a tout de suite battus en brèche. Il fait une clientèle d'enfer; l'autorité le ménage et l'opinion publique le protège.
> Il vient de recevoir la croix d'honneur.

> [In pursuit of his ambition, he consented to bow the knee to Authority. Unknown to anybody, he rendered the Prefect great service at Election time. In short, he sold, he prostituted himself. . . .
> Since Bovary died, there have been three doctors in Yonville. None of them, however, has made a success of the practice, so violently hostile has Homais shown himself to all of them. He himself is doing extremely well. The authorities handle him with kid gloves, and he is protected by public opinion.
> He recently received a decoration.]

There is no doubt that Thibaudet correctly described Flaubert's intentions. And if sheer technical power were sufficient, we should have to agree that *Madame Bovary* was one of the greatest of novels. Yet somehow we remain unconvinced by the irony as we are unconvinced by the pessimism. For Flaubert's figures will not bear the weight of the symbolism that he tried to attach to them. We cannot fail to notice that he was continually tipping the scales, trying to give these sordid provincials an importance which they were far from possessing. What he exhibits with superb accomplishment is in fact an immature cynicism masquerading as mature vision.

[1] *Op. cit.*, pp. 120, 122.

IV. L'ÉDUCATION SENTIMENTALE

FRENCH critics used to be fond of debating the comparative merits of *Madame Bovary* and *L'Éducation sentimentale*.[1] The later book is undoubtedly far more ambitious. The eminent novelist turns his back on the loves of a country doctor's wife and attempts a full-length study of high society as seen through the eyes of a rich young man. It can hardly be maintained that the result is a success or that as a work of art it is comparable to *Madame Bovary*. For the larger canvas does not suit Flaubert. Instead of providing him with greater scope, it throws into relief the limitations of his sensibility which is reduced to a pathetic trickle winding through the endless wastes of words. Love, politics, art—all wither beneath his touch and are submerged in a common futility. Pellerin, the bad painter, is a successful minor character, but as social criticism the book is a failure. 'Oh, how tired I am', he wrote in a tell-tale sentence in a letter to George Sand, 'of the ignoble worker, the inept bourgeois, the stupid peasant and the odious ecclesiastic.' The truth is that in spite of his honesty, Flaubert did not possess either the penetration or the temper which go to the making of the great social critic. His irony is almost always too heavy, too obvious. There is an undercurrent of *rancœur*, an exasperation with stupidity which is continually breaking out in crude denunciation.

We must not be misled by Flaubert's sub-titles. Whether he calls a book 'Mœurs de Province' or 'L'Histoire d'un Jeune Homme', his basic interests are the same, and the resemblances between the two books are in general more striking than their differences. Frédéric's love story does, however, introduce some interesting variations and since the claim is implicit in the book, *L'Éducation sentimentale* must be considered as a social document as well as a study of personal relationships.

In *L'Éducation sentimentale* Flaubert drew directly on his personal experience. Frédéric Moreau is a portrait of the artist and his devotion to Mme Arnoux is founded on Flaubert's own devotion to Élisa

[1] 'Pour les initiés, *L'Éducation* est le livre sacré.' (Alfred Colling, *Gustave Flaubert* (Paris, 1941), p. 288.)

Schlésinger.[1] We may suspect that Flaubert adopted this course partly to avoid the conflict which we find in *Madame Bovary* and partly to give his personal experience a wider context and a more representative significance. It could be argued that in *Madame Bovary* he was exposing what is in essence an immature state of mind, but no such excuse can be made for the failure of *L'Éducation sentimentale*. The book, indeed, belies its title. There is no 'education' and no development. Frédéric is eighteen at the beginning of the book and forty-five at the end of it; but except that he is worn out by his frivolous life, the Frédéric whom we take leave of after nearly six hundred pages is fundamentally the same as the Frédéric whom we meet on page one. For there seems to be little doubt that Flaubert was more at home with the 'literary' emotions of parts of *Madame Bovary*, and his attempt to write a novel about his own experience explains the psychological barrenness of *L'Éducation sentimentale*.

The one positive force in Frédéric's life appears to be his love of Mme Arnoux, but on closer inspection it turns out to have a different significance:

> Et ils s'imaginaient une vie exclusivement amoureuse, assez féconde pour remplir les plus vastes solitudes, excédant toutes les joies, défiant toutes les misères, où les heures auraient disparu dans un continuel épanchement d'eux-mêmes, et qui auraient fait quelque chose de resplendissant et d'élevé comme la palpitation des étoiles.

> [And they imagined a life that would be all love, and yet rich enough to fill the widest deserts; surpassing all joys, defying all sorrows, they would open their hearts to each other for hours on end. It was a life which might have become something splendid and sublime, like the twinkling of the stars.]

We recognize this as the familiar language of the romantic lover, the familiar hunt for an impossible love 'excédant toutes les joies' and producing 'un continuel épanchement d'eux-mêmes . . . comme la palpitation des étoiles'. But in this book the critical attitude which informed *Madame Bovary* is largely absent. Flaubert takes romantic love seriously and there is no trace of irony in his treatment of it. It is, per-

---

[1] Frédéric's affair with Mme Dambreuse was based on Maxime Du Camp's liaison with Mme Delessert. Flaubert deliberately shows Frédéric's conduct in this part of the book in a discreditable light in order to revenge himself on Du Camp with whom he had quarrelled. (See R. Dumesnil, *Flaubert, l'homme et l'œuvre* (Paris, 1932), pp. 361–84.)

haps, the greatest weakness of the novel that it reproduces so closely
the history of Flaubert's connection with Élisa Schlésinger and that no
attempt is made to transform the material into something more impressive. Mme Arnoux marks the stage at which the emotional development of both Frédéric and his creator was arrested. In the novel as in
life the love affair is never consummated not because of moral scruples
or because the woman would not have 'yielded' had she been pressed,
but because romantic love must of its nature be unhappy and its object
inaccessible. We may suspect that at bottom the high-minded devotion
is a defence-mechanism, a prolonged adolescence which provides a
refuge from the responsibilities of adult life.

I have spoken of the similarities between the two novels. It is interesting to compare Frédéric's *déception* when he meets Mme Arnoux again
after an absence in the country with Emma's in the presence of Léon:

> Frédéric s'était attendu à des spasmes de joie; mais les passions s'étiolent
> quand on les dépayse, et, ne retrouvant plus Mme Arnoux dans le milieu
> où il l'avait connue, elle lui semblait avoir perdu quelque chose, porter
> confusément comme une dégradation, enfin n'être plus la même. Le
> calme de son cœur le stupéfiait.

> [Frederic had been anticipating paroxysms of joy; but passionate feelings
> seldom survive a change of atmosphere, and, meeting Mme Arnoux again
> in an unfamiliar setting, he felt that her stature was somehow diminished,
> that she had suffered an indefinable deterioration—in short, that she had
> changed. His own calmness astounded him.]

Frédéric's 'spasmes de joie' resemble Emma's 'félicité profonde',
and 'le calme de son cœur' expresses an emptiness which hardly differs
from 'elle s'avouait ne rien sentir d'extraordinaire'. There is, however,
one important difference. Frédéric's 'calm' is final; it is not followed
by the *long frisson* or at any rate not until the discovery of Rosanette.

Flaubert tried to make Frédéric's story more interesting by giving
him a greater variety of mistresses. Louise, Mme Arnoux, Rosanette
and Mme Dambreuse stand for Innocence, the Romantic Idol, Nature
and Civilization. Mme Arnoux is not the only one who is a portrait
from life. We cannot identify the charming though shadowy Louise
who may have been a pure invention; but Rosanette—the only one of
the four whose vitality is genuine and who really comes to life—like
Marie in *Novembre* is to some extent a portrait of Eulalie Foucaud de
Lenglade. Although Flaubert had Maxime Du Camp and Mme
Delessert in mind when he wrote the parts about Mme Dambreuse,

she certainly plays the same role in Frédéric's life as Louise Colet did in Flaubert's. She is the woman who for a moment satisfies Frédéric sexually and to some extent emotionally or possibly socially. When she persists in buying a small box at the sale which follows the Arnoux bankruptcy, Frédéric seizes his opportunity. She is just as brutally *éconduite* as Louise Colet when she forced her way into Croisset.

The main interest, however, lies in the relation of the different women in Frédéric's mind and the way in which the different sides of his character are revealed through them:

La fréquentation de ces deux femmes faisait dans sa vie comme deux musiques: l'une folâtre, emportée, divertissante, l'autre grave et presque religieuse; et, vibrant à la fois, elles augmentaient toujours, et peu à peu se mêlaient;—car, si Mme Arnoux venait à l'effleurer du doigt seulement, l'image de l'autre, tout de suite, se présentait à son désir, parce qu'il avait, de ce côté-là, une chance moins lointaine;—et, dans la compagnie de l'autre, quand il lui arrivait d'avoir le cœur ému, il se rappelait immédiatement son grand amour.

[The companionship of the two women made, as it were, two melodies in his life: the one, gay, reckless, amusing—the other serious, almost religious; and the two strains, sounding together, continually swelled and gradually intermingled; for, if Mme Arnoux merely brushed him with her finger, his desire at once evoked the image of the other woman, since, in her case, his hopes were less remote; and if in Rosanette's company his heart should fill with tenderness, he would immediately remember his great love.]

We read of his affair with Mme Dambreuse:

Il n'éprouvait pas à ses côtés ce ravissement de tout son être qui l'emportait vers Mme Arnoux, ni le désordre gai où l'avait mis d'abord Rosanette. Mais il la convoitait comme une chose anormale et difficile, parce qu'elle était noble, parce qu'elle était riche, parce qu'elle était dévote,—se figurant qu'elle avait des délicatesses de sentiment, rares comme ses dentelles, avec des amulettes sur la peau et des pudeurs dans la dépravation.

[With her he did not feel that all-embracing rapture which impelled him towards Mme Arnoux, or the happy turmoil of the emotions into which Rosanette had flung him at first. But he desired her as a singular, almost unattainable object, because she was noble, because she was rich, because she was devout. He attributed to her a refinement of feeling as exquisite as her lace; he felt she would wear holy medals next her skin, and turn modest suddenly in the midst of debauchery.]

Frédéric's *dépravation* is uncommonly like Emma's *corruption*, and neither is the sign of a mature outlook.

It is not surprising that Frédéric has moments of revolt against Mme Dambreuse's curious charms:

> Il reconnut alors ce qu'il s'était caché, la désillusion de ses sens. Il n'en feignait pas moins de grandes ardeurs; mais pour les ressentir, il lui fallait évoquer l'image de Rosanette ou de Mme Arnoux.

> [Then he acknowledged what he had until then refused to admit—the disillusion of his senses. This did not prevent his simulating the most passionate ardour; but in order to feel it, he had to call up the image of Rosanette or Mme Arnoux.]

I do not think that Flaubert was a profound psychologist or that his work added materially to the discoveries about human nature made by his predecessors, but technically these passages are undeniably original. Without precisely revealing fresh combinations of feelings, they do throw a new light on our mental processes, on the formation of different states of mind. For it seems to me that Flaubert's insight into the association of ideas, the way in which the character's emotions for different women crystallize into images which alternately blend and clash, reinforce and destroy one another, anticipates some of Bergson's researches and points the way to Proust and Joyce. The *deux musiques* looks forward to the *petite phrase* of Vinteuil's sonata and Swann's love for Odette; Rosanette and Mme Arnoux are present in Frédéric's mind in the same way as Andrée and Albertine are in the mind of the narrator in *A la Recherche du temps perdu*.

One of the worst faults of *L'Éducation sentimentale* is its diffuseness. There are pages when words revolve like pieces in a kaleidoscope without forming any pattern. Then, suddenly, each of the pieces falls into place and the pattern is there:

> Frédéric l'observait. La peau mate de son visage paraissait tendue, et d'une fraîcheur sans éclat, comme celle d'un fruit conservé.

> [Frederic watched her. Her lustreless skin seemed to be stretched over her face; it had freshness but no bloom, like a preserved fruit.]

The homely image is a shrewd comment not only on Mme Dambreuse, but on the society which produced her. This time every word is 'right'. The *tendue* makes us feel the strain under which all these people were living. The 'fraîcheur sans éclat', reinforcing the implications of 'la peau mate', suggests the curious artificiality of their lives, lives without genuine vitality depending on cosmetics and patent medicines; and though they possessed undeniable virtues, they were the virtues of 'un fruit conservé'.

This sentence acquires a symbolical value and in the manner of the novelists who followed him, Flaubert refers back to it later in the book, playing on its latent implications:

> Outre sa visite du soir, il lui en faisait quelquefois une autre vers la fin du jour; et il avait une gradation de joies à passer successivement par la grande porte, par la cour, par l'antichambre, par les deux salons; enfin, il arrivait dans son boudoir, discret comme un tombeau, tiède comme une alcôve, où l'on se heurtait aux capitons des meubles parmi toute sorte d'objets. . . .

> [Apart from his evening visit, he often paid her another in the late afternoon; and he experienced an ascending scale of pleasures as he passed in succession through the front door, the hall and the two drawing-rooms. At length he reached her boudoir, which was as quiet as a tomb, and warm as an alcove. One stumbled against padded furniture among a whole medley of objects. . . .]

The *tombeau*—a word that Flaubert sometimes used too melodramatically—gives the right sense of atmosphere here and the 'tiède comme une alcôve' the feeling of warm, stuffy, airless life. It is caught up a few pages later when we read:

> Il semblait à Frédéric, en descendant l'escalier, qu'il était devenu un autre homme, que la température embaumante des serres chaudes l'entourait, qu'il entrait définitivement dans le monde supérieur des adultères patriciens et des hautes intrigues.

> [As Frederic went down the staircase, he felt that he had become a different man, that the heavily perfumed air of conservatories surrounded him, that he had finally made his way into the higher world of patrician liaisons and aristocratic intrigues.]

The 'serres chaudes' refers back to 'tiède comme une alcôve' and the 'fruit conservé'. The different *gradations* described in the middle passage enable the author to get underneath the skin of his hero, making us feel his snobbish satisfaction as he disposes, one after another, of the different 'obstacles' which separate him from his lady's couch. But the boudoir—the goal for which he is making—is ironically also a *tombeau* because Frédéric's love contains the seeds of its own dissolution. 'En descendant l'escalier' in the last passage is also ironical. It is the moral *descent* which appears to lead *up* to the 'adultères patriciens' and the 'hautes intrigues'.

In another place we are told of Frédéric's departure from one of his meetings with Mme Dambreuse:

> Il huma dans la rue une large bouffée d'air; et, par besoin d'un milieu moins artificiel, Frédéric se ressouvint qu'il devait une visite à la Maréchale.

> [All the same, he drew in a large mouthful of air in the street; and feeling the need for a less artificial environment, he remembered that he owed a visit to Rosanette.]

The tug-of-war between Mme Dambreuse and Rosanette symbolizes the conflict between a dying society and what is real and vital in Frédéric's own make-up.[1]

These passages recall an interesting comment on Rosanette's *cabinet de toilette*:

> On voyait, tout de suite, que c'était l'endroit de la maison le plus hanté, et comme son vrai centre moral.

> [It was obvious at once that this was the most important room, the focal point, as it were, of the house.]

This sentence seems at first to place the *poule de luxe* with the same finality as Mme Dambreuse; but this time Flaubert is not completely successful. He should have begun, one feels, with a brief description of the *cabinet de toilette* and this sentence should have been the climax of a passage in which every object had its place. Instead, the process is reversed. It is the opening sentence and is followed by.

> Une perse à grands feuillages tapissait les murs, les fauteuils et un vaste divan élastique; sur une table de marbre blanc s'espaçaient deux larges

[1] Compare Mr. Edmund Wilson's interesting comment: 'Her [Rosanette's] liaison with Frédéric is a symbol of the disastrously unenduring union between the proletariat and the bourgeois of which Marx had written.' (*The Triple Thinkers*, p. 111.)

cuvettes en faïence bleue; des planches de cristal formant étagère au-dessus étaient encombrées par des fioles, des brosses, des peignes, des bâtons de cosmétique, des boîtes à poudre; le feu se mirait dans une haute psyché; un drap pendait en dehors d'une baignoire, et des senteurs de pâte d'amandes et de benjoin s'exhalaient.

[The walls, the armchairs, and the enormous spring divan were covered in chintz, with a bold pattern of leaves; on a white marble table stood two large basins in blue faience; the glass shelves above were loaded with bottles, brushes and combs, sticks of make-up, and powder boxes; a tall cheval glass reflected the fire; a cloth hung over the edge of a bath, and the scents of almond paste and benzoin filled the air.]

Flaubert was attempting something not unlike Swift's finale in the description of his mistress's boudoir, but he fails because he adopts the wrong method. His description not only robs individual objects of their significance, it destroys the effect which he has already created in the admirable opening sentence.

The preoccupation of the nineteenth-century novelists with the physical appearance of the external world, their obsession with the impact of material reality on their sensibility is a curious phenomenon. The great French writers of the past had displayed a singular lack of interest in the external world and in 'Nature'; their whole attention was focused on the drama going on inside the mind. Feelings were determined by the clash of personalities, never by the sense of being hemmed in by unending rows of houses. We have little idea what their characters looked like, what sort of clothes they wore or what sort of houses they lived in. Descriptions of their persons were for the most part purely formal; clothes and nature were only interesting in so far as they illuminated the inner drama. Thus we have Phèdre's:

Que ces vains ornements, que ces voiles me pèsent!

and Antiochus':

Dans l'Orient désert quel devint mon ennui.

The interest in nature which emerged during the eighteenth century was a reaction against the excessively civilized order of the seventeenth century. It is not surprising that this feeling should have developed into nature-worship or that nature should later have been regarded as a sanctuary, a refuge from the horrors of industrial civilization. It has not, perhaps, been sufficiently remarked that the converse is also true. Nineteenth-century materialism—the preoccupation with buildings, money and clothes—was a desperate attempt to find something solid and enduring, something which one could touch and feel, in a world of dissolving values. In Baudelaire it produced great poetry of a new kind and even Balzac's interest in the physical is a sign of vitality. Flaubert's preoccupation was of a different order. 'Pour qu'une chose soit intéressante,' he remarked in a letter to Alfred Le Poittevin, 'il suffit de la regarder longtemps.'[1] L'Éducation sentimentale is in the main an illustration of the falsity of this disastrous maxim:

> La plaine, bouleversée, semblait de vagues ruines. L'enceinte des fortifica-
> tions y faisait un renflement horizontal; et, sur les trottoirs en terre qui
> bordaient la route, de petits arbres sans branches étaient défendus par des
> lattes hérissées de clous. Des établissements de produits chimiques alter-
> naient avec des chantiers de marchands de bois. . . .

> [The straggling houses on the plain looked vaguely like a ruined city.
> Beyond rose the level ridge of the fortifications; on the muddy footpaths
> fringing the road stood small, branchless trees, protected by wooden
> frames studded with nails. Chemical factories alternated with timber
> merchants' sheds. . . .]

This extract—there is a great deal more of it—is taken from an account of one of Frédéric's journeys to Paris; but Flaubert uses precisely the same method in other contexts. The first thing that strikes us is the writer's complete lack of interest in what he is describing. The next is the manner in which the objects are set down, one after another, like a catalogue. 'La pleine, bouleversée, semblait de vagues ruines' is a good description of the process. For the whole scene disintegrates into 'vagues ruines', into a mass of inanimate objects which are without any relation to one another or to the observer. Instead of words becoming things as they must do in good prose, things become words and the words fall on the page like lumps of lead, meaninglessly. Flaubert's Paris is simply a confused mass of bricks and mortar. It is not comparable to Baudelaire's Paris or to Joyce's Dublin or Conrad's London in The Secret Agent.

Flaubert himself seems to have been aware that there was something wrong and in other places he is obviously at pains to cover the gaps:

[1] Correspondance, I, p. 192.

Mais le soleil se couchait, et le vent froid soulevait des tourbillons de poussière. Les cochers baissaient le menton dans leurs cravates, les roues se mettaient à tourner plus vite, le macadam grinçait; et tous les équipages descendaient au grand trot la longue avenue, en se frôlant, se dépassant, s'écartant les uns des autres, puis, sur la place de la Concorde se dispersaient. Derrière les Tuileries, le ciel prenait la teinte des ardoises. Les arbres du jardin formaient deux masses énormes, violacées par le sommet. Les becs de gaz s'allumaient, et la Seine, verdâtre dans toute son étendue, se déchirait en moires d'argent contre les piles des ponts.

[But the sun was now setting, and a cold wind stirred up eddies of dust. The coachmen thrust their chins down into their neckcloths, the wheels turned faster, the asphalt grated; and all the carriages swept down the long avenue at a brisk trot, jostling, swerving, overtaking; then, at the Place de la Concorde they scattered. The sky behind the Tuileries took on the hue of its slate roof. The trees in the gardens became two solid masses, tinged with purple at the top. The lamps were lit; and the pale green expanse of the Seine broke into shot silver against the piles of the bridges.]

This passage has the same faults as the previous one, but Flaubert's subterfuges are not without interest. His use of three verbs together all expressing movement—'se frôlant, se dépassant, s'écartant'—was a favourite trick and it is employed here to give the monotonous prose a specious life. This also applies to the colours. Flaubert had little eye for colour. It is a sign of his lack of sensibility that he nearly always chose the dull, commonplace colours like *violacées* and *verdâtre*. The last sentence like so many in Flaubert reminds one uncomfortably of a crude coloured lithograph.

The late Jean Prévost has spoken of Flaubert's style 'qui rend tout immobile',[1] and in reading him we constantly have the impression that the tempo of life is being deliberately slowed down, that a strange immobility is stealing over human feelings which stiffen and die, crushed beneath the impact of their surroundings. Turn, for example, to the account of Frédéric's and Rosanette's visit to Fontainebleau:

Les résidences royales ont en elles une mélancolie particulière, qui tient sans doute à leurs dimensions trop considérables pour le petit nombre de leurs hôtes, au silence qu'on est surpris d'y trouver après tant de fanfares, à leur luxe immobile prouvant par sa vieillesse la fugacité des dynasties,

---

[1] 'Son style, qui rend tout immobile, est la plus singulière fontaine pétrifiante de notre littérature, et une source pleure sous ce marbre.' (In *Problèmes du roman*, p. 26.)

L

l'éternelle misère de tout;—et cette exhalaison des siècles, engourdissante et funèbre comme un parfum de momie, se fait sentir même aux têtes naïves. Rosanette bâillait démesurément. Ils s'en retournèrent à l'hôtel.

[There is a peculiar melancholy about royal residences, which is probably due to their inordinate size, compared with the number of their inhabitants, or to their silence, which is somehow surprising after the trumpets that have sounded there, or it may be because of their fixed and motionless splendour, which proves by its antiquity the transience of dynasties, the inevitable decay of all things; and this emanation of the centuries, numbing and deathly as the smell of a mummy, affects even the shallowest mind. Rosanette was yawning vastly. They went back to their hotel.]

Flaubert's starting point is the 'mélancolie particulière' which the visitors experience when confronted by historic monuments. It is connected at once with their physical proportions, with the 'dimensions trop considérables pour le petit nombre de leurs hôtes', with the silence and the 'luxe immobile'. Size is linked with age and the 'mélancolie particulière' transformed into 'l'éternelle misère de tout'. The repetition and the use of the heavy Latinized vocabulary give the prose its soporific quality; we feel the 'exhalaison des siècles' enveloping the visitors and overpowering them. The whole experience peters out in a sense of vacancy, in 'Rosanette bâillait démesurément'. The reader himself feels tempted to yawn as Frédéric and Rosanette suddenly turn for home, their minds a blank.

This no doubt is a description of a particular incident, but the method is characteristic and it enables us to understand the curious dullness of L'Éducation sentimentale. Flaubert's obsession with bricks and mortar, with distance, size and shape, turns his characters into ridiculous dwarf-life creatures who move convulsively through this dead silent world like the figures in an animated cartoon.

It is, indeed, of a film that the book continually reminds me—a film of inordinate length which in spite of good 'shots' and even good 'sequences' has almost every fault that a film can have. There are times when the picture is out of focus, when the sound-track degenerates into an incoherent mutter or fails altogether, or when the camera goes tracking interminably over the roofs and façades of buildings, nosing in and out of doors and windows and prying into backyards without the mind being able to grasp the significance of what is being shown. At other times it dwindles into a jerky, meaningless flicker. Then, suddenly, a scene is thrown into sharp relief, some object assumes, for a moment, immense significance, only to be swallowed up again in the endless meandering.

The discussion of these passages leads to other considerations. On the first page of *L'Éducation sentimentale* Flaubert describes the departure of the boat which is carrying Frédéric away from Paris to his home town:

> Enfin le navire partit; et les deux berges, peuplées de magasins, de chantiers et d'usines, filèrent comme deux larges rubans que l'on déroule.

> [The boat sailed at last; and the banks of the river, crowded with ware-houses, yards and factories, slipped by like two wide ribbons being unrolled.]

A few pages later we read:

> . . . et l'ennui, vaguement répandu, semblait alanguir la marche du bateau et rendre l'aspect des voyageurs plus insignifiant encore.

> [. . . boredom, vague yet pervasive, was abroad; the movement of the boat seemed slower and the passengers looked even more insignificant than before.]

The first image is not altogether a happy one and in the second the artifice is, perhaps, too evident; but the contrast between the two, between the brittle jerky movement of the first and the slow heavy movement of the second, reflects the peculiar rhythm of the book. It is a twofold rhythm, a sense of life trying vainly to break through the heavy monotony of the style and achieving only a few jerky spasms. The phenomenon described in the second example—the sudden feeling that life has come to a standstill—is not an uncommon one, but Flaubert gives it a personal interpretation. The *ennui* is transformed into something tangible which smothers feeling, striking at the roots of life and reducing everything to the same drab level of monotony.

> The whole of the first book [wrote Thibaudet of *l'Éducation sentimentale*] preserves this rhythm of water flowing, of this boat on a river where Frédéric lets the floating images of the life that he is making for himself go their own way. . . . The theme of water is taken up again in the description of the carriages going down the Champs-Elysées. Everything, in the picture borne away by the liquid continuity of the imperfects, flows towards the Seine, goes to meet the river which carries away all.[1]

---

[1] *Gustave Flaubert*, pp. 165, 166.

Thibaudet is speaking of the passage beginning 'Mais le soleil se couchait . . .' which has already been discussed. I think that it will probably be felt that the 'continuité liquide des imparfaits' is a misleading description of the rhythm of the novel and that faults of style rob the 'rivière qui emporte tout' of the tragic significance with which Thibaudet tries to invest it. But though Thibaudet seems to me to be too indulgent in his interpretation of Flaubert's symbolism, the suggestion that there is a link between the journeys by water and the journeys by coach is an interesting one. The whole of L'Éducation sentimentale is in a sense an account of a journey through life, but a journey in which the traveller is a spectator rather than an actor, in which life is *seen* from the deck of a ship or the inside of a coach instead of being *lived*, emphasizing the paucity of Frédéric's contacts with life and not the richness of his experience:

Un peu plus loin, on découvrit un château, à toit pointu, avec des tourelles carrées. Un parterre de fleurs s'étalait devant sa façade; et des avenues s'enfonçaient, comme des voûtes noires, sous les hauts tilleuls. Il se la figura passant au bout des charmilles. A ce moment, une jeune dame et un jeune homme se montrèrent sur le perron, entre les caisses d'orangers. Puis tout disparut.

[A little further on a mansion came into view, with a pointed roof and square turrets. There was a garden in front of the house, and avenues stretched back, like dark tunnels, under the tall lime-trees. He pictured her strolling past the shrubberies. At that moment a young lady and a young man appeared on the steps, between the orange-trees in their tubs. Then the whole scene vanished.]

This passage, which is quoted by Thibaudet, is taken from the account of Frédéric's journey to Nogent, but it does not seem to me to support his conclusions. The description of the ancient château, where Frédéric imagines himself wandering with Mme Arnoux, introduces romantic associations which are suddenly focused in the precise image of 'une jeune dame et un jeune homme . . . entre les caisses d'orangers'. The young couple is a symbol of 'Life' beckoning to Frédéric from the river bank. Then, with characteristic abruptness, the vision disappears. The 'Puis tout disparut' makes us feel that Frédéric has missed his chance; life has escaped him, as it always will, and the jerky restless movement reasserts itself.

This passage, in which 'Life' is significantly symbolized by 'young love among the orange groves', illustrates the dream-like quality of

Frédéric's journey. For *le rêve* plays the same part in his psychology as it does in Emma's. There is a continual movement away from comfortless actuality towards the 'oranges groves' and the 'pays à noms sonores' of the dream-world. There are moments when the dream changes into an hallucination or a nightmare, as it does in the accounts of parties in both books. Actuality disintegrates to reveal the hideous and terrifying shapes of the nightmare:

Presque toutes portaient un bouquet de violettes à la main. Le ton mat de leurs gants faisaient ressortir la blancheur humaine de leurs bras; des effilés, des herbes, leur pendaient sur les épaules, et on croyait quelquefois, à certains frissonnements, que la robe allait tomber. Mais la décence des figures tempérait la provocation du costume; plusieurs même avaient une placidité presque bestiale, et ce rassemblement de femmes demi-nues faisait songer à un intérieur de harem. . . .

[Almost everyone carried a bunch of violets. The dead colour of their gloves intensified the natural whiteness of their arms; ribbons and pearls hung down their shoulders; sometimes, when one shivered, her dress seemed about to fall. But the daring of their costumes was counterbalanced by the respectability of their faces; some wore an expression of almost animal complacency, and this assemblage of half-naked women made him think of the inside of a harem. . . .]

This illustrates very well the alternation of nightmare and reality. The procession of women with their violets suggests some strange rite which is emphasized by 'le ton mat de leurs gants', then relieved by the 'blancheur *humaine* de leurs bras'. The feeling that their clothing may suddenly fall off takes us back to the world of the nightmare where one's trousers are always falling down. We come back again to reality in 'la décence des figures' only to switch to the nightmare with its fearful shapes in 'une placidité presque bestiale' and the 'intérieur de harem'.

The best illustration of all, however, is the account of the fancy dress ball at the Maréchale's:

Alors, toutes les femmes, assises autour du salon sur des banquettes, se levèrent à la file, prestement; et leurs jupes, leurs écharpes, leurs coiffures se mirent à tourner.

Elles tournaient si près de lui, que Frédéric distinguait les gouttelettes de leur front;—et ce mouvement giratoire de plus en plus vif et régulier, vertigineux, communiquant à sa pensée une sorte d'ivresse, y faisait surgir d'autres images, tandis que toutes passaient dans le même éblouissement, et chacune avec une excitation particulière selon le genre de sa beauté. La Polonaise, qui s'abandonnait d'une façon langoureuse, lui inspirait l'envie de la tenir contre son cœur, en filant tous les deux dans un traîneau sur une plaine couverte de neige. Des horizons de volupté tranquille, au bord d'un lac, dans un chalet, se déroulaient sous les pas de la Suissesse, qui valsait le torse droit et les paupières baissées. Puis, tout à coup, la Bacchante, penchant en arrière sa tête brune, le faisait rêver à des caresses dévoratrices, dans des bois de lauriers-roses, par un temps d'orage, au bruit confus des tambourins. . . . Mais la Débardeuse, dont les orteils effleuraient à peine le parquet, semblait recéler dans la souplesse de ses membres et le sérieux de son visage tous les raffinements de l'amour moderne, qui a la justesse d'une science et la mobilité d'un oiseau. Rosanette tournait, le poing sur la hanche; sa perruque à marteau, sautillant sur son collet, envoyait de la poudre d'iris autour d'elle; et, à chaque tour, du bout de ses éperons d'or, elle manquait d'attraper Frédéric.

[Then all the women, who had been sitting on sofas round the room, got up quickly in a line; and their skirts, their scarves, their head-dresses began to revolve.

They came so close to Frederic that he could even see the drops of sweat on their foreheads; and this dizzy, spinning movement, growing ever faster and more rhythmic, aroused a kind of intoxication in his mind, filling it with strange thoughts, while the women swept by him in a single, dazzling whirl; and each, with her special beauty, excited a different desire. The Polish girl's languorous surrender to the dance made him long to hold her to his heart, while they travelled together in a sleigh over a snow-covered plain. The Swiss girl, waltzing with her body upright and her eyelids lowered, opened to him vistas of quiet joy in a chalet beside a lake. Then suddenly the Bacchante, bending her dark head backwards, made him dream of ravenous kisses among groves of oleander, in thundery weather, to the murmur of tabors. . . . But the *débardeuse*, whose light toes scarcely skimmed the floor, seemed, with her supple limbs and serious face, to suggest all the refinements of modern love, which combines the precision of a science with the restlessness of a bird. Rosanette was dancing with her hand on her hip; her wig bobbed up and down on her collar, scattering powder all around her; at every twirl she almost caught Frederic with her golden spurs.]

The ritual element is introduced by the dancers all filing into the ball-room. The connection between the 'mouvement giratoire de plus en plus vif et régulier, vertigineux' and the movement of the journeys is evident. Frédéric, as usual, is a spectator—naturally he does not dance —but this time it is life which revolves about him. Its shapes suddenly draw near to him, beckoning to him, then move away tantalizingly. The movement of the dance merges into the imagined movement of the sledge gliding over the snows, changes to the calm of a Swiss lake, then to the 'bois de lauriers-roses' and ends with the refinements of 'modern love'. Rosanette, who is described later among the débris of the party as 'fraîche comme au sortir d'un bain . . . les joues roses, les yeux brillants', is a symbol of the Natural Woman, and the way in which the ends of her gold spurs keep just missing Frédéric stands for his intermittent contacts with reality.

I have dwelt at some length on passages which are not always in themselves of great intrinsic value because of the light that they throw on Flaubert's sensibility. Certain conclusions emerge from the analysis of these different passages. Flaubert had no gift for *direct* description. His descriptive prose is almost invariably dull and lifeless. His sensibility lacks freshness and he has no power of making us see material things in a new way or of selecting what is significant in the scene before him. His originality appears rather in sudden glimpses into the *moral* significance of a person or a place such as we find in the comment on Rosanette's *cabinet de toilette*, in the critical appraisal of a section of society that we find in the account of la Vaubyessard or in the passages in which he reshapes feelings which are largely derived from his own reading as he does in Emma's 'daydream'. I think that we must go on to say that his sensibility was not simply limited and intermittent, but was undoubtedly defective. It was a sensibility which only touched life at comparatively few points, and we have seen from his descriptions of urban life that there was a wide variety of situations in which it failed to register at all.

The implications of this criticism are far-reaching. Mme Dambreuse is practically the only character who has any roots in the society which Flaubert is studying and she is the only point at which there exists a tenuous relationship between Frédéric and this society. For one of the main weaknesses of the book is the gap between the account of Frédéric's *amours* and the account of society. The social life, the political meetings and the revolutions which Flaubert described so laboriously are no more than a drab and uninteresting background for what is after all a series of not very exciting liaisons.

These conclusions seem to me to be confirmed by the famous opening of Part III, chapter 6:

Il voyagea.

Il connut la mélancolie des paquebots, les froids réveils sous la te.
l'étourdissement des paysages et des ruines, l'amertume des sympathi
interrompues.

Il revint.

Il fréquenta le monde, et il eut d'autres amours encore. Mais le souvenir
continuel du premier les lui rendait insipides; et puis la véhémence du
désir, la fleur même de la sensation était perdue. Ses ambitions d'esprit
avaient également diminué. Des années passèrent; et il supportait le
désœuvrement de son intelligence et l'inertie de son cœur.

[He travelled.

He knew the melancholy of the steamboat; the cold awakening in the
tent; the tedium of scenery and ruins; the bitterness of interrupted friendship.

He came back.

He went into society. He had other loves still. But the ever-present
memory of the first destroyed their savour; and, besides, the violence of
desire, the flower of sensation itself, had withered. His intellectual ambitions
had also dwindled. Years passed; and he endured the idleness of his mind
and the stagnation of his heart.]

This is undoubtedly one of the most accomplished pieces of prose in
the whole of Flaubert's work and in its way it is a complete success.
For like the passage from *Madame Bovary* discussed earlier in this chapter,
it is an artistic whole. The feelings are completely dissolved into the
images. There is no impression either that feelings are being released
for which no adequate words can be found or that words are being used
to conceal a failure of sensibility. The short, sharp sentence: 'Il voyagea'
marks a break with the old life, the life which had ended with the
violent death of Dussardier during the riots, and concentrates the attention on the 'remedy'. The 'blanks', which Proust rather perversely
described as the most beautiful thing in the book, prolong the effect of
the words, suggest long periods of time passing, vast distances traversed.
The weariness and boredom of life on a liner lead to the cold and loneliness of camping expeditions in the desert. For Frédéric becomes the
Romantic Traveller seeking escape from urban civilization; but, as we
should expect of a hero whom his creator described in a moment of
exasperation as 'l'homme de toutes les faiblesses', the famous sights—
fresh landscapes, historic ruins—only produce a vague *étourdissement* in
the blasé traveller. They are death-symbols which replace the life-
symbols of Frédéric's earlier journeys. The attempt to escape from his

own isolation, to integrate himself into society dissolves into 'l'amertume des sympathies interrompues'.

'Il revint' has the same emphasis as the opening sentence. It marks the failure to rebuild and the sudden return. The next sentence describes the resumption of the empty, frivolous life which had driven him away. The third explains the fundamental immaturity of his outlook and his love for Mme Arnoux is seen for what it is—an adolescent admiration which has prevented development and adaptation. The remarkable phrase, 'et puis la véhémence du désir, la fleur même de la sensation était perdue', shows Flaubert—always more successful when describing disintegration and collapse—at his best. The sensation is presented with startling clarity, linking spiritual and physical destruction. The final sentence welds the two into a whole: 'le désœuvrement de son intelligence et l'inertie de son cœur.'

The passage has the internal coherence and economy of a seventeenth-century *tirade*, moving with mathematical precision from one feeling to another, from the mood of boredom and loneliness to the mood of complete vacuity. The friction between one set of feelings and another ends by destroying all feeling. It was because Flaubert excelled in descriptions of *inertie* that the second part of the passage is still more impressive than the first. His 'Symbolist' technique was never used with better effect. A whole life is crowded into these few sentences. It is an admirable example of Flaubert's art certainly, but it knocks the rest of the book sideways, standing out with a sombre splendour against a drab and colourless background.

> It is the tragedy of nobody in particular [Mr. Edmund Wilson wrote of *L'Éducation sentimentale*] but of the poor human race itself reduced to such ineptitude, such cowardice, such weak irresolution—arriving, with so many fine notions in its head, so many noble words on its lips, at a failure which is all the more memorable because those who have failed are hardly conscious of having done so.[1]

Flaubert would have been highly gratified by these kind words; but though they may very well describe his intention, they seem to me to underline the immense gap between intention and execution. For his characters simply will not bear the social significance that he tries to attach to them. The doubts that one felt about *Madame Bovary* become certainties. *L'Éducation sentimentale* seems to me to be profoundly lacking in the famous French maturity, in that wisdom which is so abundantly present in *Adolphe* and gives it its peculiar place among modern

[1] *The Triple Thinkers*, pp. 113–14.

L*

novels. All Flaubert's characters—the principals as well as the minor characters—are *ratés*. They are doomed to failure from the start, but no one is less able than their creator to explain how or why this is so.

While I do not feel able to share Mr. Wilson's high opinion of the book, I do not think that it can be dismissed as a worthless failure, as a mere example of the *platitude bourgeoise*, as some critics would have us believe.[1] It is a work of importance in its way and for many of Flaubert's admirers it remains his masterpiece. For these readers it is a great book because it seems to them to express better than any other the contemporary 'mess', the widespread disillusionment which has followed the collapse of traditional beliefs. The book does, to be sure, leave us with a sense of waste, a slow corrosion spreading over all feeling; but we also have the impression that the situation is an artificial one which depends on an incomplete analysis of the *données* and that the true explanation is to be found in the aberrations of the author's own personality, in the cultivation of a highly refined sentimentality which is concealed behind a certain bluntness, a certain matter-of-factness in the writing.

French critics may have valid reasons for their preference, but I find something sad in the excessive admiration for the book in Anglo-Saxon countries, and the readiness to accept its author as the interpreter of the modern world to itself seems to be the sign of a fundamental lack of self-confidence. There is no doubt that Anglo-Saxon readers are altogether too inclined to identify themselves uncritically with Flaubert's characters, to admire them because they are *ratés*, to see in them the reflection of their own personal failures.

---

[1] Compare Henry James's view: '*L'Éducation sentimentale* is in comparison with *Madame Bovary* mechanical and inanimate . . . the book is in a single word a *dead* one. *Madame Bovary* was spontaneous and sincere; but to read its successor is, to the finer sense, like masticating ashes and sawdust . . . elaborately and massively dreary.' (*French Poets and Novelists*, pp. 203, 209–10.)

V. STYLE AND LANGUAGE

D'autres ont écrit bien mieux que lui, et ne sentent pas l'huile. On ne suit pas sur la page la gomme et le canif. . . . Dans tout ce qui'il fait, on retrouve le morceau de concours et parfois le pensum.

André Suarès

'I MUST confess', wrote Proust of an article of Thibaudet's to which he was replying

> I must confess that I am astounded to find a man being treated as having little gift for writing who by the entirely new and personal use which he made of the past definite, the past indefinite, the present participle and of certain pronouns and prepositions, has renewed our vision of things almost as much as Kant with his Categories, his theories of Knowledge and the Reality of the external world. It is not that I prefer Flaubert's books or even his style among all others. For reasons which would take too long to develop here, I think that metaphor alone can give a sort of eternity to style; and there is not, perhaps, in the whole of Flaubert, a single fine metaphor. Far more than that, his images are generally so feeble that they scarcely rise above those which his most insignificant characters could invent.[1]

It is not difficult to see where this 'defence' leads us. It means that the nineteenth-century view of Flaubert as the supreme artist in prose has been abandoned and his contribution reduced to what can only be called technical devices in the narrow sense. Now there is after all something in this. When we think of Flaubert's greatest achievements —the Comices Agricoles is the most striking example—we feel that we are witnessing not so much an exhibition of the novelist's art as the feats of a great literary engineer.

Yet we must not underrate what he did accomplish. Proust was certainly not exaggerating when he said that he had 'renewed our vision of things almost as much as Kant with his Categories'. Flaubert was the greatest technical master of the century and his influence on his successors was decisive. Without him they might not have written at all, and

[1] Both articles originally appeared in the *Nouvelle Revue Française* (*Chroniques*, pp. 193-4).

if they had their works would have been much less impressive than they
are. For he was virtually the inventor of what is loosely called 'the
contemporary novel'. A great deal of time has been wasted discussing,
developing and explaining Emma Bovary's 'character', but Flaubert's
novel is in no sense an imaginary biography. In his hands the novel was
essentially an experience which must be felt as a whole, an emotional
pattern in which the characters are simply strands. His greatest triumphs
lie not in the too famous purple patches or in his landscapes, but in his
symbolism, in the adaptation of language to character and in the introduction of the recurring image.

I have already discussed Flaubert's symbolism and the language of
his characters. The recurring image, which is closely connected with his
symbolism, is in some ways the most fruitful of all his innovations
because it has influenced poetry as well as prose fiction and it points
the way to the 'themes' of Proust and Joyce.

We have seen that the drive in the cab in *Madame Bovary* is an ironical
comment on the daydream earlier in the book, but there is also a
reference to another incident. When Emma is packing for the removal
from Tostes to Yonville-l'Abbaye, she comes across her wedding
bouquet. A piece of its wire pricks her finger, reminding her of her
unhappy position, and in a moment of exasperation she throws it into
the fire:

> Il s'enflamma plus vite qu'une paille sèche. Puis ce fut comme un buisson
> rouge sur les cendres, et qui se rongeait lentement. Elle le regarda brûler
> . . . et les corolles de papier, racornies, se balançant le long de la plaque
> comme des papillons noirs, enfin s'envolèrent par la cheminée.

> [It flared up quicker than dry straw. Soon it was no more than a glowing
> twig in the cinders, slowly falling to ash. She watched it burn. . . . The
> paper leaves shrivelled, hung like black butterflies upon the fire-back, and,
> in a few moments, flew up the chimney.]

The 'papillons noirs' evidently look forward to the 'papillons blancs'
of the second scene. The burning of the bouquet stands for the symbolical annihilation of Emma's marriage and her home. At Yonville she is
seduced by Rodolphe and only his defection, when they are on the
point of eloping, prevents her from actually breaking up the home. Her
second liaison with Léon is in fact the beginning of the end. Her
extravagance on his account leads to ruin, suicide and the destruction of
the family. The appearance of the 'butterflies' is therefore an indication
of the way in which the book should be read.

When Rodolphe calls on Emma six weeks after the Comices Agri-coles in order to put his plan of seduction into operation, we read:

Elle était seule. Le jour tombait. Les petits rideaux de mousseline, le long des vitres, épaississaient le crépuscule, et la dorure du baromètre, sur qui frappait un rayon de soleil, étalait des feux dans la glace, entre les découpures du polypier.

[She was alone. Dusk was falling. The short muslin curtains over the window intensified the twilight, and the gilt mouldings of the barometer, touched by a gleam of sun, drew sparks of fire from the mirror which hung between the fretted elaboration of the coral ornament.]

Forty pages later, Charles turns to his wife for consolation after the amputation of Hippolyte's leg:

'Assez!' cria-t-elle d'un air terrible.
Et s'échappant de la salle, Emma ferma la porte si fort, que le baromètre bondit de la muraille et s'écrasa par terre.

['For heaven's sake, don't begin that!' she cried, and the expression on her face was terrible.
Running from the room, she slammed the door so violently that the barometer jumped from its nail on the wall and crashed to the ground.]

In the first passage, the sun gleaming on the barometer is a sign of 'fair weather', of rising passion. In the second, it is the prelude to disaster.

The same method is employed in the description of the guide at Rouen Cathedral. The first time we meet him he stands like the cathedral for stability and his explanations, which seem interminable to the impatient lovers, delay the 'fall'. Emma does not see him again until the Sunday on which she pays her last visit to Rouen in a desperate attempt to raise a loan:

Elle arriva sur la place du Parvis. On sortait des vêpres; la foule s'écoulait par les trois portails, comme un fleuve par les trois arches d'un pont, et, au milieu, plus immobile qu'un roc, se tenait le suisse.

[She reached the open space in front of the Cathedral. The congregation was just coming out from vespers. A crowd of worshippers was flowing through the three doors like a river running beneath the triple arches of a bridge. In the middle, motionless as a rock, stood the beadle.]

He is still a sign of stability, but he stands there like a reproach and a barrier. Emma is outside the cathedral, an outcast from respectable society which is represented by the worshippers leaving the church.

Towards the close of *L'Éducation sentimentale*, Louise goes to call on Frédéric at his Paris flat and is told by the concierge that he no longer sleeps there. She realizes that this is the end of her hopes:

> Et le petit carreau de la loge retomba nettement, comme une guillotine.

> [And the little square window of the porter's lodge fell to with a slam, like a guillotine.]

Even a cursory reading of Flaubert is sufficient to show that each of his books is a 'forest of symbols'. His use of them was a habit of mind —a habit in which he was inclined to indulge to excess. For there is scarcely a sentence which does not refer to something which has happened earlier in the book or which is about to happen, or which does not contain some carefully calculated allusion.

When we turn from style in the broad sense to the actual language in which Flaubert wrote, our impression of his achievement is less favourable. He obtained some of his most striking effects by a skilful manipulation of the past indefinite and the past definite, by those arresting short sentences or those adverbs placed at the end of a sentence after a comma. A present participle stands for the permanence of the country and an imperfect for the transitoriness of the humanity passing through it; a switch from the imperfect to the past definite produces one of those startling changes of tempo for which Flaubert is famous; a well placed adverb is wonderfully successful in fixing an impression. When he writes in *Madame Bovary*

> Puis elle se mettait à crier, horriblement.

> [Then she began to scream, horribly.]

the cry echoes indefinitely in our minds. The famous close of *Hérodias* describes the slaves carrying away the head of St. John the Baptist:

> Comme elle était très lourde, ils la portaient alternativement.

> [As it was very heavy, they carried it alternately.]

where the use of the imperfect and the final adverb have the effect not merely of prolonging movement, but of suggesting unending movement through space.

In another place he writes:

Ce fut comme une apparition:
Elle était assise, au milieu du banc, toute seule. . . .

[It was like a vision:
She was sitting, in the middle of the bench, all alone. . . .]

This is Frédéric's first sight of Mme Arnoux. The five opening words mark a sudden change of tempo, as Frédéric comes upon her in the middle of his aimless wandering round the boat, and they fix our attention on the apparition, compellingly. The punctuation of the next clause intensifies the impression, makes us feel the onlooker, who is completely *ébloui*, coming back to his senses and slowly taking in the details of the scene.

Flaubert possessed a distinctive style certainly, but we only have to read a few pages to see how largely he depends on devices which are constantly in danger of degenerating into tricks. It is right and proper that a novelist should make the fullest use of the resources of grammar and syntax, but Flaubert's effects are often too nicely calculated. The number and range of his devices are extremely limited and they are repeated endlessly. I do not see how we can avoid the conclusion that the normal process of composition is reversed. Instead of the perception or the emotion creating the form, grammatical subtleties are used as a substitute for them; the scene is carefully built up from outside. That is why even the most successful passages leave us with a vague sense of uneasiness, a feeling: 'Yes, it's very brilliant, but it seems to lack something.' In writing of him, I have been struck by the way in which words like 'accomplished', 'device', 'trick' and 'successful in its way' naturally present themselves to the mind; and in discussing his finest passages I have felt a reluctance to declare firmly: 'This is great prose.' There is a continual contrast—it is here that Flaubert reminds me of Jules Laforgue—between the maturity of the expression and the immaturity or thinness of the feelings expressed. We feel that the fine passages are not the result of an original sensibility forging its own instrument, but of artful contrivance, of technical accomplishment pushed to its furthest limits.

There is an account of one of Emma's early meetings with Charles which is worth looking at:

Elle le reconduisait toujours jusqu'à la première marche du perron. Lorsqu'on n'avait pas encore amené son cheval, elle restait là. On s'était dit adieu, on ne parlait plus; le grand air l'entourait, levant pêle-mêle les petits cheveux follets de sa nuque, ou secouant sur sa hanche les cordons de son tablier, qui se tortillaient comme des banderoles. Une fois, par un temps de dégel, l'écorce des arbres suintait dans la cour, la neige sur les couvertures des bâtiments se fondait. Elle était sur le seuil; elle alla chercher son ombrelle, elle l'ouvrit. L'ombrelle, de soie gorge-de-pigeon, que traversait le soleil, éclairait de reflets mobiles la peau blanche de sa figure. Elle souriait là-dessous à la chaleur tiède; et on entendait les gouttes d'eau, une à une, tomber sur la moire tendue.

[She always saw him out, accompanying him to the top of the outside flight of steps. If his horse had not yet been brought round, she waited with him there. Good-byes had been said, and not a word passed between them. The wide spaces of air were about them, bringing disorder to the wanton curls at the back of her neck, or blowing the apron strings in a flurry of streamers round her waist. One day in particular he remembered, a day of thaw, when the bark of the trees about the yard was all astream with moisture, and the snow was melting on the roofs of the outbuildings. She was standing on the threshold, and went to fetch her parasol. She opened it, and the sun, striking through the fabric which was of the colour of a pigeon's breast, threw flickering lights upon the white skin of her face. She smiled within its shadow at the damp warmth of the day, and he could hear the drops of water falling one by one upon the tight-stretched silk.]

Henry James and Mr. Murry have both paid tributes to this passage with its vowel sounds, its delicate rhythms all leading up to the final image of the drops falling, one by one, 'sur la moire tendue'. Certainly it is one of the loveliest passages that Flaubert ever wrote, a passage which no anthologist could resist; but it cannot for a moment be pretended that it is an organic part of the book; it is simply there, a splendid piece of virtuosity, bearing little relation to anything which went before or comes after it. It is a description of an early spring day which is remarkable for its freshness and its delicate artistry. The reasons for its success are not altogether without interest. It succeeds because it does not try to do too much, because its language is simple and it does not attempt to convey any profound experience. This is brought home when we compare it with a more ambitious passage in which Flaubert tries to disentangle complex feelings:

Le lendemain fut, pour Emma, une journée funèbre. Tout lui parut enveloppé par une atmosphère noire qui flottait confusément sur l'extérieur des choses, et le chagrin s'engouffrait dans son âme avec des hurlements doux, comme fait le vent l'hiver dans les châteaux abandonnés. C'était cette rêverie que l'on a sur ce qui ne reviendra plus, la lassitude qui vous prend après chaque fait accompli, cette douleur, enfin, que vous apportent l'interruption de tout mouvement accoutumé, la cessation brusque d'une vibration prolongée.

[The morrow was, for Emma, a day of mourning. A black mist seemed to lie over everything, drifting aimlessly across the surface of objects, while the misery in her heart moaned eerily, like winter wind in an empty house. She was in the mood which afflicts one when one dreams of things that have gone, never to return. She felt in her bones the sort of lassitude which deadens the heart when something has come to an end. She felt the pain that strikes one when an accustomed rhythm has been broken or when some prolonged vibration ceases.]

This passage, which Faguet somewhat oddly described as the work of 'un très grand poète', is from the chapter describing Emma's feelings after Léon's departure for Paris.[1] The first sentence is unexceptionable. It is when the novelist sets to work to probe the mood that his difficulties begin. The *atmosphère noire* might pass, but we naturally expect it to be broken up into its component parts and clarified by what follows. It is here that the first breakdown occurs. For what are we to think of 'le chagrin qui s'engouffrait dans son âme avec des hurlements doux'? It does not seem to bear much relation to the *atmosphère noire*, but to be a fresh start, another statement *about* Emma's feelings. Flaubert's metaphor, so far from illuminating what is happening in Emma's mind, is an evasion of the difficulty. This impression is strengthened by the wind blowing through the abandoned châteaux. It is a romantic cliché which introduces ready-made feelings and solicits a response which has nothing to do with Emma or Léon. The opening of the next sentence is no more than an amplification of the romantic aura which has been introduced from without and is extraneous to the situation. The *rêverie* and the *lassitude* are both borrowings from the vocabulary of the Romantics and their history is not a very creditable one. 'Cette douleur, enfin' seems to betray a sense that something is wrong, as though the writer were saying: 'I know the *atmosphère noire* and the *chagrin* are a bit vague, but you know what I mean—*douleur*, that's the word I'm after.' He is right of course. The last eleven words

[1] *Flaubert* (Paris, 1889), p. 155.

succeed in expressing exactly how Emma felt, and *douleur* is as good a label as any other; but it is idle to pretend that they have any logical connection with what has gone before.

There is another example on the next page:

Dès lors, ce souvenir de Léon fut comme le centre de son ennui: il y pétillait plus fort que, dans un steppe de Russie, un feu de voyageurs abandonné sur la neige.

[Henceforth, her memory of Léon was, as it were, the very core and centre of her exasperation. It sparkled more brightly than a traveller's fire lit and left on the snows of the Russian steppe.]

The opening phrase is admirable in its clarity, but the cliché which follows ruins its effect. 'Le centre de son ennui' is a precise statement of the relations between Emma and Léon and the part his memory plays in her emotional life; but instead of developing its implications, the comparison with the fire burning in the steppes allows its force to evaporate. It is simply a repetition of the opening statement in much less impressive terms. The 'steppe de Russie' is a mere counter; it has none of the emotive life of Racine's 'Orient désert'. It is, unfortunately, characteristic of Flaubert's metaphors that instead of concentrating, they tend to disperse emotion.

There is a still more interesting instance in *L'Éducation sentimentale*:

La contemplation de cette femme [Mme Arnoux] l'énervait, comme l'usage d'un parfum trop fort. Cela descendit dans les profondeurs de son tempérament et devenait presque une manière générale de sentir, un mode nouveau d'exister.

[To look at this woman took away his strength, like a too powerful perfume. This emotion penetrated the depths of his being; it became a sort of general attitude of mind, a new mode of existence.]

It is a perfect example of the contrast between the maturity of expression and the immaturity of the feelings expressed. There is no valid relation between the 'manière générale de sentir' and the 'parfum trop fort'. The relation is a purely grammatical one and is only made possible by the sleight of hand in 'Cela descendit dans les profondeurs de son tempérament'.

Flaubert's achievement consists very largely in the invention of a technique for displaying a self-consciousness of a new kindtimate, an in awareness not only of the individual's own feelings or of his environment, but of the constantly changing effect of other people on him, the endless variations of mood—sudden inexplicable joy, sudden inexplicable sadness, sudden unmotivated *ennui*. It is Flaubert's sense of the intimate play of feeling and of the individual's inability to control or direct his feelings which has had such a decisive influence on later novelists, particularly on Henry James and Conrad and, at a different level, on Virginia Woolf. James and Conrad were both far greater writers than their master, but their approach to the problem of human relationships was essentially the one practised by Flaubert and it is inconceivable that they could have produced the masterpieces they did without his example.

The excellence of 'le centre de son ennui' and 'une manière générale de sentir', in their context, underlines the fatal lack of precision in Flaubert's language when he turns to the detailed analysis of a mood. A *tirade* of Racine's, a chapter of Constant or Stendhal resembles a mathematical formula. A mood or emotion is gradually broken up into its component parts and with each step our understanding of the character's feelings deepens. It is only occasionally that Flaubert is successful. He does not work at a deep level and his successes lie for the most part in the presentation of secondary feelings, in the analysis of comparatively simple states of mind which enables him to make articulate feelings which had been missed by less self-conscious artists. 'Emma', we are told, 'cherchait à savoir ce que l'on entendait au juste dans la vie par les mots de *félicité*, de *passion*, et d'*ivresse*, qui lui avaient paru si beaux dans les livres.' It is a neat description of one of her creator's central problems. The basic emotions—*ennui, chagrin, tristesse* and the rest—never are defined. They are words of limitation which prevent analysis from being brought to bear on the deeper levels of the mind. It is for this reason that Flaubert's principal characters are strangely lacking in centrality. They are not genuine creations, but a series of different and sometimes conflicting moods which are arbitrarily labelled 'Emma' or 'Frédéric'. They are in the main composed of feelings which are borrowed from the Romantics or from the novelist's personal experience and are not always transmuted into something new. It may have been this failure to penetrate life that Flaubert was thinking of when he spoke of his own lack of *innéité*.

The failure was not purely a personal one. It was caused by changes which had taken place in French sensibility and to which I referred in my opening chapter. These changes produced a situation in which only a very great writer could have succeeded; but unhappily Flaubert did not possess either the character or the intelligence which would have

enabled a writer of the first magnitude to triumph over the very real
difficulties.

Mr. Murry has spoken of Flaubert as 'a broad, big-boned, lovable,
rather simple-minded man, with the look and the laugh of a farmer'.
It seems to me that Flaubert was indeed born with a certain native
strength and directness, a toughness commonly associated with the
Norman, but that these natural qualities became atrophied by excessive
self-analysis and his sensibility blunted by his cloistered, bookish life.
For every now and then simple, direct feelings do break through the
mannered prose and we catch a glimpse of a different and in many ways
a more impressive Flaubert who might have made a more enduring
contribution to literature. These qualities are most apparent in the short
story, *Un Cœur simple*. The passages which follow are from Flaubert's
account of Félicité:

Elle se levait dès l'aube, pour ne pas manquer la messe, et travaillait
jusqu'au soir sans interruption; puis, le dîner étant fini, la vaisselle en
ordre et la porte bien close, elle enfouissait la bûche sous les cendres et
s'endormait devant l'âtre, son rosaire à la main. Personne, dans les mar-
chandages, ne montrait plus d'entêtement. Quant à la propreté, le poli de
ses casseroles faisait le désespoir des autres servantes. Économe, elle
mangeait avec lenteur, et recueillait du doigt sur la table les miettes de son
pain,—un pain de douze livres, cuit exprès pour elle, et qui durait vingt
jours.

En toute saison elle portait un mouchoir d'indienne fixé dans le dos par
une épingle, un bonnet lui cachant les cheveux, des bas gris, un jupon
rouge, et par-dessus sa camisole un tablier à bavette, comme les infirmières
d'hôpital.

Son visage était maigre et sa voix aiguë. A vingt-cinq ans, on lui en
donnait quarante. Dès la cinquantaine, elle ne marqua plus aucun âge;—
et, toujours silencieuse, la taille droite et les gestes mesurés, semblait une
femme en bois, fonctionnant d'une manière automatique.

[She used to rise at dawn in order not to miss Mass, and work until
evening without interruption; then, when dinner was over, the washing-
up done and the door shut fast, she used to cover the log with cinders and
drop off to sleep with her rosary in her hand. No one, when it came to
bargaining, was more stubborn. As for cleanliness, her shining saucepans
were the despair of other servants. She was thrifty, ate slowly, and picked
up with her fingers on the table the crumbs of her loaf—a loaf weighing

twelve pounds, which was baked specially for her and lasted three weeks.

At all seasons of the year, she wore a kerchief of printed calico which was fixed to her back with a pin, a bonnet hiding her hair, grey stockings, a red petticoat and over her bodice an apron with a bib, like hospital nurses.

Her face was thin and her voice shrill. When she was twenty-five years old, she looked forty. From fifty onwards the years no longer left their mark on her—and, always silent, with her erect figure, her regular movements, seemed like a woman made of wood who worked automatically.]

Un Cœur simple is Flaubert's only perfect work of art. It is the only one of his books in which he was content to be himself, to write directly from his experience, and it is free from the weaknesses which spoil the novels. Félicité has a poise, a centrality, which is lacking in Emma and Frédéric. Flaubert has achieved for once a genuine artistic detachment, has managed to portray the enduring qualities of the Norman peasant. There is no gap between the character and the milieu. Félicité is firmly rooted in the community and she is convincing in a way that practically no other character of Flaubert's is. There is no hesitation, no fumbling. She is simply there.

In this passage every word is right. Her piety, her industry, her hard bargaining and simple life, her essential toughness—they are all there. The 'femme en bois, fonctionnant d'une manière automatique', is an example of Flaubert's personal imagery which for once is an undeniable success. It reinforces the 'recueillait du doigt sur la table les miettes de son pain', and the slow, deliberate gesture is admirably brought out by the placing of the words and the punctuation. Superficially, *Un Cœur simple* expresses the same *tristesse* as the novels, but the experience seems to me to be of a different quality, to be both deeper and more mature.

There is another passage in the story which deserves attention:

Elle avait eu, comme une autre, son histoire d'amour. . . .

Ils se rencontraient au fond des cours, derrière un mur, sous un arbre isolé. Elle n'était pas innocente à la manière des jeunes demoiselles,—les animaux l'avaient instruite;—mais la raison et l'instinct de l'honneur l'empechèrent de faillir.

[She had had, like any other person, her love story. . . .

They used to meet at the bottom of the yard, behind the wall, under a solitary tree. She wasn't innocent after the fashion of young ladies—the animals had taught her;—but reason and a sense of honour prevented her from falling.]

It would not be possible to improve on the economy and directness of this and Flaubert's matter-of-factness adds to its effectiveness. Once again every word is right and in the right place. The *raison* and the *honneur* stand for robust moral certitudes and the contrast—with *jeunes demoiselles*—gives *innocente* exactly the right nuance. 'Les animaux l'avaient instruite' represents something which is normal and healthy, and the contrast with the unhealthy imaginings of Emma and Frédéric, which give some of the pages of the novels their torrid sex-laden atmosphere, is striking:

> . . . et tout à coup, devant cette femme laide qui avait dans la taille des ondulations de panthère, Frédéric sentit une convoitise énorme, un désir de volupté bestiale.

> [. . . and suddenly, in the presence of this ugly woman who yet had the sinuous body of a panther, Frederic felt an overpowering lust, a longing for bestial enjoyment.]

The repression of normal feelings explains the strain of brutality which runs through Flaubert's works, the glee with which he dwells on the word *adultère* or tells us: 'N'importe! Elle n'était pas heureuse, ne l'avait jamais été.' It explains, too, the 'pointe d'imagination sadique' which Sainte-Beuve discerned in *Salammbô*—that strange sadistic orgy —and which drew a hurt protest from its author.[1]

> Flaubert [wrote M. Stanislas Fumet in an interesting essay], Flaubert weighs and measures the soul, isolates its different aspects. He searches on his palette for a colour for each of its vibrations. We have to admit that from time to time the result is as beautiful as a picture of Manet's; but we stop short at the style and the form. It is a picture with its frame; it is no longer uncontrolled life.[2]

[1] See his letter of December 1862, printed in the appendix to the definitive edition of *Salammb*ˆ. He did not deny the charge, but remonstrated with Sainte-Beuve on the ground that this suggestion might harm the reputation of a writer who had already been prosecuted for writing an immoral book.
    The criticism applies with far more force to *La Tentation de saint Antoine* which can, perhaps, only be discussed at the psychoanalytical level. The following samples speak for themselves:
    'Avec une pierre tranchante il [Atys] s'émascule, puis se met à courir furieux, en levant dans l'air son membre coupé.'
    'Alors un vertige prend les Dieux. Ils chancellent, tombent en convulsions, et vomissent leurs existences. . . . Ils arrachent leurs attributs, leurs sexes. . . .'
    'Et il [Hilarion] lui fait voir, tout au fond de l'avenue sur le seuil d'une grotte illuminée un bloc de pierre représentant l'organe sexuel d'une femme.'
[2] *Problèmes du roman*, p. 272.

The balance sheet is an interesting one. When we look at Flaubert's three principal works as a whole, we are struck at one and the same time by their variety and their monotony. He did not possess any more than Balzac a style in the assured sense of the classic artist. He was the product of an age of experiment and its instability is reflected in the different styles in which he wrote. His books are in the main a series of tableaux, a patchwork of different moods. There are impressive scenes, penetrating psychological aperçus, but they remain unco-ordinated or, as M. Fumet puts it, *la vie incontrôlée* is absent. We have the impression that many of the scenes are not simply composed from without, but that instead of following one another inevitably in response to some inner compulsion, the artist has carefully arranged a series of pictures round his studio so that they will catch the best light. It is this, perhaps, which explains the sense of hollowness at the centre, the moral confusion of these books. Flaubert often displays glimpses of genuine moral insight, but they are glimpses and no more. He remains unable to organize them and tries to fill the gap by imposing a conventional morality which is totally at variance with his own nihilism and which is expressed in the endless repetition of the word *adultère*.

VI. CONCLUSION

Ce qui me semble beau, ce que je voudrais faire, c'est un livre sur rien, un livre sans attache extérieure qui se tiendrait de lui-même par la force interne de son style, comme la terre sans être soutenue se tient en l'air, un livre qui n'aurait presque pas de sujet ou du moins où le sujet serait presque invisible, si cela se peut.

Flaubert in a letter to Louise Colet.

'C'EST ce genre de tristesse, fait de la rupture des habitudes et de l'irréalité du décor', wrote Proust, 'que donne le style de Flaubert, ce style si nouveau quand ce ne serait que par là.'[1] A certain clumsiness of expression is perhaps in danger of obscuring genuine profundity here. For Proust's comment contains three separate observations which together go to the heart of Flaubert's experience and explain his hold over contemporary readers.

'La rupture des habitudes' echoes some words of Flaubert's which I have already quoted: Emma's 'l'interruption de tout mouvement accoutumé, la cessation brusque d'une vibration prolongée' and Frédéric's 'l'amertume des sympathies interrompues'. Almost all Flaubert's principal characters are people whose ties with the community in which they were born have been broken and who try in vain to rebuild their lives through fresh personal relationships. One after another these relationships break down and the characters are oppressed by a sense of their own rootlessness and isolation, of living in a world in which they have no part.

This sensation is closely linked with what Proust calls 'l'irréalité du décor'. For I suspect that he was referring to that absence of any organic relation between material things and their tendency to disintegrate to which I have drawn attention. This double breakdown of personal and material relations, this feeling of imminent collapse, 'cette pourriture instantanée des choses où elle s'appuyait', produces the pervasive *tristesse* which gives Flaubert's work its distinctive tone.

There are several respects in which we may concede that Flaubert introduced 'presque une manière générale de sentir', but though his *tristesse* is the most famous, it seems to me to be in many ways the least valuable and to have been responsible for a great deal of the over-

[1] *Op. cit.*, p. 199.

valuation of his novels, particularly of *L'Éducation sentimentale*. The word is too comprehensive and, in so far as it suggests that a single emotion is common to all Flaubert's books, it is misleading. It is used for lack of a better term to describe experiences which differ considerably in value. It is applied equally to the valid emotions that we experience in reading the best parts of *Madame Bovary* or *Un Cœur simple*, and to the most 'massively dreary' parts of *L'Éducation sentimentale*. With the exception of a few scenes, the *tristesse* of *L'Éducation sentimentale* is personal in a bad sense. It does not arise from the contemplation of events; it is generated from within and envelops the events which the novelist is describing. It is the vagueness of this central experience which creates the illusion of actuality and which makes it so seductive, a continual invitation to the reader to project into it his personal disappointments, his own unhappy love affairs, his own world weariness. For Flaubert's characters reflect the *novelist's* failure to penetrate the core of experience and to differentiate between one experience and another. He simply transmits his own emotional poverty to them without proper critical examination.

In spite of its faults, *Madame Bovary* remains a remarkable novel, but place it for a moment beside *Adolphe* or *Le Rouge et le noir* and the contrast is glaring. All the older novelists started with a belief in man. Their definition might be limited as Mme de La Fayette's was; it might be incomplete as Laclos' was, or it might be a bold essay in the exploration of a particular emotional problem which is only complete on the last page of the book as Constant's solitary masterpiece is. Yet all these writers had an answer to the question: 'What is man?' The result is that there is no faltering, no blur in their work. Their books belong to a great tradition and each of them has a place in it; each of them takes us a stage further in the unending voyage of discovery, adding something to our knowledge of human nature.

It was left to Flaubert to proclaim that his particular vocation was to pull down what they had built:

> J'ai pris plaisir [he said in one of his letters] à combattre mes sens et à me torturer le cœur. J'ai refusé les ivresses humaines qui s'offraient. Acharné contre moi-même, je déracine l'homme à deux mains, deux mains pleines de force et d'orgueil. De cet arbre au feuillage verdoyant, je voulais faire une colonne toute nue pour y poser tout en haut, comme sur un autel, je ne sais quelle flamme céleste.[1]

> [I have taken pleasure in fighting against my senses and torturing my heart. I have refused the human exaltations which presented themselves to

[1] Quoted by Mauriac in *Trois grands hommes devant Dieu*, p. 159.

me. Inflamed against myself, I uproot man with two hands, two hands
filled with strength and pride. Out of this tree with its verdant foliage, I
wanted to construct a naked column in order to place on the very top of
it, as though on an altar, I know not what celestial flame.]

It is an illuminating commentary on his work as a whole. There is
something disconcerting about the violence of the destructive process,
the savage satisfaction which he derives from 'je déracine l'homme à
deux mains, deux mains pleines de force et d'orgueil', and the extreme
vagueness of the goal, the 'je ne sais quelle flamme céleste'.

M. Colling has suggested that his work can be divided broadly into
two groups—the novels of 'contemporary life' and the novels of
'escape' into the past or into legend. He recognizes that the novels of
contemporary life show a progressive concern with disintegration and
collapse.

> This imperishable book [he writes of l'Éducation sentimentale] is the book
> of failure par excellence. Flaubert devoted five years of his life, applied the
> whole of his energy, turned the radiance of a talent which had reached its
> highest peak of perfection to the task of recording the bankruptcy of a
> man and of a generation. A disconcerting prodigy![1]

In an ingenious analysis of Bouvard et Pécuchet, the same critic draws
attention to the curious relationship between the novelist and his
principal figures. He thinks that they somehow took possession of him,
that he was invaded by their bêtise which infected and ultimately
killed him.

M. Colling's classification is in the main convincing, but in one
respect he seems to me to do more than justice to Flaubert. I find it
difficult to accept the view that the impulse to escape from life is confined to the novels dealing with history and legend. In reading the
novels of contemporary life, I constantly have the impression that he
was running away from something, that he was refusing to face
certain fundamental issues. The Romanticism of parts of Madame
Bovary is a refuge in the same sense as the Carthage of Salammbô; his
insistence on 'impersonality' and the mechanics of style was a subterfuge, a deliberate attempt to divert attention from the problems of the
inner life—the problems which were later to engage Proust—and to
direct it to something which was largely external.

There is plenty of evidence to support the view that he was moving
towards a position of complete nihilism, nor is there anything very

[1] Op. cit., pp. 284–5.

surprising about it. We cannot fail to be struck by his fundamental uncertainty on all major issues, by an incapacity for social thinking and by a lack of what can only be called intelligence. He had no gift for constructive thought. His books contain shrewd comments on society, but they are invariably destructive. He hated the bourgeoisie from which he came and which provided him with his material, and he hated the proletariat. He seems like Baudelaire to have been at heart a patrician, but his appreciation of the achievements of aristocracy was of a different order from Baudelaire's. His work betrays a progressive loss of all sense of positive values and an increasing tendency to drama-tize his private manias which destroyed him. What has not been suffi-ciently remarked is that the nihilism on which he was inclined to insist too much—'Je doute de tout et même de mon doute', 'Je ne crois à rien, pas même à moi, ce qui est rare'—was in itself a subterfuge. For whether M. Colling's hypothesis is correct or not, it is clear that had Flaubert survived *Bouvard et Pécuchet* there would have been nothing left for him but to sit down and write his novel on nothing. It was precisely what he wanted. It was the one hope of complete escape from himself.

All this can be said, but Flaubert remains a figure of capital impor-tance in the development of the novel. When you criticize a little man his work simply disappears, but the great writer possesses a toughness and resilience which enable him to survive criticism. You can criticize Flaubert's uncertainty and confusion, his defective sensibility and his emotional poverty, but a great deal still remains. I think we should add that a great deal remains for which we must feel grateful, particularly at a time when the novel of personal relationships, which was pecu-liarly Flaubert's field, threatens to give place to novels describing the mass movements of what he contemptuously called 'the ignoble worker'. It is difficult to insist on his technical originality without the risk of giving a false impression. Technical development can never be a purely mechanical process. An advance in technique means that a writer has discovered a new way of regarding and presenting experi-ence. What is startling in Flaubert is the immense gap between the elaborate apparatus which he devised and the comparatively uninterest-ing experiences which are in fact presented. We cannot escape the con-clusion that he marks the point at which the focus shifts from the artist's *experience* to his *method*. His technical innovations have been extremely fruitful; but when we compare him with Henry James and Conrad, with Proust or even with Joyce, it is difficult to see any community of feeling between them. The relationship is a technical one; they have borrowed and perfected the tools which he forged to give an incomparably finer expression to their experience than would otherwise have been possible. If his emotional development had kept pace with his technical development, he would have been one of the greatest novelists of all time. As it is, he seems to me to be a great technician, a great literary engineer rather than a great novelist.

PROUST

Pour ce qui me concerne tout au moins, Proust aura été le révélateur le plus effrayant que je pouvais rencontrer sur moi-même.

Jacques Rivière

I. A NEW VISION

'UN univers nouveau s'ouvrait à moi,' wrote Léon Pierre-Quint of his discovery of Proust. He spoke not only for himself, but for a whole generation. To those of us who grew up between the wars, Proust's work was a revelation, an unforgettable experience which modified our sensibility. It introduced us to a world whose existence we had barely even suspected, gave us a new insight into the depth and complexity of the human heart and offered us an interpretation of man which seemed at first to be totally different from that of the classic novelists. This world may appear remote from our own, but by identifying ourselves with it, as we must in reading Proust, we are liberated from our stereotyped ways of seeing and feeling. His vision has been compared to looking at life through a microscope, but its effect is more lasting. Once we have shared it, nothing can ever look exactly the same again.[1]

It is not easy to define this vision. Ortega y Gasset has described Proust as 'the inventor of a new distance between ourselves and the world of things'.[2] This puts the emphasis in the right place. He has had a good deal of attention from professional philosophers who have written absorbing studies of the importance of his contribution to philosophy. Proust may have provided the philosopher with valuable data, but his novel is an experience and not an epistemological problem. His conception of reality and his theory of knowledge are only interesting to the critic in so far as they illuminate the tensions and stresses of his book. For his revelation is *psychological* and not *metaphysical*. His search for *la vraie vie*—the reality which he believed was concealed behind the transitory world of appearances—may sometimes remind us of K's attempts to gain admission to 'the castle' in Kafka's novel, but the resemblances are superficial. He had little in common with a novelist like Kafka who invented a world where the ordinary laws governing human conduct seem suddenly to have been suspended, leaving us with a sense that events are at once fatally predetermined and unpredictable. Proust plays havoc with time and place; the order

---

[1] Compare, 'My work is not microscopic: it is telescopic' (Proust).
[2] *Hommage à Marcel Proust* (Les Cahiers Marcel Proust, 1), (Paris, 1927), p. 291.

of our emotional reactions is often reversed; but we know that his
characters could never be called upon to defend themselves against
unknown charges in the presence of invisible judges.

Proust's art is immensely subtle, but it is very firmly rooted in the
soil of France. He himself speaks of

> . . . une tradition à la fois antique et directe, ininterrompue, orale,
> déformée, méconnaissable et vivante.

> [. . . a tradition at once ancient and direct, unbroken, oral, deformed,
> unrecognizable, and alive.]

We are aware on almost every page he wrote of that ancient France
with its thousand years of civilization, its cathedrals, its village churches,
the wide undulating plains with the peasants working in the fields, the
orchards and the apple blossom, the châteaux in their parks dimly
visible behind the hedges of lilac, of that France which is symbolized
by the one word: 'Combray'.

For in spite of the extraordinary impact of his sensibility, in many
ways Proust's world resembles our own. It is simply that we are looking
at everything from a new and unexpected angle. This is how he
describes a shower of rain:

> Un petit coup au carreau, comme si quelque chose l'avait heurté, suivi
> d'une ample chute légère comme de grains de sable qu'on eût laissé tomber
> d'une fenêtre au-dessus, puis la chute s'étendant, se réglant, adoptant un
> rythme, devenant fluide, sonore, musicale, innombrable, universelle:
> c'était la pluie.

> [A little tap at the window, as though some missile had struck it, fol-
> lowed by a plentiful, falling sound, as light, though, as if a shower of sand
> were being sprinkled from a window overhead; then the fall spread, took
> on an order, a rhythm, became liquid, loud, drumming, musical, in-
> numerable, universal. It was the rain.]

Although this is a description of a common phenomenon which we
have all observed, Proust manages to convey an impression of freshness and novelty. We hear a small tap on the window as though something had knocked lightly against it. It is followed by a shower of light,
dry taps like grains of sand, and we wonder vaguely whether the
people above have upset something. The sound seems to spread,
becomes regular instead of intermittent, acquires a rhythm—Proust's

Picture Post Library

MARCEL PROUST

use of the present participles swimming into one another to give a sensation of immediacy and continuity was clearly learnt from Flaubert—the 'dry' sound gives place to a 'fluid' sound which is 'sonore, musicale, innombrable, universelle'. The piled adjectives make us feel the isolated taps merging relentlessly into a single sound which swells into a roar and seems to envelop us. Then, with a shock, we realize—'It's the rain'. The last clause has been described by one critic as a *phrase-détonation*. At a stroke the charged, stifling atmosphere, which has become intolerable, clears. We experience an immense sense of release.

In another place he looks at a sunbeam playing on a balcony and this is what he sees:

> Devant la fenêtre, le balcon était gris. Tout d'un coup, sur sa pierre maussade je ne voyais pas une couleur moins terne, mais je sentais comme un effort vers une couleur moins terne, la pulsation d'un rayon hésitant qui voudrait libérer sa lumière.

> [Outside the window, the balcony was grey. Suddenly, on its sullen stone, I did not indeed see a less negative colour, but I felt as it were an effort towards a less negative colour, the pulsation of a hesitating ray that struggled to discharge its light.]

Only a writer belonging to the age of Impressionism would have described the dull stone as *maussade* and have written of colour as Proust does here. It is not a mere 'impression'. We feel him trying to penetrate the composition of the colours, giving the scene a strange poetic life of its own.

An old lady is out walking in the park and suddenly she has a stroke:

> Elle était apparue, bien qu'à côté de moi, plongée dans ce monde inconnu au sein duquel elle avait déjà reçu les coups dont elle portait les traces quand je l'avais vue tout à l'heure aux Champs-Elysées, son chapeau, son visage, son manteau dérangés par la main de l'ange invisible avec lequel elle avait lutté.

> [She had appeared to them, although I was still by her side, submerged in that unknown world somewhere in which she had already received the blows, traces of which she still bore when I looked up at her a few minutes earlier in the Champs-Elysées, her hat, her face, her cloak left in disorder by the hand of the invisible angel with whom she had wrestled.]

M

We are suddenly aware that we are all prisoners in our private worlds which are separated from one another by almost insurmountable barriers. The *monde inconnu* is a psychological world. The child knows that his grandmother is battling alone on the other side of one of these barriers with *l'ange invisible* and trying to conceal from him the ravages of her stroke.

Then the grandmother dies:

> ... ainsi, dans un désir fou de me précipiter dans ses bras, ce n'était qu'à l'instant, plus d'une année après son enterrement, à cause de cet anachronisme qui empêche si souvent le calendrier des faits de coïncider avec celui des sentiments, que je venais d'apprendre qu'elle était morte.

> [.... and so, in my insane desire to fling myself into her arms, it was not until this moment, more than a year after her burial, because of that anachronism which so often prevents the calendar of facts from corresponding to that of our feelings, that I became conscious that she was dead.]

It is only a year later that he 'realizes'. It is an example of the way in which Proust reverses the conventional order of our emotions and substitutes the rhythm of our real feelings for time.

He writes of Swann's love for Odette de Crécy:

> ... son amour s'étendait bien au delà des régions du désir physique. La personne même d'Odette n'y tenait plus une grande place.

> [... his love extended a long way beyond the province of physical desire. Odette's person, indeed, no longer held any great place in it.]

The ready-made categories are again brushed aside. We have to adjust ourselves to a 'love' where there is scarcely room for the *person* of the beloved.

Yet when we return to Proust in middle life, it is often with a sense of disenchantment. We no longer seem to enjoy him as much as we did in the past; the vision which once illuminated his pages appears to have vanished or grown dim; we are so oppressed by the *longueurs* and complexities of the later volumes that we may even cease to be receptive to the poetry of *Swann* or to a *trouvaille* like this:

> Le temps des lilas approchait de sa fin; quelques-uns effusaient encore en hauts lustres mauves les bulles délicates de leurs fleurs, mais dans bien des parties du feuillage où déferlait, il y avait seulement une semaine, leur mousse embaumée, se flétrissait diminuée, et noircie, une écume creuse, sèche et sans parfum.

[Lilac-time was nearly over; some of the trees still thrust aloft, in tall purple chandeliers, their tiny balls of blossom, but in many places among their foliage where, only a week before, they had still been breaking in waves of fragrant foam, these were now spent and shrivelled and discoloured, a hollow scum, dry and scentless.]

There is no mistaking the debt to the *Mémoires d'outre-tombe*, but Proust has transformed what he borrowed into something new and achieved an effect which was beyond the powers of Chateaubriand. For Chateaubriand was very much the product of the Romantic Movement. We often feel in reading him that 'Nature' was largely a pretext for turning loose feelings which somehow float unattached on the page. There is nothing of the sort in Proust. On the contrary, we are impressed by the complex organization of the passage, by the acuteness of his perceptions and by a hard intellectual core underneath. We have an almost painful sensation of the fragile beauty of the lilacs which comes to stand symbolically for the fading of childhood and of life itself. 'Combray', the first section of the novel, is indeed an account of the childish paradise which is gradually lost, and it is not for nothing that the description of the lilacs occurs some forty pages before the incident at Montjouvain. Nor are the three adjectives at the end of the passage there for euphony or emphasis. The winding sentence makes us feel that life is being slowly throttled, that its gleam is fading, as it moves inevitably to its dying fall. We find ourselves looking all round the shattered blooms and seeing that in fact no life remains, only a dry, shrunken, blackened, scentless mass.

It is even possible to become so submerged in the apparently endless paragraphs and the interminable subordinate clauses that we are blind to the remarkable virtuoso in prose who could write:

. . . les phrases, au long col sinueux et démesuré, de Chopin, si libres, si tactiles, qui commencent à chercher leur place en dehors et bien loin de la direction de leur départ, bien loin du point où on avait pu espérer qu'atteindrait leur attouchement, et qui ne se jouent dans cet écart de fantaisie que pour revenir plus délibérément,—dans un retour plus prémédité, avec plus de précision, comme sur un cristal qui résonnerait jusqu'à faire crier, —vous frapper au cœur.

[. . . those long-necked, sinuous creatures, the phrases of Chopin, so free, so flexible, so tactile, which begin by seeking their ultimate resting-place somewhere beyond and far wide of the direction in which they started, the point which one might have expected them to reach, phrases

which divert themselves in those fantastic by-paths only to return more
deliberately—with a more premeditated reaction, with more precision, as
on a crystal bowl which, if you strike it, will ring and throb until you cry
aloud in anguish—to clutch at one's heart.]

The sentence seems to *perform* the curve which it describes. It reaches
its culminating point at the word *délibérément*, pauses, then turns
menacingly towards us, and, with a ruthlessness punctuated by the
words *prémédité*, *précision* and *crier*, swoops down upon us and buries
itself, with a shock, in our 'heart'.

We have to decide whether the reason for our disenchantment lies
in ourselves or in the work, whether *A la Recherche du temps perdu*
is the great novel it was once thought to be or is simply a repertoire
of astonishing phrases buried in an inert, unreadable mass of words.

Hostile critics have been quick to allege that Proust was the product
of a dying aristocracy, the laureate of a society which vanished at the
outbreak of the second world war and that his attitude is no longer
capable of interesting us, is indeed incomprehensible. The truth seems
to me to be less simple than that. It is always difficult to judge a contemporary and almost impossible in the case of a writer of the bulk
and complexity of Proust. Now that he has been dead nearly thirty
years, however, we are in a better position to see his work in perspective.

Violent changes in taste are usually due to one of two causes. They
may be the result of the snobbish depreciation from which D. H.
Lawrence has suffered or they may be due to the fact that the writer
was overrated in his lifetime as Virginia Woolf undoubtedly was
in hers.

There is, however, a third alternative. The appearance of a really
original work of art produces three separate reactions in the public:
perplexity, enthusiasm, neglect. The perplexity is caused by the difficulty of accustoming ourselves to a new vision; enthusiasm is the
reward of perseverance; and neglect follows when we have absorbed
it, or as much of it as we can for the time being. It may be that Proust's
vision was as original as it once appeared, but that we have grown so
used to it that it has become part of our make-up and needs to be
rediscovered.

That, broadly, is the thesis which I propose to defend here, but the
part played by non-literary factors in Proust's sudden eclipse and his
early revival must not be overlooked. 'There is an egalitarian bias
native to this age', wrote Professor Brogan during the last war, 'that
must be overcome if Proust is to be approached in a proper spirit of

willingness to listen, to be converted. His characters are, for the most part, rich and idle and vicious.'[1] In the nineteen-thirties these words would have been damning: to-day they are a positive commendation. Now that levelling down has been elevated into a political first principle, we are more conscious of what was valuable in the aristocratic societies of the past. We are growing weary, too, of the *littérature engagée*. It is a relief to turn to a writer who doesn't take sides and who has virtually nothing to say of political and economic problems. That is why there is something immensely fascinating about Proust's world, about the fabulous creatures—'rich and idle and vicious'—of whom he wrote. The bustle and gaiety of the age, the parties and the spectacle of the gorgeous Laure Hayman, the famous *cocotte*, passing, as some one put it, 'dans sa gloire impure', offer a momentary escape from our own sordid plight.

This has, to be sure, little to do with the literary merits of the novel, but it is of great importance. It predisposes the reader in favour of Proust. He feels better able to face the *longueurs*, more capable of making the effort to delve beneath the surface and to recapture the strange charm of his first reading.

---

[1] In an article reprinted in *French Personalities and Problems* (London, 1946), p. 25.

II. THE NOAH'S ARK

When I was very small, there was no character in the Bible whose lot seemed to me to be as wretched as Noah's because of the flood which kept him a prisoner in the ark for forty days. Later on I was often ill and for days on end I, too, had to stay in the ark. I understood then that Noah was never able to see the world so well as he did from the ark in spite of the fact that it was closed and darkness covered the earth.

Les Plaisirs et les jours

MARCEL PROUST was born in Paris on 10 July 1871, and was the elder of two sons. His father came of a middle-class provincial Catholic family. Dr. Adrien Proust was the first of the family to leave his native Illiers and seek his fortune in Paris where he became a distinguished surgeon. Proust's mother belonged to the prosperous Jewish family of Weil.

'This little being', writes Mme de Gramont of the novelist, 'was to contain at once all the earthy savour of the Prousts of Illiers and the whole of the Biblical soul of his maternal ancestors.'[1] There can be little doubt that the mixture of races played a decisive part in the formation of his character and the development of his art. From his father he derived his feeling for the historic France which gives his novel its strength and solidity; from his mother his exceptionally delicate nervous sensibility, and possibly his interest in clans and coteries.

In spite of pronounced differences of opinion, Proust was devoted to both his parents and did not leave the parental home until his mother died in 1905, two years after his father. He was, however, essentially his mother's son as his brother, Robert, was his father's; and it is the influence of her family which is preponderant in the novel.[2] At the age of fourteen he was asked in a questionnaire: 'What is your idea of misery?' He replied: 'To be separated from *maman*.' He was passionately fond of his mother and her death was the greatest sorrow of his life.

[1] *Marcel Proust* (Paris, 1948), p. 9.
[2] Mme de Gramont, who knew the family, describes Robert, who followed his father's profession, as 'l'image de la force, de la santé et de l'équilibre'. She may be right in suggesting that the fact that Marcel was born in the anxious days following the French defeat tipped the scales in favour of his mother. (*Ibid.*, p. 9.)

At the age of nine he had the first of the attacks of asthma from which he suffered all his life. Proust's ill-health has always been something of a mystery. There has been a tendency to regard him in some quarters as a lifelong martyr to asthma, but it may be doubted whether this view is entirely correct.

Doubtless [writes an American critic] this asthma was a nervous disorder and one is permitted to suspect that it was a sympathetic device rather than a cause of the peculiarities of his temperament. It enabled him in childhood to claim, from his mother especially, the extravagant affection which he demanded, and in later life it served as an excuse for fantastic habits which he doubtless did not want to give up. But it was real enough nevertheless and it marked the first step in that progressive retirement from active life which was to constitute the course of his outward existence. The little Marcel—it was thus that he continued until his dying day to be known—must make a life of his own since he obviously could not share the life of his fellows.[1]

There seems to be a good deal of truth in this diagnosis. Proust was certainly a sick man, but one cannot help feeling that the development, if not the origin, of his sickness was in some way *voulu*. For it must be remembered that his isolation from the world was essential for writing the sort of masterpiece that he did in fact write and that from a very early age he regarded himself as a dedicated man. He loved the social world, but once he had collected his material he may have felt the need to justify his retirement from it to himself.

This view appears to be supported by the opinion of one of the specialists who attended him.

I consulted Mohlen [we find him writing in one of his letters], the doctor who with Faisan is considered the best. He told me that my asthma has become a nervous habit and that the only way of curing it would be to go to an anti-asthmatic establishment in Germany where they would break the habit of my asthma—[I say would] for I shall certainly not go—as one breaks the habit of morphine in a morphine-addict.[2]

Proust was educated at the Lycée Condorcet and the Sorbonne. The Lycée Condorcet seems to have been much more civilized than the other famous French lycées. The discipline was mild—too mild for the

[1] Joseph Wood Krutch, *Five Masters* (New York, 1930), pp. 260-1. (See also footnote on p. 342 below.)

[2] Princesse Marthe Bibesco, *Au bal avec Marcel Proust* (Les Cahiers Marcel Proust, 4) (Paris, 1928), p. 38.

parents of some of the pupils—the masters were intelligent and there was plenty of intellectual life. It was here that Proust made friends with Robert de Flers, Jacques Bizet, Daniel Halévy and Léon Brunschwicg, and launched a college magazine with them. According to his biographers, he had already begun to form his famous style while still at school to the delight of an intelligent master and the scandal of a stuffy school inspector when Proust was invited, as the prize pupil, to read aloud his weekly essay during the visitation. It was also at the lycée that Proust first became interested in natural history—an interest which had a considerable influence on his mature style.

Proust's father wanted him to take up law or diplomacy and at the University he read law and political science. He displayed little interest in those subjects, and in spite of some opposition from his parents it was eventually agreed that he need not follow a profession.

It can hardly be said that the University played as important a part in his intellectual formation as the lycée, but he did make one valuable acquaintance there. He met Bergson, whose *Essai sur les données immédiates de la conscience* had appeared in 1889, and went to some of his lectures which stimulated his interest in philosophical problems. The link between the two men was strengthened when, a little later, Bergson married Mlle Neuberger, a relative of Proust's on his mother's side.

Proust's family was very well off and from adolescence he showed an immense relish for social life.

At fifteen [writes Léon Pierre-Quint] we find him in the *salon* of Mme Straus sitting like a faithful little page at her feet on a great plush footstool. The prominent personalities of the Third Republic who came to visit the lady of the house did not fail to bestow a few minutes' attention on her youthful favourite. They compared him to the handsome Italian princes in Paul Bourget's novels. At home his mirror was framed with invitation cards; and a famous courtesan sent him a book bound in silk from one of her petticoats.[1]

The same writer provides us with another glimpse of him at the age of twenty:

He had large, bright black eyes with heavy lids which slanted a little to one side. His expression was one of extreme gentleness which fastened itself

[1] *Marcel Proust: sa vie, son œuvre* (new edition, Paris, 1935), p. 18. (The courtesan was Laure Hayman and the book Bourget's *Gladys Harvey*, of which she was the heroine.)

for long moments on any object at which he looked. His voice was still gentler, a little out of breath with a slight drawl which bordered on affectation yet managed to avoid it. He had long thin black hair which sometimes obscured his forehead and which never turned white. But it was the eyes which held one's attention—those immense eyes with mauve circles, tired, nostalgic, extremely mobile, which seemed to move and follow the secret thoughts of the speaker. On his lips was a continual smile, amused, welcoming, hesitating, then fixing itself unmoving on his lips. His complexion was matt, but at that time fresh and rosy. In spite of his small black moustache, he reminded you of a great lazy child who was too knowing for his years.[1]

As a young man he entertained his friends on a lavish scale either at his parents' house or at the most expensive restaurants. On these occasions he used to have his own meal before the dinner so that he could talk more freely and he would move round the table, sitting first beside one guest, then another. 'His imagination', said Pierre-Quint, 'worked on concrete data and was controlled by his observation.' He had already adopted the practice of minute observation of the appearance and gestures of his friends, which was to serve him in writing his novel. He used to make notes on tiny scraps of paper for future use. He also became as a young man a famous mimic and often delighted the company with his impersonations of friends. Among the victims was the writer, Comte Robert de Montesquiou, who provided some—but only some—of the material for Charlus.[2] It is recorded that on one occasion Proust went to a party simply to observe the Comte de Sagan's monocle; that on another he visited a woman friend to ask her to let him see a hat which she had worn twenty years before and was very surprised to learn that she no longer had it.

Proust's first book was published in 1896.[3] *Les Plaisirs et les jours* is a collection of stories, poems and sketches. It seems to have been influenced by Baudelaire—the poems on painters and musicians are a pastiche of *Les Phares*—and by the prose of Jules Laforgue, Huysmans

---

[1] *Ibid.*, pp. 51-2.

[2] On the genesis of the characters, see André Maurois, *A la Recherche de Marcel Proust* (Paris, 1949), pp 147-66. It appears that one of the other models for Charlus was a certain Baron Jacques Doazan. J-E. Blanche records that Montesquiou and Doazan were 'at daggers drawn' because the Count had stolen the *baron de l'empire's* 'boyfriend'. (*Mes Modèles* (Paris, 1928), p. 102.)

There are strange discrepancies in the spelling of proper names in the works of Proust's French critics. In cases of doubt I have followed M. Maurois who seems to be the most reliable of the novelist's biographers in this respect.

[3] It was also the year in which *Matière et mémoire* was published.

M*

and the later Symbolists.[1] There has been some difference of opinion about its value. Proust's contemporaries dismissed it as the work of a youthful dilettante, but later critics have emphasized its importance for an understanding of the novel and have claimed to detect a distinctive note which points to the future author of *A la Recherche du temps perdu.* If Proust had written nothing else the book would probably have long since been forgotten, but it is certainly not without merit. It was not perhaps altogether an exaggeration to write, as Anatole France did in his preface:

> He displays a sureness of aim which is surprising in so young an archer. He is by no means an innocent, but he is so sincere and so true that he becomes naïve and in this way he pleases us. There is in him something of a depraved Bernardin de Saint-Pierre and an ingenuous Petronius.[2]

For underneath the period décors and the preciosity we are conscious of the writer's gift of analysis, a very intense sensibility and the unrest which we shall meet again and again in the novel. We also recognize some of the main themes of the novel. 'La Mort de Baldassare Silvandre, Vicomte de Sylvanie' is the story of a handsome and wealthy aristocrat who is slowly dying of an unnamed disease, and it introduces the character of the prisoner-invalid. 'La Confessoin d'une Jeune Fille' is the death-bed confession of a girl who takes the wrong turning, drives her mother to her death and then shoots herself. It is probably the most interesting piece of work in the book. I think that those critics are right who have argued that it is a portrait of the artist as a *jeune fille* and it certainly looks forward to Mlle Vinteuil. 'La Fin de la Jalousie' deals with a subject whose importance needs no emphasis while other sketches describe fashionable life. Over them all broods a personal nostalgia and a sense of personal guilt which breaks through again and again in Proust's accounts of the different *amours* of his hero and his characters in *A la Recherche du temps perdu.*

In 1900 Proust's parents left the Boulevard Malesherbes and went to live at 45 Rue de Courcelles. It was the year in which John Ruskin died. Proust had already become interested in him and he paid his tribute to the dead writer by publishing a short essay called 'Pélerinages Ruskiniens en France' in the *Figaro.*[3] Although Proust could only read English with considerable difficulty, he set to work with the help of

[1] Laforgue's *Moralités légendaires* had been collected in 1887.

[2] It was Mme Straus who persuaded France to write the preface and it is thought that it was in part her handiwork.

[3] Reprinted in *Chroniques.*

his mother and friends to translate Ruskin into French. His translation of *The Bible of Amiens* with an introduction and notes appeared in 1904 and *Sesame and Lilies* two years later.[1] It has been said that Proust's mother and grandmother introduced him to the great French classics of the seventeenth century and that Ruskin introduced him to the Middle Ages. That is undoubtedly true, but critics who claim that he was directly influenced by Ruskin's aesthetic theories and his prose style are on less certain ground. Ruskin certainly played an important part in Proust's formation, but his real influence was probably indirect. He awakened something that was already latent in Proust, and it was through him that Proust became aware of his true vocation.

On the death of his mother, Proust went to live at the flat at 102 Boulevard Haussmann where much of his novel was written.[2] It was the end of the society man and the beginning of the recluse. The famous cork-lined room was constructed. It was decorated by a portrait of Proust at the age of twenty by Jacques-Émile Blanche and an Infanta by Velasquez. Proust had always been extremely sensitive to noise. When, as a young man, he had spent his summer holidays by the sea at Cabourg—the Balbec of the novel—he had engaged not only a room for himself, but the four rooms above, below and on either side so that he would not be disturbed by the sound of other guests in the adjoining rooms. In the Boulevard Haussmann the windows were kept permanently closed. The long room was lighted by a single globe and the walls retained their musty brown colour because Proust, who was completely unadapted to the needs of practical life, never managed to find a decorator to do them in up some more attractive colour. He seldom left his prison except at night. When he was seized with a nostalgic desire to see the hawthorn blossom or the water-lilies, he would drive into the country in a carriage which was completely closed to prevent the scent of the flowers from bringing on an attack of asthma, and looked at the countryside through the windows.

Yet the work went on. He used to send for his friends—usually at night—and interrogate them minutely about fashions, clothes and social events. On the rare occasions on which he ventured out to attend some reception at which he felt that he would obtain valuable

[1] The two introductions were rewritten and combined in the long essay called 'Journées de Lecture' in *Pastiches et mélanges*.

[2] He remained there until 1919 when he was turned out by the new landlord to whom his aunt, Mme Catusse, had sold the freehold without telling her nephew. He then spent some months in a flat in the Rue Laurent-Pichat before going to live in a furnished flat on the fourth floor at 44 Rue Hamelin which, as he said, 'costs 16,000 francs and is more or less like a servant's room'

material for his book, the strain was so great that the outing was often paid for by weeks of prostration.

His practice of questioning people about the world was not confined to his friends. He would spend hours—sometimes as much as two or three hours at a stretch—with the head waiters of the Ritz, the Wéber and the Hôtel des Réservoirs at Versailles, documenting himself on the appearance and behaviour of the guests.

In his own home Proust was looked after by his devoted servant Céleste. Later, members of her family and her husband, Odilon Albaret the taxi-driver, were added to his staff.

In spite of his wealth, he spent practically nothing on himself. He wore his suits for three years. As he grew older, he spent more and more time in bed, writing his book propped up on his pillows and scattering the finished sheets over the room. When he got up, he usually wore an old dressing-gown which he only replaced when it was literally falling to pieces. His wealth and his modest requirements did not prevent him from constantly imagining—it is another neurotic trait—that some disaster on the Stock Exchange had reduced him to penury.

The writing of the novel and visits from friends were not the only occupations of his later years. Prince Antoine Bibesco has suggested that in his reclusion Proust felt the need of greater contact with the outside world than was provided by either of these activities and that this made him an indefatigable correspondent. His view is supported by the letters themselves. A few—a very few—contain precious information about the composition of the novel, but the vast majority are concerned with other matters or deal only with the surface of literary life. He kept his friends carefully informed about the disastrous state of his health. He would have liked to arrange a little dinner at the Ritz; but after the previous one he was poorly for weeks, so it will have to be a bedside dinner. He really feels that he is on his last legs; he nearly killed himself the other day by getting in a muddle with his pills and taking the wrong dose. There are little tiffs and misunderstandings. Proust is terribly upset about that preface he was going to write for a book of Jacques-Émile Blanche's; he goes into the most elaborate details which greatly adds to the confusion. He also directs literary operations from his bed. He writes to Souday about his review of the latest volume of the novel or angles for favourable notices of a book by one of his friends. Naturally, everything goes wrong and to his horror the *Nouvelle Revue Française* prints a notice which is little short of an *éreintement*. He chides Gallimard over his slowness in reprinting *A l'Ombre des ieunes filles en fleurs* and goes into a frenzy when his brother reports that none of the provincial booksellers has ever heard of *Sodome et Gomorrhe*. And why will that wretched printer persist in putting a circumflex on the word 'Sodome'!

Those of Proust's friends who have written biographies or memoirs of him have all spoken warmly of his extraordinary charm of manner, his gentleness and his generosity. On one occasion, for example, M. Paul Morand happened to tell him that he was about to consult a well-known and very expensive Paris specialist. The following day he was surprised to receive a large sum—much larger than the consultant's fee—from the novelist. It was useless for him to say that he did not need it. After a protracted correspondence, he was obliged to accept to avoid giving mortal offence to the donor and had to resort to all sorts of ruses in order to be allowed to repay it. Nor was Proust's generosity restricted to his friends. The munificence of his tips was legendary and an embarrassment to the guests whom he entertained in restaurants. When, at the end of one of these dinners, Proust had distributed lavish rewards to all the waiters who had served him, he suddenly beckoned to a boy who had been watching the proceedings. 'Come, Marcel,' said one of the guests. 'He's done nothing for us.' 'Never mind,' came the answer, 'he looked so sad standing there seeing what the others were getting.'

In spite of these tributes, when we consider the different portraits of the man which have come down to us, we feel that there is something missing, something which eludes us, a gap between Proust and his book. Can this gentle suffering recluse, this generous and warm-hearted if exacting friend, really be the same person who wrote those extraordinary accounts of jealousy and vice? Can there be any connection between him and the exasperating hero of the novel who seems bent on torturing himself and his friends with his horrifying suspicions, who employs friends and servants to spy on his mistress and who finally nags her into suicide?

The glimpses that we have of Proust sometimes remind us of the manner in which he presents his own characters. We have the impression that we are turning over the pages of a family album, glancing at the faded photographs of the novelist at different periods of his life. There are gaps in the collection. We see him clearly enough at the age of fifteen sitting at Mme Straus's feet and again at the age of twenty; but the later pictures, instead of being clearer, are more conventional. Then we come across this:

> Illness had profoundly changed him. His face was pale, the ends of his moustache were of unequal length. His nose had a pinched appearance, his

cheeks were sunken and his eyes more brilliant. When he was not in bed, he received his visitors in a snuff-coloured dressing-gown. He felt the cold more than ever and wore strips of cotton wool over his shirt collar, cotton gloves on his hands and woollen slippers on his feet. His fumigating apparatus gave out a suffocating smell. He looked like some fabulous necromancer in his laboratory. The dead whom he raised were people whom he had known and whom he brought back to life in his novel.[1]

It is still the portrait of the recluse, but by using the word 'necromancer' Proust's biographer has, probably without realizing it, introduced a fresh and slightly sinister impression. Another observer actually uses the word 'sinister'.

I see again that sinister room in the Rue Hamelin, that black hearth, that bed with an overcoat for a blanket, that waxen mask out of which you would have said that our host was watching us eat and of which only the hair seemed to be alive. . . . Proust seemed already to be more than half engaged in the realm of non-being, turning into that enormous, proliferating mushroom which was nourished by his own substance, by his work—*Le Temps retrouvé*.[2]

The impression is confirmed by two other accounts of Proust written towards the end of his life:

From time to time he strokes the sides of his nose with the edge of a hand which appears dead, whose fingers are oddly stiff and extended. Nothing is more striking than this clumsy, insane gesture which seems like the movement of an animal or a madman.[3]

His face is fixed like a mask against the wall as though refusing to allow the soft, fallen features and the eyes circled by the vampire of solitude to be reflected in the mirrors. When he stood up, his shirt front and dress coat gave him the appearance of a dead man propped upright in his coffin. Without appearing to see anything, was he ramming everything down into his laboratory of decomposition?[4]

M. Buchet describes these as the portraits of a 'monster', but the term needs qualifying.

[1] Pierre-Quint, *op. cit.*, p. 70.
[2] François Mauriac, *Du Côté de chez Proust* (Paris, 1947), pp. 41–2.
[3] André Gide, *Journal*, p. 694.
[4] Clifford Barney in a letter quoted by Édmond Buchet, *Écrivains intelligents du XXe siècle* (Paris, 1945), p. 41.

I seemed to discover in the cruelties of the man [wrote Maurice Sachs] the cruelties of the child and to understand that the whole of *A la Recherche du temps perdu* is the work of a sort of child-monster whose mind possessed the whole of man's experience and whose soul was only ten years old.[1]

There is something monstrous about the man which is reflected in the more sombre parts of the novel, but we are somehow aware of the *enfant-monstre* behind it. Proust was almost a dual personality. The gentle suffering recluse was real, but so was the unsavoury being who haunted the slaughter-houses in the hope of seeing a calf killed, who would have rats pricked with hatpins in his presence and who indulged in other peculiarities which will be discussed in their proper place.

Swann was published by Grasset at the author's expense in 1913 and attracted little attention. Proust went on working on his novel throughout the war, but published nothing more until *Swann* was reissued by Gallimard in 1917. *A l'Ombre des jeunes filles en fleurs* followed in 1918 and was awarded the Prix Goncourt the next year. This was the beginning of Proust's *gloire*. In spite of a good deal of detraction, particularly in his own country, he became almost overnight a European celebrity.

Le Côté de Guermantes and the first part of *Sodome et Gomorrhe* appeared in 1920. The second part of *Sodome et Gomorrhe* came out in 1922 and was the last part of the novel to be published during its author's lifetime. He died on 18 November 1922. *La Prisonnière* was published in 1923, *Albertine disparue* in 1925, and *Le Temps retrouvé* in 1927.

To most of us Proust's life must appear depressing and in some ways repellent. Yet artistically there is a curious rightness about it. We have the impression that everything in it conspired to help him to write the book which he had been born to write, transforming this life into what M. Sartre would call a 'destiny'. He enjoyed the economic independence which was essential to the writing of that particular book. Whatever the causes of his mysterious illness, that too was essential to the undertaking; and his parents died at exactly the right time. In 1905 he was already fully conscious of his vocation, had amassed a great deal of material for the novel and was ready to begin writing it. He realized, however, that his parents would have been profoundly grieved by its content, and if they had lived his affection for them might very well have led him to postpone the start until it was too late.

[1] *Le Sabbat* (Paris, 1946), p. 286.

III. *A LA RECHERCHE DU TEMPS PERDU*

1. *Structure*

WHEN we look up at the sixteen volumes of *A la Recherche du temps perdu* standing in a row on our shelves, their white covers worn and tattered or neatly bound in yellow buckram, we find ourselves wondering what Proust wrote about, what he was trying to do, what sort of a book this is and what is its 'message'.

We know that he brought 'a new vision' to the novel, but this recognition is only the first step in the exploration of his work. There have been plenty of attempts to define his aims and genius, some provided by the novelist himself or by his narrator and others by his critics: 'The story of an invisible vocation.' 'A new sensibility.' 'Analysis pushed to the point at which it becomes creative.' 'An intimate diary.' 'The views, the generalizations of the most *penetrating* moralist who has ever existed in literature.' 'The book is written in the form of a novel, but it belongs rather to the category of memoirs.' 'Situated half-way between the novel and memoirs, the population of Proust's world belongs to both.' 'The memoirs of Saint-Simon of another period.'[1]

It is a tribute to the richness and variety of Proust's work that all these definitions contain a measure of truth and that, with two possible exceptions, they do not contradict one another. Yet it must be confessed that when we first approach it, the novel presents an appearance of considerable confusion. It opens with the narrator's recollections of his childhood at Combray, switches towards the close of the first volume to a long account of Swann's love affair with Odette de Crécy which took place before the narrator was born; returns in volume three to his childhood memories and his first love affair with Swann's daughter Gilberte, and describes a seaside holiday at Balbec where he meets Albertine Simonet and the *jeunes filles en fleurs*. Two volumes are devoted to the Guermantes family and to Marcel's infatuation for the Duchess, three more to the world of the homosexuals and the love affair with Albertine.[2] At the end of *Sodome*

---

[1] The authors of these comments are Proust, Middleton Murry, Conrad, Pierre Abraham, Mauriac, Albert Feuillerat, Pierre Abraham, Proust.

[2] In future I shall refer to the narrator as Marcel.

336

et Gomorrhe his attention is largely concentrated on Albertine. Her death and his jealousy occupy four more volumes. *Le Temps retrouvé* deals with the changes that have taken place in society since the war and with the theory of art which underlies the whole work. All through the sixteen volumes there are elaborate accounts of dinner parties, receptions and the life of the 'worldlings'.

The principal difficulty is to discover the connection between the brilliant social life and the private love affairs of the individuals which are described with an even greater wealth of detail.

Proust's critics have been very conscious of the difficulty. It was fashionable at one time—particularly among critics writing before publication of the novel was complete—to pretend that it was formless, was as loosely constructed as Saint-Simon's Memoirs and its content determined by the evolution of the society in which it was written.[1] When *Le Temps retrouvé* appeared, opinion swung to the other extreme and we were invited to admire the extraordinary artistry of the book's construction.

A further change of opinion occurred in 1934 when M. Albert Feuillerat published a book called *Comment Marcel Proust a composé son roman*.[2] When he first planned his novel, Proust intended it to be complete in two volumes of six or seven hundred pages each, but the work swelled to such proportions that it actually contains over four thousand pages and would almost certainly have been much longer had he lived.[3] It is well known that he practically re-wrote large parts of it in proof. M. Feuillerat succeeded in examining proofs of the early volumes and compared them with the published text. He argued that Proust's revisions, which sometimes involved substantial alterations in the personality of his characters and other inconsistencies, completely disrupted the classic proportions of the original plan and destroyed the unity of tone and atmosphere which is one of the most remarkable and attractive qualities of *Swann*. There was also a pronounced change of style. M. Feuillerat, indeed, speaks of two distinct styles. There is the poetic, evocative style of *Swann* and the intellectual, analytical style of the later volumes in which, significantly, phrases like *Je sentis* are replaced by *Je compris*, in which direct experience is overlaid or interlarded with the wisdom and reflections of a lifetime, is interspersed with treatises and maxims on life, love and art which are worthy of the greatest moralists. This gives them an extraordinary richness, but it

---

[1] Some of the most discerning, however, like Benjamin Crémieux and Pierre-Quint, foretold that a plan would emerge when publication was complete.

[2] (*Yale Romanic Studies*), New Haven, 1934.

[3] The estimate varied. See *Correspondance générale*, IV, pp. 39–41.

also confuses the reader. For he is never sure whether Marcel is a boy or a man, and a good many incidents which clearly belong to childhood are accompanied by reflections which could only have been made by a grown man with a wealth of worldly experience behind him.

When he came to draw up his balance sheet, M. Feuillerat decided that though there had undoubtedly been considerable loss, it was outweighed by the gain. It was these changes, however, which made him conclude that the finished work should be described as memoirs rather than as a novel.

The book is certainly an outstanding contribution to the study of Proust, but it seems to me that M. Feuillerat goes further than is warranted by the facts. There are undoubtedly inconsistencies, but the main alterations in the personality of the characters were very far from being fortuitous. They sprang from the novelist's theory of the immense difficulty of ever knowing another person.[1] Nor was Proust's method of composition altogether as haphazard as M. Feuillerat seems to suggest. In a letter written to Paul Souday in 1922, he could declare that the novel was so 'meticulously composed' that the last chapter of the last volume was written immediately after the first chapter of the first volume.[2] The truth is that Proust was not a writer who produced 'social criticism', a sociological treatise or memoirs in the form of a novel; he succeeded, as practically no other novelist has done, in *combining* the methods as well as the findings of the novelist and the memoir-writer. His characters do, as Abraham suggested, belong to the world of both and this makes him unique among twentieth-century novelists.

Although we must concede that the later volumes do not possess the formal beauty of *Swann* or its strange, haunting poetry, this should not prevent us from doing justice to the skilful construction of the first two volumes. For they are as carefully and elaborately constructed as Joyce's *Ulysses*. 'It is so complex,' said Proust himself, 'that its meaning will not be revealed until all the themes have begun to combine.' The word 'theme' is an important one. The construction of the book is largely musical and Mr. Edmund Wilson has well described the famous first sentence—'Longtemps, je me suis couché de bonne heure'—as the opening chord in a vast symphony.[3] In the first three pages, Proust refers to nearly all the principal 'themes' of the book: childhood,

[1] See the very interesting letter in *Lettres de Marcel Proust à Bibesco* (La Guilde du Livre, Lausanne, 1949), pp. 175-7. (This book was originally issued to members of a Swiss book society and was not available to the general public when this was written. I am indebted to Mr. Harold Nicolson for his kindness in lending me his copy.)

[2] *Correspondance générale*, III, p. 72.   [3] *Axels' Castle*, p. 132.

memory, time, love, music, art, sleep, society, the historic France. In these first two volumes each of the principal themes is picked up again, isolated, examined, dropped, then taken up again in the later volumes and 'combined'. The description of the magic lantern, with Golo advancing towards the castle of Geneviève de Brabant, at the beginning of *Swann*, looks at first like a random childhood memory, but it turns out to be a complex image which keeps on recurring.[1] It introduces the Guermantes who, as we are told later in the book, were descended from Geneviève de Brabant. It also introduces the theme of the 'prisoner' and appears to be the first direct reference to art. It thus prepares the way for the famous incident of the *madeleine* which marks the end of the 'Overture' and the beginning of the symphony proper. In the volumes which follow Marcel's experience in eating the *madeleine* is frequently referred to and compared with similar experiences; in *Le Temps retrouvé* the experience is finally and fully analysed. It is in *Swann*, too, that we first hear the *petite phrase* of Vinteuil's sonata which becomes the *air national* first of Swann's love for Odette, then of Marcel's for Albertine.[2] The incident of Vinteuil's daughter and her friend is suddenly and apparently gratuitously introduced, but Montjouvain becomes the symbol of the homosexual relationships which occupy so much of the book and might almost be described as the entrance to the cities of the plain. When we reach the end of the second volume of *Swann*, we see that it had to come where it does because Swann suspects Odette of homosexuality as Marcel later suspects Albertine.

M. Robert Vigneron has called the first section of the novel 'Combray or the Perfect Circle'.[3] He reminds us that it not only opens and closes with Marcel lying in bed at Combray, but that it is a panorama of all the rooms in which he has slept. That was undoubtedly Proust's intention and it is possible to push M. Vigneron's analysis a good deal further. There are a number of references to 'circles' in the first twenty pages which can scarcely have been accidental:

Un homme qui dort, tient en cercle autour de lui le fil des heures, l'ordre des années et des mondes. Il les consulte d'instinct en s'éveillant

[1] It turns up, significantly, as we shall see, at the end of *Le Temps retrouvé*.
[2] In one of his letters Proust tells us that Vinteuil's sonata, in which the *petite phrase* occurs, was based among other works on a sonata of Saint-Saëns' for piano and violin, a prelude of Wagner's, a sonata of Franck's and a *ballade* of Fauré's. (*Lettres de Marcel Proust à Bibesco*, pp. 153–4.)
[3] See his two articles: 'Structure de *Swann*: Prétentions et Défaillances' (*Modern Philology*, Vol. XLIV, No. 2, November 1946); 'Structure de *Swann*: Combray ou le Cercle Parfait' (*Modern Philology*, Vol. XLV, No. 3, February 1948).

et y lit en une seconde le point de la terre qu'il occupe, le temps qui s'est écoulé jusqu'à son réveil; mais leurs rangs peuvent se mêler, se rompre.

. . . quand je me réveillais ainsi, mon esprit s'agitant pour chercher, sans y réussir, à savoir où j'étais, tout tournait autour de moi dans l'obscurité, les choses, les pays, les années.

Ces évocations tournoyantes et confuses ne duraient jamais que quelques secondes. . . .

[When a man is asleep, he has in a circle round him the chain of the hours, the sequence of the years, the order of the heavenly host. Instinctively, when he awakes, he looks to these, and in an instant reads off his own position on the earth's surface and the amount of time that has elapsed during his slumbers; but this ordered procession is apt to grow confused, and to break its ranks.

. . . when I awoke like this, and my mind struggled in an unsuccessful attempt to discover where I was, everything would be moving round me through the darkness: things, places, years.

These shifting and confused gusts of memory never lasted for more than a few seconds. . . .]

In this image the speaker is at the centre of a circle watching 'hours, years, worlds, things, countries and (again) years' revolve round him. Yet a doubt creeps in. Proust refers more than once in his writings to the impact of the Kantian categories on our experience.[1] He finds himself wondering whether the circular movement is real, whether the objects which surround him are really motionless or whether their immobility is imposed on them by 'l'immobilité de notre pensée en face d'elles'. The words, 'mais leurs rangs peuvent se mêler, se rompre', in the first passage strike me as particularly important. Combray stands among other things for the 'charmed circle' of childhood and the first section possesses a strange geometrical beauty. M. Feuillerat would no doubt argue that no 'circle' could resist Proust's methods of composition; and certainly Montjouvain looks already like a bulge. Now it seems obvious that the 'perfect circle' of Combray could never have been maintained all through the novel, that the child was bound in the end to break out of it. There are, however, other 'circles' in the book— prisons, railways and the circle of towns.[2] We might feel inclined to

[1] See the opening of the essay on Flaubert in *Chroniques* and *Le Côté de Guermantes*, II, p. 171. (Quoted on pp. 299 and 21 above.)

[2] Compare: 'Du point de départ au point d'arrivée, le cercle se ferme si parfaitement que l'itinéraire indispensable qui passe par Combray, Balbec, Sodome et Gomorrhe en paraît abrégé et comme survolé.' (Crémieux, *Du Côté de Marcel Proust*, p. 54.)

suggest that they are concentric circles, but a moment's reflection shows that this is misleading. The book is really a pyramid of circles which grow smaller and smaller as one approaches the summit. It is almost impossible to classify them exactly because time and memory play a complicated part in the scheme. What happens is that you break out of the circle of childhood only to find yourself in another smaller circle; and the process continues as you approach the apex of the pyramid. But there is a two-way movement or, more accurately, the illusion of a two-way movement because you are constantly trying to return to the first and largest circle through memory. We can see how Proust goes to work by comparing the careers of Swann and Marcel.

Un Amour de Swann sometimes appears to be an admirable short novel which has little to do with the rest of the book, but Proust himself was careful to draw attention to the parallel between Swann's affair with Odette and the coming one between Marcel and Albertine. One critic has declared that Swann is Proust's Jewish and Marcel his Catholic side, but I suspect that the connection is deeper than that.[1] The story of Swann's liaison is used partly to cover the period preceding Marcel's birth, but its main purpose is to facilitate Proust's peculiar angle of vision. For Swann is in a sense the base of the pyramid. Proust tells, from an objective point of view, the story of a cultured man of the world in society and shows how he allows a love affair with a courtesan to cut him off from his own circle. He follows Odette into the narrower circle of the Verdurins' *petit clan*, is eventually ostracized by them and driven back into himself. In the case of Marcel and Albertine the story is re-told from a subjective point of view, or rather re-told from inside at much greater length and with much greater wealth of detail. For Marcel's pursuit of Albertine takes him through the narrowing circles of the cities of the plain until he, too, finds himself alone in his room brooding over the infidelities of his dead mistress as Swann had brooded over the connection between Odette and Forcheville long after he had ceased to love her. With Marcel and Albertine the focus shifts from society to the effect of love on the individual. The feeling that we are approaching the top of the spiral or the pyramid from inside explains the peculiar sense of oppressiveness, of life unfolding and feelings evolving with greater and greater intensity in a smaller and smaller physical space.

.   .   .   .   .

[1] Marcel speaks of 'ce premier Swann dans lequel je retrouve les erreurs charmantes de ma jeunesse'. 'We know', writes Spitzer, 'that Swann is nothing but a variant of the narrator (*eine Variante des erzählenden Ich*).' (*Op. cit.*, p. 389.)

I have spoken of the apparent difficulty of perceiving the connection between the personal lives of Proust's characters and the social life which occupies so much of their time. A glance at the definitions of his genius shows that the list divides into two groups. One stresses the personal, the other the social element in his experience; and his critics do tend as a rule to give slightly greater prominence to one or other of these factors. The novelist himself avoided doing so. Marcel describes the novel as 'the story of an invisible vocation'; but he also calls it 'the memoirs of Saint-Simon of another period'; and unless we realize that it is both, we shall not appreciate it to the full. It is, indeed, the story of an artistic vocation, but of a vocation which manifested itself at a particular moment of history in a particular society and which tempts me to call it the vocation of the twentieth-century artist. Now you cannot have an artistic vocation without a subject, and the evolution of society is just as much Proust's subject as Swann's love affair with Odette de Crécy or Marcel's with Albertine.

In Proust's world—a world in which, significantly, religion has no place—art represents the spiritual element and society what Fernandez calls 'a sort of counter-spirituality'.[1] Thus we are told that Albertine and Andrée symbolized 'the incapacity of people of the world to make a valid judgment in intellectual matters'. And the thing that wrecked Mme de Villeparisis's social position was not her liaison with M. de Norpois; it was, says Proust, her intelligence, 'an intelligence which was almost that of a writer of the second order far more than that of a woman of the world'. Proust used the word 'vocation', and he meant exactly what he said. The novel describes the conflict between a genuine vocation and a series of false vocations represented by social life, love and friendship.[3] This helps us to grasp the full significance of Swann. The contrast between Marcel and Swann is not confined to their love affairs. Marcel's vocation is a true one: Swann is the 'socialite', the dilettante who is always going to write that book on Vermeer— Proust's 'favourite painter'—and dies without doing so.[2] And as the story unfolds we come to see that Swann belongs to the past, that he is submerged in 'lost time' while Marcel moves forward by virtue of his vocation towards 'time regained' which is identified with *la vraie vie*.

[1] *Proust* (Paris, 1944), p. 115.

[2] 'You know that Vermeer has been my favourite painter since I was twenty.' (Proust in a letter to J-L. Vaudoyer, *Correspondance générale*, IV, p. 87.)

[3] Since this was written, Prince Antoine Bibesco has published some interesting observations on Proust's views of love and friendship and on his illness which 'was not very serious'. (See 'The Heartlessness of Marcel Proust' in *The Cornhill Magazine*, No. 983, Summer, 1950.)

2. *The Memoirs of Saint-Simon of Another Period*

It is one of the inherent difficulties of Proust's conception of time that all the events in his book seem to take place on the same plane and that we have practically no sense of succession. When we reach *Le Temps retrouvé*, we realize with a shock that all the characters have suddenly changed, have become old, battered and semi-idiotic. Yet the book is a study of French society from 1880 to 1919 or, as Crémieux put it, it is an essay on the transformation of that society. The word 'transformation' is important. The society which Proust describes is in no sense static; it is in a perpetual state of evolution, and his greatness does not consist least in the way in which he shows the connection between the changes in manners, sensibility and human relationships. Elstir, whose art is analysed in a masterly passage, stands for Impressionism or the 'new painting', Vinteuil for the 'new music'. Berma, the celebrated actress, and Bergotte do not stand merely for the 'old' and the 'new' literature, but for the continuity between them. Proust is at pains to underline this continuity by making Berma play Phèdre and Bergotte write a book on Racine and by the innumerable references in the novel to the French classics, particularly to Mme de Sévigné, Saint-Simon, Racine and the great nineteenth-century authors, who are seen to be a living force.[1]

The same is true in less exalted spheres. 'He introduces into his work all the novelties of the period,' said Crémieux: 'modern military theories, the telephone, the motor-car . . . with the result that it assumes the appearance of a *summa* of French life.'[2]

These are what may be called the *grandes lignes* of Proust's work and we need to keep them constantly in mind in reading him.

We are inclined to think of him exclusively as the historian of the aristocracy and the upper classes. The society of *A la Recherche du temps perdu* certainly seems strange and remote from our own preoccupations. There is not a sentence in the book to suggest that economic problems even exist or that, with the exception of an ageing courtesan, anyone could possibly have *ennuis d'argent*. In an age of department stores, we feel inclined to rub our eyes when we read of Swann's birthday present of fruit to the Princesse de Parme. He was not, we are told, very

---

[1] M. Feuillerat shows that Bergotte is one of the characters who underwent 're-vision' in a very unfavourable sense. He suggests that when the character was first invented Proust had in mind Anatole France who had, as we know, written a Preface for *Les Plaisirs et les jours*, and that he modified it because his subsequent relations with that writer were a good deal less cordial.

[2] *XXe siècle* (Paris, 1924), pp. 56-7.

experienced in choosing fruit and asked a cousin of his mother's to do it for him. She explains with pride that she did not buy all the fruit from the same shop, but from different shops each specializing in a particular fruit—the grapes from Crapote, the strawberries from Jauret and the pears from Chevet.

It is these things which gave rise to the legend that Proust was a snob who only knew one section of society. Nothing could be further from the truth. He had good reasons for concentrating on the Faubourg Saint-Germain:

> Whether we like it or not [wrote Ramon Fernandez] as soon as a society is formed in France, whatever the rank and ideas of its members, it reproduces the characteristics in a more or less modified form and more or less caricatured of the society of the Faubourg Saint-Germain which it sometimes claims like the members of the *petit clan* to despise. . . . In order to acquire a social sense . . . it is therefore opportune to frequent the milieu which provides the key and the syntax of fashionable social life. . . . The frequentation of the Faubourg Saint-Germain enables us to reconstruct in their true perspective and their hierarchy all the French *salons* including Jupien's shop and the concierge's flat.[1]

Proust does indeed see French society as a hierarchy with the Faubourg Saint-Germain at the top imposing its pattern on society as a whole. The salons themselves form a hierarchy within this hierarchy which begins with Mme Verdurin, the symbol of the vulgar aggressive middle class which emerged from the industrial revolution, goes on to Mme de Saint-Euverte, then to the Duchesse de Guermantes and reaches the pinnacle with the Princesse de Guermantes. It is not difficult to see that Proust's picture is by no means a favourable one. This is how he describes the Duc de Guermantes:

> . . . dans les manières de M. de Guermantes, homme attendrissant de gentillesse et révoltant de dureté, esclave des plus petites obligations et délié des pactes les plus sacrés, je retrouve encore intacte après plus de deux siècles écoulés cette déviation particulière à la vie de cour sous Louis XIV et qui transporte les scrupules de conscience du domaine des affections et de la moralité aux questions de pure forme.

> [. . . in the manners of M. de Guermantes, a man who melted one's heart by his courtesy and revolted it by his harshness, I found still intact

[1] In his introduction to Charles Daudet, *Répertoire des personnages de 'A la Recherche du temps perdu'* (Les Cahiers Marcel Proust, 2), (Paris, 1927), pp. xvi–xvii. See also the same author's *Proust*, chapter v.

after the lapse of more than two centuries that deviation typical of court life under Louis XIV which transfers all scruples of conscience from matters of the affections and morality and applies them to purely formal questions.]

It is a criticism not simply of an individual or even of a period, but of the representative of an ancient line whose weaknesses are at least as old as its fame. In this world Marcel's grandmother and his mother are certainly intended to represent genuine human values—the values of decency, kindness and uprightness—in contrast to the 'socialites'; and there is no mistaking the writer's intention when the woman who keeps the public lavatory in the Champs-Élysées speaks to the grand-mother of 'my salon', and emphasizes the care with which the 'guests' are chosen; or again when the Duke and Duchess give the dying Swann his congé because the Duke suddenly discovers that his wife is wearing the wrong-coloured shoes which she must change at once or they will be late for somebody's soirée.

The working classes and the peasantry are not studied with the same minute care as the aristocracy, but they are undeniably there and they play an important part in the construction of the novel. Françoise, the old servant, stands as surely as Molière's servants for the robust common sense of the peasants and she fits into the background of the feudal France which is constantly evoked. There are moments when she is expressing her disapproval of Albertine in which she reminds us of the *confidents* of the classical tragedians who warn their masters and mistresses against some hazardous undertaking. This does not mean that Proust merely provides glimpses of the different strata of society. One writer has used the expression 'human flora' to describe his approach and the society which he portrays is seen as a living organism. The close relations between the different strata are suggested by his fondness for metaphors drawn from natural science, geology and above all from botany which give the impression of human solidarity, of an immensely complex network of social relationships. This impression is heightened by Proust's flair—it was helped by his prodigious memory and his histrionic gifts—for the peculiarities of speech which belong not merely to the different classes, but to people in the different sub-divisions of those classes.

It is time now to examine some concrete examples of Proust's method. We know that Rivière regarded him as the heir of the classical tradition and Mr. Edmund Wilson as the first important novelist to apply the principles of Symbolism in fiction. The account of Swann's visit to Mme de Saint-Euverte's is an illustration not merely of the way in which he blends classicism and Symbolism, but of the way in which the methods of the classical dramatist are adapted to criticize contemporary society. Proust reveals himself as a master of social comedy and the emphasis on word and gesture is used to balance his subjectivism. Swann arrives somewhat late for the party:

> . . . pour la première fois il remarqua, réveillée par l'arrivée inopinée d'un invité aussi tardif, la meute éparse, magnifique et désœuvrée de grands valets de pied qui dormaient ça et là sur des banquettes et des coffres et qui, soulevant leurs nobles profils aigus de lévriers, se dressèrent et, rassemblés, formèrent le cercle autour de lui.

> [. . . he now noticed, for the first time, roused by the unexpected arrival of so belated a guest, the scattered pack of splendid effortless animals, the enormous footmen who were drowsing here and there upon benches and chests, until, pointing their noble greyhound profiles, they towered upon their feet and gathered in a circle round about him.

The writing is deliberately stylized. The tone recalls the 'heroic comedies' of the seventeenth century with its ironic contrast between 'la meute éparse, magnifique et désœuvrée' and 'leurs nobles profils aigus de lévriers'. For Proust works at two contrasted levels. We are conscious at once of the surface décor, the *magnifique, désœuvrée* and *nobles*, and the animals underneath. The impression we have is like that of a circus, but a circus with 'human' animals. Nor should we miss the significance of the 'greyhounds' crowding in on the belated guest and forming a slightly oppressive circle round him as though he were a vanquished 'prey'; it is intended to bring out the peculiar atmosphere of the salons which is at once perceptible to Swann. The allusion is continued in the brilliantly comic passage which follows:

> L'un d'eux, d'aspect particulièrement féroce et assez semblable à l'exécuteur dans certains tableaux de la Renaissance qui figurent des supplices, s'avança vers lui d'un air implacable pour lui prendre ses affaires. Mais la dureté de son regard d'acier était compensée par la douceur de ses gants de fil, si bien qu'en approchant de Swann il semblait témoigner du mépris pour sa personne et des égards pour son chapeau.

> [One of them, of a particularly ferocious aspect, and not unlike the headsman in certain Renaissance pictures which represent executions, tortures, and the like, advanced upon him with an implacable air to take his

'things'. But the harshness of his steely glare was compensated by the softness of his cotton gloves, so effectively that, as he approached Swann, he
seemed to be exhibiting at once an utter contempt for his person and the
most tender regard for his hat.]

The comic greyhounds lead naturally to the comic executioner. It is
characteristic of Swann's mode of thought that he always sees life in
terms of art and it is, perhaps, the secret cause of his ineffectualness.
There is an undercurrent of disillusionment here which looks forward
to the moment when, mounting the elaborate staircase, Swann will tell
himself that he is entering a world from which Odette is excluded.
The footman is an 'executioner' because he is felt to be the person who
divides Swann from Odette. The masterly final sentence stresses the
importance which the world he is entering attaches to externals and its
disregard for the serious, human feelings which are the source of
Swann's distress.

A quelque pas, un grand gaillard en livrée rêvait, immobile, sculptural,
inutile, comme ce guerrier purement décoratif qu'on voit dans les tableaux
les plus tumultueux de Mantegna, songer, appuyé sur son bouclier, tandis
qu'on se précipite et qu'on s'égorge à côté de lui.

[A few feet away, a strapping great lad in livery stood musing, motionless, statuesque, useless, like that purely decorative warrior whom one sees
in the most tumultuous of Mantegna's paintings, lost in dreams, leaning
upon his shield, while all around him are fighting, bloodshed and death.]

As Swann begins to mount the staircase which leads up to the rooms
where the reception is being held, the prose takes on a ceremonial,
ritual tone. The words *immobile, sculptural, inutile* stress once again the
uselessness and the artificiality of social life which is contrasted with the
'tumultuous' life of the emotions. For everything depends on weight
and size:

D'autres encore, colossaux aussi, se tenaient sur les degrés d'un escalier
monumental que leur présence décorative et leur immobilité marmoréenne
auraient pu faire nommer comme celui du Palais Ducal 'l'Escalier des
Géants' et dans lequel Swann s'engagea avec la tristesse de penser qu'Odette
ne l'avait jamais gravi.

[Others again, no less colossal, were disposed upon the steps of a monumental staircase which, by their decorative presence and marmorean im-

mobility, was made worthy to be named, like the god-crowned ascent in the Palace of the Doges, the 'Staircase of the Giants', and on which Swann now set foot, saddened by the thought that Odette had never climbed it.]

The point is driven home when we learn, a page or two later, that the expensive, liveried servants do not form part of the hostess's normal establishment, but are simply engaged for the evening in the hope that her reception will make the right impression on the condescending aristocrats who look in for a few moments.

Swann thinks longingly of another staircase and another world which are less splendid but more real than this:

Ah! avec quelle joie au contraire il eût grimpé les étages noirs, malodorants et casse-cou de la petite couturière retirée, dans le 'cinquième' de laquelle il aurait été si heureux de payer plus cher qu'une avant-scène hebdomadaire à l'Opéra le droit de passer la soirée quand Odette venait. . . .

[Ah, with what joy would he, on the other hand, have raced up the dark, evil-smelling, breakneck flights to the little dressmaker's, in whose attic he would so gladly have paid the price of a weekly stage-box at the Opera for the right to spend the evening there when Odette came. . . .]

The extreme virtuosity of the writing is admirably maintained:

Parvenu en haut de l'escalier . . . Swann passa devant un bureau où des valets, assis comme des notaires devant de grands registres, se levèrent et inscrivirent son nom.

Il ne restait plus à Swann qu'à pénétrer dans la salle du concert dont un huissier chargé de chaînes lui ouvrit les portes, en s'inclinant, comme il lui aurait remis les clefs d'une ville.

[Coming to the top of the staircase . . . Swann passed by an office in which the lackeys, seated like notaries before their massive registers, rose solemnly to their feet and inscribed his name.

Swann had now only to enter the concert-room, the doors of which were thrown open to him by an usher loaded with chains, who bowed low before him as though tendering to him the keys of a conquered city.]

The point of the story is still to come. The elaborate ceremonial is finished at last. The doors open and this is what Swann sees:

Swann retrouva rapidement le sentiment de la laideur masculine, quand, au delà de la tenture de tapisserie, au spectacle des domestiques, succéda celui des invités.

[He speedily recovered his sense of the general ugliness of the human male when, on the other side of the tapestry curtain, the spectacle of the servants gave place to that of the guests.]

The 'ugliness' of the guests is a symbol of moral corruption and the ceremonial which leads up to the discovery is aimed at displaying their worthless, frivolous lives.

Proust makes brilliant use of the impressionist method when he goes on to describe the different monocles worn by the men:

... le monocle du général, resté entre ses paupières comme un éclat d'obus dans sa figure vulgaire, balafrée et triomphale, au milieu du front qu'il éborgnait comme l'œil unique du cyclope, apparut à Swann comme une blessure monstrueuse qu'il pouvait être glorieux d'avoir reçue, mais qu'il était indécent d'exhiber. . . .

[. . . the General's monocle, stuck like a shell-splinter in his common, scarred, victorious, overbearing face, in the middle of a forehead which it left half-blinded, like the single-eyed flashing front of the Cyclops, appeared to Swann as a monstrous wound which it might have been glorious to receive but which it was certainly not decent to expose. . . .]

The allusion to the Cyclops suggests that all these people are 'one-eyed'. Then the novelist turns on the *romancier mondain*

qui venait d'installer au coin de son œil un monocle, son seul organe d'investigation psychologique et d'impitoyable analyse.

Le monocle du marquis de Forestelle était minuscule, n'avait aucune bordure et obligeant à une crispation incessante et douloureuse l'œil où il s'incrustait comme un cartilage superflu dont la présence est inexplicable et la matière recherchée. . . .

. . . M. de Palancy qui avec sa grosse tête de carpe aux yeux ronds, se déplaçait lentement au milieu des fêtes, en desserrant d'instant en instant ses mandibules comme pour chercher son orientation, avait l'air de transporter seulement avec lui un fragment accidentel, et peut-être purement symbolique du vitrage de son aquarium. . . .

[who had just fitted into the angle of eyebrow and cheek his own monocle, the sole instrument that he used in his psychological investigations and remorseless analyses of character.

The Marquis de Forestelle's monocle was minute and rimless, and, by enforcing an incessant and painful contraction of the eye over which it was encrusted like a superfluous cartilage, the presence of which there was inexplicable and its substance unimaginable. . . .

. . . M. de Palancy, who with his huge carp's head and goggling eyes moved slowly up and down the stream of festive gatherings, unlocking his great mandibles at every moment as though in search of his orientation, had the air of carrying about upon his person only an accidental and perhaps purely symbolical fragment of the glass wall of his aquarium. . . .]

The description of M. de Palancy is a reference back to the 'greyhounds', but the comparison is all in favour of the servants with their *nobles profils aigus*. It is not simply that his monocle reminds us of an aquarium; the whole building is suddenly seen as an aquarium in which hideous fish circle round and round, hopelessly shut off from *la vraie vie*. For in this scene Proust accomplishes two things. He makes us feel that through his liaison with Odette Swann's old milieu has become strange and foreign to him; but we also see that its strangeness and unpleasantness, which Swann perceives for the first time, are real.

From this we must turn to a remarkable passage in *Le Temps retrouvé*:

Ainsi, dans le faubourg Saint-Germain, ces positions en apparence imprenables du duc et de la duchesse de Guermantes, du baron de Charlus avaient perdu leur inviolabilité, comme toutes choses changent en ce monde, par l'action d'un principe intérieur auquel on n'avait pas pensé, chez M. de Charlus l'amour de Charlie qui l'avait rendu esclave des Verdurin, puis le ramollissement, chez Mme de Guermantes, un goût de nouveauté et d'art, chez M. de Guermantes un amour exclusif comme il en avait déjà eu de pareils dans sa vie que la faiblesse de l'âge rendait plus tyrannique. . . .

[Thus, in the Faubourg Saint-Germain, the positions in appearance impregnable of the Duc and Duchesse de Guermantes, of the Baron de Charlus had lost their inviolability, as everything changes in this world by the action of an interior principle to which no one had given thought—with M. de Charlus the love of Charlie, which had made him the slave of the Verdurins, then a softening of the brain, with Mme de Guermantes a taste for novelty and art, with M. de Guermantes an exclusive love of a kind of which he had already known similar examples in his life and which age had rendered more tyrannical. . . .][1]

In the account of Swann's visit to Mme de Saint-Euverte's Proust uses the method of the *novelist* to expose the corruption of high society; in the passage from *Le Temps retrouvé* he is deliberately using the method

[1] My translation.

of the *memoir-writer* to sum up the decline and fall of the exclusive world of the Faubourg Saint-Germain.[1]

The last passage is a lucid statement of Proust's aims as a social critic. He records the disintegration of the old aristocracy, the invasion of the Faubourg Saint-Germain by the bourgeoisie and the beginning of the general levelling down between all classes which followed the First World War. His novel is, indeed, the account of an immense *déclassement* which is the result—this is the important point—of 'the action of an interior principle' and which has some unusual features.[2]

The world to which we are introduced at the beginning of the novel is as rigidly organized as the world of the *ancien régime*, is in fact a survival of feudal times.

> The bourgeois [writes Proust in the first chapter of *Swann*] considered society as though it were composed of closed castes where everyone, as soon as he was born, found himself assigned to the same rank as that occupied by his parents.

Any attempt to move out of one's sphere, whether upwards or downwards, was regarded with the utmost disapproval. The different castes are isolated from one another and know nothing of one another's lives. Marcel's parents have no idea that Swann, whom they patronize, is an intimate friend of the Prince of Wales, and when something of the truth leaks out, they regard his social activities with a mixture of incredulity and disapproval. The contrast between 'Swann's way' and the 'Guermantes' way' is intentional; they stand for two different social spheres which are normally shut off from one another and which lie in 'opposite directions':

> For there were, in the environs of Combray, two 'ways' which we used to take for our walks, and so diametrically opposed that we would actually leave the house by a different door, according to the way we had chosen: the way towards Méséglise-la-Vineuse, which we called also 'Swann's way', because to get there, one had to pass along the boundary of M. Swann's estate, and the 'Guermantes way'. Of Méséglise-la-Vineuse, to tell the truth, I never knew anything more than the way there, and the strange people who would come over on Sundays to take the air

[1] Compare: 'Proust exaggerates to the point of improbability this vision of the reversal of values and takes the same malign pleasure, displays the same vindictive insistence in smirching the social purity of this world that he brought to the denunciation of the silliness and selfishness of the Guermantes.' (Feuillerat, *op. cit.*, p. 243.)

[2] 'Ce qui caractérisait le plus cette société, c'était sa prodigieuse aptitude au déclassement.' (*Le Temps retrouvé*, II, p. 137.)

in Combray. . . . As for Guermantes, I was to know it well enough one day, but that day had still to come; and, during the whole of my boyhood, if Méséglise was to me something as inaccessible as the horizon, which remained hidden from sight, however far one went, by the folds of a country which no longer bore the least resemblance to the country round Combray; Guermantes, on the other hand, meant no more than the ultimate goal, ideal rather than real, of the 'Guermantes way', a sort of abstract geographical term like the North Pole or the Equator. And so to 'take the Guermantes way' in order to get to Méséglise, or vice versa, would have seemed to me as nonsensical a proceeding as to turn to the east in order to reach the west. . . .

But, above all, I set between them, far more distinctly than the mere distance in miles and yards and inches which separated one from the other, the distance that there was between the two parts of my brain in which I used to think of them, one of those distances of the mind which time serves only to lengthen, which separate things irremediably from one another, keeping them for ever on separate planes. And this distinction was rendered still more absolute because the habit we had of never going both ways on the same day, or in the course of the same walk, but the 'Méséglise way' one time and the 'Guermantes way' another, shut them up, so to speak, far apart and unaware of each other's existence, in the sealed vessels—between which there could be no communication—of separate afternoons.

When we had decided to go the 'Méséglise way' we would start (without undue haste, and even if the sky were clouded over, since the walk was not very long, and did not take us too far from home), as though we were not going anywhere in particular, by the front door of my aunt's house, which opened on to the Rue du Saint-Esprit. . . .

If the 'Méséglise way' was so easy, it was a very different matter when we took the 'Guermantes way', for that meant a long walk, and we must make sure, first, of the weather.

These passages illustrate the care with which Proust originally planned his novel. 'Swann's way' is easy because people are moving in their own social sphere; the difficulty and distance of 'Guermantes' way' look forward to the 'impregnable positions' which fall in the last volume. Social distances are expressed here in terms of spatial distances, but they are also seen to involve 'mental' distances 'which separate things irremediably from one another' and lives which are so different that they might be enclosed 'in sealed vessels'.

It is true that, as Crémieux suggests, these distances are finally overcome and the book closes with the fusion of the Guermantes and

Swann worlds, but Proust's interpretation is a subtle one. He is not interested merely in one form of *déclassement* which belongs to a particular epoch, but in something much older and much more complex. For society is not divided simply into the aristocracy, the bourgeoisie and the *peuple*. Within the main social classes, we detect a tendency to form other groups. We read of the Verdurins' *petit noyau*, *petit clan*, *petit groupe*, as we read of the *bande* of the *jeunes filles en fleurs*. These groups are the reverse of the natural groups like the family—we are told of Mme Verdurin that 'elle haïssait les familles (ce dissolvant du petit noyau)'—and they have their 'orthodoxy' and their 'faithful'. In order to belong to the Verdurins, 'one thing was sufficient, but it was necessary: a tacit assent to a *credo* . . . the Verdurins felt . . . that this spirit of inquiry and the demon of frivolity might through contagion prove fatal to the orthodoxy of the little church. . . .'

The Verdurins' orthodoxy rests on snobbery, but there is a much more potent factor at work in the other groups. The overmastering interest which transcends the ordinary class-distinctions and which is responsible for the formation of the 'band' of *jeunes filles* is the sexual connection whether in its normal or its abnormal form. We can say therefore that one of the principal themes of Proust's novel is not merely a *déclassement*, but a *déclassement* in which the sexual factor is either the agent of destruction or the means of social advancement.

Nearly all the main characters have a foot in more than one world, but Swann's position is unusual. For Swann, the connoisseur and the friend of the Prince of Wales, does not owe his position to birth or directly to the fortune amassed by his father on the Stock Exchange. He is the patrician, the intellectual aristocrat who is admitted to the highest circles on account of his intellectual and social gifts. It is in this respect that his position most closely resembles Marcel's, but his race seems to count for something in his ascension. The exclusive caste, which assumes the proportions of an obsession in the book, is characteristic of the Jews, but their rootlessness is a no less pronounced characteristic. Swann mixes with the highest society because he is not attached to the commercial middle class into which he was born by any of the normal social ties, but it is precisely his rootlessness which tempts him to make the return journey, to separate himself from his aristocratic friends for the sake of his taste in women. He shares with Marcel himself a tendency—it is another and a very unpleasant racial characteristic—to regard women as a 'commodity' which has its price:

> . . . these were, as often as not, women whose beauty was of a distinctly 'common' type, for the physical qualities which attracted him instinc-

N

tively, and without reason, were the direct opposite of those that he admired in the women painted or sculptured by his favourite masters. Depth of character, or a melancholy expression on a woman's face would freeze his senses, which would, however, immediately melt at the sight of healthy, abundant, rosy human flesh.

When he stops going to the house of a society friend, she only discovers by accident that she has been 'dropped' when she comes across a letter of farewell to her cook who was the reigning mistress; and in the end he completes his social ruin by marrying Odette.

His daughter, Gilberte, outstrips the triumphs of her father, marries Robert de Saint-Loup and becomes a Guermantes by marriage. Saint-Loup has an extraordinary love affair with a woman named Rachel whom Marcel has met in a brothel. After his marriage he shares the tastes of his aristocratic uncle, Baron de Charlus, and even takes up with the Baron's lower-class 'boy-friend'. Charlus, who must rank as one of the great characters of fiction, is in the same position.

One of the funniest scenes in the book is the evening at the Verdurins when Charlus agrees to bring some of his aristocratic friends. He usurps the functions of his hostess and receives the guests himself. They behave with an insolence which is characteristic of their ancient line and, pointing a finger at the wretched lady of the house, ask: 'Who's that? Is that woman Mme Verdurin?' These social triumphs are not confined to the middle classes. The lift-boy at Balbec confides in Marcel that his sister is well placed with a 'rich gentleman', learns the piano and adopts very peculiar methods of showing her contempt for the class which she has abandoned. The informant goes on to add that the enterprising father has also succeeded in placing his younger brother with an Indian prince where he has embarked on an elegant career as *tapette*. But the greatest *déclassement* of all is reserved for the last volume where we learn with shocked surprise that Mme Verdurin has become by her third marriage—the Princesse de Guermantes. The last, the most 'impregnable' position of all in the Faubourg Saint-Germain has fallen.

We have observed the tendency in Proust's work of society to subdivide into a vast number of sects, groups, cells, clans and bands; and we have also seen that in many cases the common interest which binds them together is sexual, as it certainly is with the *jeunes filles en fleurs*. One of the most curious achievements of the book is the novelist's anatomy of homosexuality. He speaks of the homosexuals as forming

a freemasonry far more extensive, more powerful and less suspected than that of the Lodges, for it rests upon an identity of tastes, needs, habits, dangers, apprenticeship, knowledge, traffic, glossary, and one in which the members themselves, who intend not to know one another, recognize one another immediately by natural or conventional, involuntary or deliberate signs which indicate one of his cogeners to the beggar in the street, in the great nobleman whose carriage door he is shutting, to the father in the suitor for his daughter's hand, to him who has sought healing, absolution, defence, in the doctor, the priest, the barrister to whom he has had recourse. . . .

These volumes are a remarkable contribution to sociology. Proust describes with minute care the behaviour, dress and even the peculiar manner of speaking of the homosexuals, giving us the impression of a vast secret society or, to use his own word, a vast 'freemasonry', whose tentacles extend into every corner of society and produce the strangest *déclassements* of all.

When we read of the disreputable diplomat, M. de Vaugoubert:

Ayant passé d'une débauche presque infantile à la continence absolue datant du jour où il avait pensé au quai d'Orsay et voulu faire une grande carrière, il avait l'air d'une bête en cage, jetant dans tous les sens des regards qui exprimaient la peur, l'appétance et la stupidité.

[Having passed from an almost infantile corruption to an absolute continence dating from the day on which his thoughts had turned to the Quai d'Orsay and he had begun to plan a great career for himself, he had the air of a caged animal, casting in every direction glances expressive of fear, appetite and stupidity.]

we might reasonably take it for a piece of social criticism in the manner of Saint-Simon, the master with whom Proust is most often compared. When the same criticism is repeated in slightly different words thirty pages later:

La carrière diplomatique avait eu sur sa vie l'effet d'une entrée dans les ordres. Combinée avec l'assiduité à l'École des Sciences Politiques, elle l'avait voué depuis ses vingt ans à la chasteté du chrétien.

[The career of diplomacy had had the same effect upon his life as a monastic profession. Combined with his assiduous frequentation of the School of Political Sciences, it had vowed him from his twentieth year to the chastity of a professing Christian.]

a doubt arises. What might pass in the earlier passage for a detached irony now appears as a note of frustration, as though the writer were trying to solve a personal problem by caricaturing it in one of his characters. The suspicion is strengthened by the crude description at the same party of Marcel's enthusiastic acceptance of a friend's invitation to visit some time in the future a particularly 'smart' brothel. This note of frustration is really the clue to the interpretation of the later volumes of *A la Recherche du temps perdu*.

Proust's biographers have been curiously reticent about their hero's sexual life. It is true that they hint that, during the years when he was a brilliant young man of the world before his work and his illness turned him into a recluse, he had considerable success with women; but to read them one might suppose that after 'sowing his wild oats' he was vowed to a chastity as absolute as M. de Vaugoubert's and for nobler reasons.[1] Now it does not call for great powers of divination to see that the author of *A la Recherche du temps perdu* was profoundly homosexual, but unless this is realized a great deal of the later volumes are meaningless. It has often been hinted that 'Albertine' was a boy, but it is only very recently that the story of Proust's personal peculiarities has been made public.[2] It is by no means an edifying story, but it has an obvious bearing on the novel.

It will be recalled that in the novel Charlus set up a male brothel in the name of Jupien—a former paramour and his servant and companion during his dotage—who acted as manager. In some of the least agreeable pages in the novel, Marcel describes a visit to this establishment and his view of the proprietor chained to a bed being flagellated. According to Sachs, the facts on which Proust drew were somewhat different. The brothel or, as it was called, the *établissement de bains*, certainly existed, but its proprietor was none other than Proust himself and the nominee his devoted servant Albert.

Sachs is certainly not an unimpeachable witness, but his account of Proust's clandestine activities and their effect on his work is highly plausible.[3] We do not know to what extent Proust himself was *pratiquant*, but he appears to have been a *voyeur* which perhaps explains why Marcel always observes the most scandalous incidents in the book—they are invariably homosexual incidents—from a concealed position. Proust's establishment, which was known as Les Bains du Ballon d'Alsace, is said to have been frequented by some of the highest personages in the land. Proust, who had often seen them at the Ritz, saw a very different side when they visited the Bains, which has an obvious

[1] For a correction, see Maurois, *op. cit.*, pp. 114–27. [2] Sachs, *op. cit.*, pp. 275–89.
[3] The substance of this story is confirmed by Mme de Gramont, *op. cit.*, pp. 209–10.

bearing on his presentation of character and on his attitude towards the aristocracy which becomes more and more hostile as the novel progresses.

> Very few of Proust's characters are healthy or even normal beings [writes M. Buchet]. Even those who appear to be at first—Albertine and her friends, Gilberte and Saint-Loup—turn out in the end to be inverts. The story is told that one day Proust was discovered on his knees in his room collecting the manuscripts of his work, giving a final look at his characters and crying out in tears, as though he had just made a discovery which horrified him: 'They're all like that.'[1]

The later volumes of the novel certainly record a universal drift towards the Cities of the Plain. Mr. Edmund Wilson has compared Proust's supposed denunciation of the homosexuals to the tone of the Old Testament prophets and puts it down to his Jewish blood. This seems to me to be a simplification. Proust's attitude is much more complex. The truth is that there is no denunciation, that on the pretext of explaining sexual aberrations Proust contrives, indirectly, to excuse them and is never tired of expatitating on Charlus' 'moral qualities'.[2] This does not mean that his attitude was wholly indulgent or that there was no conflict in the presentation of his material. Nearly everything that he writes about homosexuality betrays a profound sense of guilt, and what Mr. Wilson takes for 'denunciation' might more accurately be described as a tone of 'lamentation'. Yet even here his attitude is ambivalent. In one place he writes:

> . . . rapprochant la mort de ma grand'mère et celle d'Albertine, il me semblait que ma vie était souillée d'un double assassinat. . . .

> [. . . thinking at once of my grandmother's death and of Albertine's, it seemed to me that my life was stained with a double murder. . . .]

---

[1] *Op. cit.*, p. 71. The one notable exception is the narrator. In the remarkable conversation recorded in his *Journal*, Gide reports Proust as saying to him in 1921: 'You can tell everything . . . but on condition that you never say: *I*.'

'Far from denying or hiding his uranism,' writes Gide of the same meeting, 'he displays it, and I might almost say: prides himself on it. He said that he had never loved women except spiritually and had never experienced love except with men.' (*Journal*, p. 692.)

[2] He seems to have taken the view that the causes of homosexuality were purely physiological and that it should therefore be regarded as a misfortune rather than a vice. In spite of the admissions to Gide, however, his attitude was disingenuous. (See Maurois, *loc. cit.*)

The intention of this passage is only fully apparent when we place it beside another from *Sodome et Gomorrhe*:

Au reste peut-on séparer entièrement l'aspect de M. de Charlus du fait que les fils n'ayant pas toujours la ressemblance paternelle, même sans être invertis et en recherchant des femmes, ils consomment dans leur visage la Profanation de leur mère. Mais laissons ici ce qui mériterait un chapitre à part: les mères profanées.

[Not that there need be any connection between the appearance of M. de Charlus and the fact that sons, who do not always take after their fathers, even without being inverts, and though they go after women, may consummate upon their faces the profanation of their mothers. But we need not consider here a subject that deserves a chapter to itself: the Profanation of the Mother.]

It is a pity that Proust never wrote his chapter on the *mères profanées*, but he has said enough to reveal his line of thought. In all love, he thinks, particularly in its unnatural forms, man is driven on by the urge to destroy the person he loves. The man who loves women feels obscurely that possession is a violation of the mother-figure and this feeling is enormously intensified in the case of the homosexual who outrages not only his mother, but Woman herself. This is also true of the Lesbians who feel that they are profaning the father-figure. In the account of Mlle Vinteuil and her friend at Monjouvain, the desire of profanation assumes a ritual form and relations between the two women are preceded by Mlle Vinteuil spitting on the photograph of the father to whom she was devoted and whose death had been hastened by the discovery of his daughter's tastes.[1] Finally, in the description of Marcel's visit to Charlus' establishment we are shown a priest, who was among the clients, about to leave without paying. Jupien introduces a note of grisly comedy by shaking his purse and crying: 'Pour les frais du culte, monsieur l'abbé.'

Proust speaks constantly of 'prisons', 'prisoners', 'captives' and 'cages'. The words are of great significance, but their significance is only apparent when they are considered in relation to the little 'groups', 'clans' and 'bands'. For these sects are at once cells and secret societies which are founded on mutual interest and 'prisons' because they cut the 'faithful' off from intercourse with the rest of society, as Mme Verdurin is always at pains to keep her faithful away from people of a

[1] He explains that Mlle Vinteuil's 'sadism' is not the result of vice, but of 'sentimentality', and argues that sadists are really sentimentalists.

higher social sphere whom she calls the *ennuyeux*.[1] For Vaugoubert diplomacy was a 'prison' because it prevented him from joining the homosexuals; but the strangest example is the imprisonment of Albertine.[2] Consider the following passages from *La Prisonnière*:

. . . Albertine, que d'ailleurs je ne trouvais plus guère jolie et avec laquelle je m'ennuyais, que j'avais la sensation nette de ne pas aimer. . . .

Son charme un peu incommode était ainsi d'être à la maison moins comme une jeune fille, que comme une bête domestique qui entre dans une pièce, qui en sort, qui se trouve partout où on ne s'y attend pas. . . .

Je n'aimais plus Albertine.

Albertine s'était étonnamment développée, ce qui m'était entièrement égal. . . .

[. . . Albertine, in whom for that matter I could no longer see any beauty and who was beginning to bore me, with whom I was clearly conscious that I was not in love. . . .

Her somewhat disturbing charm was, in fact, that of taking the place in the household not so much of a girl as of a domestic animal which comes into a room, goes out, is to be found wherever one does not expect to find it. . . .

I was no longer in love with Albertine.

Albertine had developed in an astonishing way, a thing that was a matter of indifference to me.]

When we ask why he was so determined to keep prisoner a woman whom he neither loved nor found attractive, this is the answer:

J'avais pu séparer Albertine de ses complices et, par là, exorciser mes hallucinations.

[I had been able to separate Albertine from her accomplices and in that way exorcize my hallucinations.]

The whole story of this enforced detention of the woman is a curious and sinister myth of a crumbling society trying desperately to convince itself of its own normality, to stop its drift towards perversion and col-

---

[1] Swann's is 'expelled' from the *petit clan* for defending some of his aristocratic friends whom Mme Verdurin classed an *ennuyeux*.

[2] According to Maurois there was a succession of 'prisoners' at Proust's home—well-favoured but not very competent male secretaries, the last of whom was 'released' on the eve of the publication of *Sodome et Gomorrhe*. (*Op. cit.*, pp. 211–12.)

lapse. The writer invents a woman whose vices are his own; he con-gratulates himself on his forcible prevention of practices which in secret he envies and, at the same time, by changing the object of desire into a woman, tries to conceal the roots of the evil from himself. Nor should we overlook the significance of the consultations with the Duchesse de Guermantes over Albertine's clothes. It is not the adorn-ment of the bride, but a form of fetichism, a solemn incensing of the twofold being who is at once the symbol of normality and perversity.

There has been a good deal of speculation about Albertine's sex, but Sachs is certainly right in saying that 'the sex of Proust's heroine is not clearly defined. She is love itself and anyone can invest her with the image of the person who is dearest to him.'[1] But this comment over-looks one important point. Proust speaks somewhere of the *néant* which is behind all love. His interest in homosexuality was dictated largely but not wholly by personal factors. For homosexuality is essentially a symbol of sterility and frustration, of that nihilism which colours much of the novel.

The figure of M. de Charlus has been rightly praised as a great comic creation in which Proust outdoes Dickens and Balzac on their own ground. There is, indeed, a savage farce about his account of the dissolu-tion of the middle-aged homosexual; but when we look into it, we find that the irony is seldom disinterested. It seems to me that Proust displays the same ambiguous attitude towards him as he does towards Albertine and that these two characters are really complementary. He invests another with his own vices and shows how ugly they are; but Charlus inspires in his creator the same conflict as Albertine, the same mixture of dislike and envy. For there is little doubt that secretly he envied both Charlus and Morel who, under cover of an engagement to a very normal young woman, carries on his appalling intrigue with Charlus as well as with Saint-Loup and Albertine whom he supplies with *petites filles* after first corrupting them—he seems to have been very versatile—does in short what Proust would like to have done himself. That is why the novelist was determined to punish the pair of them.

When we come to the end of the novel, we find that though Proust's characters still cling to 'class' and 'family', these things have lost much of their importance and have been replaced by the 'groups', 'cells' and 'bands' which did so much to undermine them. And no doubt the final glimpse of Charlus who has fallen into a state of idiocy—he is ironically compared to King Lear—demonstrates, and is intended to demonstrate, the decline and fall of the aristocracy through a vice which is some-times said to belong peculiarly to periods of decadence; but we are

[1] *Op. cit.*, p. 282. (Compare Feuillerat, *op. cit.*, p. 217, and see p. 391 below.)

forced to admit that Proust's criticism is largely neutralized by his own complicity and by the absence of 'moral values' with which he is often reproached. When we compare this part of his novel with the end of Baudelaire's *femmes damnées*, where the moral attitude is completely fused into the poetic image, we realize why Baudelaire's poetry has in this respect a maturity, a finality, for which we shall look in vain in Proust's novel.[1]

We observe the same failings in his views of society as a whole. His study of society is undoubtedly an impressive performance. He possessed an extraordinary insight into the workings of the social organism, and his account of the impact of the Dreyfus Affair and the war on it is particularly impressive; but this is no reason for minimizing his deficiencies. I have described him as a 'social critic', but I feel that the proper term is 'social analyst'. He records the disintegration of the aristocratic élite and its absorption by the bourgeoisie. He himself attributed it to 'the action of an interior principle', but the truth is that the aristocracy succumbed to the absence of any constructive principle, to a moral inertia which assumed the forms of perversion, frivolity, snobbery and unintelligence. M. Feuillerat comments on Proust's growing rancour towards the aristocracy, but he does not explore its causes. They are not difficult to discover and they are very important. Compared with the urbanity of Stendhal or the extreme moral rectitude of Constant, Proust's attitude is often no more than a lamentable exhibition of petty spite. He disliked the aristocracy because he thought that they had let the side down and the Verdurins in. His acrimony was probably intensified by the fact that his health condemned him to reclusion, missing what fun was still to be had. Nor are his positive standards impressive. It is true that the grandmother, the mother and Françoise stand for decency, but they do so at an elementary level. They represent the human qualities which are an indispensable minimum in any reasonable society. Although Proust spoke contemptuously of the 'néant de la vie de salon' and of society as 'un spectacle sans cause', there is no reason to suppose that he had any higher ideal or that he would not have been perfectly at home in the 'social aquarium'. That is why 'social analyst' rather than 'social critic', which implies a different scale of values, seems the proper term for him.

---

[1] Gide reports Proust as asserting that Baudelaire was a homosexual and displaying indignant surprise when Gide denied it. (*Journal, loc. cit.*)

N*

3. An Invisible Vocation

Nearly all the great French masters have been men who liked to discuss and explain their art, to discover how their effects were achieved; but I cannot think of any writer who has gone as far as Proust. The artist's vocation is a recurrent theme in the novel; a substantial part of *Le Temps retrouvé* is devoted to the analysis of his own method, his peculiar vision and the place of art in life. Yet there is a marked difference between his approach and that of other writers. The pages of *Le Temps retrouvé* in which he discusses his art are not an abstract treatise on æsthetics like Joyce's at the end of *A Portrait of the Artist as a Young Man* and Marcel's treatment of his vocation is far more impressive than Gide's in the *Faux-Monnayeurs*. Art is not merely one of the principal themes of the novel; the theories on which it is based and indeed the actual writing of the book are part of the novelist's experience.

It is therefore necessary at this point to say something of the incident of the *petite madeleine* and the *mémoire involontaire* which is the pivot of the whole theory:

Il y avait déjà bien des années que, de Combray, tout ce qui n'était pas le théâtre et le drame de mon coucher, n'existait plus pour moi, quand un jour d'hiver, comme je rentrais à la maison, ma mère, voyant que j'avais froid, me proposa de me faire prendre, contre mon habitude, un peu de thé. Je refusai d'abord et, je ne sais pourquoi, me ravisai. Elle envoya chercher un de ces gâteaux courts et dodus appelés Petites Madeleines qui semblent avoir été moulés dans la valve rainurée d'une coquille de Saint-Jacques.

[Many years had elapsed during which nothing of Combray, save what was comprised in the theatre and the drama of my going to bed there, had any existence for me, when one day in winter, as I came home, my mother, seeing that I was cold, offered me some tea, a thing I did not ordinarily take. I declined at first, and then, for no particular reason, changed my mind. She sent out for one of those short, plump little cakes called *petites madeleines*, which look as though they had been moulded in the fluted scallop of a pilgrim's shell.]

He then goes on to relate the strange experience which he had when he dipped the *madeleine* into his tea and put it in his mouth. We feel the resistance—the unconscious resistance—when his mother persuades him to have some tea *contre mon habitude*. We feel, too, his mental weariness in the slow, dragging sentence

Et bientôt, machinalement, accablé par la morne journée et la perspective d'un triste lendemain, je portai à mes lèvres une cuillerée du thé où j'avais laissé s'amollir un morceau de madeleine.

[And soon, mechanically, weary after a dull day with the prospect of a depressing morrow, I raised to my lips a spoonful of the tea in which I had soaked a morsel of the cake.]

Then there is a sudden change of tone, a sense of immense excitement coupled with great watchfulness:

Mais à l'instant même où la gorgée mêlée des miettes du gâteau toucha mon palais, je tressaillis, attentif à ce qui se passait d'extraordinaire en moi. Un plaisir délicieux m'avait envahi, isolé, sans la notion de sa cause.

[No sooner had the warm liquid, and the crumbs with it, touched my palate than a shudder ran through my whole body, and I stopped, intent upon the extraordinary changes that were taking place. An exquisite pleasure had invaded my senses, but individual, detached, with no suggestion of its origin.]

The experience takes the form at first of a feeling of intense but inexplicable happiness:

Il m'avait aussitôt rendu les vicissitudes de la vie indifférentes, ses désastres inoffensifs, sa brièveté illusoire, de la même façon qu'opère l'amour, en me remplissant d'une essence précieuse: ou plutôt cette essence n'était pas en moi, elle était moi.

[And at once the vicissitudes of life had become indifferent to me, its disasters innocuous, its brevity illusory—this new sensation having had on me the effect which love has of filling me with a precious essence; or rather the essence was not in me, it was myself.]

He begins to speculate about the source of his experience and to analyse it. It is linked to the taste of the *madeleine*. He eats another spoonful. Then he realizes that the source lies not in the cake, but in himself:

Il est clair que la vérité que je cherche n'est pas en lui, mais en moi.

Although the experience is started by the mechanical action of eating the cake soaked in tea, the artist is *passive*:

> Un plaisir délicieux m'avait envahi . . . je sens tressaillir en moi quelque chose qui se déplace, voudrait s'élever, quelque chose qu'on aurait désancré à une grande profondeur; je ne sais ce que c'est, mais cela monte lentement; j'éprouve la résistance et j'entends la rumeur des distances traversées.

> [An exquisite pleasure had invaded my senses. . . . I feel something start within me, something that leaves its resting-place and attempts to rise, something that has been embedded like an anchor at a great depth; I do not know yet what it is, but I can feel it mounting slowly; I can measure the resistance, I can hear the echo of great spaces traversed.]

The close of the passage is perhaps the most remarkable part of it. We feel the strange forces stirring at a level far below that of the conscious mind, struggling to reach the surface from the *grande profondeur* where they are 'anchored'; and we are also aware of the immense *psychological* distances which they must traverse. The 'meaning' of the experience suddenly becomes clear to him:

> Certes, ce qui palpite ainsi au fond de moi, ce doit être l'image, le souvenir visuel, qui, lié à cette saveur, tente de la suivre jusqu'à moi.

> [Undoubtedly what is thus palpitating in the depths of my being must be the image, the visual memory which, being linked to the taste, has tried to follow it into the conscious mind.]

The experience originates in an association of ideas. The taste of the *madeleine* recalls the taste of the *madeleine* which his aunt Léonie used to give him when he was a child at Combray. He had temporarily 'forgotten' the past except for the nightly drama of his mother's kiss, and it is this past which is suddenly recreated and is trying to escape from the depths of his being where it is imprisoned.

The focal words of the passage are *souvenir visuel*. He sees the old grey house in which his aunt lived, and with the house the town, its square, its streets:

> Comme dans ce jeu où les Japonais s'amusent à tremper dans un bol de porcelaine rempli d'eau, de petits morceaux de papier jusque-là indistincts qui, à peine y sont-ils plongés s'étirent, se contournent, se colorent, se différencient, deviennent des fleurs, des maisons, des personnages consis-

tants et reconnaissables, de même maintenant toutes les fleurs de notre jardin et celles du parc de M. Swann, et les nymphéas de la Vivonne, et les bonnes gens du village et leurs petits logis et l'église et tout Combray et ses environs, tout cela qui prend forme et solidité, est sorti, ville et jardins, de ma tasse de thé.

[And just as the Japanese amuse themselves by filling a porcelain bowl with water and steeping in it little crumbs of paper which until then are without character or form, but, the moment they become wet, stretch themselves and bend, take on colour and distinctive shape, become flowers or houses or people, permanent and recognizable, so in that moment all the flowers in our garden and in M. Swann's park, and the water-lilies on the Vivonne and the good folk of the village and their little dwellings and the parish church and the whole of Combray and of its surroundings, taking their proper shapes and growing solid, sprang into being, town and gardens alike, from my cup of tea.]

The Japanese flowers were no doubt suggested by the sight of the tea-leaves floating round the cup. The accumulation of the four verbs, 's'étirent, se contournent, se colorent, se différencient', seems to be another device borrowed from Flaubert, but Proust uses it with greater artistry. He gives us a deliberately 'indistinct' picture of the dried paper flowers falling into the bowl, opening, revolving, revealing their colours, assuming separate shapes. With the switch to the three substantives, the 'indistinct' image suddenly becomes sharp and precise. We have a vivid sensation of 'flowers, town, people' tumbling pell-mell out of the cup. 'Consistants et reconnaissables' looks back to 'indistincts' and forward to 'prend forme et solidité'. We see every detail of the picture—Swann's park, the water-lilies in the Vivonne, the people, the church. These details merge again into the generalized image of 'tout Combray et ses environs', making us feel the landscape unfolding before us; while the repeated 'ville et jardins' deftly emphasizes the contrast between the wide panorama and the cup from which it has emerged.

The whole passage is a remarkable piece of psychological observation, a description of the creative act as it takes place in certain writers. It is repeated at intervals throughout the book; but though the content is always similar, the incident which starts it is always different. On one occasion it is the sight of the three belfries at Martinville, on another the scent of the hawthorn or of the mouldering wood. Finally, in *Le Temps retrouvé*, it is the unequal paving-stones and the rough towel on which Marcel dries his hands.

Proust does not claim that his experience is unique. On the contrary, he states explicitly that he has observed the same phenomenon in Chateaubriand's *Mémoires d'outre-tombe*, in Gérard de Nerval's *Sylvie* and in Baudelaire's poetry. He might, indeed, have quoted the famous passage from Baudelaire's diaries:

> Dans certain états de l'âme presque surnaturels, la profondeur de la vie se révèle dans le spectacle, si ordinaire qu'il soit, qu'on a sous les yeux. Il en devient le Symbole.

For in what Dandieu calls his *états privilégiés*, it is precisely this that happens. The inner meaning of life becomes clear to him. Incidents, which seemed to belong to the world of time and chance and to which he had paid little attention, are abstracted from that world and become part of a timeless world in which they acquire immense significance.

The fruits of Proust's experience are certainly impressive and the pages in which he describes Aunt Léonie are among the most memorable in the book. Yet we sometimes have the impression that he tried to use the theory of the *mémoire involontaire* to prove too much and that it could not really have been the staple of the novel as he contrived to suggest. His conception of time and all that it implies was very different from Bergson's *durée*. It was of the essence of his experience that it was fragmentary, intermittent, discontinuous. The extraordinary novelty of his vision depends very largely on sudden switches from the surface of experience to a deeper level and back again. That is why the magic lantern, the Japanese flowers, snapshots and 'photographs taken by our sensibility' are key-images, or what Proust himself called *phrase-types*, in the novel. It must be remembered, however, that the book is concerned not so much with isolated experiences as with a particular attitude of mind. Proust deliberately adopted a passive standpoint towards the phenomena of experience and played down intelligence because he was convinced that intelligence distorted experience by imposing artificial categories, and that what we call 'personality' was very largely an abstract construction which excluded too much.

There are naturally grounds on which he can legitimately be criticized. He does tend in the final volume to surround his experience with an aura of mystery and it is his own fault if this has led to misunderstanding and encouraged bad habits on the part of his critics. For some of them have used the word 'mystic' to describe his experence. It is a technical term borrowed from theology which has no application to art and might with advantage be removed from the vocabulary of literary criticism. But though there appears to be no resemblance between the *content* of Proust's experience and that of the religious mystics, there is one important parallel. The religious mystic believes that he has had an immediate experience of the Absolute—theologians speak of an experimental knowledge of God without the intermediary of a concept —but Proust pursued a *psychological* absolute. It was, as we shall see, precisely because he sought an absolute in those realms of experience in which there can be no absolute and no finality, that all his work has a perpetual underlying tension.

'Il n'a pas eu de peine à faire voler en éclats le mannequin cartésien au grand scandale de plusieurs bons esprits,' said Dandieu of Proust.[1] The connection between the philosophy of a period and its art is a close and intricate one, but we may doubt whether it is altogether correct to speak of a novelist 'smashing the Cartesian mannequin to pieces'. It seems rather that the philosopher and the artist are themselves the products of changes in the human mind, and it is from this point of view that we should approach the art of Proust.

Although 'the Cartesian mannequin' is a somewhat mechanical figure, Descartes himself inaugurated the philosophical revolution which led logically to Proust. Classical theories of art are based on the classical metaphysic, on the belief in a fixed unchanging reality which it is the artist's business to 'represent'. Modern art is based on one or other of the idealist systems, on the assumption that 'reality is a synthesis of the thing perceived and the perceiving subject. Descartes' determination 'de ne chercher plus d'autre science que celle qui se pourrait trouver en moi-même' is the moment at which the mind turns away from the outer world and concentrates on its own processes.

There is, however, nearly always a time-lag between philosophical changes and changes in men's theories of art. It was not until the second half of the nineteenth century that the Cartesian philosophy began to yield its real fruits, and by then it had been powerfully reinforced by Kant's *Critique of Pure Reason*. 'What does it matter', said Baudelaire, 'what the reality outside me is made of provided that it helps me to feel that I am and what I am?' 'What is the conception of pure art?' he asked in another place, and replied: 'It is to create a suggestive magic which contains both subject and object, the external world and the artist himself.'[2]

Baudelaire spoke scornfully of *le beau unique et absolu*, but it was left to the poet Jules Laforgue to reveal the full implications of his master's theories in a remarkable essay on Impressionism:

[1] *Marcel Proust: sa révélation psychologique* (Paris and Oxford, 1930), p. 137.
[2] *L'Art romantique* (Conard Edition), p. 119.

DOUBLE ILLUSION OF ABSOLUTE BEAUTY AND ABSOLUTE MAN. INNUMERABLE HUMAN KEYBOARDS. The old æsthetic drivelled alternatively about these two illusions—absolute, objective Beauty—absolute, subjective man, Taste.[1]

With a stroke of his pen, Laforgue demolishes *l'homme absolu* of the classical ages and replaces him by the *innombrables claviers humains*. He observes that

> Each man is, according to his moment in time, his racial and social milieu, his individual moment of evolution, a particular keyboard on which the external world plays in a particular fashion. My keyboard is perpetually changing and there is no other which is absolutely identical with mine. All keyboards are legitimate.

He concludes:

> On a aujourd'hui un sentiment plus exact de la Vie en nous et hors de nous.[2]

These are claims with which Proust would certainly have sympathized. It is easy to see the connection between his *vraie vie* and Laforgue's *Vie en nous*; but the connection between his *moi successifs* and Laforgue's *innombrables claviers humains* is still more striking. For they both see life as a succession of 'moments' which are never the same and which never return. 'Je m'étais rendu compte', said Proust in *Le Temps retrouvé*, 'que seule la perception grossière et erronée place tout dans l'objet, quand tout est dans l'esprit. . . .' And a few pages later he speaks of the 'caractère purement mental de la réalité'. We can, it appears, know what is going on inside our minds, but the crudity and the element of error in our external perceptions prevent us from knowing the outer world. The objects which we appear to see are only interesting in so far as they play a part in the creation of a reality which is 'purely mental' and in which subject and object are merged.

The artist's attempt to free himself not merely from classical conceptions of man, but from the classical categories of experience, presents obvious dangers. Yet the theory of man as a perpetually changing keyboard, trying to seize the unique moment of experience, was also extremely fruitful. It was a genuine movement of liberation. In Proust's work the absence of any formal discipline lies in the fact that he does not attempt to impose any interpretation on the actual experience; and one

---

[1] *Mélanges posthumes* (Paris, 1903), p. 140.   [2] *Ibid.*, pp. 141-2.

of the reasons why his analysis of love is so extraordinarily original is that he divested himself of all preconceived ideas.

This should help us to dispose of the vexed question of the supposed influence of Bergson on Proust.

> Proust [wrote Pierre-Quint] seems to have lived, felt and personally experienced the whole of the Bergsonian philosophy.[1]

Proust himself never accepted this view. In an interview which he gave to Élie-Joseph Bois and which was published in *Le Temps* on 12 November 1913, he said:

> I should not be in any way ashamed to describe my books as 'Bergsonian novels' if I thought they were, for in every period literature has tried to attach itself—after the event naturally—to the reigning philosophy. But it would not be accurate, for my work is dominated by the distinction between the *mémoire volontaire* and the *mémoire involontaire*, a distinction which is not only not to be found in M. Bergson's philosophy, but is even contradicted by it.[2]

In a letter written to Camille Vettard in 1922 he was still more explicit. He spoke of possessing a 'special sense' which he compared to 'a telescope brought to bear on time'. He went on:

> I have tried to make conscious unconscious phenomena which, completely forgotten, are sometimes deeply buried in the past. (When I come to think of it, it is perhaps this special sense which has sometimes produced affinities between Bergson and myself—since people say that it is so—for so far as I can judge, there has been no direct suggestion).[3]

The word 'affinities' is an important one.[4] A great writer's art cannot be explained by casual references to a few other writers and thinkers who were roughly contemporary with him and who happened to write in a similar style. It is, as I have suggested, almost always the culminating phase of a long period of development which has been going on unnoticed not merely for years, but for centuries. It is idle to speak of the 'influence' of Bergson or, for that matter, of Freud on

[1] *Op. cit.*, p. 34.
[2] The interview is reprinted almost in full in Robert Dreyfus, *Souvenirs sur Marcel Proust* (Paris, 1926). (See p. 289.)
[3] *Correspondance générale*, III, pp. 194–5.
[4] In French the crucial phrase is: 'C'est peut-être, à la réflexion, ce sens spécial qui m'a fait quelquefois rencontrer . . . Bergson.'

Proust. The philosopher and the psychologist no less than the novelist were themselves the products of changes which had taken place in the European mind, and their theories moulded by subjective factors to a greater degree than is sometimes admitted. That is why they turned out to be moving in the same direction without there being any question of what Proust called 'direct suggestion'. Bergson and Proust both reacted against the rigid categories of the nineteenth century. They both felt that the emphasis on pure intelligence left out too much. Bergson was reacting against the determinism of nineteenth-century thinkers, Proust against the dreary realism of novelists like Zola. For in spite of their immense industry, their extraordinary attention to physical detail, the realists and the naturalists failed completely to capture *la vraie vie*. So it was that Bergson's philosophy ruined the foundations of determinism and Proust's novel equally ruined the foundations of naturalism.

I have stressed these philosophical changes because they are essential to an understanding of the book. Proust's study of society and his analysis of passion are immensely fascinating, but they are only factors in the central drama. The most important word in his title is the word *recherche*.[1] The novel is the pursuit of an absolute, an experience which would be untouched by the devouring action of time. Philosophical idealism had made Proust profoundly sceptical about man's knowledge of the external world—we find ourselves continually recalling his references to Kant—and he turned his eyes inward. He tried to find in himself some principle of unity, something which would fix the perpetually changing *moi*. He tried to reach this unity first through personal relationships—they are perhaps the most dangerous of the 'false vocations'—then through art; and the novel records in the main the vicissitudes of this strange pursuit.

4. *People*

Proust's scepticism was largely responsible for his peculiar method of presenting 'character' which is different not merely from that of the classic novelists, but of his own contemporaries. In the classic novelists character—*l'homme absolu*—is in general one of the *données*. The novelist begins by 'creating' characters, but once they have been created they do not undergo any fundamental change. All their adventures or experiences are the outcome of character and of the friction of one

[1] Proust was by no means happy over the title of the English translation and complained that the word 'remembrance' distorted his meaning.

character on another. The modern writer has no doubt discarded the theory of fixed unchanging character and instead portrays the psychological development of characters who are completely different at the end of the book from the beginning. It should be emphasized that the change is real; it is not, as it sometimes is with the classic writers, that different facets of the main characters are only revealed as the result of the experiences which are described in the book.

The concept of a fixed unchanging character is common to the writers of classical antiquity, the Middle Ages and the English and French novelists of the eighteenth century. In Fielding and Smollett, in Marivaux and Laclos, there is, properly speaking, no development of character. The novelist starts with a special knowledge of his character and he reveals it to the reader by inventing a series of situations in which they become involved.

A different approach, however, can already be discerned in the dramatists as well as in the principal French novelists of the seventeenth century. Although strictly limited, there is development in Corneille Molière, Racine and Mme de La Fayette. The Alceste who abandons society in search of an *endroit écarté* in the fifth act of *Le Misanthrope* is certainly different from the fiery reformer of Act I, though his 'change of heart' is the logical outcome of the *données*. Corneille's characters undergo a moral growth and become 'integrated'; Racine's and Mme de La Fayette's suffer complete moral collapse.

Another change occurs at the close of the eighteenth century. There is a strong autobiographical element in Constant and Stendhal, but comparatively little development. Their characters are all trying to discover what sort of people they are and their discoveries are the outcome not so much of action, situation and their relations with other people as of solitary analysis in a silent room or in prison.

Proust's approach differs from all these writers or rather he combines a number of different approaches and produces a new standpoint and a new method. The classical novelists were convinced that in spite of his changing moods, man was essentially *one*. Proust was equally convinced that he was *many*. His characters are composed in layers or, if one prefers, they are all to some degree multiple personalities. The only way of bringing out this complexity and of dealing with the very real problem of our knowledge of other people was to apply the method of the memoir-writer to his characters. They are constructed by direct observation, by encounters between Marcel and the other characters at different periods of their lives and in different situations, but als ὸ by gossip and hearsay. This enables Proust to present them from a large number of different angles and to show that the same person may

appear completely different to different people. We remember the
incident of Saint-Loup's mistress:

> Suddenly Saint-Loup appeared, accompanied by his mistress, and then,
> in this woman who was for him all the love, every possible delight in life,
> whose personality, mysteriously enshrined in a body as in a tabernacle,
> was the object that still occupied incessantly the toiling imagination of my
> friend, whom he felt that he would never really know, as to whom he was
> perpetually asking himself what could be her secret self, behind the veil of
> eyes and flesh, in this woman I recognized at once 'Rachel when from the
> Lord', her who, but a few years since—women change their position so
> rapidly in that world, when they do change—used to say to the procuress:
> 'To-morrow evening, then, if you want me for anyone, you will send
> round, won't you. . . .'
>
> I realized also then all that the human imagination can put behind a
> little scrap of face, such as this girl's face was, if it is the imagination that
> was the first to know it; and conversely into what wretched elements,
> crudely material and utterly without value, might be decomposed what
> had been the inspiration of countless dreams if, on the contrary, it should
> be so to speak controverted by the slightest actual acquaintance. I saw that
> what had appeared to me to be not worth twenty francs in the house of ill
> fame, where it was then for me simply a woman desirous of earning twenty
> francs, might be worth more than a million, more than one's family, more
> than all the most coveted positions in life if one had begun by imagining
> her to embody a strange creature, interesting to know, difficult to seize
> and to hold. No doubt it was the same thin and narrow face that we saw,
> Robert and I. But we had arrived at it by two opposite ways, between
> which there was no communication, and we should never both see it
> from the same side.

At the end of his Memoirs Saint-Simon describes his book, with the
superb confidence of his century, as a *miroir de vérité* which he could not
publish during the lifetime of his victims because of the 'universal con-
vulsion' which so strong a dose of truth would cause. Proust was always
trying to arrive at 'truth', but it would never have occurred to him to
make the same claim for his book as Saint-Simon. On the contrary, he
is at pains to emphasize that our knowledge of other people is always
relative. In one of his letters he compares his presentation of character
to a town seen from a train. While the train follows its winding track,
the town sometimes appears on our right and sometimes on our left.
In the same way, he says, the different aspects of the same character
will appear like a succession of different people. Such characters, he

adds, will later reveal that they are very different from the people for whom we took them, as often happens in life for that matter.[1] The account of Saint-Loup's mistress shows how closely Proust's practice followed his theories:

> No doubt it was the same thin face that we saw, Robert and I. But we had arrived at it by two opposite ways, between which there was no communication, and we should never both see it from the same side.

This seems to me to be a complete answer to those critics who have claimed that Proust's presentation of character was inconsistent and unconvincing. It is no accident that we often have the impression that we are in a vast room of distorting mirrors which reflect the same person simultaneously from different and often contradictory angles. All of them give us a glimpse of the truth, but none of them the whole truth. In this way Proust subjects us to a series of shocks. We are introduced to Saint-Loup as the sympathetic representative of the old aristocracy, the hero who at once rejoins his old regiment on the outbreak of war only to discover that he either is or has become a rabid homosexual. The effect of this is not merely to emphasize the complexity of human nature and the elusiveness of 'personality', but to introduce a moral relativity. Proust is very careful not to judge his main characters. They simply appear in a series of different guises, some of them creditable, others highly discreditable. The *jeune héros* who eventually dies gloriously on the field of battle is the same man who carries on the nefarious traffic with Morel and visits Charlus' *établissement*.

Proust employs a different method still with Marcel and to a certain extent with Swann. It looks at first like the method of Constant. He is certainly trying to answer the same question as the nineteenth-century novelist: 'What sort of a man am *I*?' But he is also trying to answer a number of still more urgent and still more searching questions: 'What is love?' 'What is jealousy?' 'What is personality?' 'What is time?' 'What is reality?' It is one of the signs of Proust's greatness that his problems are always treated concretely. His analysis of love and jealousy is very profound, but it could never be said of him as it was—mistakenly in my opinion—of Racine and Molière that he dealt with the 'abstract emotions' or that he shows us the Lover and the Jealous Man as generalized figures. For in his novel, the correspondence between the lover and the jealous man and the individual who is in love and is jealous is absolute.

[1] *Letters de Marcel Proust à Bibesco*, p. 175.

5. *The Prisoner*

It will be apparent from what has already been said that Proust's art
is largely subjective. He is constantly telling us of his attempts to reach
la vraie vie and it is a struggle in which all his characters in a greater
or lesser degree are engaged. His work with its arguments, its method
of trial and error, sometimes reminds us a little oddly of Descartes'
doute méthodique, but there is one great difference between the seventeenth-century philospher and the twentieth-century novelist. Descartes'
'doubt' is a means of arriving at a truth which he knows exists; but
from the first Proust makes us doubt the very existence of *la vraie vie*
or, if we do not actually doubt its existence, we certainly doubt whether
it is attainable. For in this world values are necessarily relative to the
person who suffers the experience. Our interest lies less in the goal than
in the pursuit—the *recherche*—and its vicissitudes. The nature of the
struggle is evident from a passage in *Swann*:

> Si mes parents m'avaient permis, quand je lisais un livre, d'aller visiter
> la région qu'il décrivait, j'aurais cru faire un pas inestimable dans la con-
> quête de la vérité. Car si on a la sensation d'être toujours entouré de son
> âme, ce n'est pas comme d'une prison immobile; plutôt on est comme
> emporté avec elle dans un perpétuel élan pour la dépasser, pour atteindre
> à l'extérieur, avec une sorte de découragement, entendant toujours autour
> de soi cette sonorité identique qui n'est pas écho du dehors mais retentisse-
> ment d'une vibration interne.

> [Had my parents allowed me, when I read a book, to pay a visit to che
> country it described, l should have felt that I was making an enormous
> advance towards the ultimate conquest of truth. For even if we have the
> sensation of being always enveloped in, surrounded by our own soul, still
> it does not seem a fixed and immovable prison; rather do we seem to be
> borne away with it, and perpetually struggling to pass beyond it to break,
> out into the world, with a perpetual discouragement as we hear end-
> lessly, all around us, that unvarying sound which is no echo from without,
> but the resonance of a vibration from within.]

This passage explains the peculiar *angoisse* which is always throbbing
just below the surface of Proust's novel. Then, from time to time, it
suddenly, unexpectedly produces an eruption. We feel a note of hope
behind 'la conquête de la vérité' which is at once stifled by 'entouré de
son âme'. It is not a tangible prison from which he can escape; the
prison itself is mobile and just at the moment when his *élan* seems about
to carry him outside the closed circle, when he is on the point of reaching freedom, he hears 'cette sonorité identique' and realizes, with fresh

discouragement, that there is no escape. For the 'echo' is not even a sound from the outside world, but the 'retentissement d'une vibration interne'.

We can begin to appreciate now how closely the two sides of Proust's world are connected. We have already seen that when he describes, or appears to describe, society objectively, the principal characters always turn out to be 'prisoners'—prisoners of a social class, prisoners of the little 'groups' or 'bands' into which they have formed themselves or simply prisoners of their own vices.

The great myth of the nineteenth century was the 'outsider' myth; the great myth of the twentieth century is the myth of the 'prisoner'. The real hero of A la Recherche du temps perdu is the Prisoner. The Prisoner is not Swann or Charlus or even Albertine, but Marcel himself. The heroes of Stendhal are cut off from society by their own exceptional gifts of intelligence and sensibility; but they are always attacking. Julien Sorel disrupts the precarious balance of French society in 1830 and Fabrice del Dongo disorganizes the eighteenth-century political pattern which in the miniature police state of Parma has become rigid and hard. Proust's hero, too, is endowed with exceptional gifts of intelligence and sensibility. He, too, is in a sense an 'outsider', but he is the outsider who failed to make his escape and was trapped in his extraordinary mobile prison. Stendhal's view of life implies a philosophy of action, Proust's a highly personal form of quietism. Marcel does not possess the power of attack which is common to Julien and Fabrice; he is the passive victim who is exposed to almost every conceivable kind of pressure and obsession known to human society. For he is the prisoner not so much of 'clans' and 'groups' as of emotions, habits, of his own sensibility and, ultimately, of time. I think we can add that the symbolical figure who dominates the novel is not simply the Prisoner, but the Artist-Prisoner who after many false starts and misfortunes comes to see that the only hope of escape lies in his 'vocation'. That is why Proust's withdrawal from the world to meditate on time and memory stamps him as the twentieth-century artist.

M. Maurice Muller has described the book with felicity as

This psychological comedy in which the characters are Love, Jealousy, Falsehood, Habit, Forgetting, Memory which are incarnate in a being who is very much alive, the narrator—a comedy which is subject to laws which are subtle, but implacable. . . .[1]

[1] De Descartes à Marcel Proust (Collection 'Être et Penser'), (second edition, Neuchâtel, 1947), p. 63.

The main drama is of course the Prisoner's attempts to escape from himself, from a prison which seems to have no exit, to attain a truth which will make him free. Now inside this main drama there is a series of 'psychological comedies' which are endlessly repeated. They are played out between M. Muller's six characters who assume the proportions of obsessions. When Proust tells us that what is dangerous in love 'is not the woman but the habit', we know that we are witnessing the scene between Love and Habit which merges into the scene between Love and Forgetting or Love and Memory. Then there is a sudden switch:

> L'amour n'est provoqué que par le mensonge et consiste seulement dans le besoin de voir nos souffrances apaisées par l'être qui nous a fait souffrir.

> [Love is provoked only by falsehood, and consists merely in our need to see our sufferings appeased by the person who has made us suffer.]

The tension always rises steeply in the scenes between Love and Falsehood. For Falsehood is one of the principal characters in the novel.

It has been pointed out that Proust displayed a particular interest in doctors, diplomats and servants. His interest is very understandable. They are people who are obliged to adopt a professional attitude, are constantly telling 'diplomatic lies'. They therefore become for the novelist incarnations of Falsehood. Then we gradually realize that social relations are simply 'a tissue of lies'. Falsehood exists at different levels, appearing sometimes as a series of concentric circles and at others as the mental obstacle which hinders the search for 'truth' and maintains *angoisse*. The doctors, diplomats and servants are minor characters in Proust's comedy. They underline the main theme and give Marcel an opportunity of studying their 'technique' so that he will have a better chance of catching his mistress out. Charlus plays many roles, but in this particular context he represents the Lie at a rather higher level than the 'professional liars'. His whole life has become an elaborate lie in order to conceal his sexual aberrations and he provides Marcel with a still better example of the way in which the liar goes about his business. At the centre of the circle stands Albertine. We suspect that the whole of her life, too, is a lie and that she is trying to conceal the same anomaly as Charlus. The drama now becomes much more complex. Jealousy enters the scene. In his endeavours to discover whether Albertine was or was not a Lesbian, Marcel himself is driven to lying; and we find in the end that he is playing a sort of triple role: *Amour—Jalousie—Mensonge*. This is the point at which the drama reaches its maximum intensity.

When we look back to the sentence on lies—

L'amour n'est provoqué que par le mensonge et consiste seulement dans le besoin de voir nos souffrances apaisées par l'être qui nous a fait souffrir.

we are aware of the vicious circle. Love is aroused by a falsehood. It can only be assuaged by the person who aroused it, but the person who aroused it is Falsehood. There is no way out. The most that we can hope for is one of those comfortable sayings in which Proust's work abounds. 'L'amour est un mal inguérissable.' The best moments in love contain 'la possibilité insoupçonnée du désastre'.

It is not difficult to see the bearing of this on human relations as a whole. It is commonly assumed or believed that when two people 'fall in love' they suddenly become aware of one another's personality in a new way, discover something in the personality of the loved one which is not apparent to others and makes him or her particularly sympathetic, becomes the foundation of a lifelong attachment. Now Proust's psychology is a reversal of the traditional view. You do not get to know a person to see whether you love her; you love her in order to get to know her or, to use a term which conveys Proust's double purpose, to 'possess' her. We are told, for example, of the relations between Swann and Odette that she was

Plus désireuse peut-être de connaître ce qu'il était que désireuse d'être sa maîtresse.

[More desirous perhaps to know what sort of man he was than desirous to be his mistress.]

According to this conception, love is one of the ways of trying to break out of 'prison', to reach 'truth' or to still the *angoisse* which continually afflicts you. It is naturally fraught with every kind of difficulty. It is difficult to know all those different beings who are collectively labelled 'Odette' or 'Albertine'; a profound scepticism makes you doubt whether you can ever really get to know another human being at all even if there is goodwill on both sides. Goodwill is naturally extremely rare in a world of 'lies'. You are almost certain to have a rival. Your mistress is probably a Lesbian or has spent her youth in a brothel or has some other shameful secret to conceal. At this point the comedy of Love and Falsehood turns to tragedy.

It is now possible to go on to examine in more detail Proust's conception of love and personality.

6. L'Amour

'For the medieval author of *Tristan et Iseult*,' said Ortega y Gasset, 'love is a sentiment which possesses a sharp profile. For the primitive exponent of the psychological novel, love is love and nothing more. Proust, on the contrary, describes a love affair of Swann's which is completely without the form of love. . . . Only one thing is lacking— love.

'No doubt', he goes on, 'Proust belongs to the lineage of Stendhal, "the investigator of the human heart"; but while for Stendhal the human heart is a solid body with plastic and rigid lines, for Proust it is a diffused vapour which varies from one moment to another with meteorological versatility.'[1]

It is impossible in writing of Proust to avoid the word 'love', but one cannot use it without a sense of misgiving, without feeling that some other expression like 'sexual connection' would be more accurate. Proust employs it as a blanket term to describe an emotional situation, or better an emotional equation, which is capable of almost endless variations. Its only resemblance to traditional love seems at first to lie in the fact that two people are necessary, but we shall see that even this is an exaggeration.

Proust has been criticized by conservative writers for destroying the unity of personality. I have shown that his conception of personality was largely determined by historical changes, but though history can explain, it cannot justify. The only justification is artistic. He shared Laforgue's hostility to *l'homme absolu* which he would have regarded as an abstract intellectual construction; he would have approved of the substitution of *innombrables claviers humains*; but he did not intend any more than Laforgue to launch a frivolous attack on the unity of the human person. On the contrary, his work is a plea for a more profound conception of the self which would give him a better chance of reaching the elusive *vraie vie* and revealing its mysteries. It is one of his great merits that he avoided the mistake of the nineteenth-century novelists who achieved a specious unity by 'imagining the moral qualities of their characters before the characters themselves'. Yet, ironically, his determination to be absolutely honest and not to be deceived by appearances led to the tragic discovery that he was pursuing a chimera.

[1] *Hommage à Marcel Proust*, pp. 293, 294.

The fascination and horror of his love affairs depends, indeed, on the reduction of 'the human heart' to 'a diffused vapour which varies from one moment to another with meteorological versatility':[1]

[... notre amour, notre jalousie ... se composent d'une infinité d'amours successifs, de jalousies différentes et qui sont éphémères, mais par leur multitude uninterrompue, donnent l'impression de la continuité, l'illusion de l'unité.

[... our love, our jealousy ... are composed of an infinity of successive loves, of different jealousies, each of which is ephemeral, although by their uninterrupted multitude they give us the impression of continuity, the illusion of unity.]

It follows that if the continuity and unity of emotion is an illusion, the unity of the person who suffers the emotion must be an illusion too:

Je n'étais pas un seul homme, mais le défilé heure par heure d'une armée compacte où il y avait selon le moment des passionnés, des indifférents, des jaloux—des jaloux dont pas un n'était jaloux de la même femme.

[I was not one man only, but the steady advance hour after hour of an army in close formation, in which there appeared, according to the moment, impassioned men, indifferent men, jealous men—jealous men no two of whom were jealous of the same woman.]

They are not 'jealous of the same woman' because she is nothing but a figment of the imagination:

C'est la terrible tromperie de l'amour qu'il commence par nous faire jouer avec une femme non du monde extérieur, mais avec une poupée intérieure à notre cerveau, la seule d'ailleurs que nous ayons toujours à notre disposition, la seule que nous posséderons, que l'arbitraire du souvenir, presque aussi absolu que celui de l'imagination, peut avoir fait aussi différente de la femme réelle, que du Balbec réel avait été pour moi le Balbec rêvé; création factice à laquelle, peu à peu pour notre souffrance, nous forcerons la femme réelle, à ressembler.

[It is the terrible deception of love that it begins by engaging us in play not with a woman of the external world but with a puppet fashioned and

---

[1] I naturally do not include Senor Ortega y Gasset among 'conservative' writers. For an interesting criticism from a philosophical point of view of Proust's conception of personality, see Fernandez, *Messages* (Paris, 1926), pp. 147-69.

kept in our brain, the only form of her moreover that we have always at
our disposal, the only one that we shall ever possess, one which the
arbitrary power of memory, almost as absolute as that of imagination,
may have made as different from the real woman as had been from the
real Balbec the Balbec of my dreams; an artificial creation to which by
degrees, and to our own hurt, we shall force the real woman into resemblance.]

Here is the explanation:

C'est que cette femme n'a fait que susciter par des sortes d'appels
magiques mille éléments de tendresse existant en nous à l'état fragmentaire
et qu'elle a assemblés, unis, effaçant toute cassure entre eux, c'est nous-
mêmes qui en lui donnant ses traits avons fourni toute la matière solide de
la personne aimée.

[The truth is that the woman has only raised to life by a sort of magic
spell a thousand elements of affection existing in us already in a fragmentary state, which she has assembled, joined together, bridging every
gap between them, it is ourself who by giving her her features have
supplied all the solid matter of the beloved object.]

The result of this view of personality is that love can only end in
disaster, in the sudden shattering discovery that behind the innumerable
illusions which it creates there is nothing but the void. Thus, in a
sentence which gives the heart of his experience, Proust speaks of

L'acte de possession physique—où d'ailleurs l'on ne possède rien.

[The act of physical possession (in which, paradoxically, the possessor
possesses nothing).]

He speaks in another place of 'le caractère purement subjectif du
phénomène qu'est l'amour'. It is clearly inaccurate even to use the
expression 'sexual connection' in writing of Proust because all his
characters fail to 'connect':

Les liens entre un être et nous n'existent que dans notre pensée.

[The bonds that unite another person to ourself exist only in our mind.]

There is no direct contact between the lovers; they never do succeed
in knowing one another. The beloved is nothing but *une poupée*

intérieure, the exteriorization of our own personal needs and desires which we contrive to graft on to a completely anonymous being. We like to imagine that love is an exclusive attachment for a particular woman, but we realize that

Bien souvent un amour n'est que l'association d'une image de jeune fille (qui sans cela nous eût été vite insupportable) avec les battements de cœur inséparables d'une attente interminable, vaine, et d'un 'lapin' que la demoiselle nous a posé.

[As often as not love is nothing more than the association of the face of a girl (whom otherwise we should soon have found intolerable) with the heartbeats inseparable from an endless, vain expectation, and from some trick that she has played upon us.]

The anonymity of the beloved is constantly underlined:

Quand on aime l'amour est trop grand pour pouvoir être contenu tout entier en nous; il irradie vers la personne aimée, rencontre en elle une surface qui l'arrête, le force à revenir vers son point de départ et c'est ce choc en retour de notre propre tendresse que nous appelons les sentiments de l'autre et qui nous charme plus qu'à l'aller, parce que nous ne connaissons pas qu'elle vient de nous.

[When we are in love, our love is too big a thing for us to be able altogether to contain it within us. It radiates towards the beloved object, finds in her a surface which arrests it, forcing it to return to its starting-point, and it is this shock of the repercussion of our own affection which we call the other's regard for ourselves, and which pleases us more then than on its outward journey because we do not recognize it as having originated in ourselves.]

We engage in the pursuit of an *amour exclusif*, but the beloved is not a person who satisfies the same needs and desires. She is a 'surface' which refracts our own *tendresse* as another surface might refract the light. The Prisoner is a psychological hermaphrodite trying in vain to 'possess' himself.

What we call 'love' is simply a hideous, sickening see-saw between states of 'joy' and 'suffering'. He speaks of 'l'amour et la souffrance qui fait un avec lui'.

Again:

En réalité, dans l'amour il y a une souffrance permanente, que la joie neutralise, rend virtuelle, ajourne, mais qui peut à tout moment devenir ce qu'elle serait depuis longtemps si l'on n'avait pas obtenu ce qu'on souhaitait, atroce.

[Actually, there is in love a permanent strain of suffering which happiness neutralizes, makes conditional only, procrastinates, but which may at any moment become what it would long since have been had we not obtained what we were seeking, sheer agony.]

For Proust therefore love can only mean *l'amour-maladie* and he analyses it in an extraordinary passage on Swann's attitude towards Odette:

. . . cette maladie qu'était l'amour de Swann avait tellement multiplié, il était si étroitement mêlé à toutes les habitudes de Swann, à tous ses actes, à sa pensée, à sa santé, à son sommeil, à sa vie, même à ce qu'il désirait pour après sa mort; il ne faisait tellement plus qu'un avec lui, qu'on n'aurait pas pu l'arracher de lui, sans le détruire lui-même à peu près tout entier: comme on dit en chirurgie, son amour n'était plus opérable.

[. . . this malady, which was Swann's love, had so far multiplied, was so closely interwoven with all his habits, with all his actions, with his thoughts, his health, his sleep, his life, even with what he hoped for after his death, was so entirely one with him that it would have been impossible to wrest it away without almost entirely destroying him; as surgeons say, his case was past operation.]

When at length his love dies and Swann quietly marries the mistress for whom he no longer cares to give a name to their child, this is his comment on it to himself:

Dire que j'ai gâché des années de ma vie, que j'ai voulu mourir, que j'ai eu mon plus grand amour pour une femme qui ne me plaisait pas, qui n'était pas mon genre!

[To think that I have wasted years of my life, that I have longed for death, that the greatest love that I have ever known has been for a woman who did not please me, who was not in my style!]

The truth is that his characters cannot do without love; it is the one absorbing activity of their lives, the one thing which enables them to focus this activity and which gives an appearance of unity to their personality; but once they indulge in it, they are doomed to destruction—the victims of 'un mal inguérissable' '[qui n'est] plus opérable'.

While the story of Swann in love has been generally admired in Anglo-Saxon countries, Marcel's affair with Albertine has been decidedly less popular. It looks at first like a repetition of Swann's story in which the experience is analysed in much greater detail and is much more intensely felt. In a sense this is true, but only in a sense. The difference between Swann and Marcel is not simply a difference of degree, but a difference of kind. For, writes M. Feuillerat,

Instead of the regular movements of a pendulum which accompany the anguish of a Swann or a Saint-Loup, in the case of the narrator the alternatives are complicated by a multitude of secondary movements which are themselves regulated by a contradiction. . . . So that the movements which distinguish the principal oscillations almost always subdivide producing a new play of opposites from which will emerge in turn fresh alternatives.[1]

The greater part of the account of Marcel's affair with Albertine is written in what M. Feuillerat calls Proust's 'second manner'. In place of the comparatively straightforward style of *Swann*, the analysis of almost every mood is accompanied by an elaborate disquisition on the nature of sexual passion. One could, observes M. Feuillerat, construct a whole *Art of Love* out of the passages in which the narrator, who is supposed to be a naive and inexperienced man, skilfully analyses the feelings that he experiences for Albertine. We only need to turn up the word *amour* in M. Celly's fascinating compendium to appreciate the truth of this observation.[2] It would indeed be possible to construct an *Art of Love* which would make some of the classic moralists look like children.

No people have displayed more diligence and more ingenuity than the French in analysing, classifying and labelling the different kinds and degrees of sexual passion. What is fascinating in the story of Albertine is not the account of Marcel falling in love with her, but the account of his falling out of love or what a French writer has lately called *le désamour*. The story is also a horrifying one. What is horrifying to many Anglo-Saxon readers is the fact that he is on his own admission 'l'artisan volontaire, impitoyable et patient' of his own grief. For he does not discover suddenly that he no longer cares for either Gilberte or Albertine. He makes a conscious and deliberate attempt to wreck his own happiness and he describes it with a clairvoyance which is worthy of the greatest French writers.

[1] *Op. cit.*, p. 119.
[2] *Répertoire des thèmes de Marcel Proust* (Les Cahiers Marcel Proust, 7), Paris, 1935.

'La jalousie,' said La Rochefoucauld, 'naît toujours avec l'amour; elle ne meurt pas toujours avec lui.' Jealousy is a *maladie des sentiments*. The discovery that it may survive the emotion on which it is founded is not new. What is new in Proust is to have shown the extent to which the *sentiment* can become engulfed in the *maladie* and the extraordinary way in which the *maladie* can survive the total destruction of the *sentiment*. We are told of Swann that

> Il était depuis longtemps insoucieux qu'Odette l'eût trompé et le trompât encore. Et pourtant il avait continué pendant quelques années à rechercher d'anciens domestiques d'Odette, tant avait persisté chez lui la douloureuse curiosité de savoir si ce jour-là, tellement ancien, à six heures, Odette était couchée avec Forcheville.

> [For a long time now it had made no matter to him that Odette had been false to him, and was false still. And yet he had continued for some years to seek out old servants of Odette, so strongly in him persisted the painful curiosity to know whether on that day, so long ago, at six o'clock, Odette had been in bed with Forcheville.]

The emotional life is composed of strands of feeling which one by one come undone and disappear. Swann has grown 'indifferent' to Odette and her unfaithfulness, but one spot in his personality still remains painfully *sensible*—his desire to know whether at a certain hour on a certain day many years ago she was or was not in bed with the boring Forcheville. It is a remarkable description of the way in which Swann's love has disintegrated, but it is simple compared with the startling aphorism which he introduces into the account of his liaison with Albertine:

> On n'a pas besoin d'être deux, il suffit d'être seul dans sa chambre, à penser, pour que de nouvelles trahisons de votre maîtresse se produisent, fût-elle morte.

> [We have no need of her company, it is enough to be alone in our room, thinking, for fresh betrayal of us by our mistress to come to light, even though she be dead.]

We can see now why it is an exaggeration to say that the existence of two people, of the couple, is necessary to Proust's conception of love. The different characters in the 'psychological comedy' may very well be played by a single performer, or rather the drama takes place between the solitary protagonist and the phantoms which haunt his own mind.

Proust's revelation depends on the existence of a mind which was preoccupied with its own workings to an extent that is almost undreamed of in the textbooks of the professors. He distinguished between 'notre moi permanent qui se prolonge pendant toute la durée de notre vie' and what he calls 'nos moi successifs qui en somme le composent en partie'. The *moi successifs* look at first like a succession of moods, but that is not what he meant. It is obvious that man is a person, that there is in him some principle of identity which corresponds to Descartes' 'thinking substance'; but round this *moi permanent* Proust groups the subsidiary *moi*. They are not moods; they are the different people that I have been at different moments of my life. It is here that Proust's theory of memory plays its part. The incident of the *madeleine* shows that memory is not something which I recall and which I see as belonging to the past. It is essentially a recreation of the past and a logical part of Proust's conception of time. Instead of simply surviving as memories, the people that I have been at different periods of my career come to life again and take on an independent existence of their own. The *moi permanent* is the core round which they are grouped. When my mistress abandons me, my *chagrin* is not simply heightened by a memory of a night spent with her at Balbec, a walk in the Luxembourg or the time when she was my 'prisoner' at my parents' flat. The person I was at each of those moments is resurrected in me as a separate being which intensifies my present suffering:

> . . . ainsi à chaque instant, il y avait quelqu'un des innombrables et humbles 'moi' qui nous composent qui était ignorant encore du départ d'Albertine et à qui il fallait le notifier; il fallait—ce qui était plus cruel que s'ils avaient été des étrangers et n'avaient pas emprunté ma sensibilité pour souffrir,—annoncer le malheur qui venait d'arriver à tous ces êtres, à tous ces 'moi' qui ne le savaient pas encore. . . .

> [. . . thus, at every moment there was one more of those innumerable and humble 'selves' that compose our personality which was still unaware of Albertine's departure and must be informed of it; I was obliged—and this was more cruel than if they had been strangers and had not borrowed my sensibility to pain—to describe to all these 'selves' who did not yet know of it, the calamity that had just occurred. . . .]

It is apparent from this that instead of providing the unity which he sought, the *moi permanent* is simply a precarious position which is continually undermined by the painful experiences of the *moi successifs*.

o

It is of the essence of Proust's experience that there is no absolute discontinuity between the events of the external world and those of the mental world. It is rather as though life were developing on parallel lines on either side of a partition:

> Pour que la mort d'Albertine eût pu supprimer mes souffrances, il eût fallu que le choc l'eût tuée non sulement en Touraine, mais en moi. Jamais elle n'y avait été plus vivante.

[For the death of Albertine to be able to suppress my suffering, the shock of the fall would have had to kill her not only in Touraine but in myself. There, never had she been more alive.]

These two sentences bring out the full horror of the Prisoner alone with his obsessions. For not even the destruction of the cause or the apparent cause of his obsession can release him from it. The passage goes on:

> Pour entrer en nous, un être a été obligé de prendre la forme, de se plier au cadre du temps; ne nous apparaissant que par minutes successives, il n'a jamais pu nous livrer de lui qu'un seul aspect à la fois, nous débiter de lui qu'une seule photographie. Grande faiblesse sans doute pour un être de consister en une simple collection de moments; grande force aussi; il relève de la mémoire, et la mémoire d'un moment n'est pas instruite de tout ce qui s'est passé depuis; ce moment qu'elle a enregistré dure encore, vit encore et avec lui l'être qui s'y profilait. Et puis cet émiettement ne fait pas seulement vivre la morte, il la multiplie. Pour me consoler ce n'est pas une, ce sont d'innombrables Albertine que j'aurais dû oublier. Quand j'étais arrivé à supporter le chagrin d'avoir perdu celle-ci, c'était à recommencer avec une autre, avec cent autres.

[In order to enter into us, another person must first have assumed the form, have entered into the surroundings of the moment; appearing to us only in a succession of momentary flashes, he has never been able to furnish us with more than one aspect of himself at a time, to present us with more than a single photograph of himself. A great weakness, no doubt, for a person to consist merely in a collection of moments; a great strength also: it is dependent upon memory, and our memory of a moment is not informed of everything that has happened since; this moment which it has registered endures still, lives still, and with it the person whose form is outlined in it. And moreover, this disintegration does not only make the dead man live, it multiplies him. To find consolation, it was not one, it was innumerable Albertines that I must first forget. When I had reached the stage of enduring the grief of losing this Albertine, I must begin afresh with another, with a hundred others.]

As the story of Albertine unfolds, we notice that certain words are constantly recurring: *moral, multiplier, innombrable, souffrance.*

La souffrance, prolongement d'un choc *moral* imposé, aspire à changer de forme; on espère la volatiliser en faisant des projets, en demandant des renseignements; on veut qu'elle passe par ses *innombrables* métamorphoses, cela demande moins de courage que de garder sa *souffrance* franche; ce lit paraît si étroit, si dur, si froid où l'on se couche avec sa douleur.

La complexité de mon amour, de ma personne, *multipliait,* diversifiait mes *souffrances.* Pourtant elles pouvaient se ranger toujours sous les deux groupes dont l'alternative avait fait toute la vie de mon amour pour Albertine, tour à tour livré à la confiance et au soupçon jaloux.

Même dans mon amour l'état changeant de mon atmosphère *morale,* la pression modifiée de mes croyances n'avaient-ils[1] pas tel jour diminué la visibilité de mon propre amour, ne l'avaient-ils pas tel jour indéfiniment étendue, tel jour embellie jusqu'au sourire, tel jour contractée jusqu'à l'orage?

[Suffering, the prolongation of a spiritual shock that has come from without, keeps on endeavouring to change its form; we hope to be able to dispel it by making plans, by seeking information; we wish it to pass through its countless metamorphoses, this requires less courage than retaining our suffering intact; the bed appears so narrow, hard and cold on which we lie down with our grief.

The complexity of my love, of my person, multiplied, diversified my sufferings. And yet they could always be ranged in the two categories, the option between which had made up the whole life of my love for Albertine, swayed alternately by trust and by a jealous suspicion.

Even in my love, had not the changing state of my moral atmosphere, the varying pressure of my beliefs, had they not one day diminished the visibility of the love that I was feeling, had they not another day extended it beyond all bounds, one day softened it to a smile, another day condensed it to a storm?]

The French have always used the word *moral* in a wider sense than its literal English equivalent, but in these passages Proust seems to me to introduce a fresh nuance. The term is emptied of its ethical content

[1] He is referring to *désirs* mentioned earlier in the passage.

and assumes a purely quantitative significance. A *cruelle souffrance morale* is nothing but a very intense form of suffering and we can see how it is reinforced by the words *multiplier* and *innombrable*.[1]

In another place he remarks of Albertine's suspected infidelities at a time when she was still living with him:

> Mais je ne voulais ni faire de la peine, ni me fatiguer, ni entrer dans la voie terrible des investigations, de la surveillance multiforme, innombrable.

> [But I had no desire either to give pain to another, or to tire myself, or ⟨to⟩ enter upon the terrible course of investigation, of multiform, unending vigilance.]

The focal words are again *multiforme* and *innombrable*. For the physical acts of spying and investigation defeat their own ends. They intensify instead of removing the suffering because they are of their essence disruptive. They lead to an extension of the area of suffering and ultimately to the dispersal of the suffering personality which makes action unthinkable. This becomes evident when, after Albertine's death, Marcel has inquiries made about her both at Balbec and in Touraine. The report of her activities at the *établissement de bains* at Balbec slinking through the grey dawn with an unknown woman friend and her adventure with the *petite blanchisseuse* in Touraine assumes a nightmare quality; and her words to the washer-girl—'Tu me mets aux anges'—echo hollowly in the 'prison' that he has built himself. The extreme state of dissolution to which he is reduced is well illustrated by another passage:

> . . . le spécifique pour guérir un événement malheureux . . . c'est une décision; car elle a pour effet par un brusque renversement de nos pensées, d'interrompre le flux de celles qui viennent de l'événement passé et prolongent la vibration, de le briser par le flux inverse de pensées inverses, venu du dehors, de l'avenir.

> [. . . the specific remedy for an unfortunate event . . . is a decision; for its effect is that, by a sudden reversal of our thoughts, it interrupts the flow of those that come from the past event and prolong its vibration, and breaks that flow with a contrary flow of contrary thoughts, come from without, from the future.]

[1] 'Mais, réveillant les sentiments d'attente jadis éprouvés à propos d'autres jeunes filles, surtout de Gilberte, quand elle tardait à venir, la privation d'un simple plaisir physique me causait une cruelle souffrance morale.'

But all his 'decisions' remain subjective events which never issue in action; the result is no more than a collision between two impulses coming from different directions.

The words *souffrance* and *angoisse*, which are continually recurring in the later volumes of the novel, are of particular interest. Proust possessed an extremely subtle intelligence and a wide knowledge of life, but the more we study him the more evident it becomes that, compared with his intelligence, his sensibility was curiously limited. I have said that for Proust love was an emotional equation which was capable of almost endless variations, but the truth is that though some of the factors are capable of variation, there is one which is common to all the permutations. It is not simply that *souffrance* is the constant factor; it is always *the final term in the emotional equation*. When he writes:

> L'amour suivant une technique infaillible resserre pour nous d'un mouvement alterné l'engrenage dans lequel on ne peut plus ni ne pas aimer, ni être aimé.

> [Love, following an unvarying procedure, sets going with an alternating movement the machinery in which one can no longer either refrain from loving or be loved.]

the words *infaillible*, *resserre* and *engrenage* convey an oppressive sensation of someone caught in a remorseless machine and being slowly crushed by the *mouvement alterné*. But it would be perfectly possible to rewrite the sentence, vary the terms and still preserve the *souffrance* that we experience:

> L'amour suivant une technique infaillible resserre pour nous d'un mouvement alterné l'engrenage dans lequel on ne peut plus *aimer ni oublier*.

Instead of being caught in the alternating movement of 'no longer able not to love or be loved', the victim is 'no longer able to love or forget'. The answer is still *souffrance*; and this suffering nearly always contains a strong element of self-pity. These limitations in Proust's sensibility explain the extraordinary monotony of parts of his novel. The mind is continually surprised and delighted by the skill with which he varies the initial term of his equation, but there is something very exhausting about the way in which the emotional pressure always falls in the same place.

Proust's strength and weakness, however, are virtually inseparable. We are told of an elderly Jewish homosexual:

Il aimait d'ailleurs tout le labyrinthe de couloirs, de cabinets secrets, de salons, de vestiaires, de garde-mangers, de galeries qu'était l'hôtel de Balbec. Par atavisme d'oriental il aimait les sérails et quand il sortait le soir, on le voyait en explorer furtivement les détours.

[He loved moreover all the labyrinth of corridors, private offices, reception rooms, cloakrooms, larders, galleries which composed the hotel at Balbec. With a strain of Oriental atavism he loved a seraglio, and when he went out at night might be seen furtively exploring its purlieus.]

This description of the fascination of the winding corridors and secret rooms of the old-fashioned hotel corresponds closely to Proust's conception of the mind. For Proust the mind is indeed a labyrinth where the Prisoner is condemned to wander unceasingly, pursuing his phantoms and looking for an outlet which does not exist. The longer he spends there, the more thoroughly he explores the galleries of the labyrinth, the more desperate his position and the more terrifying his obsessions become:

J'étais torturé par l'incessante reprise du désir toujours plus anxieux, et jamais accompli, d'un bruit d'appel; arrivé au point culminant d'une ascension tourmentée—dans les spirales de mon angoisse solitaire. . . .

[I was tortured by the incessant recurrence of my longing, ever more anxious and never to be gratified, for the sound of a call; arrived at the culminating point of a tortuous ascent through the coils of my lonely anguish. . . .]

It is a perfect example of the 'spiral movement' of the latter part of the novel. We are aware of the Prisoner's progressive withdrawal further and further into his 'prison' until in a passage like this we have an almost frightening sense of mental claustrophobia. Proust's strength and weakness are inseparable because the sense of revolving more and more rapidly in a smaller and smaller physical space is only made possible by his very acute and very limited sensibility.

It will be remembered that in the fairy-tale of the Prince and the Sleeping Beauty it is the 'outsider' who sets the 'prisoner' free. There is nothing of the sort in Proust. In his first chapter he describes the lantern slide showing the sinister figure of Golo advancing towards the Princess's castle. In the last chapter he evokes the same image; but Golo is still in the same place outside the castle, a symbol of the terrors which haunt the Prisoner's mind, of the hallucinations which he is incapable of exorcizing.

'This part of *A la Recherche du temps perdu*', writes M. Feuillerat of the affair between Marcel and Albertine, 'is the richest and most tormented love story in literature.'[1] It deserves the praise that he gives it, but as usual there is a reservation to be made. Ortega y Gasset's comment applies even more forcibly to Marcel than to Swann. 'Only one thing is lacking—love.' For Marcel's 'love' is purely cerebral. He describes Albertine somewhere as *un être de fuite*, and this puts the matter very neatly. The characters remind us of beings on opposite sides of a glass partition. They are continually moving desperately towards one another, flattening their faces longingly against the glass, trying frantically to 'connect'. For just as they are unable to enter into one another's minds, so there is no physical contact between them, no warmth, no kindliness, no satisfaction. The mental isolation—the impossibility of really knowing the woman whom we imagine that we love—is accompanied by a shattering physical isolation.[2]

Would Albertine have come back to him? Did she go away because he did not see that she was a *jeune fille à marier*, did not offer her the one chance of escape from her vice? Was he or was he not responsible for her suicide? They are questions to which he can find no answer.

> Rapprochant la mort de ma grand'mère et celle d'Albertine, il me semblait que ma vie était souillée d'un double assassinat.

Weighed down by guilt, he collapses and goes away from Paris to 'forget'.

When, some years later, he emerges from his retirement, it is to find that all at once the world he knew has grown old and that he too is an old man. Albertine is at last 'forgotten'. He turns his attention to his novel. We remember that 'the last chapter of the last volume was written immediately after the first chapter of the first volume'. When we take leave of Marcel he is about to sit down and write the novel which we have just read. He has explained the theory on which it is based and his one fear seems to be that he may die before the book is written, that he may like Swann disappear into 'lost time'.

It is probable that Proust himself was haunted by the fear of dying before he had time to finish his novel, but Marcel's fear does not arise solely from the fact that death may deprive the world of a masterpiece.

[1] *Op. cit.*, p. 217.
[2] 'Il se passait entre Albertine et moi la chose suivante (j'entends la chose vue par moi, de mon côté du verre qui n'était nullement transparent et sans que je puisse savoir ce qu'il y avait de vrai de l'autre côté). . . .'

I have spoken of the part played by the actual writing of the novel in the artist's experience. I think that we can now go on to say that in this world the act of writing possesses a moral function. Art is the Prisoner's one chance of escape, the one chance of 'exorcizing his hallucinations'. Redemption lies in transmuting his experience—his guilty experience —into timeless art; it is his way of making amends to the *mère profanée* as Mlle Vinteuil's friend makes amends to the *père profané* by establishing the text of his unpublished works which would otherwise have been lost to the world.

The aim of the final volume is therefore to explain how 'lost time' is transformed into 'time regained'. It is scarcely an exaggeration to say that the novelist introduces a new 'hero' in the closing pages. This hero is *le Temps retrouvé* which is invested with a capital letter. The final paragraph is one of Proust's outstanding achievements as a master of French prose:

> Si du moins il m'était laissé assez de temps pour accomplir mon œuvre, je ne manquerais pas de la marquer au seau de ce Temps dont l'idée s'imposait à moi avec tant de force aujourd'hui, et j'y décrirais les hommes, cela dût-il les faire ressembler à des êtres monstrueux, comme occupant dans le Temps une place autrement considérable que celle si restreinte qui leur est réservée dans l'espace, une place, au contraire, prolongée sans mesure, puisqu'ils touchent simultanément, comme des géants, plongés dans les années, à des époques vécues par eux, si distantes,—entre lesquelles tant de jours sont venus se placer—dans le Temps.

> [If at least, time enough were allotted to me to accomplish my work, I would not fail to mark it with the seal of Time, the idea of which imposed itself upon me with so much force to-day, and I would therein describe men, if need be, as monsters occupying a place in Time infinitely more important than the restricted one reserved for them in space, a place, on the contrary, prolonged immeasurably since, simultaneously touching widely separated years and the distant periods they have lived through— between which so many days have ranged themselves—they stand like giants immersed in Time.]

The word 'time' occurs in the opening sentence of the novel and we hear it all through the book, now softly and now more loudly; but in the closing paragraph—the climax of the whole novel—it sounds like a great bell; a bell warning the writer that his end is drawing near, but at the same moment transfiguring events, giving them an importance outside the petty 'time' of everyday experience and placing them in the eternal Time which transcends time. The passage begins gently reminding us of an invocation or a prayer addressed to 'Time' to spare him and closes with the final chord—the final chord of the 'symphony' which began at Combray—*dans le Temps*. And the sound reverberates in the mind long after we have shut the book.

That at any rate seems to have been Proust's intention, but we must not be misled by his consummate virtuosity. His theory of time and art is very fascinating, but in spite of its immense psychological interest, *Le Temps retrouvé* is something of a tour de force. Marcel was overcome with guilt, was horrified by a life 'souillée d'un double assassinat'. He felt the need to make reparation even if it were only to a false god; he tries to invest his experience with some transcendental significance in order to remove the *souillure* and resorts to a sleight of hand. We are grateful for the new vision, for his psychological revelation and for what is undoubtedly a very great achievement; but we do not need to accept this personal profession of faith. The conflict between art and life, the spiritual and 'counter-spirituality', and the conception of the artist as prisoner are a restatement of a perennial problem. The contemporary artist is necessarily a prisoner who attempts to transform the *données* of the actual world and his success does not depend on 'escape', still less on the highly personal interpretation which Proust appears to impose on experience in this last volume. His apotheosis therefore remains the final, dramatic attempt of the Prisoner to escape. And it fails.

IV. STYLE

'THE long sentences with their hesitations and parentheses', writes Mr. Bernard Wall, 'expressed the nerves and sensitiveness of the writer travelling back through the corridors of memory. . . . Proust adapted and strained conventional French syntax but he in no way tampered with words or endeavoured to become more "vivid" by being less refined. . . . He did not struggle against this limitation or endeavour to introduce vitality by exploring the possibility of slang and dialects. In this way he was unlike Joyce: the effect he wished to give was not vitality.'[1]

It is an interesting comment, but I am not sure that it is entirely fair to Proust. He was both traditional and an innovator, but his strength and his limitations were essentially French. It is not altogether true to say that he did not explore the possibilities of slang and dialects. One of his more interesting innovations was precisely the study of the manner of speech not merely of servants, but of people like Brichot and Norpois whose language belongs to a particular stratum of society or a particular calling; and their peculiarities are related to the classical background of which we are always aware in the novel and which serves as a standard by which the present is measured. It remains true, however, that the distinctive feature of his style was its syntax. It was moulded to the experience which he had to communicate; it set the whole tone of the novel and it was admirably designed to reflect Proust's strange patterns of feeling and his still stranger obsessions. In this he was simply running true to form. The early work of Laforgue and to a certain extent of Rimbaud contains a great deal of verbal experiment, but the French language does not lend itself to the invention of words to the same degree that English does. Laforgue and Rimbaud abandoned most of their verbal experiments in their later and more mature work which is based like Proust's on modifications of traditional syntax and on originality of imagery.

The importance of imagery must not be underrated. Mr. Eliot has suggested that there is a parallel between the conceits of the English Metaphysical Poets and the French Symbolists, but his hints have not

---

[1] *These Changing Years* (London, 1947), p. 35.

been followed up. The Metaphysicals were preceded by Lyly and the Euphuists. Euphuism was simply a form of preciosity. It was not of great intrinsic importance, but its very exuberance did act as a liberation. It encouraged later writers to go into unexpected places in their search for images which would give a more exact expression to the complex feelings which they were trying to convey. I do not want to suggest that the English Metaphysicals had any influence on the Symbolists which would clearly be absurd, but it is evident that there was a parallel between the situations in which they found themselves and the methods which they chose to solve their artistic problems.[1] The seventeenth century and the nineteenth century were both periods in which civilization was undergoing revolutionary changes. The poets had to translate fresh experiences into words and they succeeded in establishing relations between different spheres of experience where before them there had seemed to be no relation.

> ... the truth [said Proust] will only begin to emerge from the moment that the writer takes two different objects, posits their relationship, the analogue in the world of art to the only relationship of causal law in the world of science, and encloses it within the circle of fine style. In this, as in life, he fuses a quality common to two sensations, extracts their essence and in order to withdraw them from the contingencies of time, unites them in a metaphor, thus chaining them together with the indefinable bond of a verbal alliance.[2]

Proust's words seem to me to describe an element which is common to the Metaphysicals, the Symbolists and to the novelist himself. We do not find in the French writers the verbal felicities of the English writers of the seventeenth century, but we do find the same sort of imagery. The effectiveness of many of their images lies in the unexpected discovery of this mysterious *rapport* between 'two different objects'. The Metaphysicals drew heavily for their images on astronomy and mathematics, the Symbolists on the products of urban civilization, Proust on biology and botany. His descriptions of the encounter between Charlus and Jupien and of Albertine sleeping are too long to set out here, but they deserve careful study because they show more clearly

---

[1] This view is implicit in Crémieux's description of Proust's style as a *classicisme impressionniste* as well as in an American critic's assertion that the metaphysical element is 'something basic in all poetry' and that there is a sense in which 'all poetry is *symbolist* poetry'. (Cleanth Brooks, *Modern Poetry and the Tradition* (London, 1948), pp. 48, 67.)

[2] *Le Temps retrouvé*, II, p. 40. (English translation p. 239.)

than the brief comparisons which follow the extent to which Proust's
personal imagery was a way of apprehending experience:

1.   The spider love, which transubstantiates all. . . . (Donne.)
                    As Lines so Loves oblique may well
                    Themselves in every Angle greet:
                    But ours so truly *Parallel*
                    Though infinite can never meet.
                                        (Marvell.)
      L'amour cause ainsi de véritables soulèvements géologiques de la
pensée. (Proust.)
      A force de penser tendrement aux hommes on devient femme, et une
robe postiche entrave vos pas. (Proust.)
2.   . . . les vagues terreurs de ces affreuses nuits
                    Qui compriment le cœur comme un papier qu'on froisse.
                                        (Baudelaire.)
                    La rouille ronge en leurs spleens kilométriques
                    Les fils télégraphiques des grandes routes où nul ne passe.
                                        (Laforgue.)
      M. de Palancy . . . avait l'air de transporter seulement avec lui un frag-
ment accidentel, et peut-être purement symbolique du vitrage de son
aquarium. (Proust.)
                    When the evening is spread out against the sky
                    Like a patient etherized upon a table. . . .
                                        (T. S. Eliot)
3.   . . . les lèvres découvrant d'un accent circonflexe rose pâle une denture
      aux gencives d'un rose plus pale encore, en un sourire des plus crucifiés.
      (Laforgue.)
      . . . le petit coquillage de pâtisserie, si grassement sensuel, sous son plis-
sage sévère et dévot. (Proust.)
      Broken hoops on the shore; at the land a maze of dark cunning nets;
further away chalk-scrawled back-doors and on the higher beach a drying-
line with two crucified shirts. (Joyce.)

In the first set of examples Donne establishes a connection between
'love', the 'spider' and 'transubstantiation'. Love corrodes the emotions, changing their substance from 'manna to gall'. Marvell uses
geometrical terms to express an absolute emotional frustration. Proust
draws on geological upheavals to express the *bouleversement* caused by
love to human thought and in the second passage describes how the
homosexual's anomaly causes him to trip over a psychological 'skirt'.
In the next set, Baudelaire gives a new sharpness to 'terror' by the

homely image of the paper being crumpled. Laforgue's *spleens kilo-métriques* identifies his *ennui* with the miles of rusting telegraph wires. The rust rots the metal as industrial life rots the capacity to feel. The light flashing on M. de Palancy's monocle in the airless salon is suddenly associated with an aquarium; the worldlings appear as monsters swimming blindly round and round their glass prison which is a symbol of society. Eliot makes us feel that the eclipse of day is like the patient losing consciousness on the operating table. In the last set, Laforgue's deliberately artificial 'circumflex' coupled with *un sourire des plus crucifiés* makes us feel the effect of strain on Salomé's face during her celebrated dance. Proust, contemplating the moulding on the *madeleine*, feels that it is at once 'sensual' and *dévot*. Joyce's 'crucified shirts' emphasize the sense of immense dereliction of the shore during Stephen's walk.

These passages cover a wide range of experience and they are certainly not of equal value, but the process behind each of them has a certain similarity. It would, perhaps, be too sweeping to say of them, as Mr. Eliot has said of the Metaphysicals, that the writers 'possessed a mechanism of sensibility which could devour any kind of experience': but they all succeed in a greater or lesser degree in establishing relations between realms of experience which seemed to have nothing to do with one another. They are not making 'comparisons'; the images have for the most part become part of the writers' interior landscape as surely as Proust's 'prisons', 'circles' and 'spirals'. And this assimilation of fresh and unexpected images is a growth of sensibility.

'The parentheses', said Spitzer, 'are peepholes from which the novelist looks at the action and his readers, nods and makes signs to them, and through which the readers can look back at him.'[1] It is an illuminating comment which emphasizes the extent to which Proust's parentheses and, indeed, the whole of his syntax are functional. The long winding sentences with their continual qualifications make us feel the solidarity of past and present and the way in which the past is recreated in the present through memory. There is a backward and forward movement as the narrator passes through the corridors of memory, retraces his steps to emphasize a particular aspect of experience or to take in something which appears superficially to have been overlooked during the first journey until, at the close of the sentence, we have the impression that a particular event has been examined from every possible angle and all its potentialities have been exhausted. The parentheses form a running commentary on the main experience, but

[1] *Op. cit.*, p. 388.

at the same time they are woven into it. For there are nearly always two voices—the voice of the narrator carrying on his unending monologue and the voice of the commentator who addresses himself directly to us, explains what is happening, asks us whether we have understood and sometimes, without waiting for an answer, plunges into a fresh series of explanations and illustrations.

Describing the confusion which has arisen over Gilberte's change of name, he writes:

Ce souvenir me causa une douleur aiguë mais brève, et tandis que le concierge cherchait sa femme, je songeais surtout—pensant à Mlle d'Éporcheville et comme dans ces minutes d'attente où un nom, un renseignement qu'on a on ne sait pourquoi adapté à un visage, se trouve un instant libre et flotte, prêt s'il adhère à un nouveau visage, à rendre rétrospectivement le premier sur lequel il vous avait renseigné inconnu, innocent, insaisissable, —que la concierge allait m'apprendre que Mlle d'Éporcheville était au contraire une des deux brunes.

[This memory caused me a keen but transient pang, and while the porter went in search of his wife, my chief anxiety—as I thought of Mlle d'Eporcheville, and since in those minutes spent in waiting in which a name, a detail of information which we have, we know not why, fitted to a face, finds itself free for an instant, ready if it shall adhere to a new face to render, retrospectively, the original face as to which it had enlightened us strange, innocent, imperceptible—was that the porter's wife was perhaps going to inform me that Mlle d'Eporcheville was, on the contrary, one of the two dark girls.]

He begins with a simple statement that a memory of Albertine caused him a sharp, short pain; dispatches the *concierge* in search of his wife; then, at 'je songeais surtout', he breaks off, turns to the reader and explains the suffering and sense of indecision that we feel while waiting for an important piece of information. In the last clause the narrator takes up the thread again and goes on with his speculations about the answer he is likely to receive.

The opening paragraph of Chapter II of *Albertine disparue* is a particularly good example of the merits of Proust's style as an instrument for expressing his obsessions:

Ce n'était pas que je n'aimasse encore Albertine, mais déjà pas de la même façon que les derniers temps. Non, c'était à la façon des temps plus anciens où tout ce qui se rattachait à elle, lieux et gens, me faisait éprouver une curiosité où il y avait plus de charme que de souffrance.

[It was not that I was not still in love with Albertine, but no longer in the same fashion as in the final phase. No, it was in the fashion of the earliest times, when everything that had any connection with her, places or people, made me feel a curiosity in which there was more charm than suffering.]

It looks at first like an analysis of the word *aimer*, and the procedure of breaking it up into its component parts resembles, superficially, that of the classic French writers. He begins by comparing the way in which he once loved her with the way in which he loves her now. But there is a difference. He is not defining the word *aimer* alone; he is also defining the word 'Albertine'. We realize that 'Albertine' is not so much a person as a complex of different factors, an emotional situation —'tout ce qui se rattachait à elle, lieux et gens.'

Aimer therefore becomes *une curiosité* which was provoked by a situation' in which there was more 'charm' than 'suffering'.

We must look next at the construction of the paragraph. It goes on:

Et en effet je sentais bien maintenant qu'avant de l'oublier tout à fait, avant d'atteindre à l'indifférence initiale, il me faudrait, comme un voyageur qui revient par la même route au point d'où il est parti, traverser en sens inverse tous les sentiments par lesquels j'avais passé avant d'arriver à mon grand amour. Mais ces fragments, ces moments du passé ne sont pas immobiles, ils ont gardé la force terrible, l'ignorance heureuse de l'espérance qui s'élançait alors vers un temps devenu aujourd'hui le passé, mais qu'une hallucination nous fait un instant prendre rétrospectivement pour l'avenir.

[And indeed I was quite well aware now that before I forgot her altogether, before I reached the initial stage of indifference, I should have, like a traveller who returns by the same route to his starting-point, to traverse in the return direction all the sentiments through which I had passed before arriving at my great love. But these fragments, these moments of the past are not immobile, they have retained their terrible force, the happy ignorance of the hope that was then yearning towards a time which has now become the past, but which a hallucination makes us for a moment mistake retrospectively for the future.]

The first sentence of the paragraph expressed a mood of doubt. 'It was not that I did not still love Albertine, but already . . .' The position is suddenly clarified. He knows what he feels and is able to assert roundly: 'No, it was in the manner of an earlier period. . . .'

It becomes still clearer in the third sentence when the words: 'En

effet je sentais bien . . .' give the whole tone a 'lift'. The negatives
vanish. He realizes that his goal—his emotional goal—is 'indifférence'.
The whole paragraph is characteristic. We notice the continual qualifications. 'It was not thus, but . . .' His feelings are clarified by a process
of amplification and extension like a goldsmith beating a piece of gold
into a thinner and thinner sheet, then working a very delicate pattern
on it.

The commonplace words, 'l'oublier tout à fait', are at once transformed into 'atteindre à l'indifférence initiale'. The last word is of the
utmost importance because it qualifies 'indifférence'. It is not just indifference, but the first stage of indifference. The word *atteindre* suggests
the image of the traveller—travel, especially by train, is a recurring
motif throughout the novel—but this journey is a particular sort of
journey. It is not a circular tour, but a journey from one fixed point to
another. The suggestion of the single line was evidently the result of
Proust's experience of the *petits trains* in the provinces, but here it
takes on a curious overtone; it gives us a sense of constraint; it is a
narrow one-way track so that he cannot avoid seeing the different
stopping places which he passed on the outward journey—the journey
from *indifférence* to the *grand amour*—when he makes the return journey
from the *grand amour* to *indifférence*.

The next sentence makes a further qualification with the familiar
'but'. 'Mais ces fragments, ces moments du passé ne sont pas immobiles.'

The *fragments* and the *immobiles* lead us with a shock to *la force
terrible*. The word *initiale* in the previous sentence now assumes a more
complex meaning. It is not merely 'the first stage' of indifference; it is
'the original state of indifference' in which he began and which is now
called 'l'ignorance heureuse de l'espérance'. He recaptures the momentary hope with *s'élançait*, but it emphasizes that his love was no more
than an illusion which is cruelly dissipated by *hallucination*.

The fifth sentence is a link between his present feelings and an actual
event:

Je lisais une lettre d'Albertine, où elle m'avait annoncé sa visite pour le
soir et j'avais une seconde la joie de l'attente. Dans ces retours par la même
ligne d'un pays où l'on ne retournera jamais, où l'on reconnaît le nom, l'aspect de toutes les stations par où on a déjà passé à l'aller, il arrive que,
tandis qu'on est arrêté à l'une d'elles en gare, on a un instant l'illusion
qu'on repart, mais dans la direction du lieu d'où l'on vient, comme l'on
avait fait la première fois. Tout de suite l'illusion cesse, mais une seconde
on s'était senti de nouveau emporté: telle est la cruauté du souvenir.

[I read a letter from Albertine, in which she said that she was coming to see me that evening, and I felt for an instant the joy of expectation. In these return journeys along the same line from a place to which we shall never return, when we recall the names, the appearance of all the places which we have passed on the outward journey, it happens that, while our train is halting at one of the stations, we feel for an instant the illusion that we are setting off again, but in the direction of the place from which we have come, as on the former journey. Soon the illusion vanishes, but for an instant we felt ourself carried away once again: such is the cruelty of memory.]

The remembrance of actual journeys in the *petit train*, which simply amplifies and refines upon what he has already said, prepares the way for the dying fall of the final words.

I felt tempted to say that this passage reflects perfectly the movement of Proust's sensibility—the movement which once made Mr. Aldous Huxley speak of 'an endless masturbation like Proust's horrible great book'; but this would be a simplification. The novel is constructed, as it were, in slabs. Proust starts each section by defining a particular mood or with a performance of one of his 'psychological comedies'. He chooses an image for the purpose, but this image becomes a talisman which leads from one association to another. So it is with the 'return journey', the 'line' and the 'stops'.

In a passage which I have already quoted, Proust speaks of the 'anachronism which so often prevents the calendar of facts from coinciding with that of feelings'. In the passage from *Albertine disparue*, time is abolished and feelings are expressed in spatial terms. In order to communicate his experience to the reader, the novelist draws on images—familiar images—borrowed from the external world; but the railways and the *petit train* are transported into the inner world and become part of its landscape, become the means of exteriorizing a subjective experience.

The 'journey', as one might expect, is a failure. Three paragraphs later he begins:

La première de ces étapes commença au début de l'hiver, un beau dimanche de la Toussaint où j'étais sorti. Tout en approchant du Bois, je me rappelais avec tristesse le *retour* d'Albertine venant me chercher du Trocadéro, car c'était la même journée, mais sans Albertine.

[The first of these halting-points began with the coming of winter, on a fine Sunday, which was also All Saints' Day, when I had ventured out of doors. As I came towards the Bois, I recalled with sorrow how Albertine had come back to join me from the Trocadéro, for it was the same day, only without Albertine.]

Two paragraphs later still, we come on this sentence:

Comme je suivais les *allées* séparées d'un sousbois. . . .

[As I followed the paths separated by undergrowth. . . .]

Proust has made a determined effort to convince himself that feelings move in straight lines, that he can retrace his steps by simply returning to his point of departure. It is an illusion. The 'indifference' which follows an unhappy love affair can obviously never be the same as the 'indifference' which preceded because the experience must have changed the actors in the drama. The imaginary 'single line' suddenly turns out to have innumerable branch lines which, far from taking him back to his starting point, all lead to dead ends. For there is no way out and no way back. We are still in the labyrinth with its network of galleries, its blind alleys which never take us anywhere.

V. THE PLACE OF PROUST

'THE fascination of Proust's novel is so great', writes Mr. Edmund Wilson, 'that, while we are reading it, we tend to accept it *in toto*. . . . It is only in the latter part of his narrative that we begin seriously to question what he is telling us. . . . With Proust we are forced to recognize that his ideas and imagination are more seriously affected by his physical and psychological ailment than we had at first been willing to suppose.'[1]

No great writer escapes severe criticism at one time or another, and it would have been strange indeed if a novelist whose impact on contemporary sensibility was as great as Proust's had proved an exception. It is part of his achievement that he presents such a huge target that the merest beginner can scarcely fail to hit the card and even score an outer or two. In Proust's case, however, there has been a curious consensus of opinion among his critics. Mr. Wilson comments on the effect on his work of his physical and mental health. Abraham observed that 'with Proust as your guide, you lose the use of a part of yourself; your perspicacity and subtlety gain in the process; your humanity atrophies'.[2] Fernandez argued that the novel 'does not establish a hierarchy of values and shows no spiritual progress from beginning to end'.[3] M. Jacques Maritain adds that 'to have been written as it should have been written, Proust's work would have needed the inner light of an Augustine'.[4] These views have been reinforced by Proust's fellow-novelists. The late L. H. Myers said that he treated 'all sorts of sensibility as equal in importance, and all manifestations of character as standing on the same plane of significance'.[5] M. Mauriac, who greatly admires his work, feels bound to point out that 'the lack of moral perspective impoverished the humanity created by Proust, narrowed his world' and that 'Dieu est terriblement absent de l'œuvre de Marcel Proust'.[6]

In literary criticism terms like 'healthy', 'sick' and 'normal' should

---

[1] *Axel's Castle*, pp. 164–5.
[2] *Proust* (Recherches sur la Création Intellectuelle), (Paris, 1930), p. 17.
[3] *Messages*, p. 147.   [4] *Art et scolastique* (new edition, Paris, 1927), p. 330
[5] Preface to *The Root and the Flower* (London, 1935), p. 10.
[6] *Du Côté de chez Proust*, pp. 67, 66.

only be used with the greatest circumspection. It is true that Proust's work does not possess the poise and the resilience of Stendhal's or its gaiety and humanity. Their absence undoubtedly helps to explain why Proust is not a novelist of the same calibre as Stendhal, but we must remember that his aim was very different, that his peculiar qualities were incompatible with Stendhal's. He was, we know, an invalid for most of his life and his cloistered existence left its mark on his novel; but it is no exaggeration to say that his illness was part of his literary vocation, that only a man who was suffering from an illness which was partly physical and partly nervous, partly real and partly imaginary, could have written the book that he did in fact write. His sickness was in the fullest sense a function of his genius.[1]

A similar reply might be made to Proust's other critics. The price of his 'perspicacity' and 'subtlety' was life in 'the Noah's ark' where his humanity atrophied. Fernandez explained that when he spoke of 'spiritual progress', he meant 'unification interne dont le contraire est la multiplicité étalée *partes per partes*'. It is evident from this that had Proust concentrated on 'internal unification' his book would be very different from the work that he left us. For the core of his experience in the later volumes is undoubtedly a sense of dissolution, of the exhaustion and collapse of the moral being who is trapped in his labyrinth. The truth is that self-examination can only be pushed to the point to which Proust pushed it by a person who adopts a position of absolute spiritual neutrality, who divests himself of all accepted views of the world, morality and the emotions, and simply turns his mind inwards and starts like Descartes all over again. 'My novel', said Proust, 'is not a work of reasoning; its least elements were furnished by my sensibility.'[2] The contrast between 'reasoning' and 'sensibility' suggests that the contemporary writer tends to be a moral anarchist. His work is both an experience and an experiment, and he goes inevitably into dangerous places. It was this attitude which enabled Proust to push the exploration of personal sensibility to its extreme lengths.

It is probable that most of Proust's readers prefer *Swann*. It is a perfectly legitimate view, but it is not without its dangers. Although he insisted on the unity of his work and though it is, theoretically, a single novel, he certainly attempted as many different things as novelists who have filled a whole row with different books. It can, I think, be argued that in *Swann* his experience is more universal and that *La Prisonnière* and *Albertine disparue* are studies of an exceptional 'case'; but I for one

[1] See his own defence in *Guermantes*, I, p. 272.
[2] *Lettres de Marcel Proust à Bibesco*, p. 177.

would hesitate to say that *Swann* is superior to either in an absolute sense. His work is extremely rich and varied. It does not simply offer different rewards to different minds; it offers different rewards to the same person in different moods and at different times. It can be read as a novel which possesses many of the virtues—particularly in the comic scenes—which are traditionally associated with Balzac and Dickens whom Proust greatly admired. It can also be read as memoirs, as an intimate journal, as a clinical treatise or as the commonplace book of a great moralist—I use the word in the French sense—which you can open almost at random and be sure of coming across profound reflections on many of the fundamental human problems. You may have read a passage a dozen times before, but you find that you have still not exhausted it; the words echo in your mind, distilling their essence slowly like those of the other great French moralists.

All this makes the 'placing' of Proust a matter of considerable difficulty. It is not enough to say that his strength and weakness are inseparable. The impression that he makes on our mind is contradictory; we are aware of the coexistence of opposites—richness and poverty, variety and monotony, breadth and narrowness. He possessed a great knowledge of life, but somehow it always leads back to the self, back to the case in its cork-lined room. He was endowed with that immense psychological insight which belongs characteristically to the French tradition and he made startling discoveries; but it remains true, as Myers observed, that he treated 'all sorts of sensibility as equal in importance, and all manifestations of character as standing on the same plane of significance'. It can hardly be claimed that he possessed the range, the finality or the profound humanity of the greatest writers. Compare him with Stendhal and you are conscious of the superb sensibility of the nineteenth-century master and of the limitations of Proust's own sensibility. Yet when you put him beside Balzac or Flaubert, you feel that he was a greater writer than either of them, that he was more civilized and that his outlook, for all its peculiarities, was more adult than theirs. His book is often boring and inconsistent; his analysis of the human situation suffers from the grave defects which are inseparable from the invert's approach and the personal *faiblesses* out of which he constructed his book are the reverse of attractive; but this is no reason for underrating what he did accomplish. The new sensibility and the new vision are real and their effect is lasting. He was not merely a great European novelist. 'He has his place', as Mauriac put it, with greater nicety perhaps than he realized, 'beside the greatest European novelists and it shall not be taken from him.'

'THE FRENCH DIALOGUE'

'THE FRENCH DIALOGUE'

I SPOKE in my opening chapter of the danger of generalizing about society from the experience of particular writers; but so long as we realize that the picture is necessarily partial and incomplete, there is no reason why we should not draw tentative conclusions about the views of man and society which appear in some of the most representative French novelists.

What are properly described as novels are works of fiction dealing with amorous adventures, written in prose with art for the pleasure and instruction of readers. . . . Thus the entertainment of the reader, which appears to be the aim of the skilful novelist, is subordinated to the principal aim which is the instruction of the mind and the correction of manners; and novels are more or less regular according to the degree in which they approach or depart from this definition and this aim.

But to return to myself. I was thinking more modestly about my book and it would not even be true to say that I was thinking of those who would read it as my readers. For, as I have already shown, they would not be my readers, but the readers of themselves, my book being only a sort of magnifying-glass like those offered by the optician of Combray to a purchaser.

The first of these passages is taken from Huet's letter *On the Origin of Novels* which was published as an introduction to Mme de La Fayette's *Zaïde*,[1] the second from *Le Temps retrouvé*. They give a good idea of the changes which took place in the theory and practice of novel-writing during the two hundred and fifty years which separate them.

The seventeenth-century novelist had no doubt about the nature and function of his medium. In early times, observes Huet, the novel was a love story written in verse. 'Love must still be the principal subject of the novel', but though it is essentially a 'fiction' it is written in prose because that is the convention of the century. The writer is no less clear about its function. Its aim, we are told in a sentence which echoes Dryden, is 'the pleasure and instruction of readers'. The novelist possesses a taste and wisdom which do not necessarily belong to all his

[1] Pierre-Daniel Huet (1631–1721), scholar and Bishop of Avranches.

readers and this makes his work an *école de vie* for 'the instruction of the mind and the correction of manners'.

It is apparent from her novels and from the introduction (which presumably reflected her views) that Mme de La Fayette's experience is primarily a social one. She sees man as a social being who has a definite place in the community. She does not think that society is perfect, but she clearly believes that in the main the organism is sound. We must not place too narrow an interpretation on the words 'pleasure and instruction'. Her books are not moral fables disguised as novels, and she never tips the scales. She is concerned with the double problem of *conduct* and *conscience*. Her ideal is martial glory and public service —we remember that she commends one of her characters as having 'une égale capacité pour la guerre et pour les affaires'—and compared with this the other virtues ranked decidedly low.

Society imposes certain rules of conduct which, generally speaking, are absolute. A man may be unfortunate in love, have an unhappy home or an *inclination* for his friend's wife, but none of these things must be allowed to interfere with his martial exploits or his administrative duties. The great threat to society lay in passion whether 'legitimate' or not. She admired the *mariage de raison* because it appeared to exclude the danger of any interference with public life. A love match like the Prince de Clèves's was almost certain to end in disaster and to rob society of a valuable warrior or an important administrator.

Mme de La Fayette has been compared both to Corneille and to Racine, but it is clear that her view of life differed from theirs. Her ideal is, to be sure, an heroic one—the subordination of inclination to duty, of the individual to the community; but as we might expect of a contemporary of Racine's she was not merely aware of the dangers of passion; she saw that the battle which Corneille's characters had fought and won had become a losing one. The conduct of the Prince and Princesse de Clèves is exemplary, but they are no longer masters of conscience and the internal conflict destroys them both.

Marivaux's study of society possesses greater width than Mme de La Fayette's; but though he too regards it as fundamentally sound, the society which he describes is altogether less impressive. The focus shifts from *moral* to *social* experience. The ideals of martial glory and public service have vanished. The great aim of his characters is to 'arrive', to integrate themselves in the social organism without offering anything in return. They can think of nothing better to do than indulge in gallantry which has lost all its fire and none of its charm, or make a successful marriage.

Rousseau and Laclos present one of those violent contrasts for which the French tradition is remarkable. They both waged war on convention, but their methods were very different. Rousseau believed very firmly in the innate goodness of emotion and he simply used the novel to preach individualism and rebellion. His influence was twofold. It was positive in so far as it provided a release for feelings which were excluded or denied by the rationalists, and negative in so far as it produced a reaction against the views which he sponsored. It accounts, as we have seen, for Laclos' astringency and his anti-individualism.

Laclos himself remains something of an enigma. A good deal of his criticism of society remains valid, but his claims to be regarded as a moralist are unproven. He is so dispassionate that the effect of his book depends almost entirely on the dispositions of the reader to whom it may be either a warning or a temptation; and his failure to realize his positive values suggests that at bottom they were no more than a sentimentalized variation of the convention that he was attacking.

> I wished to paint in Adolphe [said Constant] one of the principal moral maladies of the century. . . . This malady of the spirit is commoner than is usually thought and many young people have symptoms of it. The decrepitude of civilization has seized them; thinking to learn from the experience of their fathers, they have inherited their satiety. Thus, while the novels of the past described passionate men and unyielding women, the novels of the present day are filled with women who give in and men who leave them. Their authors do not realize the reason for this change; but the most mediocre like the most distinguished instinctively obey a truth of which they are unconscious.
>
> It is not only in emotional attachments that this moral feebleness, this incapacity for lasting impressions becomes apparent. In nature everything holds together. Fidelity in love like religious belief or an enthusiasm for liberty is a form of strength. Now we have no strength left. We no longer know how to love, how to believe or how to will. Each of us doubts the truth of what he says, smiles over the vehemence of his assertions and foresees the end of what he feels.[1]
>
> At a distance [he writes in another place] the image of the suffering that we inflict appears vague and confused like a cloud through which it is easy to pass. We are encouraged by the approbation of a society which is completely factitious, which replaces principles by rules, emotions by conventions and which hates scandal because it is importunate and not because it is immoral, for it gives vice quite a friendly welcome provided that there is no scandal.[2]

[1] Preface to the second edition of *Adolphe*.
[2] Preface to the third edition of *Adolphe*.

It is at once apparent that in these passages Constant makes a fresh approach to the moral problem. His predecessors had criticized the society of their time, but they had also found much to admire and a good deal remained intact after their attacks. There had been nothing comparable to Constant's onslaught and his denunciation of a decrepit civilization fostering moral maladies and rotting the moral fibre of the individual. His point of view has nothing in common with Rousseau's. There is no vagueness, no sentimental yearning for mountain landscapes and 'the simple life'. His charges are specific. There is no plea for a return to a community of gentle savages. He does not condemn society for being society; he condemns it because it is rotten; and he knows exactly why he is on the side of the individual in the conflict with society.

We have already seen that Constant's integrity and his extreme moral rectitude played a part of immense importance in his magnificent novel, but this does not mean that his outlook was without its drawbacks. In the conflict with society the individual was doomed to defeat. His clear-sightedness could not save him from the ravages of the *maladie morale*. It could not teach him 'how to believe, how to love or how to will', and he simply ended his career as a broken man who had become 'étranger pour tout le monde'.

If Stendhal's *étranger* is a much more vital figure, it is largely because his creator was free from the limitations of Constant's puritanism. For puritanism is only capable of what may be described as negative solutions. It is essentially a system of restraints. It has no conception of the good life and turns its victims into guilty men. Stendhal's criticism of society is far-reaching, but he had an immense capacity for enjoyment and an apparently inexhaustible sense of impish fun. He was untouched by any feelings of guilt and remorse, and he would have found Constant's *maladie morale* as incredible as the eighteenth-century writers. His conception of the *étranger* is a *position de combat* and his vision of the new élite—'the happy few'—offers a positive solution for which there was no place in the puritan ethic. This gives his work an extra-literary importance. I can think of no other nineteenth-century writer except Rimbaud who has become so much a part of the fibres of our being. No one—not even Baudelaire—has added to or improved on what Stendhal offers. His views are, if anything, more actual to-day than at the time when his novels were written; and they still represent the only conceivable solution for the intellectual in a democratic society.

It will be seen [said Stendhal] that egotism—I mean *sincere* egotism—is a way of portraying the human heart in the knowledge of which we have made gigantic strides since 1721, the date of the *Lettres persanes* by that great man whom I have studied so much—Montesquieu.[1]

Moral problems cannot be divorced from technical problems. Stendhal's definition of egotism is a reply to those critics who have accused him of irresponsible individualism and a description of the originality of his approach to the novel. His strength like Constant's lies to a great extent in the fact that he combined the classic writer's power of analysis with that deeper awareness of the inner life which was, perhaps, the Romantic Movement's principal contribution to literature. There must always be a certain correspondence between the writer's personal sensibility and the sensibility of his age, but in the eighteenth century the correspondence was too close. The writer was moulded by society instead of imposing himself on it and creating fresh patterns of feeling. That is why we are continually haunted by the sense that Marivaux and Laclos worked too close to the surface. Constant and Stendhal produced a change of direction. They made the inner life their starting point and moved outwards, examining society in the light of their own scheme of values. Their attitude was in no sense an 'escape' or a 'retreat' from life. Their personal systems had been worked out in opposition to society. Constant's *sanctuaire intime* and Stendhal's *rêverie* were not merely essential elements in the 'good life'; they were vital positions for which they were prepared to fight in order to preserve them against the encroachments of society.

I think that it will now be apparent that Stendhal's definition of the novel as a violin bow follows naturally from his own practice and that it points over the heads of Balzac and Flaubert to Proust. For in spite of their undeniable merits, Balzac and Flaubert surrendered some of the vital positions which Stendhal had won. They lived in a civilization which had become still more decrepit, but human powers of resistance were so diminished that the conflict was virtually over. They could not identify themselves with any of the groups of which society was composed in the manner of the eighteenth-century novelists, but neither could they present a constructive alternative like Stendhal's *étranger*. They were therefore obliged to fall back on compromise. Their work is partly a realistic description of society and partly an attempt to express something personal which never quite comes across. That is why Balzac's 'vision' was stifled and Flaubert leaves us with the impression of a blur at the centre of his work. They both pay lip-service to conventional morality; but in Balzac moral concepts are mere counters and Flaubert's novels are often a hoarse, wearisome

[1] *Souvenirs d'égotisme*, p. 81.

denunciation of human *bêtise* in the name of standards in which he has ceased to believe.

This brings me back to my starting point. The ruin of traditional values and a growing pessimism led to the intrusion of politics. For in the contemporary political novel—the novel which derives from *Germinal* instead of from *Lucien Leuwen*—the good life becomes identified with the triumph of the Party and of unworthy sectarian ambitions. The 'outsider' is transformed into a 'prisoner' trying desperately to preserve the few remaining relics of civilization. When we look back at the passage from *Le Temps retrouvé* we are able to measure the extent of the losses. Civilized society is a 'spectacle sans cause' which fosters every kind of obsession and which is scarcely less menacing than party rallies or mass demonstrations. Conduct and conscience are explained in terms of obscure physiological changes. The novelist has abandoned his claims to conduct an *école de vie* for the instruction of the mind and the correction of manners. He even seems to have abandoned the claim that his work is a musical instrument which will produce fresh harmonies if we—'the happy few'—will collaborate with him. Instead, he offers us a scientific instrument—a magnifying glass—with the invitation to spend a 'life-sentence' burrowing deeper and deeper into our hidden impulses in the vain hope of reaching *la vraie vie*.

In an essay called 'Le Dialogue Français' M. André Gide has observed that all through French literature we hear a perpetual dialogue

> Not between a political right and left, but—much more profound and vital—between the ancient tradition, the submission to recognized authorities, and free thought, the spirit of doubt, of examination which works for the slow and progressive emancipation of the individual.[1]

He concludes that this 'dialogue' is responsible for the immense vitality of the French tradition. I am sure that it does account for the clarity, vigour and alertness of the French mind, but I suspect that M. Gide underestimates the dangers and the price paid by French writers. The sharp division between right and left means that every French writer is virtually forced to take sides. I do not think that the choice before him is either as simple or as innocuous as M. Gide contrives to suggest. It is not merely a choice between authority and freedom; it is a choice between two dogmatic positions. Now as soon as dogma enters the literary order, we are bound to find distortion. The writer becomes a party-man who is blind to the weaknesses of his own position and fails to appreciate the virtues of his opponents.

[1] *The Cornhill Magazine*, No. 969 (Winter, 1946), pp. 200-1.

This seems to me to explain the shortcomings of some of the novelists whom I have discussed and their inferiority to certain English novelists which M. Gide himself was careful to emphasize. For the French novelist the issues are sometimes too clear-cut, too much a matter of black and white. There is little room for the kind of moral drama which is peculiarly the sphere of the representatives of the great liberal tradition in England—George Eliot, Henry James and Conrad.

The real issue for the French novelist is, indeed, very different from the one suggested by M. Gide. The drama lies in the attempt to escape from the somewhat rigid French either/or and to find a third way. One of the greatest merits of Mme de La Fayette is to have shown that moral problems cannot be solved by a simple choice between 'right' and 'left'. If Laclos is inferior to Constant, it is partly because the author of *Adolphe* grew up outside the French tradition and refused to accept its simplifications or its neat distinctions, while Stendhal's supremacy lies very largely in the discovery of a third way which far transcends M. Gide's 'slow and progressive emancipation of the individual'.

BIBLIOGRAPHY

The lists which follow include studies of practically every aspect of the novelists' lives and work, and represent a number of different points of view. Without making any claim to completeness, they provide material for a comprehensive study of most of the writers. The work of the critics of whom I have made greatest use is discussed in the appropriate places in the text. I have therefore confined myself here to brief explanatory comments where they appeared necessary.

GENERAL WORKS AND COLLECTIONS OF ESSAYS

BOURGET, PAUL, *Essais de Psychologie contemporaine*, I. Édition définitive, Paris: Plon, 1926.
>   (Constant: Stendhal: Flaubert.)
>   *Nouvelles pages de critique et de doctrine*, I. Plon, 1922.
>   (Stendhal: Balzac.)
>   *Quelques témoignages*, I. Plon, 1928.
>   (Stendhal: Balzac.)
>   (Everything that Bourget wrote on the ninteenth-century novelists deserves careful reading.)

DU BOS, CHARLES, *Approximations*. 1ère série, Paris: Plon, 1922.
>   (Flaubert: Proust).

DUGAS, L., *Les Grandes timides*. Paris: Félix Alcan, 1922.
>   (Constant: Stendhal.)

ELLIS, HAVELOCK, *From Rousseau to Proust*. London: Constable, 1936.

FERNANDEZ, RAMON, *Messages*. Paris: Gallimard, 1926.
>   (Stendhal: Balzac: Proust.)

GREEN, F. C., *French Novelists' Manners and Ideas*. London: Dent, 1928.
>   *French Novelists from the Revolution to Proust*. Dent, 1931.

JAMES, HENRY, *French Poets and Novelists*. London: MacMillan, 1875.
>   *Notes on Novelists*. London: Dent, 1914.
>   (I stress the peculiar excellence of James's two essays on Flaubert and the four essays on Balzac in these volumes on account of their quite unjustifiable neglect in France where they seldom even appear in French writers' bibliographies. The recently published

Art of Fiction and Other Essays, Oxford University Press, 1948, contains only the later essay on Flaubert and one of the two later essays on Balzac.)

KRUTCH, JOSEPH WOOD, *Five Masters*. New York: Cape and Smith, 1931. (Stendhal: Proust.)

LANSON, GUSTAVE, *L'Art de la prose*. Paris: Librairie des Annales Politiques et Littéraires, 1908.

LE BRETON, ANDRÉ, *Le Roman au dix-septième siècle*. Paris: Hachette, 1890.

Le Roman au dix-huitième siècle. Paris: Société Française d'Imprimerie et de Librairie, 1898.

Le Roman français au dix-neuvième siècle. 1ère partie, Avant Balzac, Paris: Société Française d'Imprimerie et de Librairie, 1901. (No other parts issued.)

(A good survey of the French novel from the beginning of the seventeenth to the beginning of the nineteenth century.)

MAUGHAM, W. SOMERSET, *Great Novelists and their Novels*. Philadelphia and Toronto: The John Winston Company, 1948.

MAUROIS, ANDRÉ, *Sept visages de l'amour*. Paris: La Jeune Parque, 1946. (Revised and enlarged edition of the author's *Cinq visages de l'amour*. New York: Didier, 1942.)

MILLE, PIERRE, *Le Roman français*. Paris: Firmin-Didot, 1930.

ORTEGA Y GASSET, JOSÉ, *The Dehumanization of Art and Notes on the Novel*. London: Oxford University Press, 1948.

POULET, GEORGES, *Études sur le temps humain*. Edinburgh University Press, 1949.

PRÉVOST, JEAN (Editor), *Problèmes du roman*. Brussels: Le Carrefour, 1943.

SAINTSBURY, GEORGE, *A History of the French Novel*. 2 vols., London: MacMillan, 1917–19.

SUARÈS, ANDRÉ, *Xénies*. Paris: Emile-Paul, 1923. (Valuable notes on the style of Laclos, Stendhal and Flaubert.)

TAINE, HIPPOLYTE, *Essais de critique et d'histoire*. 2ème édition, Paris: Hachette, 1866. (Mme de La Fayette: Stendhal.)

THÉRIVE, ANDRÉ, *Le Français—langue morte?* Paris: Plon, 1923.

THIBAUDET, ALBERT, *Histoire de la littérature française de 1789 à nos jours*. Paris: Stock, 1936.

TRAHARD, PIERRE, *Les Maîtres de la sensibilité française au dix-huitième siècle*. 4 vols., Paris: Boivin, 1931–3.

MADAME DE LA FAYETTE

ASHTON, H., *Madame de La Fayette sa Vie et ses Œuvres*. Cambridge University Press, 1922.

P

CALVET, JEAN, *La Littérature religieuse de François de Sales à Fénelon* (Histoire de la Littérature Française 5). Paris: Gigord, 1938.

MAGNE, ÉMILE, *Madame de Lafayette en ménage*. Paris: Émile-Paul, 1926.

Le Cœur et l'esprit de Madame de Lafayette. Paris: Émile-Paul, 1927.

MORNET, DANIEL, *Histoire de la littérature française classique, 1660–1700*. Paris: Armand Colin, 1940.

SAINTE-BEUVE, C.-A., *Portraits de femmes*.

CHODERLOS DE LACLOS

BAUDELAIRE, CHARLES, *Juvenilia, œuvres posthumes, reliquiæ*, I (Conard Edition).

CAUSSY, FERNAND, *Laclos 1741–1803*. Paris: Mercure de France, 1905.

DARD, ÉMILE, *Le Général Choderlos de Laclos auteur des Liaisons dangereuses 1741–1803*. Paris: Perrin, 1905, new edition 1936.

GIRAUDOUX, JEAN, *Littérature*. Paris: Grasset, 1941.

GONCOURT, ÉDMOND AND JULES, *La Femme au dix-huitième siècle*. Paris: Firmin-Didot, 1862.

HENRIOT, ÉMILE, *Les Livres du second rayon*, 1926. New edition, Paris: Grasset, 1948.

BENJAMIN CONSTANT

BLANCHOT, MAURICE, *La Part du feu*. Paris: Gallimard, 1949.

DU BOS, CHARLES, *Grandeur et misère de Benjamin Constant*. Paris: Corrêa, 1946.

DUMONT-WILDEN, L., *La Vie de Benjamin Constant* (Vies des Hommes Illustres, No. 61). Paris: Gallimard, 1930.

FABRE-LUCE, ALFRED, *Benjamin Constant* (Collection: L'Homme et Son Œuvre). Paris: Fayard, 1939.

FAGUET, ÉMILE, *Politiques et moralistes du dix-neuvième siècle*. 1ère série, Paris: Lecène, Oudin et Cie, 1891.

GLACHANT, PHILIPPE, *Benjamin Constant sous l'œil du guet*. Paris: Plon, 1906.

GODET, PHILIPPE, *Madame de Charrière et ses amis*. 2 vols., Geneva: Julien, 1905. Abridged edition in one volume, Lausanne: Spes, Paris: Attinger, 1927.

JEANSON, FRANCIS, 'Benjamin Constant ou l'Indifférence en Liberté' in *Les Temps Modernes*, No. 33, June 1948.
(Existentialist criticism of Constant's theory of freedom.)

LÉON, PAUL, *Benjamin Constant* (Collection: Maîtres des Littératures). Paris: Rieder, 1930.

MELEGARI, DORA, Introduction to *Journal intime*. Paris: Ollendorff, 1895.

NICOLSON, HAROLD, *Benjamin Constant*. London: Constable, 1949.

POURTALÈS, GUY DE, *De Hamlet à Swann*. Paris: Crès, 1924.

PRITCHETT, V. S., *In My Good Books*. London: Chatto and Windus, 1942.

REBECQUE, BARONNE CONSTANT DE, *Les Mariages manqués de Belle de Tuyll*. Paris: Payot, 1940.

RUDLER, GUSTAVE, *La Jeunesse de Benjamin Constant 1767–94*. Paris: Armand Colin, 1909.

    Adolphe de Benjamin Constant (Les Grands Événements Littéraires). Paris: Société Française d'Éditions et de Techniques, 1935.

    Adolphe, edited with introduction. Manchester University Press, 1919, 1941.

SAINTE-BEUVE, C.-A., *Nouveaux lundis*, I.

    Portraits de femmes.

    Portraits littéraires, III.

    Portraits contemporains, IV.

SCHEMERHORN, ELIZABETH, *Benjamin Constant*. London: Heinemann, 1924.

SCOTT, GEOFFREY, *The Portrait of Zélide*. London: Constable, 1925.

SUARÈS, ANDRÉ, *Sur la vie*, II. Paris: Cornély, 1910.

TURNELL, M., 'Introduction to the Study of Benjamin Constant' in *The Nineteenth Century and After*, Vol. CXLIV, No. 857, July 1948.

    (Constant's religious and political views.)

STENDHAL

ALAIN, *Stendhal* (Collection: Maîtres des Littératures). Paris: Rieder, 1935.

ARBELET, PAUL, *La Jeunesse de Stendhal*. 2 vols., Paris: Champion, 1919.

    Les Amours romantiques de Stendhal. Paris: Émile-Paul, 1924.

    Stendhal épicier ou les infortunes de Mélanie. Paris: Plon, 1926.

    Premier voyage de Stendhal au pays des comédiennes (Cahiers de la Quinzaine 18ème série, No. 16). Paris: L'Artisan du Livre, 1928.

BALZAC, HONORÉ DE, *Œuvres complètes*, T. XXIII. (Calmann-Lévy edition.)

BARDÈCHE, MAURICE, *Stendhal romancier*. Paris: La Table Ronde, 1947.

BELLANGER, CHARLES, *Notes stendhaliennes*, suivi du *H.B.* de Mérimée. Paris: Éditions du Myrte, 1948.

BLUM, LÉON, *Stendhal et le Beylisme*. Paris: Ollendorff, 1914, 3ème édition, Albin Michel, 1947.

BOSSLAERS, REMI, *Le Cas Stendhal*. Paris: Droz, 1938.

BOURGET, PAUL, *Stendhal*. Paris: Champion, 1920.

CHUQUET, ARTHUR, *Stendhal-Beyle*. Paris: Plon, 1902.

COLLIGNON, ALBERT, *L'Art et la vie de Stendhal*. Paris: Baillière, 1868.

DELACROIX, HENRI, *La Psychologie de Stendhal*. Paris: Félix Alcan, 1918.

    (Influence of eighteenth-century thought on Stendhal.)

DU BOS, CHARLES, *Approximations*. 2ème série, Paris: Crès, 1927.

FAGUET, ÉMILE, *Politiques et moralistes du dix-neuvième siècle*. 3ème série, Paris: Société Française d'Imprimerie et de Librairie, 1900.

FERNANDEZ, RAMON, *Itinéraire français*. Paris: Éditions du Pavois, 1943.

FRANCE, ANATOLE, 'Stendhal' in *La Revue de Paris*, 1 September 1920, pp. 5–17.

GIDE, ANDRÉ, *Incidences*. Paris: Gallimard, 1924.
('Préface à *Armance*.')

GOURMONT, REMY DE, *Promenades littéraires*. 2ème et 5ème série, Paris: Mercure de France, 1906 and 1913.

GREEN, F. C., *Stendhal*, Cambridge University Press, 1939.

GUNNELL, DORIS, *Stendhal et l'Angleterre*. Paris: Bosse, 1909.

HAZARD, PAUL, *La Vie de Stendhal* (Vies des Hommes Illustres, No. 11). Paris: Gallimard, 1927.

HENRIOT, ÉMILE, *Livres et portraits*, I. Paris: Plon, 1923.
Stendhaliana. Paris: Crès, 1924.
(Includes the essay on Stendhal's style in the earlier volume.)

JACOUBET, HENRI, *Stendhal* (Collection: A la Gloire de . . .). Paris: Éditions de la Nouvelle Revue Critique, 1943.

JOSEPHSON, MATTHEW, *Stendhal or the Pursuit of Happiness*. New York: Doubleday, 1946.

JOURDA, PIERRE, *L'État présent des études stendhaliennes*. Paris: Les Belles Lettres, 1930.
Stendhal l'homme et l'œuvre (Collection: Temps et Visages). Paris: Desclée de Brouwer, 1934.

LEVIN, HARRY, *Toward Stendhal* (Pharo Number Three). Utah: Murray, 1945.

MARTINEAU, HENRI. *L'Œuvre de Stendhal Histoire de ses livres et de sa pensée*. Paris: Le Divan, 1945.

MARTINO, PIERRE, *Stendhal*. Paris: Boivin, 1914 and 1934.

MAURIAC, FRANÇOIS, *Petits essais de psychologie religieuse*. Paris: L'Artisan du Livre, 1933.

MÉLIA, JEAN, *La Vie amoureuse de Stendhal*. Paris: Mercure de France, 1910.
Les Idées de Stendhal. Mercure de France, 1910.
Ce que pensait Stendhal. Mercure de France, 1938.

PAUPE, ADOLPHE, *Histoire des œuvres de Stendhal*. Paris: Dujarric, 1903.
La Vie littéraire de Stendhal. Paris: Champion, 1914.

PRÉVOST, JEAN, *Les Épicuriens français*. Paris: Gallimard, 1931.
La Création chez Stendhal. Marseilles: Le Sagittaire, 1942.

ROD, EDOUARD, *Stendhal*. Paris: Hachette, 1892.

SAINTE-BEUVE, C.-A., *Causeries du lundi*, IX.
Portraits contemporains, IV.

STRACHEY, LYTTON, *Books and Characters*. London: Chatto and Windus, 1922.

STRYIENSKI, CASIMIR, *Soirées du Stendhal Club*. 2 vols., Paris: Mercure de France, 1905, 1908.

THIBAUDET, ALBERT, *Stendhal*. Paris: Hachette, 1931.
> (Useful, but not of the same calibre as the author's study of Flaubert.)

VALÉRY, PAUL, *Variété*, II. Paris: Gallimard, 1927.

ZWEIG, STEFAN, *Drei Dichter ihres Lebens*. Leipzig: Insel-Verlag, 1928. Translated as *Adepts in Self-portraiture*, London: Cassell, 1929.

BALZAC

ABRAHAM, PIERRE, *Balzac* (Recherches sur la Création Intellectuelle). Paris: Rieder, 1929.
> (Stimulating.)

ALAIN, *Avec Balzac*. Paris: Gallimard, 1937.

ALTSZYLER, HÉLÈNE, *La Génèse et le plan des caractères dans l'œuvre de Balzac*. Paris: Félix Alcan, 1928.

ARRIGON, L. J., *Les Débuts littéraires d'Honoré de Balzac*. Paris: Perrin, 1924.
Les Années romantiques d'Honoré de Balzac. Perrin, 1927.
Balzac et la 'Contessa'. Paris: Éditions des Portiques, 1932.

BALDENSPERGER, FERNAND, *Orientations étrangères chez Honoré de Balzac*. Paris: Champion, 1927.
> (Good account of the Anglo-Saxon influences on his work.)

BARDÈCHE, MAURICE, *Balzac romancier*. Paris: Plon, 1940. New abridged edition, 1947.

BARRIÈRE, P., *Honoré de Balzac et la tradition littéraire classique*. Paris: Hachette, 1928.
Honoré de Balzac les romans de jeunesse. Hachette, 1928.
> (Study of the early 'thrillers'.)

BÉGUIN, ALBERT, *Balzac visionnaire* (Petite Collection Balzac). Geneva: Skira, 1946.
> (Interesting study of the 'visionary' element in Balzac.)

BELLESSORT, ANDRÉ, *Balzac et son œuvre*. Paris: Perrin, 1925.

BENJAMIN, RENÉ, *La Vie prodigieuse d'Honoré de Balzac*. Paris: Plon, 1925.
> (A *vie romancée*.)

BERTAULT, PHILIPPE, *Balzac l'homme et l'œuvre* (Le Livre de l'Étudiant). Paris: Boivin, 1946.
> (An excellent manual.)

BILLY, ANDRÉ, *Vie de Balzac*. 2 vols., Paris: Flammarion, 1944.
> (A good life.)

BLANCHOT, MAURICE, *Faux pas*. Paris: Gallimard, 1943.

BOURGET, PAUL, *Études et portraits*, I. Paris: Lemerre, 1889.

    Études et portraits, III. Paris: Plon, 1906.

    Pages de critique et de doctrine, I. Plon, 1912.

    Quelques témoignages, II. Plon, 1933.

BOUTERON, MARCEL, *Le Culte de Balzac* (Les Amis d'Édouard). Printed for
    limited circulation, Paris, 1924.

    Muses romantiques. Paris: Plon, 1934.

        (Portrait of Mme Hanska.)

    Une Année de la vie de Balzac, 1835. Printed for limited circulation, Monaco,
    1925.

        (The greatest living authority on all matters connected with Balzac
    scholarship.)

BRUNETIÈRE, FERDINAND, *Honoré de Balzac*. Paris: Calmann-Lévy, 1906.

CERFBERR, ANATOLE and CHRISTOPHE, JULES, *Répertoire de la Comédie Humaine*,
    Introduction by P. Bourget. Paris: Calmann-Lévy, 1887.

CURTIUS, ERNST ROBERT, *Balzac*. Stuttgart and Berlin: Deutsche Verlags-
    Anstalt, 1923. French translation, Henri Jourdan, Paris: Grasset, 1933.

FERNANDEZ, RAMON, *Balzac*, Paris: Stock, 1943.

FLAT, PAUL, *Essais sur Balzac*. Paris: Plon, 1893.

    Seconds essais sur Balzac. Plon, 1894.

GOZLAN, LÉON, *Balzac chez lui*. Michel Lévy, 1862.

    Balzac en pantoufles. Michel Lévy, 1865.

        (Souvenirs by a close personal friend.)

HANOTAUX, GABRIEL, and VICAIRE, GEORGES, *La Jeunesse de Balzac*. Paris:
    Ferroud, 1903. New edition, 1921.

HOFMANNSTHAL, HUGO VON, *Die Berührung der Sphären*. Berlin: S. Fischer
    Verlag, 1931.

LE BRETON, ANDRÉ, *Balzac l'homme et l'œuvre*. Paris: Armand Colin, 1905.
        (Useful general study. Preferable to the better-known work by
    Bellessort, *q.v.*)

LEVIN, HARRY, *Toward Balzac*. New York: New Directions, 1947.

MAYER, GILBERT, *La Qualification affective dans les romans d'Honoré de Balzac*.
    Paris: Droz, 1940.

        (The most important study of Balzac's style yet made.)

MAURIAC, FRANÇOIS, *Mes Grands hommes*. Monaco: Éditions du Rocher,
    1949.

        (Enlarged edition of *Trois grands hommes devant Dieu* referred to in
    chapter on Flaubert.) ·

MORTIMER, RAYMOND, *Channel Packet*. London: Hogarth Press, 1943.

PRESTON, ETHEL, *Recherches sur la technique de Balzac Le retour systématique des
    personnages dans la Comédie humaine*. Paris: Les Presses Françaises, 1926.

        (The key work on its subject.)

PRIOULT, ALBERT, *Balzac avant la Comédie humaine 1818–1829*. Paris: Courville, 1936.

ROSNY *ainé*, J. H., *La Vie amoureuse de Balzac*. Paris: Flammarion, 1930.

RUXTON, GABRIELLE, *La Dilecta de Balzac*. Paris: Plon, 1909.
  (Balzac and Mme de Berny.)

SAINTE-BEUVE, C.-A., *Causeries du lundi*, II.

SPOELBERCH DE LOVENJOUL, VICOMTE CHARLES DE, *Histoire des œuvres d'Honoré de Balzac*. Paris: Calmann-Lévy, 1879.

Un Roman d'amour. Calmann-Lévy, 1896.

La Génèse d'un roman d'Honoré de Balzac: Les Paysans. Paris: Ollendorff, 1901.

Une Page perdue d'Honoré de Balzac. Ollendorff, 1903.
  (The first great Balzac scholar.)

STEPHEN, LESLIE, *Hours in a Library*, I. London: Smith Elder, 1874.
  (A remarkable essay in destructive criticism.)

SURVILLE, LAURE (*sister of the novelist*), *Balzac sa vie et ses œuvres*. Paris: Librairie Nouvelle, 1852.

TAINE, HIPPOLYTE, *Nouveaux essais de critique et d'histoire*. Paris: Hachette, 1880.
  (The first important critical essay on Balzac.)

ZWEIG, STEFAN, *Drei Meister*. Leipzig: Insel Verlag, 1929. Translated as *Three Masters*, London: Cassell, 1930.

Balzac. Stockholm: Bermann Fischer Verlag, 1946. English translation, London: Cassell, 1947.
  (A good life.)

FLAUBERT

BAUDELAIRE, CHARLES, *L'Art romantique* (Conard Edition).
  (Review of *Madame Bovary*.)

BERTRAND, LOUIS, *Gustave Flaubert*. Paris: Mercure de France, 1912.

BOULENGER, JACQUES, *Mais l'art est difficile*, II. Paris: Plon, 1921.
  (Important essay on 'Flaubert et le Style'.)

COLLING, ALFRED, *Gustave Flaubert* (Collection: L'Homme et Son Œuvre). Paris: Fayard, 1941.

DEMOREST, D. L., *L'Expression figurée et symbolique dans l'œuvre de Gustave Flaubert*. Paris: Les Presses Modernes, 1931.
  (A valuable piece of research into the various technical devices used by Flaubert.)

DESCHARMES, RENÉ, and DUMESNIL, RENÉ, *Autour de Flaubert*. 2 vols., Paris: Mercure de France, 1912.

DUMESNIL, RENÉ, *Gustave Flaubert l'homme et l'œuvre* (Collection: Temps et Visages). Paris: Desclée de Brouwer, 1932.
    Le Grand amour de Flaubert (Collection: Les Amitiés Amoureuses). Geneva: Éditions du Milieu du Monde, 1945.

GÉRARD-GAILLY, *Le Grand amour de Flaubert*. Paris: Aubier, 1943.
      (Incorporates the author's earlier works, *Flaubert et les fantômes de Trouville*, La Renaissance du Livre, 1930, and *L'Unique passion de Flaubert: 'Madame Arnoux'*, Le Divan, 1932. The most complete account available of Flaubert's relations with Élisa Schlésinger, but see Dumesnil *supra*.)

GOURMONT, REMY DE, *Le Problème du style*. Paris: Mercure de France, 1902.

MAURIAC, FRANÇOIS, *Trois grands hommes devant Dieu*. Paris: Éditions du Capitole, 1931.

MAYNIAL, ÉDOUARD, *Flaubert et son milieu*. Paris: Éditions de La Nouvelle Revue Critique, 1927. *Flaubert* (Collection: A la Gloire de . . .), 1943.

MURRY, JOHN MIDDLETON, *Countries of the Mind*, I. London: Collins, 1922. New edition, Oxford University Press, 1931.

PROUST, MARCEL, *Chroniques*. Paris: Gallimard, 1927.
    Pastiches et mélanges. Gallimard, 1919.

SAINTE-BEUVE, C.-A., *Causeries du lundi*, XIII; *Nouveaux lundis*, IV, X.

SEILLIÈRE, ERNEST, *Le Romantisme des réalistes: Gustave Flaubert*. Paris: Plon, 1914.

SHANKS, LEWIS PIAGET, *Flaubert's Youth 1821–1841*. Baltimore: John Hopkins Press, 1927.

STEEGMULLER, FRANCIS, *Flaubert and Madame Bovary*. London: Collins, 1939. New edition, 1947.

THIBAUDET, ALBERT, *Gustave Flaubert 1821–1880*. Paris: Plon, 1922.

VALÉRY, PAUL, *Variété*, V. Paris: Gallimard, 1944.

WILSON, EDMUND, *The Triple Thinkers*. Oxford University Press, 1938.

PROUST

ABRAHAM, PIERRE, *Proust* (Recherches sur la Création Intellectuelle). Paris: Rieder, 1930.

BÉGUIN, ALBERT, *L'Ame romantique et le rêve*. New edition, Paris: José Corti, 1939.

BIBESCO, PRINCESSE MARTHE, *Au bal avec Marcel Proust* (Les Cahiers Marcel Proust 5). Paris: Gallimard, 1928.

BLANCHE, JACQUES-ÉMILE, *Mes modèles*. Paris: Stock, 1928.

BLONDEL, C.-A., *La Psychographie de Marcel Proust*. Paris: Vrin, 1932.

BONNET, HENRI, *Le Progrès spirituel dans l'œuvre de Marcel Proust*, I. *Le Monde, l'amour et l'amitié*. II. *L'Eudémonisme esthétique de Proust*. Paris: Vrin, 1946, 1950.

BOULENGER, JACQUES, *Mais l'art est difficile!* I. Paris: Plon, 1921.

BRASILLACH, ROBERT, *Portraits*. Paris: Plon, 1935.

BRET, JACQUES, *Marcel Proust étude critique*. Geneva: Éditions du Mont-Blanc, 1946.

BROGAN, D. W., *French Personalities and Problems*. London: Hamish Hamilton, 1946.

BUCHET, ÉDMOND, *Écrivains intelligents du XXe siècle*. Paris: Corrêa, 1945.

BURNET, ÉTIENNE, *Essences*. Paris: Seheur, 1929.

CAPETANAKIS, DEMETRIOS, *A Greek Poet in England*. London: Lehmann, 1947.

CATTAUÏ, GEORGES, *L'Amitié de Proust* (Les Cahiers Marcel Proust 8). Paris: Gallimard, 1935.

CELLY, RAOUL, *Répertoire des thèmes de Marcel Proust* (Les Cahiers Marcel Proust 7). Paris: Gallimard, 1935.

CRÉMIEUX, BENJAMIN, *XXe siècle*. Paris: Gallimard, 1924.

Du côté de Marcel Proust. Paris: Lemarget, 1929.

CURTIUS, ERNST ROBERT, *Französischer Geist im Neuen Europa*. Berlin-Stuttgart: Deutsche Verlags-Anstalt, n.d. (*c.* 1925).

> (The essay on Proust, which is an outstanding contribution to the subject, was translated separately into French by Armand Pierhal and published by the Éditions de La Revue Nouvelle, 1928.)

DANDIEU, ARNAUD, *Marcel Proust: sa révélation psychologique*. Joint publication of French text, Paris: Firmin-Didot. London: Oxford University Press, 1929.

DAUDET, CHARLES, *Répertoire des personnages de 'A la Recherche du temps perdu'* (Les Cahiers Marcel Proust 2). Paris: Gallimard, 1928.

DAUDET, LUCIEN, *Autour de soixante lettres de Marcel Proust* (Les Cahiers Marcel Proust 5). Paris: Gallimard, 1929.

DREYFUS, ROBERT, *Souvenirs sur Marcel Proust*. Paris: Grasset, 1926.

FERNANDEZ, RAMON, *Proust* (Collection: A la Gloire de . . .). Paris: Éditions de la Nouvelle Revue Critique, 1944.

FERRÉ, ANDRÉ, *Géographie de Marcel Proust*. Paris: Éitidons du Sagittaire, 1939.

FEUILLERAT, ALBERT, *Comment Marcel Proust a composé son roman* (Yale Romanic Studies). New Haven: Yale University Press, 1934.

FISER, EMERIC, *L'Esthétique de Marcel Proust*. Paris: Rédier, 1933.

FRETET, DR. JEAN, *L'Aliénation poétique* Rimbaud: Mallarmé: Proust. Paris: J.-B. Janin, 1946.

> (Interesting.)

GABORY, GEORGES, *Essai sur Marcel Proust*. Paris: Chamontin, 1926.

GRAMONT, ELISABETH DE, *Robert de Montesquiou et Marcel Proust.* Paris: Flammarion, 1925.

Marcel Proust. Flammarion, 1948.

GREEN, F. C., *The Mind of Proust.* Cambridge University Press, 1949.

GREGH, FERNAND, *L'Age d'or.* Paris: Grasset, 1948.

JALOUX, ÉDMOND, *L'Esprit des livres.* 1ère série, Paris: Plon, 1923.

KINDS, ÉDMOND, *Marcel Proust* (Collection: Triptyque-Littérature 3). Paris: Richard-Masse, 1947.
   (An excellent short survey.)

LEMAÎTRE, GEORGES, *Four French Novelists.* Oxford University Press, 1938.

LE MASLE, ROBERT, *Le Professeur Adrien Proust 1834–1903.* Paris: Lipschutz, 1935.

LEON, DERRICK, *Introduction to Proust, His Life, His Circle and His Work.* London: Kegan Paul, 1940.

LINDER, GLADYS DUDLEY (editor), *Marcel Proust: Reviews and Estimates in English.* Stanford (California): Stanford University Press, 1942.

MARCH, HAROLD, *The Two Worlds of Marcel Proust.* London: Oxford University Press, 1948.

MASSIS, HENRI, *Le Drame de Marcel Proust.* Paris: Grasset, 1937.

MAURIAC, FRANÇOIS, *Du côté de chez Proust.* Paris: La Table Ronde, 1947.
   (This appears to be a revised edition of the author's earlier *Proust*, Lesage, 1926.)

MAUROIS, ANDRÉ, *Études littéraires*, I. Paris: Sfelt, 1947.

A la Recherche de Marcel Proust. Paris: Hachette, 1949. Translated as *The Quest for Proust.* London: Cape, 1950.
   (The most useful general study at present available.)

MULLER, MAURICE, *De Descartes à Marcel Proust.* 2nd edition, Neuchâtel: Éditions de la Baconnière, 1947.

MOUTON, JEAN, *Le Style de Marcel Proust* (Collection: Mises au Point). Paris: Corrêa, 1948.

MURRY, JOHN MIDDLETON, *Discoveries.* London: Collins, 1924.
   (An excellent piece of criticism.)

PIERRE-QUINT, LÉON, *Marcel Proust sa vie son œuvre.* Paris: Kra, 1924. New enlarged edition, Le Sagittaire, 1935.
   (Still indispensable.)

POMMIER, JEAN, *La Mystique de Proust.* Paris: Droz, 1939.
   (Useful essay with a misleading title.)

RIVIÈRE, JACQUES, *Nouvelles études.* Paris: Gallimard, 1947.

SACHS, MAURICE, *Le Sabbat.* Paris: Corrêa, 1946.

SAURAT, DENIS, *Tendances*, Idées françaises de Molière à Marcel Proust. Paris: Éditions du Monde Moderne, 1938. New edition, Éditions du Vieux Colombier, 1946.

Modernes. Paris: Denoël et Steele, 1935.

Modern French Literature, 1870–1940. London: Dent, 1946.

SCOTT MONCRIEFF, C. K. (editor), *Marcel Proust: An English Tribute.* London: Chatto and Windus, 1923.

SEILLIÈRE, ERNEST, *Marcel Proust.* Paris: Éditions de La Nouvelle Revue Critique, 1931.

SOUDAY, PAUL, *Marcel Proust.* Paris: Kra, 1927.

SOUZA, SYBIL DE, *La Philosophie de Marcel Proust.* Paris: Rieder, 1939.

SPITZER, LEO, *Stilstudien,* II. Munich: Hüber, 1928.

TAUMAN, LÉON, *Marcel Proust une vie et une synthèse.* Paris: Armand Colin, 1949.

VARIOUS WRITERS: *Hommage à Marcel Proust* (Les Cahiers Marcel Proust 1). Paris: Gallimard, 1927.

(Reprint of special number of *Nouvelle Revue Française* for January 1923.)

WILSON, EDMUND, *Axel's Castle.* London: Scribner, 1936.

INDEX

Abraham, P., 336, 338, 403
Alain, 226–7
Albaret, Céleste, 332
Albaret, O., 332
Anspach, Margravine of, 85–6
Arbelet, P., 13–14, 134, 135, 139

Baldensperger, F., 92
Balzac, H. de, 4, 21, 22, 184, 253, 288, 311, 360, 405; melodramatic element in novels, 211–12; formative influences, 212–13; attitude of critics, 213–14; and the English tradition, 214–15; characteristics of *Comédie humaine*, 216–22; language and style, 18–20, 222–7; *Le Père Goriot*, 228–35; *Eugénie Grandet*, 235–8; *Le Curé de Tours*, 238–41; *La Cousine Bette*, 241–5; conclusions, 246, 413.
Bardèche, M., 126, 183, 200–1, 217–18, 244
Barney, C., 334
Baudelaire, C., 19, 21, 52, 53, 54, 56, 68, 69, 70, 75, 77, 133, 138, 206, 213, 253, 288, 315, 329, 361, 366, 367, 396–7, 412
Bénichou, P., 4
Bergson, H., 284, 328, 329, 366, 369–70
Berthet, A., 259
Beyle, H., *see* Stendhal
Beyle, C. (*father of novelist*), 131, 132
Beyle, Henriette (*mother of novelist*), 131
Bibesco, Prince A., 332, 342
Bibesco, Princesse Marthe, 327
Bisson, L. A., 23
Bizet, J., 328
Blanche, J-É., 328
Blanchot, M., 213–14, 215, 230
Blum, L., 406
Bois, É-J., 369
Bouilhet, L., 258
Bourget, P., 82, 111, 147, 328
Brogan, D. W., 324–5

Brooks, C., 395
Bruneau, C., 20
Brunot, F., 20
Brunschvicg, L., 328
Brunswick, Duke of, 92
Buchet, É., 334, 357
Bussy-Rabutin, R. de, 27

Cabanis, G., 133
Camus, A., 8, 145, 159
Catusse, Mme, 331
Celly, R., 383
Chandieu, Mme de (*grandmother of B. Constant*), 84, 85
Chandieu, Henriette de (*mother of B. Constant*), 84
Charrière, Mme de, 15, 86–8, 92, 96–7
Chateaubriand, Vicomte de, 105, 108, 119, 185, 258, 323
Chevreuse, Duchesse de, 28
Christie, Mrs. Agatha, 213
Chuquet, A., 139
Cimarosa, D., 125
Colet, Louise, 254, 255, 256, 257, 263, 283
Colling, A., 280, 314, 315
Colomb, R., 164
Condé, Princesse de, 11
Conrad, J., 288, 307, 315, 336, 415
Constant, B., 12–13, 14–16, 46, 54, 60, 61, 65–6, 73, 134, 147, 161, 207, 212, 215, 240, 241, 259, 297, 307, 313, 361, 371, 373, 413, 415. Peculiar effect of *Adolphe*, 81–2; Constant and his age, 82–3; birth and family, 84; education, 85–6; and women, 86–8; instability, 89–90; *Adolphe*, originals of characters in, 92–3; moral factor in, 94–7; social criticism in, 98–100; technical qualities of, 101–3; psychology of, 104–11, 120–2; structure of, 111–14; style and imagery, 18–19; 114–19; and the French novel, 411–12

428

LIBRARY
BRYAN COLLEGE
DAYTON, TN. 37321

20772